SOCIAL MEMORY, SILENCED VOICES, AND POLITICAL STRUGGLE

Remembering the Revolution in Zanzibar

Edited by
William Cunningham Bissell
Marie-Aude Fouéré

PUBLISHED BY
Mkuki na Nyota Publishers Ltd
P. O. Box 4246
Dar es Salaam, Tanzania
www.mkukinanyota.com

In association with
French Institute for Research in Africa (IFRA)
P.O. Box 52979-00100
Nairobi, Kenya
www.ifra-nairobi.net
©French Institute for Research in Africa, 2018

ISBN 978-9987-08-317-6

All rights reserved. No part of this publication may be reproduced, stored in a retrieval system or transmitted in any form or by any means, electronic, mechanical, photocopying, recording, or otherwise, without the prior written permission of Mkuki na Nyota Publishers Ltd.

Visit www.mkukinanyota.com to read more about and to purchase any of Mkuki na Nyota books. You will also find featured authors, interviews and news about other publisher/author events. Sign up for our e-newsletters for updates on new releases and other announcements.

Distributed world wide outside Africa by African Books Collective.
www.africanbookscollective.com

This volume is dedicated to all who have struggled to make sense of the revolution, and whose recollections and reflections have made this book possible.

Table of Contents

Figures and Illustrations... ix
Acronyms xi
Acknowledgements.. xiii
Authors... xv

CHAPTER ONE
MEMORY, MEDIA, AND *MAPINDUZI*: ALTERNATIVE VOICES AND
VISIONS OF REVOLUTION, FIFTY YEARS LATER
William Cunningham Bissell and Marie-Aude Fouéré 1

CHAPTER TWO
MEMORIES OF REVOLUTION: PATTERNS OF INTERPRETATION
OF THE 1964 REVOLUTION IN ZANZIBAR
Roman Loimeier 37

CHAPTER THREE
THE VOICE OF THE REVOLUTION: REMEMBERING AND
RE-ENVISIONING FIELD MARSHAL JOHN OKELLO
Ann Lee Grimstad..79

CHAPTER FOUR
MEMORY, LIBERALISM, AND THE RECONSTRUCTED SELF:
WOLFANGO DOURADO AND THE REVOLUTION IN ZANZIBAR
G. Thomas Burgess 109

CHAPTER FIVE
"FOR US IT'S WHAT CAME AFTER": LOCATING PEMBA IN
REVOLUTIONARY ZANZIBAR
Nathalie Arnold Koenings 145

CHAPTER SIX
UNCOMMON MISERY, RELEGATED TO THE MARGINS:
TUMBATU AND FIFTY YEARS OF THE ZANZIBAR REVOLUTION
Makame Ali Muhajir and Garth Andrew Myers........................ 191

CHAPTER SEVEN
"GLITTERING SKIN": RACE, RECTITUDE, AND WRONGDOING IN ZANZIBAR
Gavin Macarthur 223

CHAPTER EIGHT
SILENCED VOICES, RECAPTURED MEMORIES: HISTORICAL IMPRINTS WITHIN A ZANZIBARI LIFE-WORLD
Kjersti Larsen 251

CHAPTER NINE
MEMORY, HISTORY, AND THE NATION AMONG THE GRIEVING COSMOPOLITANS: OMANI-ZANZIBARIS REMEMBER THE ZANZIBAR REVOLUTION, 1964–PRESENT
Nathaniel Mathews 279

CHAPTER TEN
AFRICA ADDIO, THE REVOLUTION, AND THE AMBIGUITIES OF REMEMBRANCE IN CONTEMPORARY ZANZIBAR
Marie-Aude Fouéré 311

CHAPTER ELEVEN
HEALING THE PAST, REINVENTING THE PRESENT: FROM THE REVOLUTION TO *MARIDHIANO*
Ahmed Rajab 335

CHAPTER TWELVE
CAPTURING THE COMMEMORATION: A DOCUMENTARY PHOTO ESSAY ON THE 50TH ANNIVERSARY OF THE REVOLUTION
Ania Gruca 357

Glossary 367
Index 371

Figures and Illustrations

CHAPTER THREE

Figure 1: Photograph of the *Uganda Argus* front page, 17 February 1971 (courtesy of Makerere University Library)..............................107

Figure 2: Photograph of the *Tanganyika Standard* front page, 18 February 1964 (courtesy of Makerere University Library)..107

CHAPTER SIX

Table 1: Tumbatu Island population by *shehia*/village.........219

Table 2: Key revolutionary and political events in Tumbatu, Zanzibar (1964-2010)....................... 219–220

Figure 1: Jongowe and environs 221

Figure 2: Ruins of the 12th-century Friday mosque in the city of Tumbatu..................................222

Acronyms

ANC	African National Congress
ASP	Afro-Shirazi Party
ASPYL	Afro-Shirazi Party Youth League
ASU	Afro-Shirazi Union
BLFK	British Land Forces in Kenya
CCM	Chama cha Mapinduzi
CUF	Civic United Front
DP	Democratic Party
FFU	Field Force Unit
FRELIMO	Frente de Libertação de Moçambique (Mozambique Liberation Front)
GNU	Government of National Unity
KADU	Kenya African Democratic Union
KANU	Kenya African National Union
PAFMECA	Pan-African Movement for East and Central Africa
PWD	Public Works Department
RC	Revolutionary Council
RGZ	Revolutionary Government of Zanzibar
SMZ	Serikali ya Mapinduzi ya Zanzibar
TANU	Tanganyikan African National Union
TVZ	Television Zanzibar
UPC	Uganda People's Congress
ZANU	Zimbabwe African National Union
ZNP	Zanzibar Nationalist Party
ZPPP	Zanzibar and Pemba People's Party

Acknowledgments

Edited volumes often emerge out of collaborative efforts, sparked by on-going conversations about critical issues of common concern. The revolution of 1964 still looms quite large in Zanzibari cultural and political life, and yet its legacy in social memory and popular representations has rarely been explored in any sustained way. For academics working in Zanzibar, this scholarly lacuna is all the more striking, as Zanzibaris of different generations and social locations repeatedly bring up and refer to the revolution as a source of debate in their conversations with us. While at certain moments these discussions have occurred in the public sphere, often times they were conducted behind closed doors, amongst trusted friends or colleagues, in small *baraza* groups, or well beyond the hearing of official ears. As scholars, many of us have been privileged to be included in these discussions and debates, and the debt of gratitude we owe to countless Zanzibaris for their insights and analyses cannot be repaid here. But at the very least, we are pleased to be able to foreground and frame these issues in this volume in ways that are not always possible within Zanzibar itself. We are also fortunate to include in this book quite different cohorts of scholars engaged in Zanzibar, from those who started in the 1980s right down to the present. These diverse voices, of different generations and drawn from Tanzania, across Europe, and the U.S., have greatly enriched the text and made this a truly transnational effort.

The publication of this edited volume was supported by the French Institute for Research in Africa (IFRA) in Nairobi, Kenya, and the research unit Institut des Mondes Africains (IMAF) in Paris, France. It has also benefited from a timely publication grant given by the Academic

Research Committee of Lafayette College in Easton, PA. Our gratitude also goes to the Zanzibar Government and the Zanzibar National Archives for granting research permission to all the contributors involved, enabling them to conduct field research in Zanzibar and providing access to the Zanzibar National Archives. We are grateful to all these institutions for their assistance, without which this publication would not have been possible.

This volume is dedicated to all who have struggled to make sense of the revolution, and whose memories and reflections have made this book possible. We are particularly indebted to friends and colleagues who enthusiastically got involved in this project in various ways, from sharing their views and ideas on various aspects of the history and memories of the revolution in Zanzibar to providing assistance during fieldwork. Sincere thanks go to Claire Médard, Nathalie Arnold Koenings, and Andrea Smith for their insights and comments on different parts of the manuscript. We wish to express our on-going gratitude to Professor Abdul Sheriff who has generously welcomed, supported, and sparked the critical imaginations of most of the researchers who contributed to this volume during their research in Zanzibar, and who has been very supportive of this publication project as well. As colleagues, fellow scholars, and friends of the late Jan-Georg Deutsch, we offer these essays in hopes that they will honor his many contributions to scholarship on Tanzanian history, especially his work on memory, modernity, and urban life in Zanzibar.

This volume has gained tremendously from the work of photographer Ania Gruca, who beautifully captured in images vivid moments of the life of the archipelago at different moments in time, from the intimacy of domesticity to meaningful collective ceremonies and public events commemorating the revolution. We are delighted to be able to draw on this work here.

Last, we wish to express our sincere thanks to Walter Bgoya for his enduring support and trust since the beginning of this publication project, as well as to Mkuki na Nyota's team in Dar es Salaam. It has been a pleasure to work with them to contribute to African scholarly publishing. For the thoughtful initial editing of the manuscript, we are also most grateful for the meticulous and patient work of James Waller at Thumbprint, New York City.

Authors

Nathalie Arnold Koenings is a sociocultural anthropologist, Swahili literary translator, and novelist. Her ethnographic work is focused on rural Pemba, where she is interested in cultural constructions of agency and power, the occult, and the geographical imagination. She has published articles on the occult as a central idiom in historical discourse, and on the phenomenological importance of popular song to negotiations of identity and space. Her translations of Swahili prose literature have appeared in *Words without Borders* and *Asymptote*. Koenings also holds an M.F.A. in creative writing, with a focus on African and postcolonial literature. She is the author of the novel *The Blue Taxi* and the story collection *Theft* (2006; 2008), which explore the effects of colonialism and other injustices on individuals and communities, with a particular interest in women. She is currently Associate Professor of Interdisciplinary Arts at Hampshire College.

William Cunningham Bissell is Professor in the Department of Anthropology and Sociology, Lafayette College, Easton, PA. He has written widely on sociocultural processes in Zanzibar and the Indian Ocean world, with a specific research focus on urban transformation, representation, memory, and media in diverse contexts, including the anthropology of nostalgia and the reimagining of the revolutionary past. His first book, *Urban Design, Chaos, and Colonial Power in Zanzibar* (2011), focused on the failures and contradictions of modernist colonial urban planning, while his current ethnographic work centers on transnational media, urban image-making, and the contested politics of contemporary African film festivals.

G. Thomas Burgess is an Associate Professor of History at the US Naval Academy, Annapolis. He has been researching and writing about Tanzania since the 1990s, with essays appearing in the *International Journal of African Historical Studies*, *Africa Today*, and numerous edited volumes. His most recent book, published in 2009 by Ohio University Press, was *Race, Revolution, and the Struggle for Human Rights in Zanzibar* (2009). He is currently completing a volume for Cambridge University Press entitled *Sons and Fathers: The Making of Men in Africa*.

Marie-Aude Fouéré is Associate Professor in Social Anthropology at the École des Hautes Études en Sciences Sociales (EHESS) in Paris. She published a monograph in French on interethnic joking relationships in Tanzania (2008) resulting from her PhD thesis conducted in Morogoro region. She (co-)edited several special issues of academic journals and volumes on Tanzania and East Africa in French and in English, among them her most recent volume *Remembering Nyerere in Tanzania: History, Memory, Legacy* published with Mkuki na Nyota (2015). She also worked as a consultant for UNESCO and UNHCR in refugee camps on intangible culture heritage in East Africa. Her main research interests in Tanzania cover collective memories, belonging, nationalism, print culture, museums and archives, focusing on the figure of Julius Nyerere, on *ujamaa*, and on the revolution in Zanzibar.

Ann Lee Grimstad is Professor of History at Mt. San Antonio College. She holds a BA in Religious Studies from the University of Virginia and an MA in African Studies from Ohio University. After ten years of developing curriculum for and directing study abroad programs in numerous countries in Africa, she returned to school for her PhD program in African History at the University of Florida. This research is part of her dissertation, which is an operational history of the Zanzibar revolution. She conducted the research with the help of a Fulbright-Hays Doctoral Dissertation Research Award.

Ania Gruca is a freelance documentary photographer and videographer. From 2010 to 2015 she developed a self-initiated photography project exploring Zanzibar's current state of affairs, highlighting the archipelago's economical, social, and political challenges and ongoing search for identity. At the same time her work focuses on development and social issues mostly related to the United Nations Population Fund, the French Development Agency, and the Forum for African Women

Educationalists, among others. Her work has appeared in online and print publications such as *The New York Times, The Citizen, Profil, The Jewish Week, Tribeca Trib, Der Standard* and *Zink Magazine*; it has been exhibited internationally.

Kjersti Larsen is Professor at the Department of Ethnography, Numismatics, and Classical Archaeology, Museum of Cultural History, University of Oslo where she has also been Head of Department (2003-2006). Larsen has been a visiting scholar at the Centre for Cross-Cultural Research on Women, University of Oxford; Centre d'Études Africaines, École des Hautes Études en Sciences Sociales, Paris; International Institute for the Study of Islam in the Modern World (ISIM), Leiden University. She conducts research in Muslim societies in East Africa along the Swahili coast, particularly on Zanzibar (1984-present) and in Northern Sudan, mostly in the Bayoda desert (1997-2009). Larsen has several international publications, including the monograph *Where Humans and Spirits Meet: The Politics of Rituals and Identified Spirits in Zanzibar* (2008) and the edited volume *Knowledge, Renewal and Religion* (2009). She is also the co-author of *Movement and Connectivity: Configuration of Belonging* to be published by Peter Lang, Oxford. Her main research interests include ritual and performance; knowledge, morality, and gender; everyday-life politics, collective memory, and social change; identity, mobility and connectivity in African societies and the Indian Ocean Region.

Roman Loimeier (b. 1957 in Passau) is Associate Professor at the Institute of Social and Cultural Anthropology at the University of Göttingen in Germany. He has done research in Senegal (1981, 1990-1993), Northern Nigeria (1986-1988), and Tanzania (since 2001) and has published several volumes on the history and development of Muslim societies in Africa, in particular *Islamic Reform in 20th Century Africa* (2016); *Muslim Societies in Africa: A Historical Anthropology* (2013); *Eine Zeitlandschaft in der Globalisierung: Das islamische Sansibar im 19. und 20. Jahrhundert* (2012); *Between Social Skills and Marketable Skills: The Politics of Islamic Education in Zanzibar in the 20th Century* (2009); *Säkularer Staat und Islamische Gesellschaft – Die Beziehungen zwischen Staat, Sufi-Bruderschaften und Islamischer Reformbewegung in Senegal im 20. Jahrhundert* (2001); and *Islamic Reform and Political Change in Northern Nigeria* (1997).

Gavin Macarthur graduated with a PhD in Social Anthropology from the University of Manchester in 2009. His doctoral research argues that the islands of Zanzibar are imagined in multiple cultured modes, ordering and expressing the sometimes aligned and sometimes conflicting perspectives, projects, and objectives of a number of culturally distinct populations in the Isles and elsewhere around the globe. He is currently working on a community health-focused eco-adventure tourism pilot project, working toward certain of the UN's new Sustainable Development Goals in Jeju island, South Korea and in the Black Volta region of Ghana.

Nathaniel Mathews is Assistant Professor of Africana Studies at Binghamton University in Binghamton, NY. He received his Ph.D. in African history from Northwestern University in 2016. He is currently writing a book on the transnational return migration of the Swahili-speaking Omani community from Zanzibar to Oman. He has previously published in *Islamic Africa* on Arab identity and Islamic reform in colonial Mombasa.

Makame Muhajir holds a Ph.D. in Geography from the University of Kansas and an MA degree in Planning from Curtin University in Perth, Australia. He is a geographer and urban planner with more than 20 years of professional experience in urban management, environmental planning, and civic organizational practices. He has also served as the former director of Tanzania's Department of Surveys and Urban Planning in Zanzibar (1994-2001). Muhajir was most recently an Assistant Professor and 2012-2013 Minerva Research Fellow at the United States Military Academy at West Point, New York. Prior to joining the United States Military Academy, Muhajir was a lecturer at the University of Kansas. On top of working in geography and urban planning, Muhajir's academic and professional expertise encompasses community organization, spatial analysis, as well as applied and theoretical global sustainability studies. Muhajir is currently directing the Tanzanian Community in Washington State.

Garth Myers is Distinguished Professor of Urban International Studies at Trinity College, Hartford, CT, USA. Myers has authored four books: *Verandahs of Power: Colonialism and Space in Urban Africa* (2003); *Disposable Cities: Garbage, Governance and Sustainable Development in Urban Africa* (2005); *African Cities: Alternative Visions of Urban Theory* *and Practice* (2011); and *Urban Environments in Africa: A Critical Analysis of Environmental Politics* (2016). Each book has contained at least one chapter devoted to Zanzibar. He has coedited two other books, along with more than sixty articles and book chapters on African development.

Ahmed Rajab is a Zanzibari-born international journalist, political analyst, and essayist. He graduated with honours in philosophy (Birkbeck College, University of London), holds a post-graduate diploma in Urbanisation in Developing Countries (University College, London), and a Master's degree in Modern African Literature (Sussex University). Rajab has worked for the BBC World Service, Index-on-Censorship, Africa Events, the seminal Africa Analysis (which he edited for 20 years), UNESCO as well as the UNDP. From 2006-2009 he worked in Dubai as Head of Newsroom (Middle East/Asia Bureau) for IRIN, the UN humanitarian news agency. Until recently he was based in Nairobi as Managing Director of Universal TV. In addition to being a columnist for Tanzania's premier weekly *Raia Mwema*, he now works as a consultant and is affiliated to the Kaduna-based Gusau Institute, which specializes in research and training on governance and security issues. Rajab, who has a keen interest in continental philosophy, also writes poetry. His work was included in the anthology *African New Voices* (ed. by Stewart Brown, 1997). He divides his time between Zanzibar and London.

Chapter One

Memory, Media, and *Mapinduzi*: Alternative Voices and Visions of Revolution, Fifty Years Later

William Cunningham Bissell and Marie-Aude Fouéré

During the month of January 2014, Zanzibar celebrated with considerable pomp the 50th anniversary of the revolution. The official jubilee of this epochal event in the history of the archipelago was symbolically charged, as it commemorated the coming to power of a new regime in 1964 and, with it, the foundation of a new postcolonial polity. Posters, banners, and flags were omnipresent in the public spaces of Zanzibar's capital city as well as in the main towns and villages of Zanzibar's two islands, Unguja and Pemba. *Hongera Miaka 50 ya Mapinduzi Zanzibar* ("Congratulations on 50 Years of the Zanzibar Revolution") proclaimed posters hung high on streetlights along the main roads connecting the historic center of Stone Town to the city suburbs. Below the medallion of the portrait of a smiling Ali Mohamed Shein, the incumbent president, the longstanding slogan of the regime, *Mapinduzi Daima* ("Revolution Forever"), stood out in big letters, asserting to all that the spirit of the revolution would continue to hover in the air even after the celebrations had passed. Street signs also advertised the month-long festivities marking the revolution's anniversary, which closed with military parades and the president's official address at Amani Stadium on 12 January, the official day of the revolution long ago established as a public holiday. The formal commemoration had reached a peak two days earlier with stunning midnight fireworks, which had lit the sky above the Mnazi Mmoja grounds, attracting a dense crowd.

Except for this staggering fireworks display, the state-led commemorations were manifestly not met with a great deal of popular fervor. On 9 January, for instance, a dhow race organized at the Stone Town seafront as part of the jubilee festivities attracted just a sparse group of onlookers, and three days later, at the formal ceremonies in Amani Stadium, the open-air bleachers were only partly filled, mainly with civil servants and active members of the ruling party, as few ordinary citizens attended the event. The popular disaffection with the state-orchestrated commemorations of the revolution was accompanied by criticism that the government was spending far too much on the jubilee. Often expressed sotto voce, these critical reflections also appeared on social media. Most such critiques targeted one specific government project, the Mnara wa Mapinduzi (Tower of the Revolution). This commemorative monument—a three-story circular building that would contain a shopping mall and a panorama restaurant—was then under construction right in the middle of Michenzani, a planned neighborhood of apartment blocks, situated just outside Stone Town, that was built in the late 1960s as the symbol of the revolutionary government's efforts to bring modernity to the isles. Skeptical citizens argued that the 1 billion Tanzanian shillings (over $450,000 US) channeled into the Tower project would be far better devoted to providing basic amenities like sewage, schools, and hospitals in an archipelago where the majority still live in great poverty without access to basic services. These critical views directly undercut the official communication strategy that sought to emphasize the benefits delivered by the revolutionary government since 1964, stressing the so-called *matunda ya mapinduzi*, or "fruits of the revolution." The main jubilee slogan, "Let's sustain the peace, unity, and development that are the fruits of our revolution,"[1] could be found in different versions[2] displayed in public spaces throughout the city and constituted the principal thread in President Shein's official speech (SMZ 2014). Among critics, however, this repeated invocation of the "fruits" prompted sarcastic remarks that the *matunda ya mapinduzi* were nowhere to be seen.[3]

---

1   *Tudumishe amani, umoja na maendeleo ambayo ni matunda ya mapinduzi yetu.*

2   Alternative examples that appeared on banners or signs during the run-up to the 50th anniversary include the following: *Tudumishe mapinduzi yetu kwa kupiga vita dawa za kulevya, maambukizi mapya ya Ukimwi na malaria—inawezekana* (Let's sustain our revolution by fighting against drugs, new HIV/AIDS infections, and malaria—it can be done); *Maendeleo ya bandari kuu ya Malindi Zanzibar ni matunda ya mapinduzi* (Development of the main port of Malindi, Zanzibar is one of the fruits of the revolution); *Mapinduzi ya tarehe 12 Januari 1964 yameleta huduma bora za afya ya mama na mtoto* (The revolution of 12 January 1964 brought better maternal and child health services), and so forth.

3   All ethnographic materials about the commemoration of the revolution in January 2014 presented in this chapter come from Marie-Aude Fouéré's fieldwork, conducted in collaboration with photographer Ania Gruca, whose photographs illustrate this volume.

Opening Ceremonies: Official Events and Popular (Dis)Engagement

The disjuncture and distance between the official commemorations and popular engagement is rooted in a longer history—indeed, almost as old as the revolution itself. As an official Afro-Shirazi Party (ASP) volume commemorating the 10th anniversary of the revolution noted, the ceremonies marking the uprising's first anniversary on 12 January 1965 established an official model that was to be followed in the years to come. The first anniversary was marked by the formal visits of official guests invited from almost 60 African states, friendly socialist regimes, and representatives of liberation organizations. The ASP commemorative text lists all the invited dignitaries who attended, placing great emphasis on their presence, and then concludes, "The celebration is generally planned and arranged by an official plan that seems to please these guests because when they leave they express happiness with what they have seen" (ASP 1974: 15). When treating the first anniversary ceremonies, the book makes no reference whatsoever to popular, local, or indigenous involvement in the revolutionary celebrations—an ironic absence, indeed. From the very start, then, remembering the revolution has entailed staging official performances for select audiences, with ordinary Zanzibaris relegated to the position of spectators or symbols of popular enthusiasm—a configuration of the "public" that has strong echoes of the colonial past (Bissell 1999: 128–9).

If there has always been a looming gap between official political rituals and the popular sphere, over the years other factors have intervened in Zanzibar to widen this distance. After repeated electoral conflicts in recent years, many Zanzibaris are disengaged or disillusioned by politics; during public holidays, others are caught up with social obligations, sports, worship, or material concerns closer to home, not least the real challenges of caring for kin and putting food on the table. In this sense, the political rituals of those in power can seem removed from ordinary citizens' concerns. Moreover, as elsewhere in Africa, there is in Zanzibar an increased climate of political distrust, with elites being widely suspected of pursuing the "politics of the belly" (Bayart 1993)—enriching themselves and their cronies while allowing the vast majority to languish in poverty. In the isles, suspicions about the self-serving motivations of political elites in the ruling party serve to cast official ceremonies in a cynical light—as a political spectacle whose only purpose is to mask the real, behind-the-scenes operations of power.

But there are also more specific reasons why the official ceremonies received such a lukewarm response from most of the population. While the government sought to use the jubilee as an occasion to reenact elite loyalty to the national project and to perform its ideals of national belonging, there was never any acknowledgment that the significance of the revolution, its substance and meaning, is still very much in question for diverse Zanzibaris. What happened in 1964 and the meaning of those events are still intensely contested today. How the revolution is remembered and reconstructed is a source of continuing cultural struggle—with significant sociopolitical stakes. "Commemorative activity," writes John R. Gillis (1994: 5), "is by definition social and political, for it involves the coordination of individual and group memories, whose results may appear consensual when they are in fact the product of processes of intense contest, struggle, and, in some instances, annihilation." In this regard, the 50th anniversary commemorations seemed to recall the revolution all too well—presenting an official script (Scott 2008) that marked its own primary position in the public sphere. After all, the revolutionary government consolidated its hold on power and crafted a new sociopolitical order at least in part by seeking to control how the revolution would be represented and remembered. Much like earlier annual commemorations, the 50th jubilee sought to present a monolithic face in public, never seeking to reconcile the ambiguities and ambivalences about the revolution that linger in popular memory to this day.

Since 1964, the exact history of the revolution and its meaning have been sharply contested indeed. No question, the events of 11–12 January 1964 overturned a newly elected government only one month after Zanzibar had peacefully marked its independence from Britain. While the men who seized power (and the eventual ruling party that emerged) turned the revolution into a grand narrative of liberation from colonialism and foreign oppression, other groups in society remembered and interpreted this turning point in Zanzibar's history in very different ways. The revolution brought about much more than simply a change of regime: it recast national imaginaries, redefining community, identity, and senses of belonging while altering the conditions of everyday life in profound ways. No matter whether one celebrated the revolution as a triumph or lamented it as a tragedy (or something in between), one had to recognize that it arrived with a disruptive impact, transforming the economy and cultural life, disrupting social norms, displacing citizens, and opening unacknowledged wounds caused by violence, exile, and even death.

In the decades that ensued, revolutionary authorities in Zanzibar never acknowledged the trauma unleashed by this transformation or tried to address its ongoing legacy in public. This resulted in continuing struggles to make sense of what "really happened" and what the revolution still means today. To many Zanzibaris the past remains "an enigma" (Shivji 2008: 62)—opaque and unsettled. The generation that led or witnessed the revolution is rapidly passing from the scene, and yet the struggle to define those events and to reckon with their legacy lives on. Zanzibari identity is still very much at stake, fraught with recurrent tensions: Who exactly belongs in the islands and what historical processes brought them there? What are the boundaries of the nation, and who can claim to belong to this imagined and embodied community? Where should the lines of otherness or exclusion be drawn—between opportunistic outsiders and authentic indigenes, exploiters and exploited, slavers or the enslaved, elites and subalterns, civilized and savage? Of course, these lines of difference become all the more loaded when they are mapped onto essentialized categories of religion (Muslim versus Christian) or race (whether "Arab," "African," or "Indian"). Within this contested cultural and social domain, the revolution also raised and continues to raise critical issues of sovereignty and space—particularly fraught as the 1964 union with the Tanzanian mainland remains a point of sharp contention. Political belonging and access to power are deeply intertwined with these issues of identity and cultural belonging—raising the question whether the islands should remain linked to the continent or should break away, seeking ties across the Indian Ocean or with the wider Islamic world. At the heart of these struggles are intense debates and divisions over precisely where Zanzibar belongs in the national order of things in a postcolonial world.

Reverberations of Revolution: Things That Go without Saying, Things That Cannot Be Said

This collection of essays takes the official commemoration of the 50th anniversary as its point of departure, focusing on the remembrance of the revolution and its reverberations in everyday life. As ethnographers, historians, and cultural geographers engaged with the complexities of postcolonial Zanzibar, we have been often struck by the ongoing impact of the revolution in ways great and small. Beyond any doubt, the uprising and its immediate aftermath built new conceptions of community and identity, new notions of race and cultural belonging, and new ideals of nationhood, citizenship, and sovereignty. Zanzibar had long been shaped by its location in the wider Indian Ocean world, linked to the Arabian Peninsula and South Asia by extensive migration, the monsoon trade, long-lasting social networks, and religious ties. The revolution severed many of these links, reorienting the islands toward the continent, and its effects were felt throughout East Africa and across the Indian Ocean. At the same time, the revolution placed the islands at the forefront of global debates about socialism and Cold War rivalries, African nationalism and pan-Africanism, and the politics of decolonization.

Yet while acknowledging the importance of the revolution as an historical event, we do not seek to retrace the series of events that took place during that time, their antecedents, or their eventual impact. Much less do we propose to provide a definitive historiography—as valuable a task as that might be. Rather than seeking to define the revolution and strictly establish its meanings, we intend instead to trace its continuing echoes down to today, exploring complicated legacies, diverse representations, and mediated memories. More than just focusing on commemoration, we foreground and follow cultural debates about the revolution located well off the official stage, attending to suppressed questions, submerged doubts, rumors, secrets, and things that cannot be said. By foregrounding subaltern, spatially marginalized, or silenced voices, the essays in this volume highlight the fact that both history and memory are constituted through diverse practices, voices, and perspectives. Analysing the political and social uses that these discourses serve through diverse frames, sites, and performances, the essays present the cases of underexplored places like Pemba or Tumbatu; give insight into remembrance and representations among specific communities, such as the Asians and the Omani diaspora; scrutinize the role of historical figures, such as Wolfango Dourado and John Okello, and the traces they have left behind; and, last, investigate the use of specific media and how they affect memory transmission or transform historical consciousness. In so doing, the authors attend to, and seek to understand, diverse Zanzibari voices debating what the revolution has meant in a local, national, regional, and transnational context. They give insight into local debates about how the revolution should be represented or remembered, and what it ultimately symbolizes, 50 years later, in a very different sociopolitical world.

As it opens up new frames of inquiry about the significance of the revolution, this volume draws on recent work in cultural studies of memory and commemoration, transnationalism and cosmopolitanism, state-making and nation-making, and the impact of new media, notions of race, and forms of representation. These essays embrace the idea that *"how the story is told* [of the revolution] has become as interesting and enlightening as a recounting of what actually happened" (Myers 2000: 430; emphasis in the original). Beyond the dynamics of social memory, however, we are also deeply engaged with questions of mediation: How does the past come down to us, through what media or means, and who controls the contours of what can be spoken, known, or grasped? Modes of remembrance and representation are intrinsically linked, and much more is involved than just explicit discourses or narratives. Indeed, debates about the revolution are embodied and reflected in spatial arrangements, material life, implicit social practices, and fashion, as well as in people's bodies and affects—and in silences and absence. Rather than adjudicating between the different existing representations of the revolution, we seek instead to reframe them as ongoing questions in an ethnographic mode, exploring the past as it lives now—especially crucial insofar as the islands have in recent decades been intensively reopened to global circuits of capital, people, images, and ideas.

Engaging the Past: Remembrance and Representation

Social memory has long been defined in sharp contrast with history (Halbwachs 1980; Nora 1989). But as Nathalie Zemon Davis and Randolph Starn (1989: 2) note, binary distinctions between "official" history and "organic" memory are often overdrawn, obscuring the interdependence between diverse ways of engaging the past. After all, both memory and history are historically situated and discursively constituted, even as they may be shaped by different aims, cultural contexts, and institutional settings. Rather than making reified distinctions, we are interested in exploring interrelations across a complicated landscape of remembrance and representation. As Marita Sturken observes, cultural memory and history are not so much opposed as "entangled":

> Indeed, there is so much traffic across the borders of cultural memory and history that in many cases it may be futile to maintain a distinction between them. . . . Personal memory, cultural memory, and history do not exist within neatly defined boundaries. Memory and memory objects can move from one realm to another, shifting meaning and context. Thus personal memories can sometimes be subsumed into history and elements of cultural memory can exist in concert with historical narratives. (1997: 5–6)

In focusing on the traffic between different modes of relating to the past, we are concerned ethnographically with the collisions and clashes that occur at the intersection of public commemorations, political rituals, media framings, memoirs, oral histories, ethnographic reflections, and a wide array of popular memory practices.

As this orientation suggests, personal or individual memory is always bound up with wider sociocultural frameworks—always tied to one's perspective, subject position, and place. Between any experience or event and its recollection, representation always intervenes, and the retelling makes us think about how language, discursive form, and modes of transmission inevitably influence what gets told. Memory involves both social processes and performances transmitted through diverse media, and these media forms "play an active role in shaping our understanding of the past, in 'mediating' between us (as readers, viewers, listeners) and past experiences, and hence in setting the agenda for future acts of remembrance" (Erll and Rigney 2009: 3). In other words, how the revolution is remembered is intrinsically tied up with how the tale gets told, by whom, and in what context, and with the means by which it comes down to us.

Despite its local, national, regional, and global significance, the revolution has not been the subject of any full-length scholarly exploration in recent decades. There are a few established historical narratives written at a distance (e.g., Lofchie 1965; Clayton 1981) and numerous accounts or memoirs pressing ideologically or personally motivated interpretations, as will be seen below (see Loimeier 2006, and this volume; Myers 2000). For several decades following the revolution, travel to the islands was sharply restricted, and scholarly access to sources and archives was mostly foreclosed. The ruling party tolerated little debate or dissent; inquiry itself was a risky business; and raising questions in public would surely prompt unwanted attention from the security apparatus. Even after liberalization in the 1980s, this situation was slow to change, as the revolution remained a highly charged—and politically sensitive—subject. While scholars have treated specific aspects of the revolution and its aftermath, no definitive cultural study or full-scale historical account yet exists. As G. Thomas Burgess reminds us, there is "no text [that] speaks with any authority to all islanders about their past" (2009: 7), and the lack of an authoritative set of sources has been exacerbated by the absence of open, engaged, and thoughtful debate in the Zanzibari public sphere. Certainly, one can find sharp exchanges of political charges and counter-charges, but these are often extensions of old ideological divides or the product of politically motivated tactical attacks. In this volume, Roman Loimeier provides insight into this ideological competition, showing that how the revolution is depicted, defined, and interpreted in the political and historical essays written since the revolution is strongly related both to the identity of the authors and to the context in which these writings were produced; yet what most of these texts have in common is that they seek to produce and disseminate a hegemonic interpretation of the revolution rather than recognizing the plurality of voices and entanglement of memories. What has not occurred, therefore, is any serious effort to collectively adjudicate what happened, to achieve critical distance, or to weigh different accounts and forms of evidence—hoping thereby to appreciate both the transformation produced by the revolution as well as the toll it took. Achieving a common understanding of the revolution might be a utopian wish, but public and scholarly inquiry could at least establish a shared body of elements upon which to ground further debates.

Official Stories: Constructing the Public Face of the Revolution

As the commemoration of the 50th anniversary reminds us, the revolution has always had its "official story": a more or less orthodox version of events promulgated by the party in power. This official story has never been entirely consistent, taking on quite different shadings as it has shifted over time. As Ana Maria Alonso argues,

> The contingency of history-as-action is always mitigated by the backwards gaze of history-as-representation which orders and explains, which introduces a teleology hardly evident at the time of the original events. Yet historiographies tend to conceal the effects of this gap between past and present, between contingency and necessity, occluding the process of interpretation and the conditions of its production. . . . In this project, language, whether spoken or written, conspires with history-making. Not only does the fixity of the printed word or the freezing by repetition of the spoken word aid the work of simplification and reification but also, it helps to establish the authority which re-presentations require if they are to be seen as representative. Public language, through its very publicity, acquires a measure of truth and legitimacy. (1988: 34–5)

In one of the first official accounts of the uprising, published in the *Nationalist* newspaper in Dar es Salaam on 12 January 1965, the revolution was portrayed as a popular struggle to restore democracy, provoked by the repressive "intrigues and plots of the Sultan and his political henchmen" (*The Nationalist* 1967 [1965]: 210). That is, the uprising was portrayed as a legitimate struggle against the authoritarian and antidemocratic policies of the sultan's regime, or against the electoral gerrymandering of the British. Subsequently, the revolution was more often described as broadly anticolonial or anti-imperialist. In this version, the uprising was said to overthrow an oppressive regime that had long held the majority of Zanzibaris down. The population was described as consisting of workers, peasants, and squatters who rose up to resist external domination variously described as "sultanate rule" (*utawala wa kisultani*), "capitalist exploitation" (*ubepari*), "bourgeois" or "aristocratic" power (*ubwanyenye*), "imperialism" (*ubeberu*), and "racism" (*ubaguzi*). This vocabulary, aimed at rhetorically building political legitimacy and undermining political protest, has long recurred in the official documentation of the revolutionary regime (e.g., ASP 1970). Some personal political essays also embraced these depictions. Abdulrahman Muhammed Babu, for instance, an Umma party activist and early member of the Revolutionary Council, claimed the revolution "shook the entire imperialist camp as a devastating blow to their well-planned post-colonial strategy for East Africa" (1991: 220). He also emphasized that it was driven by the popular desire to "achieve a genuinely free society—free from the shackles of slavery, of feudal landlordism, and of colonial humiliation" (1991: 220). Here, as in other versions, the freedom struggle shaded into a struggle against foreign rule (*utawala wa kigeni*)—against Arab elites, feudal lords, or the Omani sultan. In this sense, the revolution was portrayed as bringing an indigenous African nation into being: "On the date of 12 January 1964 an African Nation under the leadership of the Afro-Shirazi Party was born in Zanzibar by the Afro-Shirazi Revolution" (ASP 1974: 2). This fledgling African nation was seen as mirroring the history of population settlement in Zanzibar, as illustrated by Abeid Amani Karume's public speeches on Revolution Day in 1968: "Our origin is Tanganyika, that is where we come from. We came from nowhere else, let no one tell that to you. Tanganyika, Kenya, Uganda, Nyasa, Kongo, it is our origin."[4]

By the mid-1970s, the ASP's vanguard role and revolutionary links to the African continent had become standard fare. Third World and socialist solidarities were often invoked, and the revolution became

---

4   Abeid Amani Karume, "Hotuba za Waheshimiwa Rais wa Tanzania na Makamo wa Kwanza wa Rais kwa Kusherehekea Mwaka wa Nne wa Mapinduzi ya Zanzibar" [The Speeches of Their Excellencies the President of Tanzania and the First Vice President to Celebrate the Fourth Year of the Revolution of Zanzibar], 12 January 1968. Zanzibar National Archives, BA 68/5.

an early instance of African liberation struggles elsewhere on the continent, following Tanzania's pan-Africanist support for the ANC, FRELIMO, ZANU, and related movements. And, of course, the revolution was often described in strict class terms, as a revolution of the oppressed, dispossessed and "downtrodden" (ASP 1974: 2) against those who sought to deny them equality, dignity, or opportunity. In recent decades, this explicitly Marxist emphasis has waned, but there is still an emphasis on material concerns; in the era of multiparty politics, the revolution has been associated more with its "fruits," treated as if it was congruent with the development of infrastructure, healthcare, education, housing, and other poverty alleviation efforts. The 2015 general electoral campaign in Zanzibar beautifully illustrates this shift. The *Mapinduzi Daima!* slogan, repeated again and again during the public rallies of the CCM (Chama cha Mapinduzi) ruling party, is no longer tied up with conceptions of the Zanzibari polity formulated in Marxist or in moral terms. Electoral promises focus on tangible changes like computers at school, tarmacked roads, or new electrical power stations, thus offering citizens the perspective of a pragmatic "developmental state" (Green 2014) in place of the modernizing welfare state that was in the line of the early post-revolutionary political leaders. Yet, the string of "liberation" and "anticolonialist" images continues to be pulled publicly. In this volume, Ahmed Rajab argues that the history of the revolution continues to be used in political and partisan struggles to divide populations in ways that infuse the rhetoric of liberation with racialized discourse. This undermines recurring institutional efforts to appease sociopolitical tensions—efforts that led to the *maridhiano* (appeasement) turning point between CCM and the CUF (Civic United Front) main opposition party in 2009 and, after the 2010 election, the formation of a Government of National Unity (GNU) that raised great expectations among the population (see also Fouéré 2011; Bakari and Makulilo 2012). The 2015 election was no exception: In a political rally held in Mkokotoni on 19 September 2015, Balozi Seif Ali Idd, Zanzibar's second vice-president, associated CUF rule, in case of victory, with the return of colonial times under the sultan—a speech that, with similar repeated statements over the course of the ruling party's electoral campaign, fostered heated debates in the street *baraza* as well as on social media.

Despite these shifts in emphasis over the decades, the effort to construct and consolidate a hegemonic portrait of the revolution has remained something of a constant. In a context where the ruling party has often been congruent with the state, we can see how the regime has long sought to consolidate its support by promulgating particular representations of the revolution and casting its aims, activities, and agents in a specific light. The revolution has always been mobilized in the service of a grand narrative establishing the boundaries of political power and the legitimacy of those who "rightfully" wield it and defining the essential terms of Zanzibari identity—that is, designating who belongs and should benefit. How the revolution has been rendered and understood officially is therefore intrinsically linked to state-building (that is, to conscious efforts of creating an apparatus of control under the heel of the ruling party) and to the building of a nation (an imagined entity of common attributes and a shared sense of belonging). Seeking hegemony in the representation of the revolution has always been part and parcel of consolidating and maintaining a hold on power (Alonso 1988).

The struggle rarely occupied just proponents of the revolution and its opponents, but often took place between different factions within the revolution itself. As Ann Lee Grimstad (this volume) shows, the shifting fortunes of John Okello are very revealing in this regard. The mesmerizing (and terrifying) initial voice of the revolution over radio, Okello played a leading role in the planning and initial conduct of the takeover, but soon found himself pushed out of power, exiled from the islands, and erased from the historical frame (much as Vladimír Clementis was airbrushed out of party propaganda pictures in Czechoslovakia following his arrest and execution [Kundera 1980]). After all, how could the revolt be an authentic, indigenous Zanzibari effort to seize the reins of self-determination if it was led by an obscure and mercurial Ugandan, later relegated to the dustbin of history? Inconvenient or unruly facts had to be displaced or dismissed, while prominent players who fit the orthodox script in favor at the time were pushed into the foreground of heroic accounts. From some of the earliest narratives on, there were concerted efforts to place Abeid Karume at the forefront of the revolt (despite the fact that he had fled to Dar es Salaam shortly before the night of the revolution) and to present the ASP as the vanguard party directing the flow of events with confident precision; these efforts intensified following the assassination of Karume in 1972 (*The Nationalist* 1967 [1965]; ASP 1974; Chuo cha Siasa n.d. [1976]; Mrina and Mattoke 1980). Yet those revolutionaries who were sidelined or fell from grace after the revolution offered quite different accounts. As a member of the Umma faction, Abdulrahman

Muhammed Babu continued to interpret the revolution in orthodox Marxist terms, with the Umma party allegedly playing a central role. In his version, the Umma party "transformed the status of what until then was simply a rebellion into a revolutionary insurrection. It broadened the objectives of the uprising from a narrow, lumpen, anti-Arab, anti-privilege, anti-this and anti-that perspective into a serious social revolution" (1991: 240). The revolution, in any case, had a way of consuming its children, as many of the first generation ended up dead, exiled, or sidelined from power.

Controlling Affects, Disciplining Bodies, and Reordering Space

The symbolic power of the revolution rested on the capacity of the state and the sole ruling party to control discourses, producing authorized historical accounts or literature and poetry (Myers 2000). As Michel-Rolph Trouillot (1995: 26) reminds us, "Silences enter the process of historical production at four crucial moments: the moment of fact creation (the making of *sources*); the moment of fact assembly (the making of *archives*); the moment of fact retrieval (the making of *narratives*); and the moment of retrospective significance (the making of *history* in the final instance)." But control of representation did not simply operate through discursive tools or the control over public media. The new regime also sought to oppress and discipline bodies. As elsewhere in Africa (Bayart 2008), coercion has long been part and parcel of the struggle to achieve hegemony in Zanzibar, instilling specific affects and exercising command over bodies. In the uprising and its aftermath, perceived opponents were specifically targeted, while others were simply caught up in the chaos—imprisoned, beaten, killed, or driven into exile. Those who remained behind quickly understood what would happen to those who actively disagreed or dissented. Imposing a "terror regime of the highest order" (Bakari 2001: 106), the security apparatus penetrated everyday life to an unprecedented degree, instilling uncertainty and distrust regarding what could be said or acknowledged publicly. As those times are remembered now, Zanzibaris wryly observe that if you were in a group of more than two, at least one among you was an informer—even in discreet street-corner discussions or conversations between friends and acquaintances. A climate of denunciation, pervasive fear, suspicion, and uncertainty worked to enforce a code of silence. The life stories of those who were key actors in such an authoritarian regime offer specific viewpoints for understanding compliance and complicity. In this volume, G. Thomas Burgess recounts the life and actions of Zanzibar's first attorney general (1964–77), Wolfango Dourado, showing how much his personal memory of the revolutionary regime is tied to his ambiguous position and social status in Zanzibari society. Reordering his memories through the language of universal values and principles—in moral and legalistic terms—Dourado recasts his past actions in ways that reveal the process of discursive production of honor, respectability, and self-esteem.

Moreover, the revolution relied upon on a wide array of techniques intended to discipline bodies. The violence and corporeal punishments unleashed in places like Pemba—remembered as the "days of caning" (Arnold 2003, and this volume)—or Tumbatu (Muhajir and Myers, this volume) were one aspect of this "politics of the whip" (Bayart 1993), while military parades, marches, youth groups, and work gangs were another. "Rituals of citizenship" (Burgess 2005) aimed to ingrain loyalty to the regime, ideological engagement, and an ethics of work among the youth, notably embodied in the practices of the Young Pioneers, were tools for nation-building efforts as a whole. These techniques also served as strategies to legitimize the revolution as the foundational myth of the post-independent Zanzibari nation while seeking to justify the authority of the men in power.

The capacity of the revolutionary regime to enforce ideological conformity also had distinctly material and spatial components. The state sought to construct a new spatial infrastructure of power. It let less privileged Zanzibaris from peri-urban and rural areas move into the houses of Stone Town, the space of the former elite, which had been abandoned by those who had left for exile. It took over old buildings, notably those epitomizing the power of the overthrown sultanate, like the former palace of Beit el Ajaib, or House of Wonders, converted into the ASP ideological training school. Built in 1883 by Sultan Barghash, this monument was the "most impressive creolization of global symbols" in a cosmopolitan archipelago opened to the world, through economic networks as well as the circulation of people and ideas (Prestholdt 2008: 108). Ideals of belonging and nationhood promoted after the revolution ran against this earlier conception of Zanzibar's relation to the rest of the world. The regime also constructed new spaces, like the East German–designed blocks of public housing in Michenzani, Kikwajuni, or Kilimani, which were models for new socialist cities and symbols of modernization (Bissell 2015). These new urban territories were meant to incarnate the idea of the revolution—or to be "the physical embodiment of the revolution's social experiment" (Myers 1994: 451)—while providing palpable evidence of its embodied achievements. And what the new regime did not raze and rebuild, it simply renamed: Mao Tse Tung stadium, V. I. Lenin hospital, Lumumba college, and Fidel Castro, Haile Selassie, and Ben Bella schools. The revolution made its way into the villages, too, with diesel generators, water pumps, and television sets (Winther 2008, 2011). It entered the homes of urban Zanzibaris, as families living in newly built Western-style modern housing abandoned coal ovens for electrical cookers (Myers 1993). In some present-day memory narratives, the revolution stands for stability, broad provision of social services, housing, work, and good wages. In this script, Karume is recast as Zanzibar's "Father of the Nation" because the material and spatial components of the post-revolution modernizing programs are burnished with a positive and nostalgic glow when compared to present-day living conditions under unrestrained capitalism (Bissell 2005: 236–7).

Yet the physical and material politics of the revolutionary regime spawned inconsistencies and contradictions, especially in recent years, when the prospect of attracting international aid, foreign investors, and tourists has fundamentally undermined the regime's efforts to be revolutionary in any meaningful sense. Space has been reordered in new ways, as former public buildings have been privatized and converted into tourist facilities and poorer residents have sold their houses to external investors and wealthy exiles who build hotels or luxury homes (Bissell 2005: 220–1). These spatial transformations and changes in population and wealth tend to erase the symbols of the revolution that were once foregrounded by the state. While an orientalist Arabian Nights fantasy has been fully embraced by the tourist industry in architecture, design, and decoration, the material traces of the revolution are becoming less and less visible. (Sites where significant events took place are unmarked; monuments, signs, or other visual displays are mostly absent.) The state has been unable to sustain its modernizing project in the socialist-inspired housing blocks outside Stone Town, which are increasingly decrepit. Important sites for the revolution, such as Mtoni police station (one of the first sites targeted by the revolutionary fighters, who were after weapons) or Ziwani police headquarters were never made heritage sites or commemorated as part of a "heritage circuit" of the revolution. The Beit el Ajaib, today a national museum of Zanzibar's history and culture, and the adjacent Palace Museum both recount the glory of the past sultans, but little is told about the revolution, except for two items displayed in a room on the ground floor of the Beit el Ajaib—President Karume's light-blue Zephyr automobile and a *khanga* hung on an adjacent wall bearing a drawing of the car inscribed with the words *Ahsante gari ya muheshimiwa wetu* ("Thanks for the car of our venerable [president]"). And, in fact, the making of the new museum in the House of Wonders entailed deconstructing and carting off exhibits dedicated to commemorating the material culture of the revolution. Two open-air statues of Abeid Karume are almost invisible to the common citizen, one erected in the courtyard of CCM headquarters in Kisiwandui area and the other almost hidden behind the Bwawani hotel, once Karume's pride (Martin 1978). And no other "heroes" of the revolution are ever officially commemorated, thus revealing gaps in the official history of the revolution and how it should be publicly represented. The 50th anniversary marked an attempt to at least partly reverse the lack of material and performative symbols of the revolution in recent years. The Tower of the Revolution erected in the middle of Michenzani is meant, through its massive presence, to go against the tide of this forgetting; a *taarab* musical performance was organized on the grounds where a "fete" had taken place on the night of the revolution, next to Ziwani police station, providing cover for the revolutionaries (a historical reference that the emcee insisted upon mentioning several times between songs); and, on 10 January 2014, medals were bestowed upon the "heroes" of the revolution—all loyal ASP/CCM politicians, army officers, or high-ranking administration officials.

Dissonant and Alternative Voices

As elsewhere, this configuration of power/knowledge has established an intimate dialectic between memory and forgetting, speech and silence, and presence and absence, as revolutionary authorities since the mid-1960s have worked to stifle oppositional accounts of the revolutionary past. The voices of ordinary Zanzibaris (both those who lived through the events and those who came after) have been muted or marginalized, and the embodied and everyday experience of living with the revolution has remained unrecognized. Consolidating a hegemonic version of the revolution always entailed labeling other views as subversive counter-narratives, and striving to silence or suppress them. This was notably the case in areas like Pemba and Tumbatu, considered loyal to the pre-revolutionary regime. As shown by Nathalie Arnold Koenings (this volume), Pembans have long been thought of as not "wielding the *panga*" (machete) to liberate themselves from colonial oppression.

They have paid the price for this supposed lack of participation in the revolution, being neglected, if not intentionally overlooked, by the post-revolutionary regime in terms of socioeconomic development. Their right to fully belong to the post-revolutionary body politic has always been put into question—often in contemptuous ways—by those who made the revolution the symbol of Zanzibariness. Similarly, Garth Myers and Makame Ali Muhajir (this volume) argue that the marginalized position of Tumbatu—a tiny island off the northeastern coast of Unguja—is rooted in its specific history and identity but is also the consequence of Tumbatu people's loyalty to the overthrown Zanzibar Nationalist Party (ZNP) government. The post-revolutionary regime unleashed repression and violence against them, notably in 1969 when an alleged coup against President Karume was said to involve Tumbatu, and organized their marginalization in Zanzibar's political life and socioeconomic development. In this repressive environment, while many Zanzibaris remained unconvinced by the official script of the revolution—precisely because it was so insistently and ideologically framed—counter-memories and alternative discourses circulated only among a few trusted intimates or very close family, passed down in diffused and fragmentary forms.

Two phases can be identified in the public expression of alternative narratives. In the politicized wake of the revolution, alternative narratives were invariably cast as reactionary or alien. Thus, other ways of understanding the revolution were insistently linked with political opponents and dismissed as reflecting the ideologies of those who ended up exiled or on the losing side. The interpretation of the revolution oscillated between assertion and counter-assertion, orthodoxy and opposition. With political and economic liberalization in the mid-1980s came a proliferation of recollections and recastings of the events of 1964 (Loimeier 2006, and this volume; Fouéré 2012). Ordinary people also increasingly began recounting their personal memories or stories they had heard. In this volume, Kjersti Larsen shows how much remembrance is tied up with everyday interactions. Among some Zanzibaris of Indian origin, watching videos together unrelated to Zanzibar—notably movies from the Indian subcontinent—can spark open reflections about the revolution when scenes from a movie remind them of situations they lived through during or after the revolution, or situations that others recounted later. Quoting Michael Lambek and Paul Antze, Larsen reminds us that memory "is always found in context" (1996: xvii), but this context is made up of both micro situations of remembrance and a wider configuration that makes such micro situations possible. This echoes Gavin MacArthur's contribution about the everyday operations of words and actions that perform memory and identity. Focusing on the experience of Asians of Goan origin and depicting micro situations of interaction in which race and the right to belong are at stake, MacArthur shows the extent to which the specific understandings of the revolution that sustain today's production of Zanzibariness are tightly bound to moral conceptions of correctness, rectitude, and virtue. The past is about politics, but also morality.

In the absence of processes of review conducted publicly (whether in the form of "truth and reconciliation" commissions, reparations, or other means of moral and political reckoning), the revolution has remained enigmatic and elusive. As G. Thomas Burgess has noted, "As citizens and exiles contemplate the past, they continue to create and repeat multiple parallel stories and scripts, which variously represent the views of the Revolution's winners and losers, the islands' political establishment and its opposition" (2002: 47). Especially with the reopening of multiparty politics, how one interprets the revolution is tightly bound to party affiliation, activity, and agency, as CUF and CCM have waged a series of intensely contested and divided elections marked by violence, repression, and widespread allegations of fraud (Rajab, this volume). One's identity and political allegiances are bound up with how one depicts the revolutionary past—whether as a liberation struggle or a catastrophic loss of sovereignty; an outside invasion or indigenous uprising; an expression of African solidarity and class struggle or a racialized civil war. For many in Zanzibar these polemics promise little enlightenment—indeed, these discourses are reminiscent of the politicized times that preceded the revolution, when political rhetoric took on sharp edges and produced violent responses, marking *siasa*, or politics, as a dangerous and divisive sphere.

Searching for the "Truth": Epistemic Murk and Historical Quest

To succeed in reproducing the official ideology and political rule, the "not telling" about the revolution was as important a mechanism as its "telling"—whether in the form of narrations, performances, or materiality and space. Controlling official history went far beyond filling the public sphere with one allegedly unambiguous state-led version of the revolution and driving remembrances and interpretations that did not correspond to this official version underground. First, it entailed creating a zone of secrecy. Leaving holes in the chain of events or erasing the role of opponents and having them "disappear" from history were, among other things, part of a politics of secrecy geared toward hiding certain historical facts that may have incited resistance and created disorder. Second, secrecy went together with lies. These could be "small lies, partial truths, and deliberately ambiguous meanings" (Jay 2010, quoted in Minkley and Legassick 2000: 5) aimed at distorting the exact identity of some actors of the revolution, mixing up causes and effects, or inventing a posteriori ideological objectives for actions that were initially partly driven by chaos and arbitrariness. But obfuscation as a strategy could also consist of deliberate falsification and outright lies that, as they produced a total "reversal of the truth," sought to "install a monolithic belief system to which no alternative is possible" (Jay 2010, quoted in Minkley and Legassick 2000: 5)—a modus operandi typical of autocratic regimes.

Much as it tried, the Revolutionary Government was never able to fully impose a monolithic belief system in Zanzibar. While a multiplicity of unofficial scripts about the revolution continued to circulate underground or behind closed doors, fear and uncertainty curtailed open discussion, and pervasive secrecy and deception created an official story that remained elusive and fuzzy, full of holes and gaps. This intentional uncertainty was a means for the state to remind ordinary citizens that they were deprived of the right to know—therefore asserting power not only by crafting what can be publicly known but also by designating what should remain unknown or unspoken as well. These tactics serve as a means of impeding or blocking the formation of powerful counter-narratives of the revolution. If the official story had been consistent, detailed, and documented, oppositional narratives would have gained greater traction insofar as they would have been built by investigating, questioning, or even negating each and every detail of the official version of history, rather than having to confront uncertainties, unknowns, and unstable accounts. There has been, one may say, "a politics of epistemic murk" (Taussig 1987) produced through the constant interplay between disclosure and concealment, or truth and lies, which ultimately has proved an effective tool for the regime in power.

In this context of uncertainty, whispers, and rumors, street narratives about the "unrevealed truths" of the revolution seemed all the more convincing precisely because their underground status gave them the appearance of reliability. This is true of Internet sources, too, as they have been increasingly made accessible, but their status remains quite difficult for ordinary Zanzibaris to assess. In her essay in this volume, Marie-Aude Fouéré focuses on how the contested *Africa Addio* documentary, featuring rough footage allegedly shot a few days after the revolution and showing hundreds of dead bodies in mass graves and scattered on beaches, is increasingly being used as a potential source of information to investigate what "really happened" during the revolution despite tremendous doubts about its authenticity. The powerful appeal this movie has had on those who have seen it in Zanzibar partly derives from the government's restriction on its circulation. Indeed, many see the ban as a sign that the film contains certain truths that the state tried to conceal for many years. Yet as the authenticity of these images remains highly uncertain, the authoritativeness of *Africa Addio* as historical evidence to interrogate the revolutionary past is sharply questioned by many viewers. But at the same time, watching the film has also paradoxically triggered new ways of reflecting about how to collectively overcome the trauma of the past and imagine a post-racial Zanzibari society.

The appeal to investigate "what really happened" has always figured prominently among those who discredit the revolution. These accounts seek to unearth and set the "real facts" against distorted versions of the events, pervasive secrecy and falsification, and ideologically driven interpretations. In a context of epistemic murk, a call to know "what really happened" does not come as any surprise. This call for a consensual and factual historical account is prompted by a desire for "history" as a neutral exercise that stands outside or beyond events and can deliver the truth of what they mean. Facts, in this perspective, are seen as able to contain meanings and bear witness in some unequivocal way. We contend, however, that this conception of facts and history overlooks the very nature of the "truth," its polysemy and indeterminacy; that is, such views precisely fail to account for the political processes that served to produce certain truths about the revolution while disallowing or discrediting many others. There are always multiple versions of the truth, and they are relative, selective, and representational. The recourse to "real facts" also overlooks an important aspect of debates about the revolution—namely, that the word "revolution" itself can be used to refer to quite different historical referents depending who uses it, on which occasions, and for what purposes. In the vocabulary of semiotics, the "revolution" is a signifier that has no fixed or definite signified attached but rather ambiguous, flexible, and variable signifieds assigned by different actors according to the settings of its use. Due to the inherent polysemy and indeterminacy of words, no factual historical version will ever settle struggles over what the revolution was and what it means. Any efforts to settle these struggles by enabling different versions to converge, even when they aim for appeasement and social healing, will always consist in controlling the polysemy and indeterminacy of the signifier. As Stuart Hall observes, "[S]tatements about the social, political, or moral world are rarely ever simply true or false; and 'the facts' do not enable us to decide definitively about their truth or falsehood, partly because 'facts' can be construed in different ways. The very language we use to describe the so-called facts interferes in this process of finally deciding what is true and what is false" (1996: 202–3).

Interestingly, many of the nonofficial writings about the revolution that call for factuality and certainty proceed in ways quite similar to the regime's accounts of the revolutionary past: They bend, distort, conceal, minimize, or exaggerate some specific events or actions to the detriment of others. In this volume, however, our aim is not to sort out the works that fall under "academic historiography" from those that may be labeled differently (e.g. amateur, learned, politically oriented, revisionist, conspiratorial, etc.). Rather, we contend that, from an anthropological point of view, the divergent interpretations of the revolution that are set down on paper provide heuristic material for various reasons. First, these texts give access to diverse understandings of the social world. Some bear the traces of the violence experienced during the revolution, or the lingering traces of those traumatic times; others give insight into the political ideologies of the early 1960s and efforts to forge new postcolonial identities; and yet others tell about how exile or the diasporic condition informs political subjectivities in the wider Indian Ocean world. By situating these writings in the time and place of their production, we follow the social trajectory of their authors and examine the goals these texts were intended to serve. In this way, we argue that these works constitute irreplaceable documents to explore what people imagine to be the past. Second, these accounts can instruct us as to how particular stories of dramatic events transmitted orally can be collated, recast, recomposed, and reinterpreted to produce a new narrative. Such writings must therefore not be used as autonomous and self-sustaining documents but as composite and hybrid narratives made of multiple intertwined strands of individual remembrance, collective memories, deep-rooted ideologies, rumors and whispers, political speeches, and past images. To follow John and Jean Comaroff's insight, they must not be studied as "literary topoi"—that is, as mere content disconnected from any context—but as accounts "anchored in the process of their production, in the orbits of connection that give them life and force" (1992: 34). They need to be scrutinized, therefore, as a body of texts in dialogue even though they may have been written at different historical moments.

Adjudicating the Dead of the Revolution

This call for facts against distortion, for historical certainty against epistemic murk, is best exemplified by debates regarding the number of deaths the revolution caused. Massive violence was unleashed for days, even weeks, after the night of the overthrow of the government. It targeted people of Arab origin as well as Indians and Comorians whom the revolutionaries considered as allies of the "Arab oppressor." Attempts to control or contain the turbulence of the revolution appeared vain in the face of what a foreign observer called "terror" (Clayton 1981: 71). Several contributors to this volume remind us how the scope and scale of the killings remain uncertain, if not unknown. According to Jonathon Glassman, opponents of the revolution tend to inflate the number of deaths while its defenders minimize this figure (2011: 374n1). To this day, some earlier death toll figures seem to be gross underestimates (Lofchie, for example, cites only 68 deaths [1965: 203–4]), while the numbers given by the self-appointed leader of the insurrection, "Field Marshal" John Okello, of 7,994 people killed during the very first days of the revolution and a total of 13,635 dead and 21,462 "enemies" detained (Okello 1967: 150, 160) seem exaggerated. As Glassman notes (2011: 374n1), many subsequent writers have quoted Okello's boast of 13,000 Arabs killed, a figure that can be seen as just one of the many "apocalyptic fantasies" that fills Okello's memoirs. In any case, as Glassman observes, it is undoubtedly clear that "despite the uncertainties, numbers are often presented as if they were documented fact."

In this volume, our aim is not to solve this delicate issue, which would require a thorough and large-scale enquiry by the state, a search for bodies and mass graves, the scrutinizing of civil registers and census data, enquiries with religious leaders and families who held funerals, and the collection of individual and family stories not just in Zanzibar but also abroad. Rather, we see the growing debates about the number of deaths as an object of enquiry in and of itself, one indicative of wider sociocultural processes. First, we note that discussions about how many people were killed, and under what circumstances, have increased recently. We see these debates as undeniably tied to the diffusion of quite different interpretations of the revolution, which has been characterized as an "invasion," as "ethnic cleansing," or even as genocide. These strands of interpretation are not exactly new (see, for example, Kharusi 1969), but they seem to have gained publicity and political salience recently. These terms have become recurring tropes in the writings and social media of the opposition and exiled families (Babakerim 1994; Fairooz 1995; Shariff 2014), and they crop up locally among political opponents of the regime. Such descriptions are often associated with the diffusion of a more racialist, conspiracy-oriented conception of history in which the revolution is said to have been masterminded by neighboring Tanganyika and its then-president, Julius K. Nyerere (Ghassany 2010). Along the lines of this revisionist script, the ideological foundations of the revolution rested less upon political leanings or ideologies (such as socialism, anticolonialism, and anti-imperialism) than upon sentiments of racial revenge and religious hatred (Harding 2003; Fouéré 2014).

In this light, debates about numbers of deaths raise sociopolitical issues that numbers themselves can never manage to resolve. Even if a verifiable number of deaths caused by the 1964 uprising could be established, this figure would only indicate an order of magnitude while utterly failing to express (much less managing to address) the sense of widespread social dislocation and trauma that has continued down to this day. The social impact of the massacres is not the product of quantities but of traces that intermingle emotions, experience, memories, official accounts, oppositional rewritings, and the ways in which all of these have been mediated. The fantasy of concreteness in numbers mystifies deeper and more profound questions about how to measure loss on a mass scale. It shows that what is at stake, in debates about numbers in Zanzibar, has more to do with political struggles than with social healing. And if the revolution were officially recast a "genocide," as some advocate, this would have far-reaching legal and moral implications that would undeniably generate new types of disputes related to restitution and compensation—conjuring up ghosts of the past while replaying old enmities and conflicts in a new register.

Interwoven Temporalities: The Revolution and the Legacy of Slavery

Narratives of the revolution, whether popular, militant, or scholarly, do not speak only of the tumultuous revolutionary moment and its aftermath. They connect, upstream, to other historical periods or processes that shaped the archipelago over the long term such as slavery and the slave trade; the precolonial era of Swahili rulers before the rise and political hegemony of the Omani sultanate; the late 19th-century modernizing apogee under Sultan Barghash (r. 1870–88) of the al-Busaidi family, which accelerated the global integration of Zanzibar initiated by his father, Sultan Seyyid Said (Prestholdt 2008); and the reordering of the city space and lifestyles under British colonial rule, remembered "as a time when things worked, the law was the law, and a shilling went a long way" (Bissell 2005: 222). Downstream, memories of the revolution mix with a variety of events that have occurred since Zanzibar's independence: the economic reforms of the mid-1980s, which reopened the archipelago to the world; the turbulence, even violence, of the multiparty elections, notably in 2000–2001, when "bullets were raining" (Human Rights Watch 2002) and people lost their lives; the several critical moments of overt struggle over the legal, constitutional, and institutional arrangements of the union with mainland Tanzania; the political struggles between CCM and CUF; and, since 2010, the *maridhiano* and the power-sharing government. Yet other historical moments could be cited, as social memory associates the 1964 revolution—as an event and as a signifier—with diverse other past and latter-day moments of high significance in Zanzibari society. This profusion of associations reminds us that ordinary memories do not follow the rigid temporal divisions generally used in academic historiography, which, in the case of Zanzibar, is reflected in the ways academic histories often close on the eve of the revolution. Instead, popular modes of relating to the past connect different temporalities in fluctuating ways, concatenating the precolonial, colonial, and postcolonial times. In memories, time is stretched and aggregated, allowing rapprochements, interspersions, or even assimilations of historically distant events. What is significant about this approach to social memory is that, instead of prioritizing a specific moment over another, it emphasizes the need to connect every memory object—when constituted as a research object—to the different temporalities in which local modes of understanding and remembering intertwine.

The case of slavery and the slave trade well illustrates our argument about the entanglement of different historical types of experience and the concatenation of various temporalities in collective memories. After the revolution, the new regime turned this epochal event into a grand liberation narrative from colonialism and oppression, as we noted above. But the revolution was also cast as a liberation from the never-forgotten experience and long-term impact of slavery and the slave trade in Zanzibari society. Historian Jonathon Glassman reminds us that the "spectre of slavery" haunted some of the worst violence of 1960s Zanzibar—that is, the 1961 anti-Arab election pogroms and the 1964 revolution. Narratives of slavery were at the heart of the racial thought and racial politics that took root in Zanzibar (Glassman 2011: 92). They became a central trope of opposition between the political thinkers and activists of the two main political parties in the isles from the mid-1950s to 1963, the ZNP and the ASP. Through their respective pamphleteering newspapers, these parties disseminated interpretations of slavery that were diametrically opposed. Pioneers of a ZNP-led monarchy embodying Islamic faith and Arabocentric urban high culture, such as ZNP founding member Ali Muhsin al-Barwani, depicted slavery in Zanzibar as "entirely devoid of the cruelties that were usual concomitants in the other parts of the world" (quoted in Glassman 2011: 92), casting it not only as "benign" slavery (Cooper 1977) but also, with strong paternalist overtones, as a long-term "civilizing" process. On their side, ASP activists championed the rights of slave descendants and responded with simplistic and apocalyptic images of enslavement and oppressive slave conditions (see also Glassman 2004, 2010). This depiction of slavery was also used on public occasions, such as the political rallies held before independence, as a rhetorical device to instill fear and racial hatred. It replayed pervasive local sentiments of resentment against and fear of the "Arabs"—constructed as an essentialized group—and imaginaries of slavery that laid the ground for the building of a racial state based upon Africanness.

These opposed mythologized stories continued long after the revolution. As the ASP took power, it invoked the same motifs of liberation from colonial rule and capitalist exploitation, but it also resorted to similar narratives of justice—and revenge—against a past social order allegedly built upon the barbaric, Arab-dominated slave trade and slave ownership. To take just one example from the propaganda literature of the single ruling party in the 1970s, the depiction of slavery and the slave trade mobilized the image of the exploited clove- or coconut-plantation slave, thus reducing the variety of working conditions, social statuses, and specific worker/owner relationships to one main figuration of slavery, while also minimizing the agency of the slaves. Muhammed S. Khatib's (1975: 11) long epic poem (*utenzi*) on the liberation of Zanzibar, which was part of a Kiswahili poetry series dedicated to the glorification of the revolutionary regime, depicts the times of slavery under Sultan Seyyid Said as follows:

Utumwa ukazaliwa
Watu wakanunuliwa
Na hata kuadhibiwa
Shida kuwaelemeya

Wenyeji wakafurushwa
Mashambani kulimishwa
Kwa mateso wakachoshwa
Wengine wakajifiya

Wakapandishwa minazi
Kuwa wao ni wakwezi
Hiyo kawa yao kazi
Lazima kuabudiya

Karafuu kualimishwa
Tena kwa kulazimishwa
Hakuna kuhiarishwa
Lazima kuhudumiya.

Slavery was born
People were bought
And even tortured
Burdened by tribulations

The indigenes were evicted
Forced to till the land
They were consumed by terror
Others perished

They were forced to climb coconut trees
Becoming upward crawlers
That became their vocation
Which they had to glorify

They were taught clove planting
Again by compulsion
They had no other choice
But to obey.[5]

---

5   The free translation in English of Khatib's poem is by Ahmed Rajab.

This official discourse also repeated the 1950s stories of pregnant slaves allegedly disemboweled by Arab masters who wanted to satisfy their lovers' curiosity about what a human fetus looked like, and tales of female slaves who had to sweep the sultan's palaces with their breasts (Glassman 2010). The Revolutionary Government also designated several spaces associated with slavery—the Mkunazini slave market in Stone Town, the Mangapwani caves in northeastern Unguja—as national heritage sites, where visitors were told stories about enslavement, slave trading, and the nature of slavery that were often unsupported or contradicted by historical evidence. Conceptions of slavery that had become deeply rooted among the Africans of Zanzibar in the 1950s were remade into a tool for celebrating the revolution as a triumph and for building the political legitimacy of the post-1964 regime. These images were also recurrently used, in more or less veiled ways, in partisan contests between CCM and CUF during election campaigns in 2000, 2005, 2010, and 2015. CCM has long castigated the CUF as an Arab party—heir to the ZNP—whose aim is to restore a sultanate and a regime of slavery. And the old language of slavery has not simply been used by the revolutionary regime to perpetuate racial divisions and antagonisms in Zanzibar, thereby consolidating political support and renewing the regime's legitimacy. These discourses have also been conflated with socioeconomic representations about property and dispossession, patrician high culture and low-status popular culture, or autochthony and foreignness that have both permeated and shaped present-day socioeconomic hierarchies.

The metanarrative of slavery propagated by the ASP and the revolutionary government never fully submerged or silenced other conceptions (whether historically grounded or based upon misconceptions inherited from the 1950s) of the experience of slavery in Zanzibar. As shown by Nathaniel Mathews in his contribution to this volume, Nasser al-Riyami's recent book *Zanzibar: Personalities & Events (1828–1972)* is a good example of the resilience of narratives of the past in the present. This is especially the case among families of Arab origin, whether ancestral or mythical, who went into exile after the revolution. Al-Riyami, who belonged to a generation that did not experience the revolution directly but grew up in exile before becoming Omani citizens, depicts slavery in pre-revolutionary Zanzibar in ways very similar to how ZNP circles depicted it in the 1950s—as benign, civilizing, and beneficial to integration into Zanzibari society. In this regard, this depiction resonates with arguments developed not only along the lines of the incendiary ZNP-owned newspapers of the 1950s, as seen above, but even of literature published more recently. In 1999, Issa bin Nasser al-Ismaily published a recollection of Zanzibar history from exile, *Zanzibar: Kinyang'anyiro na Utumwa* (*Zanzibar: The Scramble and Slavery*), that dismisses the evils of slavery and the role of Arabs in the slave trade in ways that likewise recall the earlier ZNP arguments. Both al-Riyami and al-Ismaily exemplify conceptions of slavery and the slave trade that took root and prevailed in the context of exile and forced migration of people of Arab origin (see also al-Barwani 1997; Kharusi 1969). This literature does not remain confidential but circulates among the educated urban population of Stone Town. It is being referred to in debates that entangle the experience, impact, and meaning of slavery and the slave trade in Zanzibar and the epochal event of the revolution. This has been the case, for instance, at the former slave market (Glassman 2010; Wynne-Jones 2011), a site that has increasingly polarized conceptions of slavery and the slave trade in ways that are deeply connected to the trauma and disruption brought about by the revolution.

Coda: "Revolution Forever!" (*Mapinduzi Daima!*) or a Revolution Not Even Past?

"History is the fruit of power, but power itself is never so transparent that its analysis becomes superfluous," observes Michel-Rolph Trouillot in *Silencing the Past*. "The ultimate mark of power may be its invisibility; the ultimate challenge, the exposition of its roots" (1995: xix). When we move beyond the terrain of formal history to embrace memory, media, and the myriad ways ordinary citizens seek to make sense of the past, these words take on even greater resonance. Unearthing the roots of power assumes even more significance when the past itself remains largely unresolved, and the trauma and tensions of the profound transformations of 50 years ago continue to haunt the present. In strictly material terms and with regard to its political economy, the "revolution" is largely an absent presence—a figment of its former self. Devoid of any actual ideological intent to transform the fabric of society and empower workers or peasants in a classic sense, the Revolutionary Government is more committed to continuity and stability than upheaval—seeking above all, to maintain its hold on power. And yet, even as revolutionary goals are vitiated by the regime's embrace of neoliberal policies, holding onto the guise of the revolution has become paradoxically all the more critical. Representing the Zanzibar revolution and framing the ruling party in particular ways in public discourse remains a key tactic of the regime, one that is deeply contested in daily life—producing many of the complications and contradictions we explore in the pages that follow. Efforts to make sense of what happened and what it still means today is an on-going process, intrinsically linked in Zanzibar as elsewhere to the difficult struggle to bring about a more participatory society, a vibrant and open public sphere, more inclusive senses of community, and modes of belonging in a postcolonial world. In remembering and representing the revolution 50 years later, we are reminded once again of William Faulkner's classic observation in *Requiem for a Nun*: "The past is never dead. It's not even past."

References

Adam, Adam Shafi

1978 *Kasri ya Mwinyi Fuad*. Dar es Salaam: Tanzania Publishing House.

Afro-Shirazi Party

1974 *Maendeleo ya Mapinduzi ya Afro-Shirazi Party, 1964–1974*. Zanzibar: n.p.

1970 *Tumemaliza Mwaka wa Sita, 1970. Tanzania Inaendelea Mbele. Matunda ya Mwaka wa Sita wa Mapinduzi Visiwani*. Zanzibar: Shirika la Upigaji Chapa.

Alonso, Ana Maria

1988 "The Effects of Truth: Re-presentations of the Past and the Imagining of Community." *Journal of Historical Sociology* 1(1): 33–57.

Arnold, Nathalie

2003 "Wazee Wakijua Mambo!/Elders Used to Know Things!: Occult Powers and Revolutionary History in Pemba, Zanzibar." Ph.D. diss., Indiana University, Bloomington.

Anderson, Benedict

1983 *Imagined Communities: Reflections on the Origin and Spread of Nationalism*. London and New York: Verso.

Askew, Kelly

2002 *Performing the Nation: Swahili Music and Cultural Politics in Tanzania*. Chicago: University of Chicago Press.

Babakerim

1994 *The Aftermath of Zanzibar Revolution*. Muscat: privately printed.

Babu, Abdulrahman Muhammed

1991 "The 1964 Revolution: Lumpen or Vanguard?" In *Zanzibar under Colonial Rule*, ed. Abdul Sheriff and Ed Ferguson, 220–249. London: James Currey.

Bakari, Mohammed

2001 *The Democratisation Process in Zanzibar: A Retarded Transition*. Hamburg: Institut für Afrika-Kunde.

Bakari, Mohammed, and Alexander Makulilo

2012 "Beyond Polarity in Zanzibar? The 'Silent' Referendum and the Government of National Unity." *Journal of Contemporary African Studies* 30(2): 195–218.

al-Barwani, Ali Muhsin

1997 *Conflicts and Harmony in Zanzibar: Memoirs*. Dubai: n.p..

Bayart, Jean-François

2008 "Hégémonie et coercition en Afrique subsaharienne. La 'politique de la chicotte.'" *Politique africaine* 2(110): 123–52.

1993 *The State in Africa: The Politics of the Belly*. Heinemann: London, 1993. (Originally published as *L'État en Afrique. La politique du ventre* [Paris: Fayard, 1989].)

Bissell, William Cunningham

2015 "From 'Progress' to Postcolonial Relics: Modernist Architecture and Design in Africa." In *The Modernist World*, ed. Stephen Ross and Allana C. Lindgren, 164–73. London: Routledge.

2005 "Engaging Colonial Nostalgia." *Cultural Anthropology* 20(2): 215–48.

1999 "Colonial Constructions: Historicizing Debates on Civil Society in Africa." In *Civil Society and the Political Imagination in Africa*, ed. John L. Comaroff and Jean Comaroff, 124–59. Chicago: University of Chicago Press.

Burgess, G. Thomas

2009 *Race, Revolution, and the Struggle for Human Rights in Zanzibar: The Memoirs of Ali Sultan Issa and Seif Sharif Hamad*. Athens, Ohio: Ohio University Press.

2005 "The Young Pioneers and the Rituals of Citizenship in Revolutionary Zanzibar." *Africa Today* 51(3): 3–29.

2002 "Cinema, Bell Bottoms and Miniskirts: Struggles over Youth and Citizenship in Revolutionary Zanzibar." *International Journal of African Historical Studies* 35(2/3): 287–313.

Chuo cha Siasa

n.d. [1976] *Maelezo ya Nyumba ya A.S.P.* Zanzibar: n.p.

Clayton Anthony

1981 *The Zanzibari Revolution and Its Aftermath*. London: C. Hurst & Company.

Comaroff, John, and Jean Comaroff
1992 *Ethnography and the Historical Imagination.* Boulder, Colo.: Westview Press.

Cooper, Frederick
1981 "Islam and Cultural Hegemony: The Ideology of Slave Owners on the East African Coast." In *The Ideology of Slavery in Africa*, ed. P. E. Lovejoy, 271–307. London, Sage.

Croucher, Sarah K.
2014 *Capitalism and Cloves: An Archaeology of Plantation Life on Nineteenth-Century Zanzibar.* New York: Springer.

Davis, Natalie Zemon, and Randolph Starn
1989 "Introduction." *Representations* 26: 1–6.

Erll, Astrid, and Ann Rigney, eds.
2009 *Media and Cultural Memory: Mediation, Remediation, and the Dynamics of Cultural Memory.* Berlin: Walter de Gruyter.

Fabian, Steven
2013 "East Africa's Gorée: Slave Trade and Slave Tourism in Bagamoyo, Tanzania." *Canadian Journal of African Studies/La revue canadienne des études africaines* 47: 95–114.

Fairooz, Aman Thani
1995 *Ukweli ni Huu (Kuusuta Uwongo).* Dubai: self-published.

Fouéré, Marie-Aude
2014 "Recasting Julius Nyerere in Zanzibar: The Revolution, the Union and the Enemy of the Nation." *Journal of Eastern African Studies* 8(3): 478–96.
2012 "Reinterpreting Revolutionary Zanzibar in the Media Today: The Case of *Dira* Newspaper." *Journal of Eastern African Studies* 6(4): 672–89.
2011 "Chronique des élections de 2010 à Zanzibar." *Politique africaine* 121: 127–45.

Ghassany, Harith
2010 *Kwaheri Ukoloni, Kwaheri Uhuru! Zanzibar na Mapinduzi ya Afrabia* [Goodbye Colonialism, Goodbye Independence! Zanzibar and the Revolution of Afrabia]. Self published, https://kwaheri.files.wordpress.com/2010/05/kwaheri-ukoloni-kwaheri-uhuru.pdf, accessed 18 July 2016.

Glassman, Jonathon

2011 *War of Words, War of Stones: Racial Thought and Violence in Colonial Zanzibar*. Bloomington, Ind.: Indiana University Press.

2010 "Racial Violence, Universal History, and Echoes of Abolition in Twentieth-Century Zanzibar." In *Abolitionism and Imperialism in Britain, Africa, and the Atlantic*, ed. Derek Peterson, 175–206. Athens, Ohio: Ohio University Press.

2004 "Slower than a Massacre: The Multiple Sources of Racial Thought in Colonial Africa." *American Historical Review* 109(3): 720–54.

Gillis, John R.

1994 "Memory and Identity: The History of a Relationship." In *Commemorations: The Politics of National Identity*, ed. John R. Gillis, 3–24. Princeton, N.J.: Princeton University Press.

Green, Maia

2014 *The Development State: Aid, Culture and Civil Society in Tanzania*. London: James Currey.

Halbwachs, Maurice

1980 *The Collective Memory*. New York: Harper & Row. (Originally published as *La mémoire collective* [Paris: Presses Universitaires de France, 1950].)

Hall, Stuart

1996 "The West and the Rest: Discourse and Power." In *Modernity: An Introduction to Modern Societies*, ed. Stuart Hall et al., 184–227. Oxford: Blackwell.

Harding, Leonhard

2003 "Nyerere in Neuem Licht. Interpretationen in den Lebensgeschichten von Sansibaris." In *Unser Leben vor der Revolution und danach—Maisha yetu kabla ya mapinduzi na baadaye*, ed. Sauda A. Barwani et al., 493–577. Cologne: Rüdiger Köppe Verlag.

Human Rights Watch

2002 *Bullets Were Raining: The January 2001 Attack on Peaceful Demonstrators in Zanzibar*. New York: Human Rights Watch.

al-Ismaily, Issa bin Nasser

1999 *Zanzibar: Kinyang'anyiro na Utumwa* [Zanzibar: The Scramble and Slavery]. Muscat, Oman: n.p.

Jay, Martin

1999 "Mendacious Flowers." *London Review of Books* (21): 29 July.

Kharusi, Ahmed Seif

1969 *The Agony of Zanzibar: A Victim of the New Colonialism*. Richmond, U.K.: Foreign Affairs Publishing.

Khatib, Muhammed S.

1975 *Utenzi wa Ukombozi wa Zanzibar* [An Epic Poem on the Liberation of Zanzibar]. Oxford: Oxford University Press.

Kundera, Milan

1980 *The Book of Laughter and Forgetting*. New York: Penguin Books.

Lambek, Michael, and Paul Antze

1996 "Introduction: Forecasting Memory." In *Tense Past: Cultural Essays in Trauma and Memory*, ed. Paul Antze and Michael Lambek, xi–xxxviii. New York: Routledge.

Lentz, Carola

2013 "The 2010 Independence Jubilees: The Politics and Aesthetics of National Commemoration in Africa." *Nations and Nationalism* 19(2): 217–37.

Lofchie, Michael F.

1967 "Was Okello's Revolution a Conspiracy?" *Transition* 33, October–November: 36–42.

1965 *Zanzibar: Background to Revolution*. Princeton, N.J.: Princeton University Press.

Loimeier, Roman

2006 "Memories of Revolution: Zur Deutungsgeschichte einer Revolution (Sansibar 1964)." *Afrika Spectrum* 41(2): 175–97.

Makulilo, Alexander B.

2011 "The Zanzibar Electoral Commission and its Feckless Independence." *Journal of Third World Studies* 28(1): 263–83.

Mapuri, Omar R.

1996 *Zanzibar: The 1964 Revolution: Achievements and Prospects*. Dar es Salaam: TEMA Publishers.

Martin, Esmond B.
1978 *Zanzibar: Tradition and Revolution*. London: Hamish Hamilton.

Mbembe, Achille
1992 "Provisional Notes on the Postcolony." *Africa* 62(1): 3–37.

Minkley, Gary, and Martin Legassick
2000 "'Not Telling': Secrecy, Lies, and History." *History and Theory* 39(4): 1–10.

Mrina, B. F., and W. T. Mattoke
1980 *Mapambano ya Ukumbozi Zanzibar*. Dar es Salaam: Tanzania Publishing House.

Myers, Garth A.
2000 "Narrative Representations of Revolutionary Zanzibar." *Journal of Historical Geography* 26(3): 429–48.
1994 "Making the Socialist City of Zanzibar." *Geographical Review* 84(4): 451–64.

The Nationalist
1967 [1965] "The 'Official' Version of the Zanzibar Revolution, as Reported in *The Nationalist* Dar es Salaam, 12th January, 1965." Reprinted in John Okello, *Revolution in Zanzibar*, 209–222. Nairobi: East African Publishing House.

Nora, Pierre
1989 "Between Memory and History: Les lieux de mémoire." *Representations* 26: 7–25.

Okello, John
1967 *Revolution in Zanzibar*. Nairobi: East African Publishing House.

Presthold, Jeremy
2008 *Domesticating the World: African Consumerism and the Genealogies of Globalization*. Berkeley, Cal.: University of California Press.

al-Riyami, Nasser Abdulla
2012 *Zanzibar: Personalities & Events (1828–1972)*, trans. Ali bin Rashid al-Abri. Cairo and Muscat: Beirut Bookshop.

Scott, James C.
1990 *Domination and the Arts of Resistance: Hidden Transcripts.* New Haven, Conn.: Yale University Press.

Serikali ya Mapinduzi ya Zanzibar [Revolutionary Government of Zanzibar]
2014 *Hotuba ya Rais wa Zanzibar na Mwenyekiti wa Baraza ya Mapinduzi Mhe. Dk. Ali Mohamed Shein katika Maadhimisho ya Sherehe za Miaka 50 ya Mapinduzi ya Zanzibar, Tarehe 12 Januari, 2014.* Zanzibar: Serikali ya Mapinduzi ya Zanzibar.

Shariff, Ibrahim Noor
2014 *Tanzania na propaganda za udini.* N.p.: Self-published.

Shivji, Issa
2008 *Pan-Africanism or Pragmatism? Lessons of Tanganyika-Zanzibar Union.* Dar es Salaam: Mkuki na Nyota.

Sturken, Marita
1997 *Tangled Memories: The Vietnam War, the AIDS Epidemic, and the Politics of Remembering.* Berkeley, Cal.: University of California Press.

Taussig, Michael
1987 *Shamanism, Colonialism, and the Wild Man: A Study in Terror and Healing.* Chicago: University of Chicago Press.

Trouillot, Michel-Rolph
1995 *Silencing the Past: Power and the Production of History.* Boston: Beacon Press

Werbner, Richard
1998 "Beyond Oblivion: Confronting Memory Crisis." In *Memory and the Postcolony: African Anthropology and the Critique of Power,* ed. Richard Werbner, 1–17. London: Zed Books.

Winther, Tanja
2011 "Les rapports entre État et citoyens à Zanzibar. Un récit ethnographique à partir de la fourniture d'électricité." *Politique africaine* 121: 107–25.
2008 *The Impact of Electricity: Development, Desires and Dilemmas.* Oxford, New York: Berghahn Books.

Wynne-Jones, Stephanie
2011 "Recovering and Remembering a Slave Route in Central Tanzania." In *Slavery in Africa: Archaeology and Memory,* ed. Paul J. Lane and K. C. MacDonald, 317–42. Oxford: Oxford University Press.

Chapter Two

Memories of Revolution: Patterns of Interpretation of the 1964 Revolution in Zanzibar

Roman Loimeier

In the introduction to *Geschichte Afrikas im 19. und 20. Jahrhundert* (African History in the 19th and 20th Centuries), the German historian Leonard Harding (1992) remarks that historiography always tries to interpret the past from the perspective of the present. Such presentist interpretations of the past are not uniform, however: Different schools of thought compete with each other and defend their respective interpretations of the past. History and debates about the past always involve a struggle for *Deutungshegemonie*, that is, the power to define in hegemonic terms specific features of social, religious, or political life. By analyzing the Zanzibar revolution[1] and its ongoing reverberations in social memory and historical debate, we can witness this prolonged struggle for hegemony of interpretation in especially paradigmatic fashion. In fact, in the Zanzibari case, we can see how this competition to achieve a hegemonic interpretation of the revolution has been both prolonged and particularly vexed, even in the wake of the 50th anniversary of the events in question.[2]

---

[1] According to Reinhart Koselleck, the term "revolution" has a spectrum of meanings that have changed over time. Thus, "revolution" can point to a sudden change (*Umsturz*) or a civil war, as well as long-term processes of change, in particular when referring to changes of basic structures. The term is not necessarily confined to political events but may also be applied to economic developments such as the industrial revolution. Only after the French revolution, which was often seen as a "civil war," did the term increasingly come to be seen as a sudden and total change of both regime and structures of order (Koselleck 1984: 67ff). Civil war came to be seen as having a more extended and warlike character (as, for instance, in the American civil war), and was associated with the establishment of parallel structures of power and administration.

[2] Research for this contribution took place in the context of a larger research project on the development of Islamic education in Zanzibar in the 20th century (see Loimeier 2009) between 2001 and 2010. I am grateful to Prof. Abdul Sheriff, Mohamed Saleh, Harith Ghassany, Ann Lee Grimstad, as well as the editors, in particular William Bissell, for their numerous and extremely constructive comments. They have been extremely helpful in resolving some intricate problems related to conflicting representations of the revolution.

In order to properly understand this struggle to interpret the revolution in Zanzibar, it is necessary to differentiate among at least three different levels of analysis: (1) the historical chain of events leading to the revolution, as well as the revolution itself, its consequences and legacy; (2) the different patterns of interpretation of the revolution as articulated by Zanzibari as well as non-Zanzibari voices; and (3) the question as to why discourses about the revolution significantly increased following the mid-1980s, especially in terms of memoirs and other recollections. Was this discursive increase connected with political liberalization, with better access to archival material, or rather driven by an urge to transform memory into text—a socio-psychological dynamic discussed by Jan Assmann (1997) and Johannes Fried (2004)? In this chapter, I will first present a short account of the revolution before going into the details of interpretation and finally addressing the processes of transformation of memory. By offering a baseline account of the revolution I do not mean to suggest that there is a singular truth that somehow stands above and beyond various ideological versions. Instead, as a professional scholar, I have been able to draw upon a range of historical accounts that most Zanzibaris do not have regular access to. Moreover, in surveying this corpus, I have sought to highlight core features of the revolution where there is considerable consensus among different sources. I do so not in the interest of disallowing or undercutting other accounts but rather to establish a background that can serve to illuminate contrasts with alternative scripts and interpretive traditions of the revolution currently circulating in Zanzibar. While hegemony of interpretation is often sought after, it is rarely achieved; indeed, in the 1960s and 1970s, state attempts to consolidate an authoritative and official story of the revolution only served to drive underground counter-narratives shared mostly among close intimates or kin. In a repressive political climate, where certain things could never be spoken aloud, doubts, suspicions, and alternative views circulated privately, under the surface. In the face of state attempts to crudely control historical debate, many Zanzibaris concluded that the official story was incomplete, ideologically motivated, or filled with erasures and silences. This hermeneutic of suspicion has continued even as liberalization beginning in the 1980s has produced a new crop of historical analyses and memoirs focusing on the revolution. New assertions about the revolution—whether favorable to the orthodox story or framed by oppositional views—are attended by lingering epistemic uncertainties, where whispers, rumors, street narratives, and Internet sources collide and seem all the more convincing precisely because of their underground or nonofficial status.

The Revolution: Establishing a Framework of Events and Processes

Because of its brutality, the revolution of 12 January 1964 in Zanzibar shook all of East Africa, yet it should not have come as a complete surprise. Before Zanzibar's independence, which was proclaimed on 12 December 1963, the British Protectorate had already seen some years of intense sociopolitical conflict, a period of time that became known in the sultanate as the "time of politics" (Kiswahili, *zama za siasa*). The most important political players in this period were the Zanzibar National Party (ZNP, established in 1955) and the Afro-Shirazi Union (ASU, established 1957). The ZNP advocated quick independence and the restitution of the sultan's full sovereignty. However, the ZNP was split into a conservative and a progressive wing with respect to Zanzibari political perspectives: The more conservative wing, under the leadership of Ali Muhsin al-Barwani (1919-2006), represented Zanzibar's social and economic establishment and proposed to follow the politics of Nasserite Egypt. By contrast, the progressive wing, which under the leadership of Abdulrahman Muhammed Babu (1924-1996)[3] became the Umma Party in 1963, represented Zanzibar's Arab, Indian, and Comorian youth and proposed to follow Cuban, Chinese, and East German policies. The ASU, founded by Abeid Amani Karume (1905-1972) and renamed the Afro-Shirazi Party (ASP) in 1959, advocated delaying independence and

---

3   Abdulrahman Muhammed Babu was a member of an old Comorian family (al-Husayni) in the Ukutani quarter of Zanzibar Stone Town. His father, Sharif Muhammad Umar "Lyne" al-Husayni, acted as honorary consul for Portugal and maintained a popular baraza in Mkunazini. After attending Government Central School, Babu studied at Makerere and in London, and he later established connections with Cuba and China (Clayton 1981: 46). In 1957 he went to London and became the leader of the Zanzibar emigré community. He returned to Zanzibar in 1957 and became secretary general of the ZNP (1957–63). Also, he established the ZNP youth organization, the Youth's Own Union (Burgess 2002: 16), and subsequently managed to organize scholarships for studies in East Germany, China, the USSR and Czechoslovakia. By 1962, 116 students were studying in these countries, including 18 in China (Burgess 2002: 22). On account of his radical positions, he was imprisoned by the British authorities in 1962. When it became clear, in July 1963, that the ZNP was not willing to support his case against the British, he founded the Umma Party (Aley 1988: 58; Babu 2001).

represented Zanzibar's plantation workers and the urban "proletariat."⁴ This political spectrum was complemented by the Zanzibar and Pemba People's Party (ZPPP) on Pemba, led by Muhammad Shamte, which tried to mediate between the political interests of the ZNP and the ASP and represented the interests of Pemba's African "Shirazi" population.⁵

In the three parliamentary elections of 1961 and 1963, the ASP won a majority of votes on Unguja island (and a considerable portion of the votes on Pemba), yet the design of the constituencies and the British majority-voting system did not give the ASP a corresponding majority of parliamentary seats. In the end, the ZNP managed to form coalition governments with the ZPPP in July 1961 and 1963 and to keep the ASP from parliamentary power. As a consequence, the British Protectorate administration, led by the British high commissioner, T. H. Crosthwaith, officially handed over power on 10 December 1963 to a ZNP-ZPPP coalition government led by Prime Minister Muhammad Shamte. British officials believed that this new independence government was mostly invested in representing the interests of the Arab establishment—a view that many in the ASP ranks shared. As Crosthwaith confided in a later report, "At independence, power was handed over to an 'Arab-dominated' coalition, which had, however, a substantial following among the Africans. This government was prepared to support, or at any rate to bear with, the Sultanate which was in the hands of an

---

4   From its very beginning, the ASP was closely linked with the Tanganyika African National Union (TANU) in mainland Tanganyika, led by Julius K. Nyerere. In 1939 Abeid Amani Karume, the leader of the ASP, had become the secretary of the first "African" political association in Zanzibar, the African Association. It had been established in 1934 as a Zanzibari branch of the first African political association in Tanganyika, the Tanganyika African Association (TAA, est. 1929). The ties between the Zanzibar and the mainland branches of this association were formally discontinued in 1947, yet mainland politicians such as Bibi Titi Muhammad continued to visit Zanzibar, while Karume went to the mainland to meet TANU politicians (see the articles by Iliffe, Ranger, and Temo in Kimambo 1969: 158ff, 186ff, and 198, respectively, as well as Mapuri 1996: 12; for a different view see Mrina and Mattoke 1980: 45).

5   Since the 1920s and the 1930s, the term *Shirazi* had been adopted increasingly by Pembans and some groups on Unguja to distinguish themselves from "newcomers" from the African mainland, such as the Nyamwezi, Makonde, and Manyema.

inexperienced, selfish, arrogant and generally disliked young man" [i.e., Sultan Jamshid].[6]

After independence, tensions continued to rise as this new government started to implement a number of measures that seemed directed against African or mainland interests, fueling anxieties that the new state was out to privilege "Arabs" while specifically targeting Africans and ASP supporters. Thus, all servicemen of "mainland" (i.e., Tanganyikan) origin in the police force were summarily discharged, allegedly because the government was not able to finance their salaries because of a crisis in clove exports and subsequent budgetary constraints. At the same time, the government was neither able nor willing to finance these servicemen's return to the mainland—leaving a cadre of unemployed police hanging around, with the motive for opposing the regime and knowledge of security procedures. As a consequence, many of these disgruntled ex-policemen, organized by John Okello,[7] were well prepared and willing to support a revolt against the government (Clayton 1981: 53). Also, the new government started to strike out against prominent opponents, in particular the Umma Party, which was banned in early January. In order to escape imprisonment, Babu fled to Dar es Salaam on 8 January 1964 and only returned to Zanzibar on 13 January, after the successful overthrow of the Muhammad Shamte administration (Clayton 1981: 69, 77; Prunier 1998: 105). The repressive and incompetent policies of the Shamte administration thus served to speed up preparations for a coup d'état that was indeed staged in the night of 11 to 12 January 1964.[8]

The revolution and the immediate post-revolutionary developments can be divided into three distinct phases:

---

[6] BLFK Liaison Conference Reports: Report by Crosthwaith to the "British Land Forces Kenya" (BLFK) and to Duncan Sandys, Secretary of State for Commonwealth Relations, 22 July 1964 (PRO DO 185/68). This assessment of the situation is misleading, as only two ministers (Ali Muhsin al-Barwani and Dr. Idarus Baalawi) were Zanzibaris of Arab origin, while one was of Indian origin (Amirali Abdulrasul), two (Maulid Mshangana and Ibuni Saleh) of Comorian origin, and four (Muhammad Shamte, Juma Aley, Salim Kombo, Abadhar Juma Khatib and Rashid Hamadi) of Zanzibari-Shirazi origin. I am grateful to Mohamed Saleh for this addendum (see also the "Central Office of Information Reference Pamphlet," No. 60, Zanzibar, 1963).

[7] John Okello, the initial leader ("field marshal") of the revolution, was a Ugandan from Anino in Lango district. He was born in 1937 and came to Zanzibar/Pemba only in 1959. In Pemba he had different occupations and started to build small groups of followers, mostly fellow mainlanders who were equally dissatisfied with existing political structures in Zanzibar (see Okello 1967).

[8] For more on views about the incompetence and arrogance of the first government prior to the revolution, see Petterson 2002: 39–43; for a detailed account of the first days of the revolution, see Clayton 1981.

1. The actual takeover of power by the revolutionaries during the night of 11 to 12 January 1964 and the following day, when all armed resistance was broken. This initial phase essentially ended with the proclamation over state radio of Zanzibar's revolution by "Field Marshal" John Okello on the morning of 12 January.
2. A period of chaos, killings, massacres, and the flight of thousands of Arabs and Indians, and the settling of old scores, which went on for some days in Unguja and probably some weeks in Pemba, but which also subsequently brought about the downfall and exile of Okello and consolidation of the revolutionary process.
3. The period of ongoing power struggles between the different factions of the revolution, essentially Karume and his supporters in the ASP, the "moderates" in the ASP, and the radical "comrades," mostly of the Umma Party but also some ASP Youth League (ASPYL) leaders. This phase ended with the conclusion of a union agreement between Tanganyika and Zanzibar in April 1964.

The First Phase in Detail

The revolutionary uprising started under the cover of an ASP party in the Raha Leo Community Center of Ng'ambo[9] on the evening of 11 January 1964.[10] First of all, some groups of ex-police officers,[11] strengthened by disgruntled ("lumpen") youth from the Ng'ambo area, stormed the Ziwani police barracks and the adjacent Bomani headquarters. They were able to overcome resistance in this police stronghold at 5:30 am on 12 January and consequently gained access to

---

9   It should be mentioned here that in 1964 Zanzibar city was divided into two major parts: the various quarters of Stone Town (Shangani, Malindi, Mkunazini, etc.), west of the "creek" (a filled-up former inlet of the sea, mostly inhabited by Zanzibaris of Arab and Indian origin), and Ng'ambo, the "other side" (of the creek), which was also divided into a number of quarters, such as the different Mwembes (Mwembeshauri, Mwembeladu, Mwembetanga, etc.), but also Kikwajuni, Kisiwandui, Mtendeni, Mlandege, Raha Leo, Misufini, Gulioni, Saateni, Kilimani, etc., mostly inhabited by Zanzibaris of African ("Shirazi") origin, mainland Africans, and pockets of Arab and "Indian" residents.

10   For a detailed description of the first day of the revolution, see Clayton 1981, Ghassany 2010, and Petterson 2002. Mrina and Mattoke (1980: 96) claim that the revolution started under the cover of an *ngoma* party in the ASP headquarters in Kisiwandui. This can be seen as an effort to "write out" Okello's role in the revolution.

11   In fact, Okello's original fighting force was recruited mainly among mainlanders: Of 330 original fighters, only 30 were of Zanzibari origin, with the rest from Kenya or Tanganyika. This original fighting force was strengthened by a number of ex-servicemen who had been dismissed from the Zanzibar police force on account of their mainland origin. According to Okello, only 300 out of 2,300 revolutionary fighters (and a total force of 9,000 "volunteers") were of Zanzibari origin (Clayton 1981: 57).

the armory of the police station. The other Ng'ambo police post, Mtoni, where the newly formed Police Mobile Force (PMF) was stationed, probably fell into the hands of the revolutionaries even earlier, since this police post handed over keys to the armory quickly.[12] In the early hours of the morning, the revolutionaries also occupied the radio station in Raha Leo, which enabled Okello to make his first radio speech at 7:00 am, announcing the success of the revolution and the end of the Shamte government. By 10:00 am the revolutionaries had overcome the resistance in the Mazizini police station near the airport and taken over control of the fourth, and last, police station in Malindi/Stone Town.[13] At this point in time, the family of the sultan had fled to the government ship *Seyyid Khalifa*, while the members of the Shamte government were rounded up, taken prisoner, and escorted to Raha Leo (Clayton 1981: 77-8). High Commissioner Crosthwaith explained these events in the following terms, highlighting official British attitudes concerning the motivations of the revolution:

> Antipathy between the Arabs and the Africans had led to serious riots in 1961 which were only suppressed by British and Kenyan troops. A colonial Government assessment . . . foretold the likelihood of trouble after independence. Despite this warning Mohamed Shamte's government was caught unprepared by the violence of the revolution which overthrew them with almost ridiculous ease and dispatched the Sultan and his family into exile in the early hours of 12th January, 1964. Despite the intense Communist interest already referred to this uprising was not, in my view, primarily Communist inspired. It was essentially an upsurge of African nationalism motivated not by Communism but by Black African resentment at continued domination after independence by their former Arab masters.[14]

---

12   Ann Lee Grimstad, personal communication, 19 November 2013.

13   According to Wimmelbücker (2001: 299), the "massive fighting" for control of Malindi police station, as "recorded" by a number of revolutionary sources, may have been an "invention of tradition." According to him and his sources, the police station was evacuated peacefully by a British police officer at 10:00 am. Other reports maintain, however, that real fighting went on until afternoon (Ann Lee Grimstad, personal communication, 19 November 2013).

14   BLFK Liaison Conference Reports: Report by Crosthwaith to the "British Land Forces Kenya"(BLFK) and to Duncan Sandys, Secretary of State for Commonwealth Relations, 22 July 1964 (PRO DO 185/68), p. 3.

The Second Phase in Detail

On the evening of 12 January 1964, Okello proclaimed himself minister of defense while Karume[15] was declared president. Abdulla Kassim Hanga, who had organized the ASP Youth League with Seif Bakari, the president of the ASP Youth League, was named vice president, and Babu (Umma Party) was named minister of external affairs—even though Karume, Babu, and Hanga were all still in Dar es Salaam at this point and only came back to Zanzibar the next day. Other members of the ASP, such as Aboud Jumbe (Health and Social Services)[16], Othman Shariff Musa (Education)[17], Hasnu Makame (Agriculture and Finance),

---

15 Abeid Amani Karume was born on 4 August 1905 in Pongwe (Mwera mudirate), about 15 kilometers to the east of Zanzibar Town. His father came from Malawi, his mother from Rwanda. He had 28 months of primary school education, left school at the age of 15 and became a sailor in 1920. In 1938, he returned to Zanzibar for good and started to organize a shore launch service syndicate of boatsmen and small boat owners (Clayton 1981: 17). Since 1933 he had also been active in the African football clubs, in particular, the Wafalme Wapya (New Kings Football Club). In 1957, he became the leader and cofounder of the ASU. From 1964–72, he was president of Zanzibar and vice president of the union of Tanganyika and Zanzibar. He was assassinated in 1972 (see also Mwanjisi 1967).

16 Aboud Jumbe was born on 14 June 1920 in Zanzibar, went to Government Primary School from 1930–37 (to Standard VIII), then to Government Secondary School from 1938–42 (to Standard XII). From 1943 to 1945 he studied at Makerere University (English, history, geography) and acquired, in 1946, a Makerere Teacher Diploma. On 14 February 1946 he was appointed as a teacher at the Government Central School. In fact, he was the first African secondary school teacher in Zanzibar and later even became the vice principal of the King George School. He finally retired from school service in 1961 to take part in the 1961 elections and was subsequently elected a member of the LegCo (File AB 86/44). He was one of the few members of the Karume government who had a secondary school education. From 1960, he worked full time for the ASP. In 1972, he rose to become president of Zanzibar after the assassination of Karume (Burgess 1999: 34). In 1984, he was forced to retire on account of conflicts within the ruling party. His successor was Ali Hassan Mwinyi (1984–85).

17 Othman Shariff, b. 1914, was a member of the ZNU but later joined the ASP as a founding member. He was also a member of the second group of Zanzibaris to be sent to Makerere in 1940 (together with Muhammad Ali Awadh). From 1943–47, he worked as assistant veterinary officer, and from 1952 as assistant agriculture officer. On 2 January 1964, Shariff and his group of "progressives" (Hasnu Makame, Idris Abdul Wakil, and Saleh Saadalla) left the ASP, as they were not prepared to accept Karume's leading role in the party. After the revolution, however, Shariff and his followers rejoined the ASP, becoming members of the Revolutionary Council on 24 January 1964. In April 1964, Shariff was appointed Tanzanian ambassador to the United States. Both he and Abdulla Kassim Hanga were executed in Zanzibar in 1970 for having taken part in an alleged coup against Karume.

Idris Abdul Wakil[18] (Commerce), and Saleh Saadalla (Agriculture) were also proclaimed ministers. On 13 January 1964, after Karume's, Babu's, and Hanga's return from Dar es Salaam, further appointments were announced. The former ruling parties, the ZNP and ZPPP, were prohibited and replaced by a Committee of 14 (Clayton 1981: 79). The Committee of 14, which took over the leadership of the revolution after the initial hours of the uprising (before eventually being replaced, on 24 January, by the Revolutionary Council) consisted of revolutionaries of mainly mainland origin. Some of them had close relationships with the leader of the ASP, Karume. Apart from Okello, they included Seif Bakari, Yusuf Himid, Abdallah Said Natepe (who became the first chairman of the Young Pioneers in revolutionary Zanzibar; see Burgess 1999: 34), Muhammad Abdallah Mfaranyaki, Ramadhan Haji, Said Iddi Bavuai, Said Washoto, Muhammad Abdallah Ameir Kaujore, Pili Khamis, Khamis Darwesh, Khamis Hemed, Hafiz Sulaiman, and Hamid Ameir (Clayton 1981: 54; Mrina and Mattoke 1980: 94).[19]

---

18 Idris Abdul Wakil, a "Shirazi," was born in Makunduchi in 1928. From 1936–39 he attended primary school; from 1940–43 the Dole Middle School and from 1944–48 the Government Secondary School. From 1949–51, he studied at Makerere, and he was appointed to the Zanzibar civil service on 1 January 1952. In 1952, he applied for a government scholarship but was rejected; he reapplied in 1954 and was accepted for a vacation diploma course at Makerere in 1954. In 1955, he reapplied for a UK grant but was rejected again. In 1962, he retired from service, as he was also a candidate for the Legislative Council elections (File AB 86/45). After the revolution, he became minister of education for a short period of time (April–December 1964), and then, also in 1964, union cabinet minister as well as ambassador to Germany. In 1985, he became the successor to Ali Hassan Mwinyi as president of Zanzibar (until 1990). Politically, he was regarded as a "liberator," a hard-line member of the Revolutionary Council.

19 A number of leading revolutionaries of mainland origin and closely linked with Okello were already missing, at an early point of time, from the Committee of 14, as well as the Revolutionary Council: Mzee Kenya, a Tanganyikan police bugler; Joseph Mugambwa, alias Matias Simba; Mzee Muhammad; and Absolom Amoi Ingen, who was deported to the mainland in late February 1964 (Clayton 1981: 55, 122; Okello 1967: 118). Also missing from this list is Ibrahim Makungu, who became notorious in the first days, weeks, and months of the revolution as the revolution's major executioner. His brutality was attested by Markus Wolf, the East German Stasi advisor to Zanzibar, who was posted to Zanzibar in 1964 for a period of three months to train the Zanzibari "state security" (Schneppen 2003: 528). Among Makungu's most prominent victims were Amur Zahor, the inspector of police, as well as Muhammad Hamud al-Barwani and Muhammad b. Salim "Jinja" al-Barwani, all executed in the Mtoni detention camp (Bakari 2001: 111; Barwani 1997: 237). Muhammad Hamud al-Barwani had been imprisoned for the murder of Ali Sultan Mughayri in 1956; although he had been sentenced to death, this sentence was commuted to ten years' imprisonment (Mapuri 1996: 16). Muhammad Hamud's son, Hamud Muhammad al-Barwani, assassinated Abeid Amani Karume, on 7 April 1972 (Babu 1991: 266; Clayton 1981: 39).

With the takeover of power by ASP Youth League and Umma cadres through the Revolutionary Council[20] on 14 January and the following days, the revolution assumed a more organized character. At the same time, control over the course of the revolution passed from the mainland revolutionaries into Zanzibari hands.[21] In Raha Leo, which served as the new revolutionary headquarters as well as a detention site, Karume, Babu, Hanga, and the other revolutionaries quickly formed a revolutionary leadership that was called, from about 16 January, the Revolutionary Council. On 24 January, it proclaimed the first revolutionary government of Zanzibar.[22] On the same day, a new cabinet list was published that comprised eleven names. Those men, along with the nineteen other members of the Revolutionary Council, formed a leading group of thirty revolutionaries who more or less dominated Zanzibar's political development in the 1960s and early 1970s. By 24 January, it was clear, however, that Okello and his group of mainlanders

---

20 As of 24 January 1964, the Revolutionary Council consisted of the following: 1. Abeid Amani Karume (chairman), 2. Abdulla Kassim Hanga, 3. Abdulrahman Muhammed Babu, 4. Hasnu Makame Mwita, 5. Saleh Saadalla, 6. Aboud Jumbe, 7. Othman Shariff, 8. Idris Abdul Wakil, 9. Abdul Aziz Twala, 10. Hassan Nassor Moyo, 11. Seif Bakari, 12. Ramadhan Haji, 13. Abdallah Said Natepe, 14. Said Iddi Bavuai, 15. Said Washoto, 16. Yusuf Himid, 17. Mohammed A. Ameir, 18. Pili Khamis, 19. Muhammad Mfaume Umar, 20. Hafidh Sulaiman, 21. Khamis Hemed Nyuni, 22. Muhammad Abdallah Mfaranyaki (from Songea, who was deported to the mainland in late 1964), 23. Mohamed Ameir Kaujore, 24. Khamis Darwesh, 25. Muhammad Juma Pindua, 26. Khamis Abdullah Ameir, 27. Edington Kisasi, 28. Daudi Mahmoud Jecha, 29. Muhsin ibn Ali, 30. John Okello (source: Mapuri 1996: 56). Of this group, only Okello and Mfaranyaki represented the original group of revolutionaries, while all the others were members of the ASP or Umma Party (Clayton 1981: 91). This shows how thoroughly the Okello group had already been removed from power during the first days of the revolution. The early elimination of Okello and his group from power was instrumental to the efforts of the post-revolutionary governments of Zanzibar to deemphasize the role of mainlanders in the revolution and in post-revolutionary politics.

21 British intelligence (Crosthwaith) commented as follows on this development: "Although, as I know from my observation, few indoctrinated Communists took part in the revolution, with the arrival of Babu from Dar es Salaam two days later they soon manoevred themselves into the key positions in the administration which they have since held. The speed with which they did this supports the theory that has been put forward by one informed British journalist that Okello's coup merely anticipated one which Babu was planning with Tanganyikan and international Communist assistance for a slightly later date..." (PRO DO 185/68, p. 4).

22 The first Government of Revolutionary Zanzibar (as of 24 January 1964) consisted of Abeid Amani Karume (president), Abdulla Kassim Hanga (vice president), Abdulrahman Muhammed Babu (minister of external affairs), Hasnu Makame (minister for finance and development), Aboud Jumbe (minister of health and welfare), Saleh Saadalla (minister of agriculture), Idris Abdul Wakil (minister of communication and works), Othman Shariff (minister of education and national culture), Abdul Aziz Twala (junior minister in the president's office), Hassan Nassor Moyo (junior minister for communication and works), and a mainlander, Edington Kisasi (commissioner of police) (Clayton 1981: 91).

had lost their influence in the government and the Revolutionary Council. Okello himself was deported on 20 February 1964 to mainland Tanganyika (Clayton 1981: 93). In the new Revolutionary Council, led by Karume, the radical group became increasingly influential. Zanzibar was officially renamed the People's Republic of Zanzibar and Pemba, and a policy of nationalization was started that considerably changed the social demographics of Zanzibar. At the same time, anarchic killings went on for some time in the rural areas, and other acts of "revolutionary violence" and misuse of power were rampant. Although fighting in Zanzibar city was over by the evening of 12 January 1964, it continued in the countryside where acts of individual vengeance were carried out against Manga (Omani) Arabs, who had worked as plantation headmen, and Indian moneylenders. Political violence and the struggle for revolutionary control became intertwined with score-settling and racialized retribution, creating an ideological script that increasingly interpreted the revolution in racialist terms—as an "African" uprising directed against Arab and Indian oppressors. Outside Zanzibar city, some Manga Arabs tried to resist in some areas, in particular Bumbwini, Bububu, and Nungwi, but they were mostly killed in the fighting during the first days of the revolution (Clayton 1981: 77–8). On 13 January and particularly on 14 January and the following days, the revolution in fact acquired a touch of terror, expressed not only in killings but also the humiliation of representatives of the former elites, including some religious scholars,[23] and rapes and mutilations of "enemies of the revolution." Those who were killed were buried in mass graves (see Wimmelbücker 2001), and thousands of people were (allegedly)

---

23 Such as Muhammad b. Salim b. Hilal al-Barwani, a respected scholar, who was, however, liberated from detention after some days by Karume, when he inspected the detention camp (Clayton 1981: 98). Other members of the Revolutionary Council were responsible for acts of arbitrariness and violence against religious scholars and institutions. In September 1964, for instance, one member of the Revolutionary Council "entered a (Ithnasheri) mosque during a religious ceremony, accused the Imam to have held a non-authorized political rally and shot him as well as some of the Muslims present. He was, however, not punished for this crime and still occupies his position in the Revolutionary Council" (PRO DO 185/51, BLFK Liaison Conference reports; these reports actually accuse Yusuf Himid of being the perpetrator of the mosque killings). According to Clayton, the mosque killing was committed by Abdallah Mfaranyaki, who was subsequently deported to the mainland (1981: 122). Still other sources claim that Abdallah Kang'ore committed this crime (communication with Mohamed Saleh).

detained on one of the small islands off the Zanzibari coast.[24] In addition to these actions, some people took the opportunity to carry out local vendettas by pillaging Arab and Asian houses. In Zanzibar city, Okello, who still resided in Raha Leo, divided the town into districts that were distributed among his lieutenants, who organized the searching and plundering of specific houses (Clayton 1981: 79–81). As a consequence of this anarchic terror, the early days of the revolution are particularly remembered as characteristic of the revolution, even if the number of people actually killed was probably not as high as sometimes assumed (see below).

The Third Phase in Detail

After Okello had been excluded from power, the struggle for control over the development of the revolution continued between the "moderates," the "radicals," and the Karume group. The Karume group consisted mostly of ASP cadres, in particular, Seif Bakari, Aboud Jumbe, Thabit Kombo, Said Iddi Bavuai, Hassan Nassor Moyo,[25] and Abdallah Said Natepe (both members of the ASP Youth League), and others. According to Okello, Bakari[26] was, apart from Okello's own men, the major figure in the preparation of the revolution:[27]

---

24 Al-Barwani claims that besides 13,000 people killed in the Zanzibar "holocaust," 26,000 were imprisoned and 100,000 exiled, so that by his count 43 percent of the population of Zanzibar became victims of the revolution (1997: 35, 150). And these figures do not even cover the confiscation of property: Beyond the plantations and houses of the sultan's family and the al-Busaidi dynasty, the Barwani, Karimjee, Jivanji, Lamki, and Harthi families were affected most by these expropriations.

25 Hassan Nassor Moyo, a carpenter with primary school education, was sent to the USSR. After 1967 he became responsible for land reallocation policy, and he was named minister of education in 1968 (as successor to Ali Sultan Issa) (Clayton 1981: 138).

26 Seif Bakari, a tailor and button-sewer with little education, had been the chairman of the ASP Youth League and continued in this function after the revolution. Bakari was also the chairman of the intelligence and security council and, according to Markus Wolf, in charge of security. In addition, he was appointed political commissar of the army and later became responsible for the fight against smugglers and the policing of the food ration queues (Burgess 1999: 36). Also, he was the chosen successor to Karume, who preferred him and other non- or semi-educated revolutionaries to the "intellectuals," such as Hanga and Othman Shariff. Karume mistrusted intellectuals, with the exception of Aboud Jumbe and Attorney General Wolfango Dourado.

27 According to Mw. Idris (communication 25 February 2004) as well as Abdul Sheriff (communication 22 July 2004), Seif Bakari and Ibrahim Makungu were largely responsible for the massacres in 1964. Bakari and "his hard-line faction within the Revolutionary Council" are also considered to be largely responsible for the blockade of reforms in Zanzibar when Aboud Jumbe took over the Presidency in 1972, until Bakari finally accepted a union government position in Dar es Salaam in the late 1970s (Burgess 1999: 44).

It was with these men [i.e. Abdallah Mfaranyaki, Ramadhan Haji, Mzee Kenya, Said Idi Bavuai, Matias Simba, Mzee Muhammad, Absolom Amoi Ingen], and Seif Bakari, that the strategy of the Revolution was worked out. I consulted them on all plans, and the final scheme was the result of all our combined ideas (Okello 1967: 118).

Bakari and his followers in the ASP Youth League indeed seem to have played a major role in the planning of the revolution from 26 September 1963 onward, as documented in an exchange of letters between Okello and Bakari in September 1963 (as reproduced in Okello 1967: 100ff; but see also Wimmelbücker 2001: 302).[28]

Although the revolution had effectively eliminated the old Arab elite, although Karume could rely on a group of close associates such as Bakari, and, finally, although Okello's group had been marginalized at an early point of time, Karume's claim to power remained disputed in the first weeks of the revolution. A new, radical Arab and Comorian elite had come to power in the course of the revolution, threatening Karume's claim to absolute power. Even though this new elite was not large, it could wield considerable influence because of its good training and education as well as its close links with Egypt, China, Cuba, East Germany, and the USSR. Led by Babu, this radical elite comprised, among others, intellectuals and civil servants such as Ahmad "Badawi" Abubakar Qullatayn, a former customs officer;[29] Khamis Hussein Abeid, the area commissioner for Donge; A.S.-R.M. Kwacha, an ex-teacher and the general secretary of the Umma Party; Khamis Abdallah Ameir, the secretary of the Maritime and Allied Workers Union; Ali Sultan Issa (al-Isma'ili);[30] Salim Rashid; and Ali Mahfoudh—all Umma Party members (Clayton 1981: 110)—as well as some radical ASPYL members, such as Hanga and Abdul Aziz Twala. This group effectively managed to marginalize the "moderate" faction among the

---

28 Again, we encounter here the problem of diverging interpretations of the role of individual revolutionaries. For conflicting interpretations of Bakari's role in the revolution, see also Burgess 1999 and Petterson 2002.

29 Ahmad "Badawi" Qullatayn, who had become a junior minister of the revolutionary government in the late 1960s, was imprisoned in 1972, in the aftermath of Karume's assassination, for being involved in the assassination.

30 Ali Sultan Issa came from a well-known family in Pemba. He was a close friend of Babu, and in the late 1950s he became the chief representative of the ZNP in Cairo and opened ZNP offices in Havana and London. He was also able to organize 18 scholarships for studies in Cuba, which he visited in 1962 (Burgess 2002: 23). Issa was minister of education from December 1964 until 1968, when he was replaced by Hassan Nassor Moyo. He subsequently took over the Ministry of Health. From 1972–78, Issa was in prison on account of his alleged participation in the coup against Karume. He was in prison again in 1982–83.

revolutionaries, which included Othman Shariff, Hasnu Makame, Idris Abdul Wakil, and Saleh Saadalla,[31] who had all left the ASP in January 1964 (before the revolution) because it had become "too radical," but who then rejoined the ASP after the revolution (Clayton, 1981: 65ff). Following the electoral defeat in July 1963, Karume's hold on power within the ASP parliamentary delegation was uncertain; the party was divided, with Othman Shariff and others pressing for a government of national unity representing all political parties in parliament. On 26 April, however, the initial internal struggles for power began to come to an end when Karume agreed to form a union with Tanganyika—leading some to suggest that Karume embraced the union largely as a means of outmaneuvering his more radical rivals for power, marginalizing leftist and Marxist factions (Othman 2014: 197–8). The union enabled Karume to overcome the major remaining threat to his power, as many radical members of his government, such as Hanga[32] and Babu, were nominated for union government positions in Dar es Salaam (Clayton 1981: 114). As a consequence, Zanzibar's political development became increasingly dominated by Karume and his supporters (Clayton 1981: 119).

As long as the political influence of radicals such as Hanga and Babu was growing, the revolution attracted international attention and generated anxieties, as attested, for instance, by the increasing number of British navy ships off the Zanzibar coast after 16 January (Clayton 1981: 82). Not only had a conservative and allied government been replaced by a revolutionary regime, but the revolution had also been quickly recognized by the Soviet Union, East Germany, and China. Advisors, military personnel, and civilian experts from these countries soon started to arrive in Zanzibar, replacing the British expatriate officers working in the administration. From the very beginning of the revolution, British intelligence reports registered

---

31 Abdul Aziz Twala and Saleh Saadalla were executed for trumped up charges of conspiracy against Karume.

32 Abdulla Kassim Hanga (1932–69) was the vice general secretary of the ASP Youth League and a leading member of the Zanzibar African Youth Movement. He studied at the Teachers Training College, then taught at primary schools until 1958, when he went to London to study at the London School of Economics. He wanted to continue his studies in the United States but was not given a visa. Subsequently, in 1960, he went to Moscow, where he met and married Lidya Oliverovna Golden, the daughter of an American couple who had emigrated to the Soviet Union in 1930 and become naturalized Soviet citizens. He returned to Zanzibar in 1961 to become deputy secretary general of the ASP. Together with Karume, Ibrahim Saadalla, Thabit Kombo, Ameir Tajo, and Othman Shariff, he had been a founding member of the ASP in 1957 (Clayton 1981: 60; Mapuri 1996: 20; Wilson 1989: 164). He was executed in 1969 by Karume after an alleged coup attempt.

the influx of Chinese (and later East German and Russian) experts, who were to train the revolutionary forces, in particular the "People's Liberation Army" (PRO DO 185/51). A British secret service report of 22 September 1964 remarked that there were "c. 175 Chinese experts in Zanzibar, among them c. 35 military advisors" (PRO DO 185/51). Although the Umma Party had been quickly integrated into the ASP, British intelligence was particularly nervous about Babu's growing influence.[33] Babu, who was appointed revolutionary Zanzibar's first minister of foreign affairs, had indeed described "East Africa as a powder keg and Zanzibar as the fuse" (Burgess 2002: 1). The development of the revolution between January and April 1964 thus motivated the British government to develop plans for a military intervention. Despite Clayton's claim that "no consideration was given at any time to political

---

33 " . . . and there was Babu. This half-Somali half Arab figure has been noteworthy in the political scene of Zanzibar for some years. He is smooth charming and clever and his political views are far to the left. He has also received substantial financial support from China and I think Russia" (Report Bourne, PRO DO 185/51).

intervention" (Clayton 1981: 102), the British indeed had prepared a military intervention.[34]

After the consolidation of the Karume regime in the context of Zanzibar's merger with Tanganyika to form the United Republic of Tanzania, the revolutionary process may be said to have come to an end. The Umma group—the only group willing to implement some socialist policies with revolutionary consequences for Zanzibari society and economy—was effectively removed from power, its members promoted to union government positions. As a consequence, the Karume regime

---

34 Even if in the end these plans were not executed on account of Zanzibar's union with Tanganyika and the subsequent neutralization of the radical members of the Revolutionary Council in the union government, they reveal how the British position developed in this critical period. British considerations were clearly revealed in a letter from the Commonwealth Relations Office in London to the British High Commission in Dar es Salaam of 25 January 1964, which states: "We are much concerned at the possibility that Zanzibar may develop into an African Cuba under Communist control. We are therefore considering whether we ought not to seek a respectable excuse for intervening and eliminating Okello and other extremist elements" (PRO File DO 185/51). The actual plans for a military intervention coordinated by the British Land Forces in Kenya (BLFK) were to be executed by an airborne landing of the 2nd Battalion Scots Guards supported by the first battalion of the Staffordshire Regiment, both based in Kenya. These plans were developed in detail by the Commanders Committee East Africa, joint operation instruction No 2/64, "Intervention in Zanzibar, OP Shed," of 30 April 1964 (PRO DO 185/51). This plan essentially assumed that Karume would effectively be ousted by the radicals—in particular, Ali Mahfoudh's Defence Force—in an internal struggle for power. Before such an "internal coup" could occur, the British planned "to intervene by request in Zanzibar to support the Karume government in the maintenance or restoration of law and order" (PRO DO 185/51). According to British scenarios, opposition to these plans of intervention was expected to be expressed in two forms: "1.) Passive opposition through members of the "Committee of 14" in the Revolutionary Council. 2.) Active opposition from Ali Mahfoudh's Defence Forces who appear to control most, if not all, of the Russian arms: i.e. some degree of "civil war"—Babu supporters vs. Karume supporters. To counter this threat, Nyerere is expected to send additional Tanganyika Police to strengthen Karume's hand in the event of trouble. Should this prove insufficient, it is possible British troops may be asked to intervene" (PRO DO 185/51). The intervention plan then gives detailed information on the Zanzibari armed forces and their possible fighting power: "Zanzibari Police, approx. 600; Tanganyika Police, approx. 150–200 and 'Peoples Liberation Army', approx. 200–300). Of these troops an approximate number of 225–300 men are to be regarded as 'pro-BABU' (75–100 'military police' at Migombani and 150–200 'Security Force' at Chukwani, both under command of Ali Mahfoudh)." The plan then continues to present scenarios of intervention on the spot: "There are two possible plans: a) Plan A envisaging intervention at short notice using initially MRT aircraft available in Kenya only, b) Plan B envisaging intervention at a minimum of 10 hours notice, using extra Aden based MRT aircraft to provide a larger initial troop-lift." Subsequently, the plan discusses the details of immediate action after intervention and details the positions and strength of the Zanzibari armed forces (PRO DO 185/51). These plans were also defined in a paper of 29 May 1964 entitled "Plan for an intervention in Zanzibar," as dispatched from HQ BLFK to the British High Commission in Dar es Salaam, code name "Operation Shed" (PRO DO 185/51). In the end, the intervention was not necessary, as we have seen above, and the plans for a military intervention were transformed into plans for the evacuation and rescue of Zanzibari refugees. These plans received top-secret status and were unavailable to the public until disclosure in 2001 (PRO DO 185/51: Internal security and possibility of military intervention).

was free to implement its own concepts of development, which continue to impact Zanzibar today, as they essentially try to eternalize the political regime that emerged after April 1964 under the slogan *Mapinduzi Daima* ("Revolution Forever"). These efforts to achieve eternalization of the revolution are not confined, however, to political structures, but they also refer to representations of the past, as will be shown in the next section.

As a result of the revolution, Zanzibar began to shift into a socialist regime along the lines of the German Democratic Republic or People's Republic of China. Socialist housing, education, and health projects were started; foreign trade was nationalized; and national monopolies, particularly regarding the marketing of cloves, were set up. Kiswahili became the new official language of Zanzibar. Coconut palm plantations on Unguja were nationalized and partially redistributed. From 1965, the state also started a policy of disentanglement from religion and initiated the mobilization of the population in mass organizations. In addition, a number of seemingly insignificant yet symbolically important measures, such as the prohibition of rickshaws as a "symbol of feudal exploitation," were implemented, and British expatriate employees were replaced by experts from socialist countries.[35] The legacy of the revolution is noticeable even today, 50 years later—for instance, in the siren that announces the beginning and end of each working day and in the Kaunda uniforms ("*Ki-Mao*" style) of state functionaries and politicians. In addition, the institutions of the state and the revolutionary party, the Chama cha Mapinduzi (CCM, "Party of the Revolution") that emerged in 1977 from the ASP, still celebrate the legacy of the revolution and the memory of the first revolutionary president, Abeid Amani Karume, in regular manifestations. Finally, many revolutionaries and many victims of the revolution are still alive and attest to the ongoing disruption of Zanzibar in contradictory memories of the revolution.

The Intricacies of Interpretation

The process of redefining and rethinking the revolution, which has been going on since 1964, has led to quite different patterns of interpretation of the revolution among both Zanzibaris and non-Zanzibaris. These schools of interpretation focus not only on the historical events of the revolution as such but also on pre-revolutionary

---

35 One of these experts was Markus Wolf, who had been posted to Zanzibar as an officer of the East German Stasi (Staatssicherheit) for a period of three months in 1964 in order to train Zanzibar's new state security forces (Schneppen 2003: 528).

social relations, the motivations for the uprising, and its longer-term impact and legacy. Debates have swirled even on seemingly elementary issues of fact, such as how many people were killed. Al-Barwani (1996: 150), for instance, claims that the revolution cost the lives of 12,000 people,[36] while others have tried to play down the number of casualties. Babu maintains that "the real casualty figure was minimal" (Babu 1991: 241), while Ali Kettani mentions an equally ridiculous number of 70,000 people killed (Kettani 1982: 112). B. F. Mrina and W. T. Mattoke remain, by contrast, totally silent with respect to this topic (1980: 94-6). Other estimates usually range from 3,000 to 11,000 dead (Clayton 1981: 81). These numbers may be too low, as they do not include the events in Pemba.[37] British sources are, by contrast, rather vague and claim that "several thousands of people were killed in the general disorder and the paying off of old scores especially against Arab land owners and traders from whom the Africans had suffered in the past."[38]

Despite these different interpretations of the scope of revolutionary and post-revolutionary killings, the scale of the violence and the number of casualties had a shocking impact on Zanzibari society. In fact, the revolutionary and post-revolutionary killings became the foundation of a national trauma that has continued to trouble Zanzibar to this day. Thus, al-Barwani has claimed that "the 1964 massacre wiped Zanzibar off the world map as a state and the center of Islamic culture and influence in East, Central and South Africa" (1996: 2). Similar charges and countercharges have flown back and forth over the years, but there is no question that the revolution has been the defining event for those who fled Zanzibar into exile, as well as for many who stayed behind. Debates about the revolution were equally central to the political conflicts following multiparty elections in 1995, 2000, and 2005; persistent tensions about the union; the perceived erosion

---

36   Probably referring to the rather propagandistic figure given by John Okello, who had proclaimed, after only three days in power, that "enemy soldiers and persons killed numbered 11,995; only nine of my own soldiers were reported killed; 1,631 civilian Africans were killed; the total reported killed then was 13,635. . . . In addition, 21,462 enemies and stooges were detained. All jails and fenced prison compounds were full and some detainees were transferred to small islands off the coast" (Okello 1967: 160).

37   The claim that Okello's Makonde militias committed massacres in Pemba is rejected by most sources. At the same time, Pemba became famous for being oppressed in terms of arbitrary beatings, imprisonments, and torture. Yet even a number of 3,000 casualties in Zanzibar "only" would correlate to approximately 1 percent of Zanzibar's total population at that time (i.e., 350,000 persons), not taking into account several thousand refugees.

38   PRO DO 185/51, report BLFK Liaison Conference, Zanzibar and Pemba, 23/9/1964.

of Zanzibari sovereignty and anxieties about its sociopolitical place in the global order; and sharp disagreements about the social gains or lack thereof over the last half-century.

Number games such as those mentioned above, are, of course, connected with specific interests, and in particular the endeavors of the revolutionaries, especially the Umma and ASPYL cadres, to present themselves as the guarantors of stability, who were able to put an end to the random killings started by Okello and his group,[39] or, on the other hand, with the strategies of the political opposition to stress the barbaric nature of the revolution. Similar speculations and divergent interpretations exist with respect to the role of individual leaders in the revolution, such as Karume,[40] Bakari (see above), Issa,[41] and Okello (see also above), whose influence is inevitably stressed in different ways by different sources and different factions of the revolution. Thus, there seems to have been a broad consensus to

---

39 These arbitrary acts of violence happened although Babu and his group claimed control of Stone Town. Babu had in fact sent several of his supporters to East Germany, where they were trained. They brought along pictures of Babu, which in the first days of the revolution were fixed on those houses which were to be protected or which were "exempt from harassment" (communication with Gary Burgess, 19 July 2002).

40 One of the myths is that Karume personally led the revolution, while he was, in fact, still in Dar es Salaam. Revolutionary historiography created this version of history not only to boost Karume's image as a revolutionary leader but also to write out Okello's central role in the first days of the revolution, and thus to deemphasize the role of non-Zanzibaris in the revolution. This manipulation of history was important for the subsequent presentation of the revolution as a purely Zanzibarian affair. For a number of other myths, see Wimmelbücker 2001 and Barwani et al. 2003. One of the few revolutionary authors who explicitly appreciates Okello's role in the revolution and confirms that he was indeed a member of the Committee of 14 (which has been denied by other revolutionary sources) is Omar R. Mapuri (1996), a mainlander and Zanzibar's minister of education from 1986-89 and again from 1992-2001.

41 In a private conversation (22 August 2002), Issa denied responsibility for the burning of Islamic books in the course of the revolution (as was implied by Ali Muhsin al-Barwani) and even claimed to have saved the National Archive. Also, he rejects responsibility for putting an end to Qur'anic classes in government schools. As Othman Shariff, who occupied the Ministry of Education from January to April 1964, was a moderate, and as the administration of the department of education remained in the hands of British or British trained staff in 1964, the major disruption must have taken place when Issa took over the Ministry of Education from Idris Abdul Wakil in December 1964. Only during his time as minister of education was the Muslim Academy closed and Islamic classes in government schools stopped, even if individual teachers continued to insist on Islamic school prayers. The files on education in the ZNA also confirm that all institutions of Islamic learning continued to work throughout most of 1964. Issa's claims to have done nothing against Islamic education in Zanzibar must therefore be regarded as a retrospective reconstruction of personal memory. In fact, many Zanzibaris claim that he, and nobody else, was responsible for the end of Qur'anic classes in government schools (personal communication Mw. Idris, 25 February 2004).

minimize Okello's role and omit his name in official reports about the revolution, as documented, for instance, in the official version of the revolution published in *The Nationalist* in Dar es Salaam on 12 January 1965, where Okello was not mentioned (Okello 1967: 209–22; see also Mrina and Mattoke 1980: 95–6).

We also encounter vastly different interpretations of the legacy of the revolution. While some observers maintain that the role of the Umma Party has been largely overemphasized, outspoken Umma members, in particular Babu and Issa, tend to stress Umma's major role in the first days of the revolution, for instance regarding Umma Party endeavors to curb violence.[42] Also, while some revolutionaries and observers claim that after 1964 Zanzibar became East Africa's most radical regime, Tapio Nisula maintains that Zanzibar remained "a society with extreme disparities" (1999: 15) even after the revolution and despite the emigration, expulsion, or virtual elimination of thousands of Arabs and Indians and a subsequent ethnic "homogenization." Thus, there is no doubt that the 1964 revolution in Zanzibar was a watershed in the development of the society as a whole. The legacy of the revolution is felt even today, almost 50 years after the events of 1964. There are many surviving symbols of revolutionary times, as has been mentioned above, and, finally, many people who took part in the revolution, who witnessed these events and who became victims of the revolution, are still alive today and remember. They are the living embodiment of Zanzibar's multiple splits, even if many of them still do not dare to speak out publicly and relate their experiences of the revolution.

Patterns of Interpretation

The persistence of memories of the revolution has had a strong influence on the representation of the revolution to this day. But while the first texts were written almost immediately after the revolution by outsiders, the Zanzibari official perspective remained confined, in the first 20 years after the event, to a few propagandistic statements. Since the mid-1980s, the number of texts on the revolution written by Zanzibaris has increased significantly, coinciding with political and economic liberalization, the return of multiparty politics, and the reopening of the isles to external investment, information, and the exile community or their descendants. Since 1984, at least 57 accounts representing an emic perspective on the revolution have been

---

42   Abdul Sheriff, personal communication, 5 August 2003.

published, as against 24 between 1964 and 1984. At the same time, the total number of books written on the revolution so far has grown to at least 81 (see the references).[43] These new works have started to bring about a certain modification of memories. At the same time, the recent texts have also triggered a boom of memorialization and rationalization, of legitimization and delegitimization, with respect to the revolution in Zanzibar's public discourse.

When considering these accounts, we should first differentiate texts representing an emic perspective—that is, texts written by Zanzibaris and Tanzanians living inside and outside Zanzibar and in diasporic contexts, as opposed to texts written by outsiders, mostly Western academics. Second, when focusing on the emic texts, we should differentiate between texts representing the "victim" perspective and those representing the "victor" perspective, as they represent different types of local historiographic reinterpretation. The school of the "victims," represented by al-Barwani (1996), as well as the texts written by Aley (1984, 1988, and 1994), Babakarim (1994), Fairooz (1995), al-Isma'ili (1999), Khar(o)usi (1967 and 1969), Lodhi (1979 and 1986), al-Maamiry (1988), and Muhammad (1991), for instance, explicitly try to discredit the revolution. At the same time, these authors present pre-revolutionary Zanzibar as a sort of paradise on earth, which, without a revolution, would have had marvelous prospects for socioeconomic development, while barely mentioning pre-revolutionary social inequalities.

The school of the "victors" is represented by authors such as Mapuri (1996) and texts such as the manifesto on the revolution by the Afro-Shirazi Party (1965 and 1974); its successor, the Chama cha Mapinduzi (CCM); as well as texts by Babu (1991), Maliyamkono (2000), Mdundu (1996), Mosare (1969), Mrina and Mattoke (1980), Mwanjisi (1967), and Okello (1967), who defend the revolution and its legacy. These texts condemn pre-revolutionary conditions and try, with some legitimacy, to depict pre-revolutionary Zanzibar as a feudal society where Africans were still treated, implicitly or explicitly, as "slaves" by the "Arab" aristocracy. The revolution is presented as having brought about a radical reversal of these social conditions.

Finally, we should differentiate between the different theoretical and ideological paradigms of explanation and interpretation of the

---

43   Only full-length texts that discuss and focus on the revolution have been included in this analysis. I have not considered newspaper articles or Internet publications.

revolution.[44] Here, three older patterns of explanation have been joined by two more recent interpretive modes; these patterns, however, can intersect or overlap, and they might best be thought of as ideal types. A number of authors and texts also represent models of explanation that could be seen as complementing other modes of interpretation.[45] The established patterns of explanation are these:

1. The nationalist pattern, which maintains that the revolution had an essentially nationalist character and was a reaction against British colonial rule and its legacy as well as the sultanate. This argument is best represented by Aumüller (1980), Clayton (1981), Lofchie (1965), Glassman (2000), Petterson (2002), and Purpura (1997).

2. The socialist pattern, which claims that the revolution abolished the "feudal" sultanate in a class struggle and replaced a class-oriented society with an anti-imperialist socialist society (even if the revolution in its early days is often seen as a "lumpen affair" staged by "lumpen youth" that was brought under control by the experienced cadres of the Umma Party and the ASP Youth League). This position is shared by Ayani (1970), Babu (1991), Bakari (2001), Burgess (1999 and 2002), Prunier (1998), Sheriff and Ferguson (1991), Wilson (1989), and Othman (1993, 2004).

3. The racialist pattern,[46] which maintains that the revolution was essentially a rebellion of "the Africans" against the "Arabs and Indians." This position is broadly shared by Amory (1994), Crosthwaith (the British High Commissioner in 1964, PRO DO 185/68),[47] Crozon (1991), Flint (1965), Glassman (2000), Kettani (1982), Lofchie (1965), Maliyamkono (2000), Martin (1978), Mrina and Mattoke (1980), Parkin (1995), Petterson (2002), Prunier (1998), Purpura (1997), Shao (1992), and Triplett (1971), as well as a Hamburg research project on the revolution in Zanzibar as represented by Wimmelbücker (2001). The racialist pattern of explanation seems to have gained major influence as a paradigm of explanation, as both Zanzibari and non-Zanzibari sources, texts

---

44 For an extensive discussion, see Wimmelbücker 2001.

45 Some models of explanation that have not gained widespread acceptance, such as the idea of the revolution as a "British plot," are not discussed here.

46 The term "racialist" does not insinuate that these authors represent racist positions. They only stress "race" as a category of analysis.

47 Crosthwaith actually maintained that "the uprising was in essence a rebellion of (African) slaves against their (Arab) masters" (PRO DO 185/68, p. 16).

and oral accounts alike, share this interpretation. The racialist argument carried some weight, of course, as the revolutionaries themselves, in particular Okello, cultivated racialist discourses. As the revolution indeed led to the emergence of a new and prominently African (Shirazi and mainlander) elite, Zanzibaris of African descent became more visible in higher political and social positions after 1964, whereas the public visibility of Arabs, Comorians, and Indians decreased. Moreover, well into the 1970s and beyond, the Revolutionary Government often highlighted the "fruits of the revolution" (*matunda ya mapinduzi*) in terms of racial justice—pursuing Africanization in the civil service and education, Africanizing the city, and redistributing land to African smallholders, among other policies.

While these three modes of interpretation have been around for some time, two other patterns of argumentation have been developed more recently—largely since the 1990s. These recent versions either maintain that the revolution possessed all the key features of a civil war or they stress the non-Zanzibari character of the 1964 events by claiming that the revolution was not a revolution at all, but rather a coup, "imported to Zanzibar from outside" (al-Maamiry 1988: 70),[48] or an invasion of mainland forces (Ghassany 2010; extensively Fairooz 1995; see also Fairooz's argumentation in Harding 2003: 509).[49] The invasion theme has some weight on account of the indisputable importance of mainlanders in the first days of the revolution and the historical links of the ASP with mainland politicians, as well as the fact that mainland Africans contributed in significant ways to the success of the revolution, not only with respect to their participation in Okello's troops in the first days of

---

48 Babu, for instance, seems to have thought about the revolution in largely "coup" terms: "You need 17 people to make a revolution in Zanzibar" (conversation with Abdul Sheriff in London in 1979; personal communication, Abdul Sheriff, 22 July 2004).

49 In an interview with Sauda Barwani in 2003, Amani Thani Fairuz maintained, "*Siyaiti mapinduzi kwa sababu mapinduzi yanafanywa na wananchi wenyewe bila ya kushawishiwa na yoyote kutoka nje, kwa kuona maslahi yao hayaendi barabara ndipo wanapoona hawana njia nyengine ikiwa wanashindwa kwa mambo ya ballots, wanatumia mapinduzi. Lakini yalofanyika Unguja ni uvamizi, yaani kiingereza wanasema 'invasion,' wameinvade nchi kwa sababu walotumiwa katika mapinduzi hayo si wazanzibari*" (quoted in Barwani et al. 2003: 178). ["I don't call it a 'revolution' because a revolution is made by the people themselves without any pressure from outside, by seeing that their interests are not going very well; it is then, when they see they will be defeated by the ballot and there is no other way, that they utilize a revolution. But what happened in Unguja was an invasion, that is, in English, they say 'invasion' – they invaded the country because those who were used in the revolution were not Zanzibaris." Translation provided by the editors.]

the revolution but also in the form of mainland police support for the revolution or the sustained participation of mainlanders in the political development of Zanzibar after the union with Tanganyika.

The Civil War Argument

The explosion of texts on the revolution since the 1980s, as well as the increasing accessibility of archival sources (at the Zanzibar National Archives as well as at the Public Record Office in London) and processes of political liberalization in Zanzibar, have contributed to the critique of existing models of explanation of the revolution and supported the emergence of new paradigms of interpretation. Thus, Abdul Sheriff has maintained that the revolution should be understood "not as an overthrow of an Arab oligarchy by an African majority . . . but as a civil war in a society that could not find enough common ground" (Sheriff 2001: 313).[50] This argument has acquired particular importance as it is implicitly directed against the predominant political discourse of the CCM (and has implications for more recent political conflicts). With respect to ongoing debates and disputes between CCM and the oppositional CUF (Civic United Front, whose members are mostly former CCM members) on the legacy of the revolution as well as the management of power in contemporary Zanzibar, it would in fact be possible to speak about an enduring "cold civil war" that has at times reappeared after 1964, as in January 2001, when dozens of people (mostly from Pemba) were killed in days and weeks of riots and protests against the manipulation of the 2000 elections, while several thousand people from Pemba fled to Kenya. Analysts who share the civil war position, apart from Abdul Sheriff (in Mukandala and Othman 1995: 151, and again in Sheriff 2001), are Crozon (1991), Bakari (2001), and Hirschler (2001).

The argument that the revolution should really be called a civil war raises a number of questions. The "revolution argument" is supported by the fact that the uprising had been planned for some time by the ASP Youth League and Umma cadres such as Seif Bakari, who had undergone training in Cuba, East Germany, China, and the Soviet Union. ASP Youth League and Umma cadres managed to wrest control

---

50   The idea of imagining the revolution as a civil war was developed by Abdul Sheriff at a conference in Paris in the early 1990s, and subsequently repeated by Mohamed Saleh. The civil war argument was used to point out that there were not only ethnic splits in Zanzibar before 1964 but also splits within the different communities (communication with Sheriff, 22 July 2004).

from Okello's forces and to take over central positions in the government after 12 January 1964 (Burgess 2002: 41). The revolution thus adopted significant features of a socialist revolution. These socialist features were enhanced by "socialist types of politics" in the aftermath of the revolution, which were supported by a number of socialist countries, in particular China, the Soviet Union, and East Germany. These policies brought about nationalization of the large plantations, the "three acres" (Kiswahili, *eka tatu*) land distribution program,[51] state control over the import-export trade and banking, the formation of new, socialist mass organizations such as the "green shirts" or the Youth Brigades, the uniformization of society, and a socialist mass culture (see Burgess 2002b). At the same time, decisions such as the expulsion of the owners of houses or land were often enforced in rather arbitrary ways: Large plantations, for instance, were not divided into three-acre plots for the "masses" but were transformed into landholdings for the new political elite or turned into state farms.

The civil war argument, on the other hand, is supported by the fact that, in the "time of politics" of the mid- and late 1950s, Zanzibar's development was characterized by disputes between and among Zanzibar's different social and ethnic groups, which led to a significant deterioration of the political climate in Zanzibar even before the events of January 1964. In particular, a number of incidents and riots occurred in the early 1960s. In 1961 alone, 60 people died in riots in the context of the elections in that year (Glassman 2011). A significant feature of these conflicts was that they were ethnically mixed—not Arabs on the one side and Africans on the other. Rather, both the ZNP and the ASP, as well as the Umma Party and the ZPPP, enjoyed heterogeneous popular support. Thus, the revolution was not a revolution of Africans against Arabs but rather a rebellion of the marginalized against the established. That is, it was a movement largely defined by social, economic, and political factors and not by purely ethnic (or racial) categories—despite the racialist character of the early stages of the revolution (the Okello period) and despite the subsequent legitimizing claim that racial disparities were a major factor in the development of a revolutionary climate.

It should be mentioned at this point that even if a racialist paradigm for describing society had been established in colonial times, this

---

51 The three-acre plot idea was "petty bourgeois," though, and not socialist in character (communication with Abdul Sheriff, 22 July 2004).

racialist paradigm reflected British attitudes to colonial rule that were based on a hierarchy of races, topped by the British themselves ruling over an Omani-Arab aristocracy, an Indian traders and clerks class, and finally an African plantation and harbor-worker proletariat (on this issue, see Glassman 2000 and 2004). In addition, ethnic (racialist) arguments were used both in the *zama za siasa* and in the years following the revolution to delegitimize the respective other camp, in particular the sultan and his supporters, and to legitimize the revolution. Yet this racialist paradigm is not very useful for explaining social and political change: Pemba, in particular, could point to a large land- and tree-owning African ("Shirazi") population as well as a considerable number of poor Arabs. The greatest number (two-thirds of the total number) of clove trees, Zanzibar's most important source of income until the 1970s, grew in Pemba,[52] and two-thirds of these were owned by Africans (Wapemba/Shirazi). Tree and land ownership, as well as ethnic structures, were thus completely different in Pemba and Unguja.[53] Unguja's clove economy was insignificant in comparison to that of Pemba, where ownership of clove trees was much more evenly distributed among ethnic groups. Race, class, and clove tree ownership thus did *not* coincide in Pemba, although this argument has been cultivated in the apologetic literature in order to legitimize the revolution (see Bakari 2001: 51).

The misrepresentation of the ethnic and economic setup of Zanzibar's clove plantation ownership data essentially goes back to Michael F. Lofchie (1965: 87),[54] who, in his analysis of clove tree ownership and land ownership, committed the mistake of not differentiating between the islands of Unguja and Pemba: While Unguja had relatively few clove trees and the major plantations and farms were controlled by Arab and Indian landowners, Pemba had the greatest number of clove trees in the archipelago. In addition, a considerable and growing "indigenous" (i.e., "Shirazi") group of both tree- and landowners existed in Pemba. The Clove Bonus Scheme thus registered that, in the period between

---

52 In a hurricane in 1872, Unguja's clove plantations were uprooted and subsequently replaced by coconut palm plantations.

53 These calculations could be seen as another myth in Zanzibari historiography. For a general history of the plantation economy, see Cooper 1980: 125ff.

54 Lofchie's data are due to a misleading interpretation of a 1931 statistic overview of land ownership and race (Wimmelbücker 2001: 305). On patterns of land ownership and processes of expropriation of land for plantations in the 19th and 20th centuries, see Bakari 2001, Sheriff 1987, and Middleton 1961.

1922 and 1929, peasants owning less than 500 clove trees constituted 94 percent of all clove owners and that they owned 54 percent of all clove trees in Pemba (Bakari 2001: 51). Lofchie's miscalculation, and his subsequent conclusion that Arabs had a dominant position as landowners in Zanzibar (as a whole), was adopted, however, by many revolutionary authors, such as Mrina and Matoke (1980: 34) and Mapuri (1996: 91–2), for reasons of legitimation, and it was revised only in 2001 by Mohammed Bakari (see Sheriff 2001: 307; Bakari 2001: 51ff).[55]

When talking about numbers and percentages, it has to be stressed that despite racialist claims, the percentage of Arabs in Zanzibar's total population has never reached more than 17 percent, and even this percentage should be seen as an artificial number derived from colonial constructions of identities (see Glassman 2000). Thus, in all pre-independence elections, the pre-revolution ZNP-ZPPP party coalition was able to win considerable percentages of the non-Arab vote, even if the ZNP-ZPPP never won the absolute majority of votes (Sheriff 2001: 303). Zanzibar's society was thus divided, before and after the revolution, into two parts of almost equal size. There never was a clear distinction between a large number of "oppressed Africans" and a small number of "Arab oppressors," but rather there was a spectrum of different ethnic (racial) groups that were represented in all social and political spheres.[56] The revolution was thus not a rebellion of the Africans against the Arabs but rather an uprising of the "marginalized," who were, however, not necessarily African. Most members of the Umma Party, for instance, were of Arab or Comorian descent, but marginalized in political terms. The social support for the revolution therefore did not come exclusively from "Africans"—who in any case rarely constituted a unified or consistent collectivity (Bissell 2011: 37ff.). Rather, a significant feature of the revolution was the important role played by Arabs and Comorians in the first weeks. And although many Zanzibaris of Arab, Indian, and Comorian descent were expelled

---

55 The correct relationship of ethnic groups and ownership of trees and land in Unguja and Pemba has been documented by Cooper (1980: 146). He has shown that, by 1922, "Swahili" in Pemba already owned as many clove trees as Arabs, while the ratio in Unguja was 1:3.

56 The idea of the division of Zanzibari society into two almost equal parts, which blocked each other, possibly explains the formation of the idea of a third party that would eventually overcome this split. In pre-revolutionary times, both the ZPPP and the Umma Party could be seen as such a third force. The concept was kept alive by Babu until his death in July 1996. Recently, another third force has developed in reaction to the mutual CCM-CUF blockade. This political group was first called Safina but was renamed Jahazi Asili in 2005 (communication with Mohamed Saleh, 2 April 2005). On the idea of the third force, see Babu 1996: 5ff.

after 1964 or fled Zanzibar in the 1960s, a significant number of Arabs and Comorians remained. Arabs and Comorians could thus be found on *both* sides, before and after the revolution (see Sheriff 2001). In Karume's administration (1964–72), however, many revolutionaries of Arab and Comorian origin, mostly Umma cadres, were excluded from the revolutionary nomenklatura, imprisoned, and even executed in the context of alleged coup attempts. As a result, the leadership of the ASP/CCM became increasingly homogeneous over the 1960s and 1970s, and Zanzibar's "African" character became increasingly visible within the revolutionary elite.

Efforts to consolidate the revolution relate not only to Zanzibar's political structures and the public sphere, however, but also to the way in which the revolution was and is remembered or represented. Subsequent to the consolidation of the revolution, Karume and his successors (Aboud Jumbe, 1972–84; Ali Hassan Mwinyi, 1984–85; Idris Abdul Wakil, 1985–90; Salmin Amour, 1990–2000; and Amani Abeid Karume, 2000–2010)[57] were indeed able to use their official power to fix their own interpretation of history in schools, in the public representation of the revolution, and in the cult of the revolution.[58] Due to the victory of CCM in the 2005 elections, the hegemony of interpretation of the Karume

---

57 See a short characterization of the administrations of these presidents of Zanzibar in Bakari 2001: 110–18.

58 See Burgess 1999 and 2002a, b, c extensively on the revolutionary cult. The legacy of the revolution has been kept alive in multiple ways until today by the CCM as, for instance, in the instrumentalization of public festivals and celebrations, in particular in the field of sports, in the media, and in the continued existence of revolutionary structures such as Zanzibar's security apparatus and the Zanzibari secret service, as well as in the marginalization of oppositional forces, especially the Civic United Front (CUF). CUF, for instance, was accused of working for the restoration of pre-revolutionary times and the restitution of *eka tatu* land to former plantation owners. On the other hand, CUF was also accused of cultivating contacts with al-Qa'ida and other terrorist groups.

administration was extended for another five-year period, until 2010.[59] The attempts by the revolutionaries and their heirs to eternalize the revolution and to impose their own interpretation of history in Zanzibar were supported by, among other factors, the fact that a large majority of Zanzibar's religious scholars were forced into exile between 1964 and 1968, died, or emigrated voluntarily. In addition, Zanzibar's newspapers were either prohibited after the revolution (and replaced by government bulletins such as *Zanzibar Leo*) or ceased to exist for lack of readership. Abeid Amani Karume's policy of marginalizing religious scholars was not directed against Islam as such, however, but against Zanzibar's influential religious scholars and their families, who alone would have been in a position, as a moral institution, to challenge Karume's political legitimacy. Karume personally described the religious scholars' threat to his rule in the following statement: "When I hold a speech and they

---

59 For an analysis of the 2005 elections, see Feingold 2005. Because of space limitations, a proper analysis of the electoral process and the results of the elections cannot be given here. Some major reasons for the victory of the CCM (in 2005, as well as in the 2000 elections) were the exclusion of a considerable number of Zanzibari voters by way of nonregistration in the local voters' lists, the well-coordinated voting of Tanzanian security forces (often several times), and the registration of Tanzanian "mainlanders" for the elections in Zanzibar. In fact, 507,225 voters cast their votes in 2005, while only 450,000 voters were registered (IC82, 8.11.2006). Both the process of voter registration and the elections proper were marked by numerous irregularities that eventually led to a comfortable majority of 32,000 votes for the CCM. In addition, the elections were characterized by strategies of intimidation against external observers from the United States and a number of European countries and by repression of the opposition. Thus, in April 2005 the members of the *baraza* at Jaws Corner in the historical center of Zanzibar, known for their CUF sympathies, were beaten up by security forces for no other reason than their alleged sympathies for the political opposition which had again protested against irregularities in the process of voters' registration for the elections in 2005: "20 policemen beat people at random and arrested eight without explanation" (*Africa Confidential* 2005). The 2005 elections were monitored not only by international observers but also by a Zanzibari Muslim observer mission from the Uamsho ("Awakening") group. The Uamsho report mentioned that more than 2,000 people had registered more than once and that hooligan groups known as Janjaweed had disturbed both the registration process and CUF rallies. In the process of the elections, many people were not allowed to vote and were turned away from the 994 voting stations. Vehicles were spotted that transported "voters," often soldiers, to other voting places for repeated voting (see AllAfrica Global media, report 11.11.2005). The elections in 2010 were probably the first since 1995 not to be fraudulent on a grand scale. As a result, the CUF received almost 50 percent of the votes and subsequently formed a coalition government with the CCM under Ali Mohamed Shein, a CCM politician from Pemba. As a result of the formation of a CCM-CUF coalition, government, political, and parliamentary opposition has virtually ceased to exist and radical Muslim groups such as Uamsho (see Loimeier 2009) have started to fill this role. Also, demands for Zanzibar's independence, or at least a greater degree of autonomy within the union, have become stronger, supported not only by CUF but also by CCM politicians such as Hassan Nassor Moyo (communication with Samuel Mhajida, 31 October 2013). Finally, the new political situation has contributed to de-escalating public debates, with surprising results concerning the interpretation of the revolution, its legacy, and memories of revolution.

address the public as well, whom do you think will people follow?" (communication with Ahmed Maulid, 17 August 2003). The collapse of Islamic education and the emigration of most of Zanzibar's religious scholars, who had contributed to Zanzibar's cosmopolitan character before the revolution because of their varied Hadrami, Comorian, and Somali (Brawa) descent, as well as the death of many of the remaining scholars between 1970 and 1972, ended their near hegemony of interpretation of Zanzibar's history.

By Way of Conclusion: Memories of Revolution

The above considerations regarding the paradigms of interpretation of the revolution and, in particular, the question whether it was a revolution or a civil war, relate to the initial argument, namely, that the interpretation of history is often a struggle for hegemony of interpretation. As Zanzibar is a small archipelago of islands where almost everybody knows almost everybody else, representatives of the different patterns of explanation of the revolution and its aftermath are often bitterly opposed. They see striking discrepancies between their respective perceptions of the revolution, not only with regard to the different discourses on the revolution but also with regard to their biographies, both invented and real. Thus, to this day, the public discourse on the revolution is also a discourse on Zanzibar's pre-revolutionary times and the assessment of personal agency in this period of time. As all protagonists reinterpret events and try to present and legitimize their own role in the revolution, (surprising) reinterpretations of the revolution take place. These reformulations of memories are subject to constant processes of negotiation, which may transform personal memory over time.[60] The ongoing production of memories of the revolution also affects the way the revolution is represented and understood, especially insofar as numerous Zanzibaris have written about the revolution since the mid-1980s. These texts have not only triggered public reactions and debates but have also sparked new rounds of psychological rationalization and justification regarding the roles of particular individuals in the revolution. As memories are translated into writings, these representations in turn shape or stimulate further memories, disputes, and counter-narratives. A key to explaining

---

60 This seems to be particularly true of Issa, who today vehemently rejects accusations that he was responsible for distinctive anti-Islamic attitudes in the early days and weeks of the revolution (communication with Ali Sultan Issa, 22 August 2002). Issa's biography was published by G. Thomas Burgess in 2009.

the boom in text production with respect to Zanzibar's recent history may be found in an argument put forward by Jan Assmann (1997) in his work on the constitution of collective and communicative memories. Assmann claims that important historical events undergo phases of reinterpretation approximately 40 years after they occurred: "Forty years mark a borderline in collective memory: [namely] when living memory is in danger of vanishing or when forms of cultural memory are becoming problematic" (1997: 11). After roughly 40 years, he continues, adult witnesses to historical events begin to retire and to reflect more upon their lives; consequently, there is an increase in memory work as well as the urge to transmit and fix recollections for subsequent generations (ibid: 51). The growth since the mid-1980s in the number of texts on the revolution in Zanzibar shows, however, that Jan Assmann's 40-year benchmark was reached earlier in Zanzibar.[61] These accounts show how interpretations of events in the revolution have changed over time due to a process of filtering and *Rückschaufehler* ("errant memories").[62] They have consequently triggered a reaction in both media and public debates. In these texts and debates (Aley 1994; Babakerim 1994; Babu 1996; al-Barwani 1996; Fairooz, 1995; al-Isma'ili 1999; Mapuri, 1996; Mdundu 1996; Othman 2004; Ghassany 2010), the events of 1964 are rethought, re-discussed, re-evaluated and reinterpreted, and, as a consequence, existing patterns of explanation are subject to constant revision.

What has been said for the processes of transformation of personal memories is also true for the transformation of personal memories into collective memory, which is also subject to processes of negotiation, selection, modification, reassessment, filtering, revision, and/or reinterpretation of facts and events. Different schools of interpretation produce ever-new texts and explanations in their struggle for hegemony of interpretation of the revolution, and consequently they either defend or challenge established accounts. In an almost dialectical process, they trigger reactions from competing schools of interpretation that lead to subsequent disputes (see Fried 2004: 85).

---

61 I would like to point out here that Assmann's 40-year benchmark should not be taken too narrowly. Life expectancies are still much shorter in many African countries than in contemporary Europe. In Zanzibar, people often die in their 50s or 60s instead of their 70s or 80s. Thus the transition from living memory to cultural memory should be closer to 20 or 30 years.

62 In psychoanalysis, these faulty reinterpretations of personal experiences and historical events are described as "errant memories" (*Rückschaufehler*). These *Rückschaufehler* primarily help one to come to terms with mistakes, failures, and traumatic experiences and serve to remove (historical) responsibilities.

In Zanzibar, the process of negotiation of personal memories has not yet been concluded, as Karel Arnaut (2006: 15) has noted in a different context, largely due to the fact that for a long period of time "victims or witnesses found it (almost) impossible to narrate their experiences (or to find an audience for their account), while victors and executioners found it largely redundant to engage in any dialogue" and were consequently happy to ignore the memories of the defeated. As a result, the process of negotiating Zanzibar's collective memory, with a consensus regarding the revolution and its legacy, is still blocked by multiple and contradictory personal memories. This process has also been blocked by the efforts of the CCM government to eternalize or fix the official revolutionary account of Zanzibar's history.

As a result, the revolution, and the subsequent struggle to interpret and represent the revolution, may be seen as a chapter of Zanzibari history that has not yet been closed. Zanzibar's revolutionary history is still undergoing processes of negotiation that are painful for those witnesses of the time who are still alive today, as their memories of revolution remain contested or even ignored. However, a society must come to terms with its past by resolving disputes regarding the interpretation of personal memories and must find a way to reconcile these memories in order to reach a historical consensus with respect to specific events. Otherwise, the collective memory of these events will remain mutilated and will pass, in mutilated form, into "cultural" memory—that is, the long-term historical memory of a specific society. This process of passing on mutilated memories has already started in Zanzibar, as many witnesses of the time have died without having been able to transmit their personal memories. In a political context where contradictory accounts of the events of 1964 still abound, the death of contemporary witnesses constitutes a serious problem for the revision of a number of myths regarding the revolution that have been cultivated by the party of the "victors" and taught as history in schools. In the personal memories of many Zanzibaris, the revolution is still ongoing, yet, since the 1980s, this struggle has assumed all the characteristics of a civil war of memories.

References

Archival Sources: The Public Record Office, London (PRO)

Information on the revolution is available in the PRO files with access code PRO CO, some of which were classified "top secret" until recently (2001):

PRO DO 185/51: Military Intervention Zanzibar (top secret, closed until 2001)

PRO DO 185/60: Revolution/Casualties (confidential, closed until 2001)

PRO DO 185/68: Political Situation Zanzibar, British Land Forces Kenya Conference, Zanzibar and Pemba (Report by T.H. Crosthwaith, confidential, closed until 2001.)

PRO DO 214/118: East German aid to Zanzibar

PRO DO 214/119: East German aid to Zanzibar

Published Works

Africa Confidential
2005 Vol. 46, no. 10, 13 May.

Afro Shirazi-Party

1974 *The Afro Shirazi Party Revolution 1964–1974*. Dar es Salaam: Printpak Tanzania Limited.

1965 *The History of Zanzibar: Africans and the Formation of the Afro-Shirazi Party*. Zanzibar: n.p.

Aley, Juma

1994 *Enduring Links*. Dubai: n.p.

1988 *Zanzibar: In the Context*. New Delhi: Lancers Books

1984 *Twenty One Years of Leadership: Contrasts and Similarities*. Dar es Salaam: n.p.

Amory, Deborah

1994 "The Politics of Identity in Zanzibar." Ph.D. diss., Stanford University.

Arnaut, Karel

2006 "'Out of the Race': The Poiesis of Genocide in Mass Media Discourses in Côte d'Ivoire." In *Grammars of Identity/Alterity: A Structural Approach*, ed. Gerd Baumann and André Gingrich, 112–41. London: Berghahn.

Arnold, Nathalie

2003 "Wazee Wakijua Mambo!/Elders Used to Know Things!: Occult Powers and Revolutionary History in Pemba, Zanzibar." Ph.D. diss., Indiana University, Bloomington.

Assmann, Jan

1997 *Das kulturelle Gedächtnis. Schrift, Erinnerung und politische Identität in frühen Hochkulturen.* Munich: C. H. Beck.

Aumüller, Ingeborg

1980 *Dekolonisation und Nationwerdung in Zanzibar.* Munich: Weltforum Verlagsgesellschaft.

Ayani, Samuel G.

1970 *A History of Zanzibar 1934–1964.* Nairobi: Kenya Literature Bureau.

Babakerim

1994 *The Aftermath of Zanzibar Revolution.* Muscat: privately printed.

Babu, Abdulrahman Muhammed

1996 "Wanted: A Third Force in Zanzibar Politics." *Change: Magazine of Business, Politics and Economics* (Dar es Salaam) 4(7–9): 5–20.

1991 "The 1964 Revolution: Lumpen or Vanguard?" In *Zanzibar under Colonial Rule*, ed. Abdul Sheriff and Ed Ferguson, 220–249. London: James Currey.

Bader, Z. K. M. J.

1984 "The Social Conditions and Consequences of the 1964 Land Reform in Zanzibar." Ph.D. diss., Birkbeck College, London.

Bakari, Mohammed

2001 *The Democratisation Process in Zanzibar: A Retarded Transition.* Hamburg: Institut für Afrika-Kunde.

al-Barwani, Ali Muhsin

1997 *Conflicts and Harmony in Zanzibar: Memoirs.* Dubai: n.p.

al-Barwani, Sauda, et al., eds.

2003 *Unser Leben vor der Revolution und danach—Maisha Yetu kabla ya Mapinduzi na baadaye.* Hamburg: Rüdiger Köppe Verlag.

Burgess, G. Thomas

2009 *Race, Revolution, and the Struggle for Human Rights in Zanzibar: The Memoirs of Ali Sultan Issa and Seif Sharif Hamad*. Athens, Ohio: Ohio University Press.

2005 "An Imagined Generation: Umma Youth in Nationalist Zanzibar." In *In Search of a Nation: Nations and Nationalism in Tanzanian Culture and History. Essays in Honour of I. M. Kimambo*, ed. Gregory H. Maddox, James L. Giblin, 216–49. Oxford: James Currey.

2002a "Cinema, Bell Bottoms and Miniskirts: Struggles over Youth and Citizenship in Revolutionary Zanzibar." *International Journal of African Historical Studies* 35(2/3): 287–313.

2002b "Youth and the Revolution: Mobility and Discipline in Zanzibar, 1950–1980." Ph.D. diss., Indiana University, Bloomington.

1999 "Remembering Youth: Generation in Revolutionary Zanzibar." *Africa Today* 46(2): 29–52.

Central Office of Information

1963 *Zanzibar: Reference Pamphlet 60*. London: Her Majesty's Stationery Office.

Chrétien, Jean-Pierre, and Jean-Louis Triaud, eds.

1999 *Histoire d´Afrique. Les enjeux de mémoire*. Paris: Karthala.

Clayton, Anthony

1981 *The Zanzibari Revolution and Its Aftermath*. London: C. Hurst & Company.

Crozon, Ariel

1991 "Les Arabes à Zanzibar: Haine et fascination." In *Les Swahili entre Afrique et Asie*, ed. Françoise Le Guennec-Coppens and Pat Caplan, 179–94. Paris: Karthala.

Deutsch, Jan-Georg, and Brigitte Reinwald, eds.

2002 *Space on the Move: Transformations of the Indian Ocean Seascape in the Nineteenth and Twentieth Century*. Berlin: Klaus Schwarz Verlag.

Fairooz, Aman Thani

1995 *Ukweli ni Huu (Kuusuta Uwongo)*. Dubai: self-published.

Feingold, Russ

2005 "Tanzania: *Congressional Record* Statement of U.S. Senator Russ Feingold on Recent Elections in Zanzibar." allafrica.com/stories/200511030164.html, accessed 27 February 2016.

Flint, J. E.

1965 "Zanzibar, 1890–1950." In *History of East Africa*, vol. 2, ed. Vincent Harlow and E. M. Chilver, 641–71. Oxford: Clarendon Press.

Fried, Johannes

2004 *Der Schleier der Erinnerung: Grundzüge einer historischen Memorik.* Munich: C. H. Beck.

Gerhardt, Ludwig, and Harding, Leonhard

2000 SFB 520, Teilprojekt C2: "Erwerb und Verlust von politischen Handlungsspielräumen im Kontext des Übergangs von der Kolonialzeit zur politischen Unabhängigkeit, dargestellt an autobiographischen Texten aus Sansibar." Hamburg: unpublished document.

Ghassany, Harith

2010 *Kwaheri Ukoloni, Kwaheri Uhuru! Zanzibar na Mapinduzi ya Afrabia* [Goodbye Colonialism, Goodbye Independence! Zanzibar and the Revolution of Afrabia]. Self-published, https://kwaheri.files.wordpress.com/2010/05/kwaheri-ukoloni-kwaheri-uhuru.pdf, accessed 18 July 2016.

Glassman, Jonathon

2011 *War of Words, War of Stones: Racial Thought and Violence in Colonial Zanzibar.* Bloomington, Ind.: Indiana University Press.

2004 "Slower than a Massacre: The Multiple Sources of Racial Thought in Colonial Africa." *American Historical Review* 109(3): 720–54.

2000 "Sorting Out the Tribes: The Creation of Racial Identities in Colonial Zanzibar's Newspaper Wars." *Journal of African History* 41: 395–428.

Harding, Leonhard

2003 "Nyerere in Neuem Licht. Interpretationen in den Lebensgeschichten von Sansibaris." In *Unser Leben vor der Revolution und danach—Maisha yetu kabla ya mapinduzi na baadaye,* ed. Sauda A. Barwani et al., 493–577. Cologne: Rüdiger Köppe Verlag.

1992 *Geschichte Afrikas im 19. und 20. Jahrhundert.* Hamburg: Oldenbourg.

Hirschler, Kurt

2001 "Sansibar—Krise und (k)ein Ende?" *Afrika Spectrum* 3: 319–46.

Hobsbawm, Eric, and Terence Ranger, eds.

1983 *The Invention of Tradition.* Cambridge, U.K.: Cambridge University Press.

al-Ismaily, Issa bin Nasser
1999 *Zanzibar: Kinyang'anyiro na Utumwa* [Zanzibar: The Scramble and Slavery]. Muscat, Oman: n.p.

Jumbe, Aboud
1994 *The Partnership: Tanganyika-Zanzibar Union: 30 Turbulent Years*. Dar es Salaam: Amana Publishers.

Kaniki, M. H. Y., ed.
1980 *Tanzania under Colonial Rule*. London: Longman.

Kettani, Ali
1982 "Muslim East Africa: An Overview." *JIMMA* 4(2): 104–19.

Kharusi, Ahmed Seif
1969 *The Agony of Zanzibar: A Victim of the New Colonialism*. Richmond, U.K.: Foreign Affairs Publishing.
1967 *Zanzibar: Africa's First Cuba: A Case Study of the New Colonialism*. Richmond, U.K.: Foreign Affairs Publishing.

Kimambo, Isaria N., and A.J. Temu
1969 *A History of Tanzania*. Dar es Salaam: Kapsel Educational Publications.

Koselleck, Reinhart
1984 *Vergangene Zukunft: Zur Semantik geschichtlicher Zeiten*. Frankfurt: Suhrkamp.

Le Cour Grandmaison, Colette, and Ariel Crozon, eds.
1998 *Zanzibar aujourd'hui*. Paris: Karthala.

Lodhi, Abdulaziz Y., Annette Rydström, and Gunnar Rydström
1986 "The Arabs in Zanzibar: From Sultanate to Peoples' Republic." *JIMMA* 7(2): 404–18.
1979 *A Small Book on Zanzibar*. Stockholm: Författares Bokmaskin.

Lofchie, Michael F.
1965 *Zanzibar: Background to Revolution*. Princeton, N.J.: Princeton University Press.

Loimeier, Roman
2012 *Eine Zeitlandschaft in der Globalisierung. Das islamische Sansibar im 19. und 20. Jahrhundert*. Bielefeld, Germany: transcript.

2009 *Between Social Skills and Marketable Skills: The Politics of Islamic Education in 20th Century Zanzibar*. Leiden: Brill.

2006 "Memories of Revolution: Zur Deutungsgeschichte einer Revolution (Sansibar 1964)." *Afrika Spectrum* 41(2):175–97.

al-Maamiry, Ahmed Hamoud

1988 *Omani Sultans in Zanzibar (1832–1964)*. New Delhi: Lancers Books.

Maliyamkono, T. L.

2000 *The Political Plight of Zanzibar*. Dar es Salaam: TEMA Publishers.

Mapuri, Omar R.

1996 *Zanzibar: The 1964 Revolution: Achievements and Prospects*. Dar es Salaam: TEMA Publishers.

Marfaing, Laurence, and Brigitte Reinwald, eds.

2001 *Afrikanische Beziehungen, Netzwerke und Räume*. Münster: LIT Verlag.

Martin, Esmond B.

1978 *Zanzibar: Tradition and Revolution*. London: Hamish Hamilton.

McMahon, Elizabeth

2005 "Becoming Pemban: Identity, Social Welfare and Community during the Protectorate Period." Ph.D. diss., Indiana University, Bloomington.

Mdundu, Minael-Hosanna O.

1996 *Masimulizi ya Shaykh Thabit Kombo Jecha*. Dar es Salaam: Dar es Salaam University Press.

Middleton, John

1961 *Land Tenure in Zanzibar*. London: Her Majesty's Stationery Office.

Mosare, Jonathan

1969 "Background to the Revolution in Zanzibar." In *A History of Tanzania*, ed. Isaria N. Kimambo and A. J. Temu, 214–38. Nairobi: East Africa Publishing House.

Mrina, B. F., and W. T. Mattoke

1980 *Mapambano ya Ukombozi Zanzibar*. Dar es Salaam: Tanzania Publishing House.

Muhammad, Amir A.
1991 *A Guide to a History of Zanzibar*. Zanzibar: Good Luck Publishers.

Mukandala, R. S., and Haroub Othman, eds.
1995 *Liberalization and Politics*. Dar es Salaam: Dar es Salaam University Press.

Mwakikagile, Godfrey
2002 *Nyerere and Africa: End of an Era*. Atlanta, GA: Protea Publishing Company.

Mwanjisi, R. K.
1967 *Ndugu Abeid Amani Karume*. Nairobi: East African Publishing House.

Napoli, Fatma Jiddawi, and Mohamed Ahmed Saleh
2005 "The Role of Sexual Violence against Zanzibari Women in the Human Rights Conflict with Tanzania over Sovereignty." In *Resisting Racism and Xenophobia: Global Perspectives on Race, Gender and Human Rights*, ed. Faye V. Harrison, 159–72. Walnut Creek, Cal.: Altamira Press.

Niethammer, Lutz
2000 *Kollektive Identität. Heimliche Quellen einer unheimlichen Konjunktur*. Frankfurt: Suhrkamp.

Nisula, Tapio
1999 *Everyday Spirits and Medical Interventions*. Saarijärvi, Finland: Gummerus Kirjapaino Oy.

Okello, John
1967 *Revolution in Zanzibar*. Nairobi: East African Publishing House.

Othman, Haroub
2014 "Tanzania: The Withering Away of the Revolution?" In *Yes, In My Lifetime: Selected Works of Haroub Othman*, ed. Saida Yahya-Othman, 189–214. Dar es Salaam: Mkuki na Nyota and Codresia.

1995 "The Union with Zanzibar." In *Mwalimu: The Influence of Nyerere*, ed. Colin Legum and Geoffrey Mmari, 170–5. Trenton: Africa World Press.

1993 *Zanzibar's Political History: The Past Haunting the Present?* Copenhagen: Centre for Development Research.

Othman, Haroub, ed.

2001 *Babu: I Saw the Future and It Works: Essays Celebrating the Life of Comrade Abdulrahman Mohamed Babu, 1924–1996*. Dar es Salaam: E&D Ltd.

Parkin, David

1995 "Blank Banners and Islamic Consciousness in Zanzibar." In *Questions of Consciousness*, ed. Anthony Cohen and Nigel Rapport. London: Routledge.

Penrad, Jean-Claude

1995 "Emeute à Zanzibar (février 1936). La violence ambigüe." In *L'Étranger intime. Mélanges offerts à Paul Ottino*, 395–410. Saint André, Réunion: Université de la Réunion.

Petterson, Don

2002 *Revolution in Zanzibar: An American's Cold War Tale*. Boulder, Colo.: Westview Press.

Prunier, Gérard

1998 "La Révolution de 1964." In *Zanzibar aujourd'hui*, ed. Colette Le Cour Grandmaison and Ariel Crozon, 95–112. Paris: Karthala.

Purpura, Alison

1997 "Knowledge and Agency: The Social Relations of Islamic Expertise in Zanzibar Town." Ph.D. diss., City University of New York.

Ranger, Terence

1993 "The Invention of Tradition Revisited." In *Legitimacy and the State in 20th Century Africa*, ed. Terence Ranger and Olufemi Vaughan, 62–111. London: Palgrave Macmillan.

Saleh, Mohamed Ahmed

2002 "Tolerance: Principal Foundation of the Cosmopolitan Society of Zanzibar." https://www.goodreads.com/author_blog_posts/7632505-tolerance-principal-foundation-of-the-cosmopolitan-society-of-zanzibar, accessed 14 July 2016.

Schneppen, Heinz

2003 *Sansibar und die Deutschen. Ein besonderes Verhältnis 1844–1966*. Hamburg: LIT Verlag.

1999 *Sayyid Khalid bin Bargash: Three Days as a Sultan—Thirty Years in Exile*. National Museums of Tanzania Occasional Paper 13. Dar es Salaam: National Museum of Tanzania.

Shao, Ibrahim Fokas

1992 *The Political Economy of Land Reform in Zanzibar*. Dar es Salaam: Dar es Salaam University Press.

Sheriff, Abdul

2001 "Race and Class in the Politics of Zanzibar." *Afrika Spectrum* 3: 301–18.

1987 *Slaves, Spices and Ivory in Zanzibar: Integration of an East African Commercial Empire into the World Economy, 1770–1873*. London: James Currey.

Sheriff, Abdul, and Ed Ferguson, eds.

1991 *Zanzibar under Colonial Rule*. London: James Currey.

Shivji, Issa

2008 *Pan-Africanism or Pragmatism? Lessons of Tanganyika-Zanzibar Union*. Dar es Salaam: Mkuki na Nyota.

Speitkamp, Winfried

2005 *Kommunikationsräume—Erinnerungsräume. Beiträge zur transkulturellen Begegnung in Afrika*. Munich: Martin Meidenbauer.

Triplett, George

1971 "Zanzibar. The Politics of Revolutionary Inequality." *Journal of Modern African Studies* 9: 612–17.

Wilson, Amrit

1989 *US Foreign Policy and Revolution: The Creation of Tanzania*. London: Pluto Press.

Wimmelbücker, Ludger

2003 "Aspekte eines gesellschaftlichen Umbruchs: die Sansibarische Revolution von 1964." In *Unser Leben vor der Revolution und danach—Maisha yetu kabla ya mapinduzi na baadaye*, ed. Sauda al-Barwani et al., 460–92. Hamburg: Rüdiger Köppe Verlag.

2001 "Die Sansibarische Revolution von 1964: Widersprüche und Unzulänglichkeiten offizieller Geschichtsschreibung." In *Afrikanische Beziehungen, Netzwerke und Räume*, ed. Laurence Marfaing and Brigitte Reinwald, 295–308. Münster: LIT Verlag.

Chapter Three

The Voice of the Revolution: Remembering and Re-Envisioning Field Marshal John Okello

Ann Lee Grimstad

"I am Field Marshal Okello! Wake up, you imperialists, there is no longer an imperialist government on this Island; this is now the government of the Freedom Fighters."

— JOHN OKELLO, *Revolution in Zanzibar*

The Voice

It was the Ugandan self-proclaimed Field Marshal John Okello whose booming voice Zanzibaris heard over the radio on the morning of 12 January 1964 informing them that their country had undergone a revolution the night before and threatening those who might oppose it.[1] For the next two months, Okello continued his barrage of excessively violent and extreme threats on the radio, becoming the voice of the revolution. There is no other singular voice that comes to people's minds when they think about the revolution. His was a voice no Zanzibari who heard it has forgotten, even fifty years later. People comment on the timbre of his voice, saying for instance that "*aliguruma kama simba*" ("he growled like a lion").[2] They also remembered the specific contents of his threats, ranging from terrifying to ludicrous. He ranted that the sultan should kill his children and wives or otherwise the revolutionaries would "extinguish [him] from the face of the earth," and "burn [his] remains with a fierce and hungry fire" (Okello 1967: 145). The most common recollection Zanzibaris shared in interviews about Okello, however, was

---

1   The word *revolution* is generally used to describe both the overthrow of the constitutional monarchy on the night of 11–12 January 1964 and the regime that followed under the Revolutionary Government of Zanzibar. In this chapter, I am primarily using this term to designate the overthrow.

2   Interview with Ali Omar Abdalla, 3 November 2013. Abdalla worked for the Public Works Department in Vitongoji, Pemba, and met Okello when he first came to Pemba looking for work.

his ridiculous order that everyone should come outside, strip to their underpants, and lie down as he drove by in his car in the Malindi section of Stone Town.³ Yet it also appears that the psychological warfare he conducted from the radio station at the revolutionaries' headquarters in Raha Leo had a significant effect, actually intimidating people into obeying the Freedom Fighters who toppled the government on the night of 11–12 January 1964. It also appears that the verbal terror he unleashed was not due to some alleged lack of sanity on Okello's part, as many British reports concluded at the time, but instead was the result of a tactical strategy. Before the revolution, Okello told Ali Omar Abdalla in Pemba that it was more important to talk tough than to know how to use weapons,⁴ and after the revolution, he told his friend Jonathan Opio in Uganda that "even shouting was enough to topple the government."⁵ In spite of his lack of formal education and sophistication, Okello seems to have had keen insights into psychological warfare. He was well aware of the performative dimensions of political power: by acting as if he was brutal, ruthless, and utterly in charge, he knew he could wield authority that otherwise might elude his grasp. For almost two months, this strategy of terror over the airwaves provided him with a position of command he otherwise would not likely have been able to gain—even as subsequent events prove how much he overestimated the long-lasting effect of his strategy of psychological warfare.

Another example of Okello's tactical intelligence was that he knew that the British were key to the success of his venture. He grasped that the revolution would have to wait until after independence, when the British would be gone. He realized that if the revolutionaries tried to take action while the British were still there, the colonialists would send in reinforcements to protect their interests and quash it (Okello 1967: 92). Okello also made it very clear that the lives and property of Europeans were to be safeguarded in the process of the revolution. He knew that the revolutionaries had to protect British lives and property, so that the British would have no reason to intervene.⁶ These are strategic

---

3   Interview with Ali Mbamba, 23 August 2013; Fatma Jinja, 30 November 2013; and Salim Rashid, 30 October 2013. Numerous people told me this story, and Okello's instructions can also be found in the BBC Written Archives, Summary of World Broadcasts Part IV The Middle East and Africa on 14 January 1964.

4   Interview with Ali Omar Abdalla, 3 November 2013.

5   Interview with Jonathan Opio, 23 January 2014.

6   Interview with Ali Omar Abdalla, 3 November 2013. He said Okello told him this in advance of the revolution.

considerations that none of the other members of the Committee of 14 claims to have contemplated.[7] Indeed, the British discussion about possible intervention and military action in Zanzibar in January and February 1964 was couched in terms of potential threat to British lives.[8]

Both of the last living members of the Committee of 14, Ramadhan Haji Faki and Hamid Ameir, said that Okello was chosen for his voice. He was to make announcements in his clearly non-Zanzibari Kiswahili so that people would pay attention and obey. Hamid Ameir said Okello was chosen so that people would ask who was running the revolution, as it was clearly not someone from Zanzibar. And Faki insisted that if he (or one of his Zanzibari colleagues) had made the announcement, people would have laughed, saying something like, "*Kweli?* [Seriously?] *Ramadhan Haji? Yeye mshamba tu.* [He's just a hick.] He thinks *he* can overthrow the government?" By making an outsider the voice of the revolution, the revolutionaries led people to think *Wabara* (mainlanders) were now in charge, ensuring that they would follow instructions. Faki also spoke of Mau Mau and how ferocious they were, insinuating that if people thought Mau Mau were involved, there would be no resistance.[9]

In the introduction to Okello's book, Clyde Sanger insightfully wrote, "In order to diminish Okello's popularity and ease his removal, Babu, then Foreign Minister, claimed Okello had never been anything more than a sort of disc-jockey, a man given the job of broadcasting over the captured radio-station because his Kiswahili (with its Kenyan accent) would reassure the mainland governments" (Okello 1967: 7). Sanger was correct about why Okello was depicted in these revisionist terms in the aftermath of the revolution. However, Okello is also the only figure involved who has actually spoken about the planning and the events during the night of the revolution. None of the other Committee of 14 members, or any Afro-Shirazi Party (ASP) politician, or anyone else in the first Baraza la Mapinduzi (Revolutionary Council) has reported anywhere near as complete a story as John Okello. In fact, none have written memoirs, no matter how brief. Khamis Darwesh was interviewed

---

7   The Committee of 14 is a legendary group comprised mostly of Afro-Shirazi Youth League (ASYL) members who were in the first Revolutionary Council. ASP documents claim they led the revolution at the behest of Karume (ZNA BA 76/19). On the point of protecting the British, William Smith asserts that President Karume gave orders that no Europeans should be arrested (1973: 106).

8   BNA CAB 21/5524.

9   Interview with Ramadhan Haji Faki, 27 August 2013, and interview with Hamid Ameir, 25 November 2013.

for an article in *Mwananchi* in 2002, as was Hamid Ameir in 2008, and Major General Abdallah Said Natepe was interviewed for a few pages in an army history magazine but provided very little detail.[10] While Okello often exaggerates in his account, bending the story to make him look more like the man he envisioned himself to be, he provides many more specifics and explanations than anyone else. This is significant, because Okello's bravado and his histrionics over the radio are part of why he was not accepted in Zanzibar. As early as 24 January 1964, he was warned in an unsigned letter, "Your behavior is inconsistent with the requirements of the indigenous people. You are the only person boasting of having all the power in the Revolutionary Government" (Okello 1967: 177). The other members of the Committee of 14 were either born in Zanzibar or had spent much more of their lives there than Okello, and they knew that their silence would protect them, even give them power. It was a political move, on their part, as well as appropriate behavior in Zanzibari culture, where discretion, subtlety in language, and linguistic play are highly valued (Askew 2002: 76). Okello lacked the political and cultural awareness to act in a way that would have deepened his power base.

In this chapter, I critically reexamine Field Marshal John Okello's role in the revolution, exploring how he has been represented and remembered. I use oral interviews, contemporary local newspapers, online news and blogs, and archival sources and newspapers concurrent with the revolution to show how Okello is and has been viewed in Zanzibar. Having spent six months in Zanzibar, including a trip to Pemba to interview people who knew Okello, and one month in Uganda meeting Okello's family and friends from before and after the revolution, I use recent, first-hand field research to examine individuals' memories of Okello and to reintroduce him to the historiography on the Zanzibar revolution. I contrast powerful personal memories of Okello and his radio broadcasts with the relative lack of a collective memory of Okello in Zanzibar, due to his expulsion and elimination from the official record. Finally, I argue that he served as the voice of the revolution not just because of his accent and non-Zanzibari Kiswahili language but because he played a critical role as its leader. Tying this historiographical claim to current social memories, I show a recent trend in Zanzibari and Tanzanian media to restore Okello to his position in Zanzibari history.

---

10 "Hamis Daruweshi Afichua Siri ya Mapinduzi Zanzibar," *Mwananchi*, 8 September 2002; Hamid Ameir, "Shabaha ya Mapinduzi Haijatekelezwa," *Mwananchi*, Toleo Maalumu, Miaka 44 ya Mapinduzi, 11 January 2008; and Maj. Gen. Abdallah Said Natepe's two pages, see ZNA BA 74/16, Miaka 40 ya JWTZ 1964–2004.

The biographical portion of this chapter provides personal recollections that enable us to better understand the role and fate of Okello during the revolutionary moment and its aftermath.

Confusion about Okello's Identity

There are still Zanzibaris who remember Okello as he was portrayed in early press reports in January 1964: as a Kenyan Luo who had fought in the Mau Mau, or as a former Zanzibari policeman with Cuban training. My research confirms that Okello was a Ugandan Langi who did not fight in the Mau Mau and who had never been to Cuba. British archives reveal that there was no record of any John Okello in the Zanzibar police in the 1960s.[11] There is no evidence, other than his own bombastic claims on the radio, that Okello was part of the Mau Mau. Chronology further supports this assertion. Okello was in Nairobi from October 1954 until late 1955, when, by his own admission, he was put in prison (Okello 1967: 54–8). He accounts for that time—all the jobs he had and the night school he tried to attend—quite precisely in his book. When he got out of prison, he went straight to Machakos and then on to Mombasa. There was not enough time for him to have been in Mau Mau, even assuming that he, as a Langi (in the Luo ethnic family), could have made deep enough connections among the Gikuyus. Despite the rumors that he served in World War II, he had no formal military training. (Given that he was born in 1937, he was clearly not old enough to have participated in the war.) These false portrayals represent ways in which his identity was misunderstood or manipulated to provide explanations for his position of power, which was greater than most people thought it should be. Luise White contends that plausibility is a necessary component of rumors, gossip, and lies: That which is "socially conceivable" is what ends up being passed on (2000: 14). This explains recollections that Okello was a Mau Mau or soldier or policeman, because these were credible stories about a man who led a revolution. With no media or literature to provide accurate (and also plausible) biographical information, the memories remain.

Biography, Take One: Sources Close to Okello

Early Life in Uganda and Youth in Kenya

The man we know as John Okello was given the name John Etuku at birth. Gideon was his baptismal name, so he was John Gideon Etuku

---

11   BNA DO 185/59 and RHL MSS. Afr. s. 1446.

until he left home. Okello was his father's name, which John took to use in the workplace when he left home in 1953 (Okello 1967: 35).[12] He then went by John Okello for the rest of his life, but he was to use the name Gideon again in the future, when he was trying to avoid journalists after the revolution.[13] Although Okello was never in the military, he was interested in soldiers and physical strength from a young age. He ran away to try to join the military when he was seven years old (Okello 1967: 36–7). He was obviously too young to join and was returned home by the district commissioner. But Okello viewed himself as mighty, even as a young boy, and this thinking was widely accepted by others. As his half-brother, Yeko, tells it, Okello's mother's firstborn was an elephant calf. As someone born from the same womb as an elephant, Okello viewed himself as imbued with superhuman strength. He also called himself Hitler, reflecting his self-image as a powerful man.[14] His actions were often aggressive, and other boys were afraid he might beat them up. The Lango word *ger*, meaning fierce or cruel, was used by almost everyone who spoke about Okello. But Langis nevertheless liked him, and he was described as "humble" by the same people.[15] He was a good footballer; he was social, liked singing and dancing, and was well-behaved, according to his now 90-year-old sister Akello Kulusita Mary.[16] Although his brawniness was admired in Uganda but not in Zanzibar, the family reports of Okello as both cruel and well-liked are consistent with later reports of him as both despotic and concerned with protecting those in need. Okello had a convoluted personality with character traits that seem contradictory. This unexplored complexity

---

12   Interview with Akello Kulusita Mary, 22 January 2014.

13   Okello tried to avoid talking to the press after leaving Zanzibar in March 1964, and he called himself Gideon Baker from Kenya, directly lying to reporters who tried to talk with him while he was in Dar. He said he was returning to Kenya, his home, not Zanzibar or Uganda. Reporter Sammy Mdee confronted Okello, saying that they had just met in Zanzibar and that he knew that Okello was not returning to Zanzibar because he was not wanted there. Okello insisted that he was Kenyan Gideon Baker, and he knew nothing about Zanzibar ("Field Marshal's 'Double' in Dar," *Tanganyika Standard*, 4 March 1964; photo and caption, "The man with the military bearing ...," 6 March 1964).

14   Interview with Yeko Okello, 22 January 2014. Yeko explained this boast in its Langi cultural context, as admiration of power and might, not as a veneration of Hitler as a Nazi. This is important for understanding Okello's obsession with strength and domination. There are examples of people being named Hitler in other parts of British Africa as a sign of anticolonial strength, because Hitler fought the British. (Thanks to Luise White for this information.)

15   Interview with Yeko Okello, 22 January 2014.

16   Interview with Akello Kulusita Mary, 22 January 2014.

contributes to the propensity to remember or focus on only one aspect of this multifarious figure. That is to say, for those who witnessed his ruthless radio broadcasts or public floggings, there was no reason to consider that he might have had another side to him as well.

After the death of his parents, Okello and his younger brother, Ogangi Tito, were sent to an uncle's place to live in 1952. The uncle beat Okello. When asked how the younger brother fared while living with the uncle, some family members said he did just fine. The beatings of Okello, they alleged, were due in part to Okello's stubborn nature, which the uncle would not tolerate. Yet Okello refused to accept this treatment and ran away. The fact that Okello was orphaned at an early age had considerable impact on his life and outlook. Okello was told he was less important, as an orphan in his uncle's home, and that he had to make his way in the world on his own. The beatings and mistreatment made him question the fairness of the world at an earlier age than most. Okello found comfort in the biblical Beatitudes in Matthew 5:3, citing the text in his memoir: "Blessed are they that mourn, for they shall be comforted.... Blessed are they which are persecuted for righteousness' sake: for theirs is the Kingdom of Heaven. Blessed are ye, when men shall revile you, and persecute you.... Rejoice, and be exceeding glad: for great is your reward in Heaven: for so persecuted they the prophets which were before you" (Okello 1967: 41–42). This was an early sign of his spiritual sense that God was giving him a mission. It is fairly evident from his book that he had a heightened awareness of oppression and was moved by the desire to overcome injustice. David Koff, who helped Okello edit the manuscript that became his book, said that Okello struck him as someone who truly believed in the cause he was fighting for.[17]

Okello himself provides us with many examples of his learning to be strong, independent, and opposed to discrimination. He did not have an older brother to protect him, and he was beaten up by other boys when he would not "join any of their small gangs." He fought them "until they fled" and "learned young, and in a hard way, how to stand alone" (Okello 1967: 39). He also tells of how he acted as mother and father to his younger brother after they were orphaned, fetching water and doing other domestic jobs. Since his sister was already married, the boys stayed on their own for a while before their uncle came to collect them. They learned to gather mushrooms from the forest when their cruel uncle drank, beat them, and did not feed them. When Okello left

---

17   Email correspondence with David Koff, 26 June 2013.

to join the workforce, he once again saw inequality and stood up against it. He claims to have taken grievances to a district labor officer to help his worker colleagues at a cotton ginnery in Otuboi get better working conditions from their Asian bosses. While living and working in Soroti, he fairly quickly began to question why whites felt superior to blacks and why there were so many foreign owners of land and businesses in Africa. He asked himself existential and religious questions about the equality of all humankind and came up with the answer that Africans must assert themselves to overcome the status quo. He also prided himself on being a diligent and efficient worker, getting pay raises for his good work, and helping the destitute, while others were out drinking (Okello 1967: 41–51). Okello had been mistreated and taken advantage of, and he thought that was unfair and did not want others to suffer a similar fate. He had been orphaned and had lived on his own for most of his life, so he was strong and self-sufficient and had little patience for laziness or luxuries.

After working for mostly Asian bosses, moving around to various places, including Kisumu in Kenya, where he found the Luos quite similar to Langis from his home, he decided that he really wanted more education. He had only had two years of primary school because he had been unable to pay school fees, and he was beginning to see the importance of education. Unfortunately for him, he was off to a late start and was never able to get the education he desperately needed. Nevertheless, he went to Nairobi, where he heard he could take night classes while also working (Okello 1967: 54).

His time in Nairobi, beginning in October 1954, impacted him greatly, shaping his ideas about injustice in a political light. Upon arrival at the train station, he was beaten up and robbed by some white soldiers, only to be mistreated further by the white police. When he returned to the train station with Luo police, he discovered that he was not alone in this treatment. He described seeing an African mother who was beaten unconscious: "Beside her lay her aborted baby, dead as a result of the brutal behavior of the white soldiers" (Okello 1967: 55–6). He says that he met some leaders of the Land Freedom Army and later joined the Nairobi African District Congress under C. M. G. Argwings-Kodhek. He credits the political education he received during this time as something he used later, "when teaching the masses of Zanzibar." He says he realized that many Europeans hated Africans and that was why they upheld such discriminatory practices. In late 1955, he went to prison in Kenya for two years. Because this incarceration took place during the Emergency, he was in prison with Mau Mau members who were being tortured and forced to confess what they knew about the movement.[18] As Okello articulates, "I came out of prison with a deep hatred of injustice and colonialism" (Okello 1967: 55–8). Although Okello was not himself in the Mau Mau, he was clearly influenced by the movement, the fear it elicited in the British, and the brutal way in which the British dealt with it.[19]

Two more incidents in Kenya seem to have affected him similarly. When he was on the coast of Kenya in the village of Takaungu, where the powerful Mazrui family held sway, he asked some Arabs if he could rest on their verandah. They called him slave and told him that he could rest but that he could not snore—he should "sleep as quietly as a dead dog." Later, he traveled to a sisal plantation in Vipingoni, but he struggled with the social climate there, saying, "I hated to hear an Indian calling a 30 year old servant, 'boy', or an Arab shouting '*mtumwa*' (slave). It goes deep into one's nerves to hear such things" (Okello 1967: 62–3). These incidents motivated him to deeply feel the injustice of colonial rule and of the racial stratification that colonial rule upheld and reified.

The figure we see in 1959 is thus a man with two years of primary school education; a man who works hard and believes he has to fight for everything because he is an orphan; a man who is physically strong and who reveres physical strength and, perhaps, brutality; an itinerant laborer who longs for success; and a man who has been a victim of and witness to the oppression and exploitation of colonialism.

---

18   In response to the Mau Mau movement, the British declared a state of emergency in Kenya, which lasted from 1952 until 1960.

19   See David Anderson (2005) and Caroline Elkins (2005) for detailed accounts of British torture and hangings of Mau Mau and suspected sympathizers.

In Pemba and Zanzibar, Stonecutter to Revolutionary

In 1959, Okello accompanied a Luo friend to Pemba Island, where jobs were reportedly easy to secure. Friends of Okello in Pemba, particularly in Vitongoji, where he lived and worked, remembered him with fondness. In other parts of Pemba, stories differed dramatically, as Pemba suffered severely under the Revolutionary Government, but in Vitongoji, people claimed to have liked him. One of his friends who worked for the Public Works Department (PWD), while Okello worked for himself, cutting stones, said that Okello was not a drinker. He would beat his friends if they did bad things while drunk.[20] This may have earned him some moral admiration in a primarily Muslim society where drinking is not respected. Okello clearly viewed himself in a moral leadership role, as if he could and should provide guidance to others when they went astray. He also felt that the ASP needed an office in that area, so, when he moved to Unguja in 1963, he gave his house to the party.[21] The building is much larger now than it was then, but to this day it is still an office of the ruling party. Later, Okello returned to Pemba after the revolution and held public floggings to show who was in charge. Some members of the former ruling party were beaten by seven people at once.[22] In spite of this show of force, however, Okello refused to beat anyone from Vitongoji or anyone (including Arabs or Indians) he had worked with or for.[23] This is particularly striking, given how brutal the public floggings in Pemba are described as having been, with some people beaten by *bakora* (cane) one hundred times on bare skin.[24] These are just a few more examples of the duality of character we see in memories of Okello.

By the end of 1962, Okello had already decided that revolution was necessary, so he went to Unguja to see the situation there for himself (Okello 1967: 86). He moved from Pemba to Unguja in February

---

[20] Interview with Rajab Hakim Mrisho, 3 November 2013.

[21] Interview with Saleh Nassor Juma, 3 November 2013.

[22] Interview with Mohamed Aley Abdalla, 2 November 2013.

[23] People in Pemba consistently remarked upon this (interviews with Abdallah Bin Juma and Ali Omar Abdalla, 3 November 2013). Mzee Ghulum told a very specific story of an Indian soda factory owner who had fired Okello for stealing dye. Okello called him in after the revolution and asked him what he wanted. The man was terrified, but said nothing. Okello said, "Fine, but let me know if you want anything. I am in charge now and I can help you out."

[24] Interviews with Saleh Nassor Juma, Mohamed Haji Khalid, and Rufai Said Rufai, 23 October 2013, and Mohamed Aley Abdalla, 2 November 2013.

1963, about a year before the revolution.[25] While there, he was a house painter and worked in a bakery. Many different groups of people were considering and discussing revolution at this time in Unguja, so the time was ripe when Okello began to approach people with his idea. He used the Zanzibar and Pemba Paint Workers Union in order to find a cadre of semi-skilled workers to join the revolutionary ranks. He says that the first people he and two other union leaders contacted thought that the plan was to kill the sultan rather than overthrow the government (Okello 1967: 99). Many saw the sultan's leadership as another form of imperialism. The key issue for these prospective revolutionaries was getting out from under colonial oppression, an idea that Okello was fanatical about.

Biography, Take Two: Archival Sources

Threats and Mixed Messages over the Radio while Forgiving the Hypocrites

In a broadcast on 12 January 1964, after Okello announced the new republic and named ASP leader Abeid Amani Karume as its president, he requested that Karume to return to Zanzibar and assume his position in the new government. He continued to make numerous radio broadcasts during the next few days. The contrasting natures of Okello's character came out in his radio broadcasts, as well as in people's memories of him. One minute he was threatening people with prison or being shot, and the next minute he was punishing people for being violent. Some examples of these threatening and confusing broadcasts follow:

On 13 January, when instructing everyone to bring all weapons from their homes to Raha Leo headquarters, he said that the "Field Marshal is the leader of this Government, and he has ordered that cars can go out and search houses." He claimed he knew of 17 youths with weapons, who were given 20 minutes to surrender their weapons or they would be shot if sighted. Arab youth were to stay inside, as well; they also would be shot if seen out of doors. In the next sentence, however, Okello said that they should come outside with their weapons when his soldiers came to collect them and that the buildings would then be ransacked to make sure there were no more weapons hidden inside. Later that same day, 13 January, after former prime minister Muhammad Shamte and former minister of external affairs and trade Ali Muhsin al-Barwani pleaded for peace and requested that everyone maintain peace and

---

25   *Drum*, February 1967. Interview with Ali Omar Abdalla, 3 Nov 2013.

order, Okello said they no longer had the right to ask for peace, as it was now up to people to restore peace themselves.[26] But, he said, if people did not obey, he would take measures 88 times more *kali* (severe) than now. He went on to say that the army had the strength of 99,099,000 and that those who did not do as they were told would be punished. Just an hour and a half later, he reported that Sheikh Ali Muhsin was beaten and that he was very unhappy about that. Okello wanted peace, and people were not to beat up ministers, even if Muhsin was the "leader of the hypocrites."[27] Then, when Muhsin was brought to his office, Okello put his pistol to Muhsin's face and asked whether he should kill him. After Muhsin replied he should do as he wished, Okello said that his government would not oppress people, so he forgave Muhsin (Okello 1967: 152). Further, Okello was constantly making announcements demanding that people hand over weapons and vehicles to Raha Leo, as they were property of the government. There was simultaneously a significant amount of looting going on in town. Almost all stores were looted. Okello declared that this would not be tolerated: Any man caught with so much as half a bar of soap would get eight years in prison (*Daily Nation*, 14 January 1964). This threat from Okello made a lasting impression on young people; despite all the stealing, if they found something on the ground and took it, they would rather throw it away or hide it, for fear of getting caught.[28]

Okello sought freedom from oppression and was trying to lead in the midst of chaos without military training or guidance. This underdog status in a fight for justice had religious significance for Okello. He read the Bible avidly and had had dreams in which God told him to help the Africans in Zanzibar. He saw himself as a martyr for the cause of saving his people from subjugation. Okello claims he was introduced to an Afro-Shirazi Youth League (ASYL) meeting as "Our Redeemer," and he prophesied his own rejection at the hand of his followers (Okello 1967: 107, 113, 122, 186–7). Ten days after the revolution, he was on a boat from Pemba to Unguja with the Anglican bishop of Zanzibar. He asked the bishop to read him a biblical passage about the scribes and Pharisees and their hypocrisy. Okello then told the bishop, "I don't mean all those

---

26   Muhammad Shamte was the leader of the Zanzibar and Pemba People's Party (ZPPP), which had formed a coalition with the Zanzibar Nationalist Party (ZNP), led by Ali Muhsin al-Barwani, to form a government in 1963. These two men held the most powerful positions in the government that was overthrown.

27   BBC Written Archives, Summary of World Broadcasts Part IV The Middle East and Africa.

28   Interview with Mohamed Jiddawi and Nassor Hemed Nassor, 5 November 2013.

things about burning people in oil, you know." The bishop replied that "it was time to quieten things down," to which Okello responded, "Nobody tells me these things" (Smith 1973: 107–8). The last statement shows us that he had no trusted advisors he could count on. Additionally, in these instances Okello was drawing parallels between Jesus' seeking to reform a system of duplicitous rulers and Okello's own struggle against colonial domination. Although this may have been motivational for Okello, this line of thinking is not part of Zanzibaris' memories of him. It may never have even been known to Zanzibaris, as they would not have been moved by this Christian martyr concept.

The Symbolism of Mau Mau

Okello was not a participant in the Mau Mau uprising, but he used the reputation of this resistance movement to strengthen his position. On 14 January 1964, Okello proclaimed, "I was a very high ranking person in Kenya in the Mau Mau Army which knows how to make weapons … In fact, I can easily make no less than 500 guns per day. I can beyond doubt make a bomb that can destroy an area of three square miles. I can make about 100 grenades in an hour."[29] In his book, Okello reports that in a discussion with some African fishermen on his way to Unguja Island in February 1963, he explained that they would soon see "Arab colonialists eliminated." They did not believe that that was possible, remarking that "perhaps the 'Mau Mau' from Kenya" could do such a thing, but "no one can dare attack the imperialists here" (Okello 1967: 90). Both these stories help explain that Okello used the Mau Mau movement metaphorically, for its psychological value of striking fear into the hearts of both British and Zanzibaris, given the British view of the Mau Mau as atavistic savages who could not be controlled. For his African audience, Okello also claimed connection with the Mau Mau on the radio to give himself some credibility as a guerilla leader, since the Mau Mau were a symbol of African guerilla fighters who could actually bring down imperialists.[30] Given that he had no military or police training or experience, he needed to make himself look more

---

29   BBC Written Archives, Summary of World Broadcasts Part IV The Middle East and Africa.

30   It did not matter that the Mau Mau technically "lost" their campaign; they fought the British, and Kenya got its independence as a result. And East Africans knew that the British were afraid of the Mau Mau insurgents.

prepared than he was.[31] This type of misinformation was passed along not just by newspapers but even by British and American intelligence reports. Don Petterson, the vice consul at the U.S. embassy in Zanzibar at the time of the revolution, comments on the process of information gathering, indicating that the British MI5 accepted information with little discernment and the Americans banked on the good name of the MI5 and parroted it (Petterson 2002: 74–5). Despite all the evidence that he was none of these, the myths of Okello as Mau Mau fighter, Zanzibari policeman, World War II veteran, King's African Rifles soldier, and Cuban-trained revolutionary are still quite alive. That these myths persist elucidates how this untrained, uneducated man played such a fundamental role in overthrowing the government of Zanzibar. His supporters proudly claim he was a soldier because it adds to his prestige in their eyes.[32] His detractors are convinced he had military training because the idea of a barely literate mainlander, such as Okello, having the ability to topple a government of more sophisticated and better educated men was difficult to believe; this feat was incongruous with notions of Zanzibari coastal exceptionalism.

Biography, Take Three: East African Newspapers in the Aftermath of the Revolution

Immediately after the revolution, Okello was in Dar es Salaam during the Tanganyikan army mutiny. This raised suspicion among many observers about his role in the mutiny, though historical sources clearly show that he did not have anything to do with it. Okello had gained power so suddenly, and so incomprehensibly, with the Zanzibar revolution, however, that many East African leaders were suspicious of and concerned about him. On 20 February, Okello traveled to Uganda and Kenya, where he met with his family, President Milton Obote, and President Jomo Kenyatta. Kenyatta apparently teased Okello about coming through without seeing him on his way to Uganda and joked that some people told him Okello was trying to overthrow his government

---

31 All the Ugandan elders who knew Okello, as well as a Ugandan military historian, confirmed that he was never in the King's African Rifles or the Ugandan military. Additionally, Okello was not a policeman in Zanzibar (BNA DO 185/59 and RHL MSS. Afr. s. 1446).

32 His wife's son proudly told me that Okello was in KAR, and fought in World War II. Interview with Moses Onyok, 20 January 2014. Another informant said Okello was chosen to lead the revolution because he fought in World War II and was in Mau Mau. Interview with Maisara Mahoukum Iddi, 2 November 2013. Family members used his title "Field Marshal" with similar admiration.

(Okello 1967: 183). Okello claims to have been well received by Obote and by some Kenyan leaders during this trip. On his way back from the trip, however, he was detained in Dar es Salaam for a few days, and then, when he flew to Zanzibar on 9 March, he was met at the airport in Zanzibar and told he was no longer welcome there. He was flown back to Dar es Salaam. Several reports say he was flown back along with Karume for talks with Julius K. Nyerere, who was helping Karume strengthen his position (*Tanganyika Standard*, "Okello to Zanzibar and Back," 10 March 1964; Okello 1967: 184–6). Nyerere asked Okello why he used the radio to "make fierce and boastful speeches, more than was necessary" (Okello 1967: 188). Despite Okello's claim in his book that he had prophesied that he would be rejected even after being a hero, in reality, he was shocked and confused when he was actually kicked out. He was quoted as saying, "Even God must have been surprised" (Okello 1967: 89; *Tanganyika Standard*, "World Shock, says Okello," 17 March 1964). This inflated self-image may well have provided the impetus for his removal, but his political naïveté also contributed. He was unable to see this move coming or do anything to prevent it. After a time, he was able to reflect on his expulsion for his book and use his religious sentiments to describe himself as a martyr to a just cause.

Once Okello had been removed from Zanzibar, all East African leaders became wary of him. This was an indicator that they believed not only that he was the leader of the Zanzibar revolution but that he was also capable of leading more revolutions. Okello was pronounced persona non grata in Zanzibar (and later Tanzania) and declared a prohibited immigrant in Kenya, and he was jailed consistently (and for various reasons) in Tanzania, Kenya, and Uganda during the next five years. Okello was first arrested in Mwanza in northern Tanzania in October 1964, along with "Lumumbist" rebels from Congo. He was then detained in Kenya for 18 months beginning on 23 June 1965 for trying to enter the country as a prohibited immigrant. Okello then returned to Uganda and again was detained, from 3 July 1967 until 8 September 1968, under the Emergency Regulations, with no other reason given. Finally, on 3 January 1969, he was arrested on the Kenya-Uganda border while traveling on a bus bound for Nairobi. Once again, Okello was detained in Kenya as a prohibited immigrant (*Daily Nation* and *Uganda Argus*). This pervasive fear of Okello spread beyond East Africa: in Malawi, even President Dr. Hastings Kamuzu Banda claimed that his former

Foreign Minister was trying to enlist Okello's help to overthrow him (*Daily Nation*, "'Bid to Recruit Okello'–Banda," 17 November 1964).[33]

His notoriety, in the meantime, was such that when he was released from prison in Nairobi at the end of 1966, he called John Nottingham, executive director of the East African Publishing House, and asked him if the company would agree to publish his book. Okello had a secretary who had helped him write a first draft, and he brought that manuscript with him. He then spent several months living in a hotel on River Road, working on editing the book with David Koff, who was asked by Nottingham to help Okello with this task.[34]

Biography, Take Four: Views from Back Home in Uganda

When Okello returned to Uganda in 1967, he was originally still trying to get back to Zanzibar. His own actions may not have helped him escape the kind of suspicion that kept getting him put in jail. For example, Okello met with President Obote, who was from the same area as he, to see if he would be able to help facilitate a move back to Zanzibar. That did not pan out. However, Obote had his cousin and minister of information, Adoko Nyekyon, offer Okello a position in the military, with the stipulation that Okello also marry a sister of theirs. Okello refused, and from that time on he was under surveillance, and his relationship with Obote was strained.[35]

Okello was so disillusioned with Obote that when Idi Amin Dada overthrew Obote's government on 25 January 1971, Okello was pleased. In fact, he was so hopeful—and, once again, naïve—that he went to Amin's office to congratulate him (see Figure 1 on page 107, courtesy of Makerere University Library). In the social memory of the Langi, though, Amin came to Alebtong to give a speech, and Okello knelt before him in greeting.[36] His relatives criticized that move, not only when Amin's true colors became clear, but also because they believed he might have survived if he had kept a lower profile. His continued use of the field marshal title is another way in which he set himself apart publicly. The legends surrounding his title of field marshal are also

---

33 Okello seemed to have become known worldwide as an extreme revolutionary, as is shown by Werner Herzog naming a character after him in his 1972 film *Aguirre, the Wrath of God*.

34 Email communication with David Koff, 26 June 2013 and interview with John Nottingham, 21 June 2013.

35 Interview with Okello Ajoka and Jonathan Opio, 23 January 2014.

36 Interview with Okello Ajoka, 23 January 2013; interview with Akello Kulusita Mary, 22 January 2014.

part of the Ugandan memories of Okello.[37] Once again, his need for recognition and attention contributed to his downfall. As time went on and he saw how bad Amin was, Okello worked with his friend Jonathan Opio to begin recruiting people to overthrow Amin. They did so as they prepared to travel to Tanzania to ask the exiled Obote to join their plan. They did not get that far, as Okello was killed before departing Uganda.

Ugandan Memories of Okello's Death

There is no social memory of Okello's death in Zanzibar.[38] His physical removal once again is reflected in the memories. In Uganda, the collective memory asserts Okello's disappearance at the hand of Idi Amin. However, most Ugandans speak of it as legend, and are unaware of the details. Okello's family and close friends provided new details about this event.

An Acholi named Latigo is said to have been the one who betrayed Okello and Opio and got Okello killed. The two men had collected some money and sent an intermediary to go to meet Alex Ojera, one of Obote's men in Tanzania, who had been a minister in the first Obote cabinet. But that intermediary did not report back to them on the discussions, so they were suspicious of him. They collected more money to send Okello himself, since he was the leader of this group. He was supposed to go straight to Tanzania but he stopped at his home in Amugu on his way out. Meanwhile, Latigo came to Okello's home in Alebtong and was told Okello was in Amugu. Latigo then brought Amin's men to Amugu and greeted Okello and told him that a friend had arrived from Nairobi and they should go meet him in Lira. Okello agreed, but he was strangled and his body dumped in the swamp on the Aloi road just before reaching Lira.[39] There were other stories that Okello's body was thrown into the Karuma Falls rather than the swamp, but most of the stories about Okello being picked up by Amin's men are quite similar. People drove to his home area and asked where he was, and they were taken to his home at Amugu, where they collected him and drove away. In one story, it was a boy who

---

37 His cousin, Yeko, claimed that Idi Amin later took the title field marshal because he killed Field Marshal Okello (interview, 22 January 2014). Moses Onyok said Okello was the first African to hold this title. He explained that the two ways one can take this title are by overthrowing a government or killing another field marshal (interview, 20 January 2013). There is also an urban legend in which Okello joked that "now Uganda has two field marshals" and one in which Amin remarked that there cannot be two field marshals. These examples show the significance of the title and the rivalry it embellished between Okello and Amin.

38 More than one informant seemed genuinely sorry to hear the news that Okello was killed by Idi Amin.

39 Interview with Okello Ajoka and Jonathan Opio, 23 January 2014.

took the men to Okello. Okello was also reported to be waving to people as he left. That was the last time he was ever seen alive.[40]

Okello left behind two widows: Akao Erin Okello, whom he inherited in 1972 from a brother who passed away, and Lily Atim, whom he married in 1972. He had two biological children: Agnes Awilo, Erin's daughter, and Yoweri Acon, Lily's son. Yoweri died, but Agnes is still living and has children of her own.[41] Erin had five more children who were considered Okello's, according to tradition, as she never remarried after Okello's death. Lily Atim left the area and remarried.

Okello in the Media, Then and Now

Old Sources, New Views: Local Media from 1964

Okello was written out of ASP history by 1965.[42] However, East African newspapers from 1964 leave little doubt about the significance of Okello's role. The first edition of *Kweupe*, the official newspaper of the new revolutionary government, has four photos on its front cover. One is of President Karume, one of his cabinet, one of Field Marshal John Okello standing in his office in Raha Leo with weapons and bodyguards, and one of the Committee of 14, with Okello front and center (*Kweupe*, 18 January 1964). Many Zanzibaris commented on how this series of photographs alone was a significant indicator of Okello's position at that historical juncture. Additionally, on the eve of Okello's visit to Kenya and Uganda, on 18 February 1964, the *Tanganyika Standard* front page hosted a photo of President Karume and Field Marshal Okello clasping hands at the Idd al Fitr *baraza* (gathering) in Zanzibar city (see Figure 2 on page 107, courtesy of Makerere University Library). If Okello was just a mere DJ, with no following and no political sway, Karume would certainly not have felt the need to stand together with him in a public display of (fake) unity. If Okello had no influence, there also would have been no need to get rid of him. This photo demonstrates the challenge Okello posed to Karume's leadership at the time.

Most of the early reports of Okello, in newspapers and archives, were concerned with his violent broadcasts and his ambition and brute force.

---

40   Interview with Erin Okello, 20 January 2014. Okello also told his wife, Erin, that he was going to Kampala to collect building supplies rather than setting out to help Obote overthrow Amin's government.

41   His daughter Agnes Awilo resembles her father, as does one of her children, Okello Jonathan, whom she named after her father.

42   See the account in *The Nationalist*, 12 January 1965, which is reprinted in Okello 1967: 209–222.

The British, in particular, were quite concerned about how fierce and ruthless he might be. Okello's own book confirms his courage as well as his ability to kill. While he makes the exaggerated claim that 11,995 enemy soldiers and people were killed, he also describes a physical battle with a sentry at Ziwani police headquarters in which he wrested the rifle from the sentry, hit him with the butt of the gun, and killed him with its bayonet (Okello 1967: 30–2, 160). In light of all this, it is odd that we also hear two Committee of 14 members reporting that Okello was a coward. On a visit to Cuba in June 1964, Ramadhan Haji Faki and Said Iddi Bavuai told the Cuban press that Okello was no more than one of the deserters from the police barracks who tried to run away in a boat.[43] What was it that inspired such contradictory reports? This deserter story seems highly unlikely, given all that is known about Okello, and it did not catch on publicly or become a well-known story. I did not hear it from any other source, nor did Faki repeat it to me when we spoke in August 2013. In fact, at that time, Faki told me that he invited Okello to join the Committee of 14 group—a narrative that embraces rather than disparages Okello. It therefore appears that at the time they reported the vignette about Okello's cowardice, these men wanted to denigrate Okello's role in the revolution. This view is consistent with the official history that was written a few months later (see below).

Many people believed that Okello was thrown out so quickly because he thought that he was really in charge and had managed to seize a great deal of power; he wanted to be president. His desire and ambition were too much, and even those who were impressed by what he had done did not support his attempts at gaining more power. Revolutionaries were pleased with what Okello was able to accomplish, but they wanted Karume as president. This is why there was little protest over Okello's removal in March.

A video that was originally part of Keith Kyle's report on the BBC's news program *Tonight* on 7 February 1964 is now available on YouTube.[44] In it, Kyle reports on the revolution and interviews Karume, Okello, and

---

43 BNA FO 371/174035. These men also reported the same story to Jamal Nassor Adi when he was asked to research the details of the revolution for Aboud Jumbe in 1980 (interview with Jamal Nassor Adi, 7 August 2013). In this archival source, Faki and Bavuai also say that Karume and Babu had not participated in the revolution but that they were still deserving of the positions they had.

44 http://www.youtube.com/watch?v=7uPi3vh2hGE, accessed 21 October 2016.

Abdulrahman Muhammed Babu.⁴⁵ The footage has garnered much interest in Zanzibar recently, as it is one of the only available sources of video and audio footage from the time. Kyle explains the planning of the revolution and the various plots that were being developed and then questions the three leaders. Both Karume and Babu appear uncomfortable. Karume stammers a bit as he answers why a revolution was necessary, speaking in Kiswahili and to Babu rather than facing the reporter. Babu laughs nervously as he translates many of Kyle's questions and Karume and Okello's answers. Neither Karume nor Babu can answer the question of why Okello was chosen as leader of the revolution, but Okello states clearly and firmly that he was chosen by "viongozi inapenda na hawa watu wote" (leaders who were liked by all these people). When Babu translates this, he says Okello was chosen "because of his experience and the leadership which is popular to the people who organized the [revolution]." When asked about his military experience, Okello says that he got his experience and success "kwa Mungu wa Afrika" (by the God of Africa). Babu then admits that he had no prior knowledge of this revolution and repeats that the revolution succeeded because of the "God of the Africans." Today's discussions about this video are bringing Okello back to the table in the debates on the history of the revolution.

Current Blogs and Newspapers: Okello Brought Back as Leader

As recently as 2012, Okello was compared with Che Guevara in terms of his role as a revolutionary leader.⁴⁶ Joseph Mihangwa has written several pieces in the weekly *Raia Mwema* in conversation with what journalist Ahmed Rajab has written on the revolution and on Okello. Mihangwa points out that even if the ASP had won the 1963 election, the sultan would still have been in power, but that the ASP only agreed to support this system of constitutional monarchy because party leaders knew they would lead a revolution later. He notes that Karume had asked the youth to wait and work for victory at the ballot box, but that other, more radical ASP leaders, like Abdulla Kassim Hanga⁴⁷ and even Babu and his Umma

---

45   Babu had been the secretary general of the ZNP until 1963, when a dispute with its leader, Ali Muhsin, led Babu to leave the party. He formed his own Umma Party in 1963 and joined the ASP in opposing the ZNP. He was a Marxist with close ties to China and Cuba. Eighteen of his Umma Party members received military training in Cuba and joined the revolution on the morning of 12 January.

46   See, for example, http://www.raiamwema.co.tz/field-marshal-john-okello-shujaa-mapinduzi-zanzibar-asiyekumbukwa-iii (accessed 14 August 2013).

47   Hanga had lived and studied in the Soviet Union.

party did not want to wait. They, as well as Okello, had begun planning for revolution. Without summarizing all of Mihangwa's argument here, he uses much of Okello's own book for biographical information, not only reinstating Okello at the center of his historical recounting of the revolutionary event but even presenting him as a forgotten hero.

Similar revisionist views are cropping up on websites. A 2011 Zanzibar blogspot points out that Karume was called to his position (from Dar es Salaam) while Okello was the actual leader of the revolution. The author of the piece observes that the Revolutionary Government of Zanzibar (Serikali ya Mapinduzi ya Zanzibar, or SMZ) does not tell the whole story, questioning how the state could maintain that Karume was the man who led the revolution when Karume did not even know about the planned overthrow of the government. The author's pen name is Free Zanzibar People from Mkoloni Mweusi (Black Colonialism), and his main issue is that Zanzibar celebrates Karume, who yoked the isles to Tanganyika in the union, but not Okello, who risked his life for the revolution—an unusual position, given that most Zanzibaris who feel this way about the union also deeply lament the revolution itself. Though the writing lacks idiomatic expression and appropriate grammar, the author seems to support the revolution but not the union with Tanganyika. His point is, if you support the revolution, you should recognize and honor Okello and other heroes who risked their safety for it.[48]

Finally, in the issue of the newspaper *Nipashe* commemorating the 50th anniversary of the revolution on 12 January 2014, an article titled "Ushariki wa Okello Mapinduzi ya Zanzibar 1964" concludes that Okello was the leader of the revolution and that Karume was not involved in the planning or the night of the revolution. The revolutionaries would have kept Karume out of the coup for his own protection,[49] and ASYL leader and Committee of 14 member Seif Bakari refused to involve Karume until it was time for him to take over the country. The article cites interviews with former ASYL leaders Abdallah Said Natepe and Ibrahim Amani in which they discuss how Okello was introduced to the Committee of 14 and how he came to be the main speaker on radio Sauti ya Unguja (Voice of Unguja). The author also cites the mentioned previously video by Keith Kyle to argue that it shows that Okello was

---

48 http://free-zanzibar.blogspot.com/2011/07/john-okello-hakutaka-zbar-iungane-na.html (accessed 25 August 2013).

49 This is asserted by many other sources as well, including interviews documented in BNA FO 371/174035 and DO 185/59, and by Hamid Ameir, 25 November 2013.

the leader of the revolution, as he stood right there next to Karume, both of them wearing suits, being interviewed about the revolution. The article still maintains that Okello had experience as a liberator, as part of the Mau Mau, but also acknowledges that he had no formal military training. It claims that Okello had been introduced to the Committee of 14 by another ASYL member, Ali Lumumba, after Okello asked him when colonialists would leave Africa, as that seemed to be a litmus test of sorts. The idea that the sultan and the ZNP-led government of Zanzibar were imperialist overlords is one of the narratives presented by African nationalists in Zanzibar and on the mainland, as well.[50] Okello independently expressing this opinion ingratiated him with the ASYL.

This new trend of crediting Okello is generally linked to the notion that Karume did not plan and lead the revolution, as ASP party histories contend. Even though only one article explicitly associates the union with Karume and the revolution, the union is the most politically salient topic in Zanzibar today. Since Zanzibaris have been allowed to debate the constitution of Tanzania and the union openly for the past few years, the opinion that Zanzibar lost its sovereignty in the union has been stated publicly by numerous politicians. This has opened the door for Karume to be criticized for his role in the formation of the union. That is the political environment in which Okello has returned to local media memories of the revolution.

Okello in Academic Accounts and Party Histories

Numerous early reports place Okello as leader of the revolution, whether they were local newspapers, foreign newspapers, or Western intelligence and diplomatic reports.[51] Many of these initial reports included factual inaccuracies, such as describing Okello as a Kenyan Luo, as has already been discussed. However, Okello was widely acknowledged to be in charge of the overthrow of the government. Similarly, Michael Lofchie (1965), who wrote the earliest scholarship on the Zanzibar revolution, credited Okello with leading the uprising.

---

50 For Zanzibari speeches and reports on the revolution getting rid of imperialism and colonialism, see ZNA AK 10/ 9, ZNA BA 70/3, ZNA BA 74/3, ZNA AK 17/10, ZNA AK 16/48, ZNA BA 68/16, and ZNA SA 1/104. Numerous reports cite Tanganyikan president Nyerere expressing this view of the sultanate as continued imperialism; see BNA CO 822/3204, BNA DO 121/237, and BNA FCO 141/7074.

51 See *Kweupe*, 18, 21 January 1964; *East African Standard*, 17–18 January 1964; *Daily Nation* 13–14 January 1964; *Uganda Argus* 18, 20 January 1964; *New York Times*, 19, 24 January 1964; CAC, DSND 8/5; BNA DO 185/59; *The Spectator*, 24, 31 January and 7, 14 February 1964; *The Stars and Stripes*, 17 January 1964.

Yet just as Okello was driven out of Zanzibar and later Tanganyika, so too was he written out of the official history of the revolution by the ASP. The government newspaper *The Nationalist*'s account of 12 January 1965 and the official history *The Afro-Shirazi Party Revolution, 1964-74* do not even mention his name, let alone credit him in any way for the overthrow of the government. Okello's role in the revolution disturbed the narrative that it was Karume's and the ASP's revolution from the beginning. Because the SMZ came to power through the revolution, not through an election, its political legitimacy was dependent upon the revolution (Bakari 2001). If Okello were given credit for leading the revolution, Karume's role would be diminished, according to this line of thought.[52] The two exceptions were histories by non-Zanzibaris that were published after Karume's death: Esmond Bradley Martin (1978) and Anthony Clayton (1981) both follow Lofchie's example, crediting Okello with leadership of the revolution. After a period of a dearth of scholarship and other writing on the history of the revolution, the introduction of multiparty democracy in Tanzania in 1995 and the change in the political climate ushered in a new era of writing on the revolution (Fouéré 2012). For a time, it was mostly those who resented the revolution and opposed the SMZ who gave Okello credit for his leadership role. Today, however, he is given credit in local media sources, as shown above, as well as by several Zanzibaris with whom I spoke who say he certainly appeared to be in charge at the outset. Even Party authors[53] have begun to acknowledge him. This new reading of Okello's role in the revolution began, surprisingly, with Omar Mapuri's *Zanzibar, The 1964 Revolution: Achievements and Prospects*, in which the author acknowledges the mistake of early ASP materials that left Okello out of the history completely (Mapuri 1996: 51).[54] Additionally, in a recent unpublished Revolutionary Government manuscript entitled *Historia ya Baraza la Mapinduzi 1964-2012* (History of the Revolutionary Council 1964-2012), the authors cite Okello's 1967 book about who was involved in the planning of the revolution. This indicates a certain credibility being given to Okello in official SMZ materials, and thus perhaps a new approach to his role. This broadening

---

52 This is how the SMZ has viewed it: the need for a singular, political narrative. However, there were numerous groups who were discussing revolution at the time, including a group of ASP politicians. The reality is much more complex than the official discourse allows.

53 By the "Party," I am referring both to the pre-1977 ASP and to the post-1977 Chama cha Mapinduzi (CCM).

54 Other than this brief acknowledgement of Okello, this book tells the ASP side of the story.

of the official story may stem from the 2010 Zanzibar Government of National Unity. With former opposition politicians in the government, new narratives arose in the public domain, and there was an attempt to gain renewed legitimacy through processes other than the revolution.

Conclusion

Views of Okello vary dramatically, from British reports stating that he was unbalanced—"round the bend"[55]—to remembrances of his friends and family in Pemba and in Uganda saying he was a charismatic leader who protected those close to him. The difference between the stories in Unguja, Pemba, and Uganda is indicative of the time he spent in each place. In Unguja, not much is known about him personally because he was not there for very long. What people know about him is mostly drawn from his public persona. In Pemba, where he lived for five years, however, people knew him as a friend or workmate, which gave them a different sense of the man. In Uganda, Okello was seen as a strong, brave, fierce, even brutal and cruel man, but he was admired, which is why he is cast as a hero. In other words, he could not have overthrown an unjust government without being ferocious. The difference is that in Uganda, there is no debate or discussion about the character of Zanzibar's government in 1963. The independent state is assumed to have been an unjust regime entailing Arab colonial rule, hence the overthrow of such a government is clearly understood as a heroic act in the eyes of most Ugandans.[56]

Okello and many of his fellow migrant laborers had worked jobs in several countries in East Africa and can be viewed as transnational African nationalists. That is, they were pan-Africanists of the "Africa for Africans" ideology. On the other hand, Zanzibari pride in cosmopolitanism honors a type of transnationalism, insofar as trade and culture are concerned (Burgess 2009: introduction). Ironically, this respect does not extend to migrant laborers, who are equally transnational. Coastal exceptionalism was about historical connections with distant lands through a sizable trade route and a "civilized" culture, *ustaarabu* (Glassman 2011: 62). The Okello type of mobility was looked

---

55 BNA DO 185/59, Police Commissioner Sullivan is reported to have described Okello as "round the bend."

56 In an interesting parallel, the only mention of the night of the revolution itself at the 50th anniversary celebrations in Zanzibar on 12 January 2014 was made by Uganda's president, Yoweri Museveni, who thanked Zanzibaris for overthrowing a bad government.

down upon by Zanzibaris whose transnational cosmopolitanism defined them.

Finally, a significant point that has not been examined in this chapter but deserves attention is the issue of religion. Okello was a Christian who staunchly believed that he was sent by God to help the Africans in Zanzibar. He had dreams and visions that guided him in his work (Okello 1967: 132–4). Some of his friends and followers were also Christian, but the Zanzibari political leaders and most of the other Committee of 14 members were Muslim. Okello wrote that he felt the significance of this when he received threats after the revolution telling him, "You do not belong to the Muslim religion and you are leading Muslims even though you are a Christian. Also, your activities led to the death of many people on the Island, most of whom were Muslims. So, start counting your days for a time to come when Muslims will unite to expel you from the Island" (Okello 1967: 177–8). Given the current Zanzibari narrative that often castigates Christian mainlander hegemony and recasts Nyerere as *Baba wa Kanisa* (Father of the Church/Church Elder) and *Adui wa Taifa* (Enemy of the Nation) (Fouéré 2014), it is surprising that Okello's religion did not surface during my interviews.[57] Zanzibaris generally knew that he was a Christian, but that was not mentioned among the numerous character flaws that resulted in Okello's expulsion.

Numerous sources indicate Okello's leadership role in the Zanzibar revolution. The recent political climate in Zanzibar has allowed more open discussion about the revolutionary event and Okello's role in it, among other topics. Therefore, in spite of cultural reasons for Okello's rejection from Zanzibari society and political reasons for his physical removal from Zanzibar, he has returned to popular debates of Zanzibar's history. Okello's role is being vehemently debated in the media in Tanzania, but he is no longer seen as someone whose presence meant that this was not a Zanzibari revolution. Instead, it is being discussed, in part, to show that the official narrative is incomplete. This historical revision does not entail a complete rejection of that official narrative, but it points to a widening of its scope to include more details than it previously has. Many sources now discuss Okello's role in terms of practical and logistical questions about the night of the revolution as well as in relation to the revolution's violence and brutality.

---

57 These revisionist names for Nyerere play on his more conventional honorific as *Baba wa Taifa* (Father of the Nation).

References

Archival Sources

British National Archives, Kew, United Kingdom (BNA)
British Red Cross Archives, London, United Kingdom (BRC)
Churchill Archives Center, Cambridge, United Kingdom (CAC)
Makerere University Library, Kampala, Uganda (MAK)
Rhodes House Library, Oxford University, United Kingdom (RHB)
Zanzibar National Archives, Zanzibar, Tanzania (ZNA)

Published Works

Afro-Shirazi Party

1974 *The Afro-Shirazi Party Revolution, 1964–74*. Zanzibar: Zanzibar Government Printer.

Anderson, David

2005 *Histories of the Hanged: The Dirty War in Kenya and the End of Empire*. New York: W. W. Norton & Company.

Askew, Kelly

2002 *Performing the Nation: Swahili Music and Cultural Politics in Tanzania*. Chicago: University of Chicago Press.

Bakari, Mohammed

2011 "Understanding Obstacles to Political Reconciliation in Zanzibar: Actors, Interests and Strategies." In *Understanding Obstacles to Peace: Actors, Interests and Strategies in Africa's Great Lake Region*, ed. Mwesiga Baregu, 222–70. Kampala: Fountain Publishers, International Development Research Centre.

Burgess, G. Thomas

2009 *Race, Revolution, and the Struggle for Human Rights in Zanzibar: The Memoirs of Ali Sultan Issa and Seif Sharif Hamad*. Athens, Ohio: Ohio University Press.

Clayton Anthony

1981 *The Zanzibari Revolution and Its Aftermath*. London: C. Hurst & Company.

Elkins, Caroline

2005 *Imperial Reckoning: The Untold Story of Britain's Gulag in Kenya*. New York: Henry Holt and Company.

Fairooz, Amani Thani

1995 *The Truth (To Refute Falsehood)*. Dubai: self-published.

Fouéré, Marie-Aude

2012 "Reinterpreting Revolutionary Zanzibar in the Media Today: The Case of *Dira* Newspaper." *Journal of Eastern African Studies* 6(4): 672–89.

2014 "Recasting Julius Nyerere in Zanzibar: The Revolution, the Union and the Enemy of the Nation." *Journal of Eastern African Studies* 8(3): 478–96.

Ghassany, Harith

2010 *Kwaheri Ukoloni, Kwaheri Uhuru! Zanzibar na Mapinduzi ya Afrabia.* [Goodbye Colonialism, Goodbye Independence! Zanzibar and the Revolution of Afrabia]. Self published, https://kwaheri.files.wordpress.com/2010/05/kwaheri-ukoloni-kwaheri-uhuru.pdf, accessed 18 July 2016.

Glassman, Jonathon

2011 *War of Words, War of Stones: Racial Thought and Violence in Colonial Zanzibar*. Bloomington, Ind.: Indiana University Press.

Kyle, Keith

1964a "The Zanzibar Coup." *The Spectator*. 24 January.

1964b "Mutinies and After." *The Spectator*. 31 January.

1964c "Gideon's Voices." *The Spectator*. 7 February.

1964d "How It Happened." *The Spectator*. 14 February.

Lofchie, Michael F.

1965 *Zanzibar: Background to Revolution*. Princeton, N.J.: Princeton University Press.

Martin, Esmond B.

1978 *Zanzibar: Tradition and Revolution*. London: Hamish Hamilton.

Middleton, John

1992 *The World of the Swahili: An African Mercantile Civilization*. New Haven, Conn.: Yale University Press.

Okello, John

1967 *Revolution in Zanzibar*. Nairobi: East African Publishing House.

Petterson, Don
2002 *Revolution in Zanzibar: An American's Cold War Tale.* Boulder, Colo.: Westview Press.

Smith, William Edgett
1973 *Nyerere of Tanzania.* London: Gollancz Ltd.

U.S. Central Intelligence Agency
1966 "Zanzibar: The 100 Days' Revolution." www.foia.cia.gov/sites/default/files/document_conversions/14/esau-28.pdf, accessed 20 February 2014.

White, Luise
2000 "Telling More: Lies, Secrets, and History." *History and Theory* 39(4): 11–22.

Newspapers

Daily Nation
East African Standard
Kweupe
Tanganyika Standard
Uganda Argus

Figure 1: Field Marshal John Okello at General Idi Amin's Office Congratulating Him on Overthrowing President Obote, 17 February 1971 (Courtesy of Makerere University Library)

Figure 2: President Karume and Field Marshal Okello Clasping Hands at the Idd al Fitr Baraza in Zanzibar City, 18 February 1964 (Courtesy of Makerere University Library)

Chapter Four

Memory, Liberalism, and the Reconstructed Self: Wolfango Dourado and the Revolution in Zanzibar

G. Thomas Burgess

If history is written by the winners, it is remembered by the losers. The revolution in Zanzibar is no exception: After seizing power in 1964, an African nationalist regime oriented many of its efforts for the next decade toward leveling island society at the expense of Zanzibar's once dominant Arab and South Asian minorities. It established control over the public sphere, shutting down or taking over newspapers and radio broadcasting stations and propagating its version of the past in the schools. In his novel *Desertion*, Abdulrazak Gurnah imparts a taste of how the new regime set out to silence memories it found objectionable or inconvenient. The character Amin writes to his brother, who is overseas:

> We have to find a new way of speaking about how we live now. They don't like to hear people say certain things, or sing certain songs … . People have been killed. I cannot write these things. They have frightened us too much, and it would be stupid to be found scribbling what we are required not to know about … . They want us to forget everything that was here before, except the things that aroused their rage and made them act with such cruelty. (2005: 246–7)

Aside from some expatriate writers like Gurnah, for many years there were very few voices in Zanzibar critical of the revolution; those willing to call the regime to account normally did so only in confidence and to close intimates. There were reasons for such reticence. Ordinary citizens lived in fear of the state's pervasive East German-trained security apparatus. They faced arrest, torture, and imprisonment.[1] Yet even in such adverse circumstances, oppositional narratives continued to privately circulate; people continued to measure the distance between

---

1 For two complimentary accounts of postcolonial Zanzibar's atmosphere of personal insecurity, see Burgess 2009.

the rhetoric of the revolution and its desperate realities. Their narratives were and are inherently subversive, confirming the correctness of Liisa Malkki's observation about oral histories in general: They are "not only a description of the past, nor even merely an evaluation of the past, but a subversive recasting and reinterpretation of it in fundamentally moral terms" (1995: 54). Zanzibaris very often see the past as a morality tale, in which from 1964 onward they were ruled by people full of "rage" and "cruelty."

If some Africans came to reject the revolution, it was especially ruinous for the islands' non-African minority communities. In 1948 there were over 15,000 South Asians residing in Zanzibar, but by 1972 that number had been reduced to around 3,500 (Lofchie 1965: 71; Martin 1978: 69). While so many others of South Asian heritage were forced to leave Zanzibar, Wolfango Dourado stayed, and through an odd twist of fate rose to a position of stature and respect in the new regime. As both a servant and critic of the new African nationalist regime, he came to occupy an ambivalent position. His memories of the revolution are tinged with regret that he did not do more to reign in a regime that in his eyes had become unhinged. After a brief historical sketch, I will set forth below what I consider most interesting and unique about Dourado's memories of the revolution.

Background

Representing roughly three-quarters of the islands' population, Africans[2] acquired land and property during the era of British rule (1890–1963) but did not achieve anything close to parity with Arabs and Asians in terms of wealth, status, and education.[3] Though intermarriage was not uncommon, and though over 90 percent of islanders embraced Islam, communal antagonisms came to the fore in the years after World War II in an atmosphere of intense partisan acrimony.[4] Such antagonisms were

---

2   "African" is one of the more disputed ethnic and racial labels in Zanzibar. The 1948 census included both "indigenous" and immigrant populations within the category. In the colonial period, "African" most commonly referred to migrants from the East African mainland arriving in the 20th century. Yet those who claimed "indigenous" status were also generally of African continental origins, albeit more distant. "Indigenous" labels included *Waswahili, Wahadimu, Wapemba, Watumbatu,* and *Washirazi,* the last term also suggesting Persian origins. For the 1948 census results, see Lofchie 1965: 71.

3   For essays that shed light on the relationship between class and social identity in Zanzibar during the colonial period, see Sheriff and Ferguson 1991.

4   The two best secondary sources on the tensions that led to the Zanzibari revolution are Glassman 2011 and Lofchie 1965.

an outcome of colonial-era inequalities; they also fed upon memories of Zanzibar's tragic and prominent role in the pre-colonial slave trade, which brought many tens of thousands of Africans to work in the islands' lucrative clove plantations. Many Africans therefore saw independence from colonial rule as a chance to also free themselves from Arab and South Asian political, social, and economic hegemony.

Nowhere were Arabs and South Asians more established in terms of numbers, wealth, and status than in Stone Town, the western, seaward, and older half of the capital, Zanzibar city. In 1948 Arabs and South Asians constituted, respectively, 49 and 27 percent of the capital's population (Prins 1967: 19). Due to their concentration in Stone Town, a rough estimate of their preponderance there would be upwards of 90 percent. Serving in the 19th century as the regional locus of the slave and ivory trades, Stone Town by the 1940s had largely shed its violent past. It offered access to electricity, schools, and a range of consumer commodities for both locals and an increasing number of day-tripping Western tourists from ships passing up and down the East African coast. For those with time and means it was a sporting playground, with sailing, swimming, golf, cricket, tennis, football, and field hockey among the chief amusements.[5] It was also a cosmopolitan feast of the senses: cafés offered African, Arab, Indian, and Chinese dishes, and cinemas packed in audiences to see everything from American Westerns to Egyptian dramas and Indian musicals. Kiswahili, Arabic, English, Hindi, and Urdu were spoken in the streets and read in over a dozen local newspapers. Ahmed Gurnah recalls that in Zanzibar city, "several great cultures routinely mixed and exchanged goods and ways of living" (1997: 117).

The labels "Arab" and "South Asian" do not convey the diversity of peoples that settled in Stone Town from the various shores of the western Indian Ocean. Those of Indian ancestry belonged to distinct religious communities, each with their own associations. Always one of Zanzibar's smallest groups, those who migrated from the Portuguese colony of Goa numbered a mere 681 in the 1948 census, or 0.3 percent of the protectorate's total population.[6] Goans were well known for their attachment to the Catholic Church; whenever possible they sent

---

5 For how British civil servants sought to reshape Stone Town's urban space according to colonial ideas of progress and order, see Bissell 2011.

6 See Lofchie 1965: 71. In 1948, the last year for which figures from all four British territories are available, there were a reported 11,294 Goans in East Africa, compared to a total population of approximately 350,000 Indians in the region. See also Frenz 2014: 64.

their children to St. Joseph's Convent School, located along Stone Town's seafront and operated by German and Irish nuns and priests. They attended the Goan Institute, whose building served as a venue for dances, dinners, drama performances, and other social gatherings. There was also the Goan Sports Club, which fielded all-Goan cricket and field hockey teams, as well as the Goan Union, which sought to represent the tiny Goan community to the colonial state. While they continually rubbed shoulders and formed friendships with other islanders, Goans normally married among themselves, and they were immersed in a range of communal traditions, such as weekend picnics to Changu Island. While they resided in one of the most cosmopolitan spaces in East Africa, they were a tight-knit and semi-exclusive group, comparable in this respect to other small Stone Town-centered communities such as the Ismailis, Ithnasheria, and Bohora. Solidly urban and middle-class, either in status or in aspirations, they were teachers, tailors, businessmen, and shopkeepers. They operated bakeries, bars, and restaurants. But by far the most common Goan occupational category was that of civil servant in the colonial administration (Frenz 2014: 100ff.). As trusted employees who largely embraced Christianity, western clothing and education, Goans were members of Zanzibar's "colonized middle," and part of "an expanding population of South Asians who were vigorously disseminating Western ideas around the Empire" (Myers 1999: 32). According to Margret Frenz, they were "subaltern elites" occupying "liminal, interstitial positions as not-quite Indian, not-quite Portuguese, not-quite British and, increasingly, not-quite East African" (Frenz 2014: 18, 90).[7]

As Frenz also observes, tens of thousands emigrated from Goa in the decades prior to World War I, and East Africa was a popular destination. Zanzibar served as a first port of entry for many Goan migrants to the region. A community appears to have coalesced in the islands by the advent of colonial rule in the 1890s; by then, Goans owned over 100 retail shops and were able to donate considerable sums towards the construction of Stone Town's imposing St. Joseph's Catholic Cathedral, where they comprised the majority of adherents (Frenz 2014: 55, 61, 66, 98, 156). Goans sought respectability *within* colonial society and had every reason to look upon the years after independence with a certain degree of trepidation. Their worries proved warranted; within months of seizing power in 1964, Zanzibar's new revolutionary regime banned

---

[7] Frenz observes that from 1910 Goans enjoyed Portuguese citizenship, instead of the status of British "protected person," which their children possessed when born in Zanzibar or other British colonies in East Africa. A few Goans in East Africa even served as Portuguese consuls.

all ethnic associations, cutting away in one stroke a cornerstone of the Goan community. Their cherished Goan Institute, located in Stone Town's Vuga neighborhood, became a state-owned venue for musical performances. The regime also nationalized and secularized St. Joseph's Convent School, and seized control of many Goan properties and businesses. It dismissed many (though not all) Goans from the civil service. Most Goans chose to leave Zanzibar for new lives in the United Kingdom, Canada, India, or mainland East Africa. By 1976, only about 175 remained (Martin 1978: 98).

Memory, Liberalism, and the Reconstructed Self

One of those who remained was Wolfango Dourado, who despite the turmoil and anti–South Asian ethos of the revolution, served as Zanzibar's attorney general from 1964 to 1977. Possessing a law degree from Middle Temple in London, Dourado was one of the very few persons with a college education to serve the revolution. Abeid Amani Karume, president of Zanzibar from 1964 until his assassination in 1972, was known to dislike men with degrees, and on repeated occasions he publicly boasted of their absence in his government.[8] Yet he trusted Dourado, for reasons to be described below.

I met "Wolfe" in July 2005, at his home in Stone Town, and in the space of one week was able to interview him four times. Having conducted research in Zanzibar since 1996, I regretted then, and continue to do so now, that I did not approach him earlier. Dourado's memories are exceptional—they come from a rare insider both willing and unafraid to criticize the regime he served. Yet by the time I met him Dourado was 76 and in fragile health. His stamina for the interview process was limited. While he and his wife, Yvonne, were extremely gracious and supportive of the idea of a series of interviews intended to record his life and times, circumstances were not always propitious for our collaboration. I interviewed Dourado once more in 2006 and was sad to see his health had not improved. Finally, in 2009, I presented Dourado with a typed manuscript and first-person narrative taken from our previous interviews, of roughly 11,000 words in length. Not wanting to produce a mere transcript, I edited and arranged his memories in a way that made them comprehensible and accessible to the ordinary reader. In doing so I remained as close as possible to his original wording.[9] I

---

8   Zanzibar Government 1968. See also Clayton 1981: 117.

9   I employed the same methodology in the production of Burgess 2009.

also recognized, however, the manuscript's limitations: It offered only a fragmentary understanding of Dourado's life experiences. Yet Dourado read and gave his full consent to the manuscript's publication, either in whole or in part.

What motivated Dourado to speak to me, a western historian? One of his most repeated claims was that he was a good and honorable man whose misfortune it was to serve a very dishonorable regime. He presented himself as someone who sought to protect the rights of ordinary islanders yet suffered far more defeats than victories, and who was imprisoned on more than one occasion for speaking truth to power. Dourado portrayed himself as the "mouse that roared," never afraid to speak his mind, yet due to his precarious position within the regime, was forced to carefully choose his battles. Very often he remained a melancholy witness to a series of misguided revolutionary initiatives, and was reduced to making the most of an awful situation. As attorney general he could at least work within the existing system, such as it was, to ensure that Zanzibar's justice system was not entirely unjust. And so he never resigned; to do so would have meant the end of what little capacity he had to "moderate" the revolution. He went on serving and meeting with President Karume, a man for whom he had little respect yet who regularly called on his attorney general to craft dozens of his revolutionary decrees—decrees that were utterly contrary to Dourado's personal and professional notions of justice and that, he says, made him cringe.

Dourado's position within the regime is intriguing and indeed highly ambiguous; it presents obvious challenges to the historian. Yet far more interesting than trying to locate Dourado's personal complicity in serving such an authoritarian regime are Dourado's actual recollections of the past, the moral and intellectual frameworks by which he ordered such recollections, and the self he sought to fashion through memory. And for reasons that will become apparent below, I see no reason to doubt Dourado's despair that he did not do more to ameliorate suffering in Zanzibar.

Indeed, for the historian trying to understand the complexities of any period of social upheaval such as the revolution in Zanzibar, despair may sometimes prove a less problematic sentiment than pride. In Dourado's case, his memories of the revolution—those that intentionally or not serve to distance him from its worst abuses—are possible to confirm through oral and print sources. Nor did he ever seem that worried that I might actually judge him harshly for his service to the revolution.

While the "good man in a bad regime" was a common theme, Dourado's motivation for speaking to me had more to do with his desire to be accorded his "rightful" place in history. More than anything else, pride was what motivated him to speak to me. He was far more anxious about the prospect of obscurity than he was of the appearance of complicity.

I was by no means the first writer to approach him. Others had materialized during the course of his long career, westerners whom he regaled with stories, humor, and analysis. Some became friends who went on to publish laudatory reports. Don Petterson served as an American diplomat in Zanzibar from 1963 to 1965, and then returned as ambassador to Tanzania in the 1980s. He described Dourado as someone who gave his loyalty "but not his soul" to the regime, and who was outspoken "at times to the point of indiscretion." Despite his willingness to criticize, the revolutionary regime "prized" Dourado's honesty and ability so much that they never fired him. Since in his acknowledgments Petterson thanked Dourado for reviewing his book manuscript, we can be sure that Dourado was not displeased to read that he "disagreed with government actions and policies and did not hesitate to express his disagreement," even if it meant imprisonment (Petterson 2002: xi, 111).[10]

A similar image of blunt, come-what-may disregard for revolutionary sensibilities comes through in Esmond Bradley Martin's account from the 1970s. He described the attorney general in glowing terms, as "the best educated person" in government, an "exceptional man," with a reputation for hard work, "faultless integrity and willingness to help people." "Rather short in stature but not in personality," Dourado was "stimulating, provocative, [and] witty." Perhaps because of these qualities, whenever "journalists and businessmen visit Zanzibar, the government strongly suggests that they see Mr. Dourado." And yet there was another, more illicit side to these encounters with foreigners, a side that could not have pleased the authorities. After Dourado unleashed a torrent of criticisms of the regime, Martin asked how such views could be tolerated. Dourado responded that it was because no one doubted his devotion and commitment to Zanzibar (Martin 1978: 7–9).

After a three-hour lunch with Martin at the Bwawani Hotel, in which Dourado enthusiastically held forth on all matters related to Zanzibar, he insisted on taking Martin to have tea with the American vice-consul, followed by drinks at the Africa House Hotel, to watch the sunset. Then

---

10   Clearly, this was Petterson's impression from a time more recent than the mid-1960s.

he took Martin home for dinner, and to meet his wife, Yvonne. Also present at dinner were members of Zanzibar's "Goan Mafia": Goans who had managed, like Dourado, to retain high-ranking positions in the civil service. And then after dinner it was off for more drinks at the Maruhubi Palace ruins. It perhaps comes as no surprise that after this ten-hour marathon Martin would eventually acknowledge Dourado for his help in preparing his book, a book in which he dishes out nothing but praise for the attorney general (Martin 1978: x).

No doubt for Dourado these periodic sprees with curious and admiring westerners were one of the few perks of office. When I knocked on his door in 2005 he likely saw me as someone else with whom he could share his recollections, and who would inevitably come around to seeing him as others had before: As not only a good and honorable man but one of the "great men" of Zanzibar. While I was favorably impressed by his singular qualities, I was, however, concerned that he might intentionally amplify his role in island affairs. It was a continual ride between despair and pride: At one moment he presented himself as the tireless civil servant patiently seeking to influence the powerful to rule the islands with some modicum of decency and restraint. And in the next he characterized himself as a prizefighter and more than a match for the likes of Julius K. Nyerere, president of Tanzania from 1961 to 1985. Thus Dourado employed his memories to fashion two sides of the same self, which were neither incompatible nor entirely deceptive.

Moving on to the moral and intellectual frameworks by which Dourado ordered his memories, one might expect him to remember the revolution primarily as a disaster to his fellow Goans, who, while not targeted in the worst racial violence of early 1964, endured official discrimination for a decade afterward, such that the vast majority felt they had no choice but to accept exile overseas. As Garth Myers notes, "There are prices people pay when they are stranded in the interstices." Like other members of the "colonized middle," Goans very often had "no place" in the post-colonial order (1999: 32, 49).[11] One might therefore expect Dourado to dwell upon the injustices endured by "his people"; such a view of the past would be in accordance with how others in the islands have constructed their own memories. In the last years of colonial rule, African intellectuals remembered the past as a narrative

---

11 For an excellent account of African–South Asian relations in Dar es Salaam from the 1920s through the 1970s, see Aminzade 2013 and Brennan 2012. While South Asians experienced post-colonial discrimination in Tanzania and Kenya, they endured expulsion from both Uganda and Malawi.

of enslavement and oppression extending back to the 19th century.[12] They succeeded in making this one of the principal rhetorical platforms of the Afro-Shirazi Party (ASP), which ruled Zanzibar through the revolutionary era and which at official gatherings, in the schools, and through the media propagated a narrative of African exploitation by Arab "feudalists" and South Asian "capitalists."[13] Such memories of communal suffering endure to this day and continue to serve as the visceral heart of African nationalism in the islands.[14]

Yet Dourado did not dwell upon such matters; communal traumas did not dominate his recollections of the past, perhaps because he eschewed the ethnic and racial politics that have so characterized Zanzibari politics since the 1950s. He did not see wealth, opportunity, and respectability as scarce commodities to be contested, acquired, and defended through collective action and on a communal basis. He was also no doubt aware of the extent to which his fellow Goans managed, in their post-Zanzibar years, to work toward a prosperous exile in places like Canada and the United Kingdom (see Frenz 2014: 222–57). This may have decided him that it was pointless to emphasize the losses incurred by "his people." Instead, Dourado placed consistent emphasis on the general damage the revolution wrought upon island society. And while he did not ignore the adversities faced by those on the wrong side of the partisan and ethnic fence, he viewed their mistreatment as simply a manifestation of a larger problem: The willingness of revolutionary elites to abandon the forms and principles of liberal governance, and in so doing to set Zanzibar back a generation in its development. Dourado presented himself as a despondent witness to the repeated sacrifice of the rule of law upon the altar of revolution. He critiqued the regime through a universal language of human rights,

---

12 See Glassman 2011. The violence of early 1964, moreover, was in part a collective settling of scores, in which Africans avenged themselves *and* their ancestors.

13 In 1977 the ASP formed a union with the Tanganyikan African National Union (TANU), the ruling party of the Tanzanian mainland. The offspring of this union, Chama cha Mapinduzi (CCM), or "Party of the Revolution," remains in power to this day.

14 Such memories have sometimes assumed printed form; see Mapuri 1996. And for at least some of those who reject the revolution, communal traumas also color their conceptions of the past. Residents of the island of Pemba often remember the 1960s and 1970s as an era when a vindictive regime sought to collectively punish them for their lack of revolutionary enthusiasm. See Bakari 2001; Burgess 2009: 24–5, 186–201. That many remember the revolution in this way was confirmed for me in the summer of 2010 as I recorded dozens of Pemban oral histories.

which since the 1990s has attained a global currency as widespread as that of socialism in the 1960s.

And yet such apparent universalism is not without an ethnic basis. Dourado proudly recounted that Goans were unusual in colonial Zanzibar for their fluency in English, their embrace of Christianity, and their western education. Dourado's own father is representative in this respect. Migrating from Goa as a young man, he found steady employment as a civil servant in the colonial public works department. He also made a name for himself in the Goan community as an actor in various amateur theatricals performed at the Goan Institute. Dourado recalled with pleasure going as a boy to see his father appear on stage as a thief or a despot, his acting talents and command of English on full display.

Goans acquired the reputation in the colonial era of being one of the most if not the most "westernized" community in Zanzibar (Frenz 2014: 16). Dourado embraces this perception; it lies at the core of his personal identity. As a boy he attended mass daily, and he studied at St. Joseph's Convent school, where he excelled. He played cricket and field hockey, always for all-Goan teams. He spent most of his time within a fifteen-minute walking distance of his family home in Stone Town, rarely having reason to venture farther than to swim in the sea near what is now Forodhani Gardens or to borrow books from friends and libraries around town. He was raised in a household where all resources were pooled, and where he and his siblings were expected to contribute to the family welfare. Personal worth was measured by one's diligence, integrity, and adherence to Catholic teachings. With his academic gifts recognized from an early age, Dourado had every reason to believe he could rise through the civil service. And yet Dourado can in no way be described as merely careerist; perhaps taking after his father, there was a showman side to his personality, which was on full display as he shared memories of the revolution, and his personal encounters with its "great men."

In between moments of humor and theatricality Dourado expressed his critique of the revolution in liberal terms that in recent decades have become more and more familiar around the globe. It is no accident that Dourado saw great continuity between such principles and those embraced by some Goans like himself in the 1950s. Setting aside the question of the extent to which Dourado's principles are objectively his alone or representative of Goans in Zanzibar (or for that matter if they may even be described as western or universal values), it is more important to note here that Dourado structured his memories of the revolution according to an abstract creed that aspires to universalism and that is also derived from his own experience growing up in a Goan family in Stone Town during the colonial era. Dourado's recollections, then, are illustrative of memory's endless loop between the communal and the universal.

They are also founded upon a strong sense of colonial nostalgia. Dourado framed his memories according to a simple distinction between the order and progress of the colonial period and the chaos and decline of the revolution. He premised his critique of the regime upon a belief that in many ways colonial times were much better. Dourado's nostalgia is part of a larger phenomenon reported from various parts of Africa in recent years (Bissell 2005). If indeed such colonial nostalgia is an imagined construct, for Dourado it has little to do with the neoliberal present. Listening to Dourado (and some others of his generation) recite a litany of complaints about Karume and his colleagues, one gains a distinct impression that such grievances are extremely well rehearsed and have been in circulation since the traumas of the 1960s. Ever since, they have floated in time, to be snatched from the ether when necessary. For some of Dourado's generation, at least, current realities do not intrude very much upon a well-established dialectic between memories of colonialism and of the revolution.

Colonialism

Born in September 1929, Dourado was a colonial subject until his mid-30s. He speaks fondly of those years:

> To me, Zanzibar in those days was a paradise of sandy beaches and swaying palms. It was also a very cosmopolitan place; my friends included Parsees, Hindus, and a few Ithnasheria. The people got on very well together during that time. We celebrated their holidays and they celebrated ours. Zanzibaris are great huggers! Of course the Comorians were our sports rivals, because we were the leading field hockey team and when they tried to snatch the trophy from us there were all kinds of broken legs and fingers. We Goans mostly played cricket and hockey because we were not strong enough in soccer, which was very popular among the majority Africans, who were sturdy and strong. The different communities were on agreeable terms until the advent of independence, and then the local Africans were rather nasty. They were fighting for what they conceived to be their rights.

Dourado remembers a society in which the British were relatively benign masters, the shops were full, and people for the most part lived in safety and harmony. As far as he is concerned, Goans were treated with a measure of respect:

> I thought if we had to have colonialism the British were the least evil of them all. They were unassuming as our masters; they were not like South Africans who when they bossed you, they really bossed you. And some became very good friends of ours, and they did their best to try and get us Zanzibaris to get along with each other. And when they found a bright chap they pulled him out and pushed him up. They were the ones who accelerated my promotion, for example ... .
>
> We actually got on well with the Brits. Yes, they collared all the good places around town for themselves, like the golf course, the English Club, and the tennis courts which were just for them. But still they wanted to be with us, and not the other way around. The British always wanted to come to the Goan Institute and to sit and drink with us. They didn't want us at the English Club, because all their ladies would be after us, because we were sophisticated and yet also exotic. There were some romances, but it was just silent smooching because they were British wives and couldn't run away from their husbands.

If the British accorded Goans some respect, they were in no way above racism. After earning his Cambridge School Certificate, grade one, in 1946, Dourado was unable to continue his studies due to the death of his father. To help support his mother and siblings, he found employment as a junior civil servant, where he recalls experiencing job discrimination: "I was frustrated at times because people who were my inferiors were my bosses, and they refused to take instruction from me, just because they were white. They were inferior in terms of age, education, and knowledge. They were brought up with racial prejudice and I was not going to have it."[15] Nevertheless, Dourado obtained a government scholarship in 1950 to study law in the United Kingdom; he could not take advantage of this offer until 1954, when colonial officials also agreed to continue paying his salary to his family while he attended Middle Temple in London.

Dourado passed the bar exam in 1957, but not without suffering through miserably cold London winters, intense loneliness, and a nervous breakdown. He recalled days on end spent reading in his room, never venturing outside because of the cold. "I was getting very good marks, yet I was living in digs where the landlady was a grasping witch, and I was of a nature where I gave her everything she wanted, but she always asked for more and more. The result was a nervous breakdown." After a month-long hospitalization at King's College Hospital,

---

15   This compares with Ajit Singh's recollections, as a colonial-era civil servant in Zanzibar, of numerous British officials lacking in empathy, understanding, and humility (Myers 1999: 47).

... the Colonial Office rescued me: someone there wrote the second cousin of the Queen Mother on my behalf. They thought I was very friendly and able to get on with all sorts of people, and they asked her to take me in, and from day one we hit it off. She would call me "butler" because I used to lay the table, and I would also work in the garden and feed her hens, and I built a shed to store the coke for heating the whole house. She arranged for me to go to a student hostel in West London called One Hands Crescent, just next to Harrods, yet I stayed with her every holiday between each term. "Little Garlands" was the name of her place outside London, in Essex, near Colchester. She had a fine sense of humor and was a very kind woman, because she was royalty, and that's where the kindness comes. Her name was Rose Verner, and unfortunately she is blind now. Every time I think of her I have tears.

Dourado's evocation of Zanzibar as a colonial "paradise" might lead researchers to conclude he is only selectively remembering the past, that he is a good example of naïveté or "social amnesia."[16] Yet Dourado does not appear to be forgetting past realities so much as putting them within a framework of understanding that ought to be recognized as such.[17] When he compared British rule in Zanzibar to what came before or after, he did not consider it a Hobbesian world of racist exploitation and discrimination. Yes, there was racism, but there was also the beginning of a kind of meritocracy from which he was able to derive personal benefits. From his perspective, it was a time when social mobility was possible, and when it was still feasible to enjoy the warm affective ties of a Goan community that appears to bear many of the hallmarks of Ferdinand Tönnies's classic conception of *Gemeinschaft*. Certainly Dourado offers an appealing portrait of how within a few minutes of his doorstep he could walk to the sea, the school, or sports field, as well as participate in the myriad events that punctuated the ordinary Goan social calendar—something the revolution dramatically curtailed.[18] And if there were greedy British landladies and racist colonial officers, there

---

16 For one usage of this term, see Burke 1989: 97–113.

17 According to Frenz, the "contradictions within the Goan community between the experience of being colonized and supporting the colonizer, I argue, are resolved by not remembering, or by selectively forgetting, the past." See Frenz 2014: 292.

18 For at least some western tourists, wandering the streets of Zanzibar city is appealing precisely because of the whiff it offers of such affective ties. And with little comprehension of the local language, or the islands' social relations, such ties appear as alive today as any time in the mysterious past.

were also others who recognized his merit and came to his assistance. Is all this merely naïve?[19] As William Bissell asks:

> Can we then say that colonial nostalgia is just misguided history or willful misrecognition? Is it simply the result of false consciousness or fantasy? None of these characterizations seem very convincing insofar as they rest on a dubious epistemological divide between observer and observed: "we" (presumably Western, educated, and privileged) see history in the clear light of day, whereas "they" ... indulge in myths or mysticism. (2005: 222)

Nationalism

If for many Africans studying in London the 1950s were a watershed moment and period of political awakening, for Dourado they were years when he held fast to the Catholic teachings of his childhood while gaining a more sophisticated understanding of the meaning of liberalism, human rights, and the rule of law. Dourado did not embrace radically new ideas in London:[20]

> Eventually other Zanzibaris started coming in, and we had the East Africa House where I had friends there from all over East Africa .... We used to gather there and discuss everything, wildly and furiously, including politics. We knew all the answers the Conservative government did not know. If colonial subjects like myself had had more freedom to send members to speak in parliament on our behalf then we would have had no need of Hyde Park Corner, where speakers would vent their spleen against everybody. I went to listen there at first, yet I was a diehard right wing Tory, and I'm not ashamed to admit it. This was first because of my Catholic upbringing, then the influence of the German nuns, and then, strangely enough, that of the Irish Fathers. I had no interest in Marxism: it was dry as dutch. I did try and study Marxism but I couldn't go beyond a page a day. Marxism, anyway, was not fashionable among the Goans, who were specially privileged. But for the downtrodden, it was food.

Dourado's embrace of Tory politics did not escape the notice of other Zanzibaris in London at the time, including Abdulrahman Muhammed Babu, who within a few years was to become secretary general of the Zanzibar Nationalist Party (ZNP) and Zanzibar's leading socialist

---

19 Frenz suggests the disconnect between rosy memories and less than pleasant colonial realities is related to Goans' social mobility in Zanzibar and their capacity to escape traditional caste distinctions. See Frenz 2014: 292.

20 For an entirely different kind of intellectual evolution, see Ali Sultan Issa's recollections of his time in London in the 1950s in Burgess 2009: 49–54.

politician, strategist, and polemicist. Dourado recalled that in 1955 the two were standing in a crowd in Trafalgar Square as parliamentary election results were announced. Babu noticed Dourado, remembered him from Zanzibar, and was dismayed to see him cheering the news of every Tory candidate victory. A much taller man, Babu walked over to Dourado and reportedly said, intending to be humorous: "I know what to do with colonial stooges like you."

Dourado returned to Zanzibar in 1957 and resumed employment in the civil service. The following year he married Yvonne Pereira, who came from an affluent Goan family resident in Zanzibar for three generations and with whom he attended school at St. Joseph's. The two settled into one of her family's homes in Stone Town. Although Dourado claims that in the years prior to the revolution he remained aloof from nationalist politics, he defends the ZNP and praises the party's spiritual leader, Ali Muhsin al-Barwani:

> Though I was a civil servant politics was unavoidable in those days. And when I served in the early-1960s as Ali Muhsin's Principal Secretary in the Ministry of External Affairs, I could not help but get involved. Ali Muhsin was the chief leader of the ZNP, and I would rate him the best politician in East Africa: sophisticated, knowledgeable, and educated. If he were still alive today he would still be miles above the rest.
>
> Comorians, Shirazi, Arabs, and Hindus all supported the ZNP; it was a broad spectrum of people. On the other hand, we didn't have a sense of African nationalism.... We Zanzibaris were more educated, more sophisticated, and possessed a greater world outlook than on the [African] mainland. We used to call the mainlanders *washenzi wa bara*, savages of the mainland. When I got really angry at them I would say, "You are a savage born in the forest, and you will eventually die there." We said we Zanzibaris would not be ruled by people who file their teeth, or who might be descendants of cannibals. Ali Muhsin said this, and we supported his view.[21]

While westerners and others may be shocked by Dourado's aspersions of "mainlander" Africans, they nonetheless reflect a broad spectrum of ZNP rhetoric and opinion, as well as a discourse, long present in coastal East Africa, that denigrated Africans hailing from the interior as uncivilized. While the ZNP preached the virtues of multiracialism, it also scorned mainlander Africans as uncouth, unenlightened, and

---

21 This may be a reference to Julius K. Nyerere, president of Tanzania until his retirement in 1985, who in accordance with Zanaki custom, submitted to tooth-filing as a boy.

unfit to govern.[22] Dourado's views depart from the ZNP mainstream, however, in that as a Catholic he does not espouse the party's prevailing Arab-centrism or its desire to unify islanders according to a common adherence to Islam. From his perspective, Goans did not need to look to either Islam or the manners and mores of Zanzibar's Arab community for guidance in the art of civilization.

If Dourado was not particularly drawn to either Arab or African nationalism, he was not alone: Self-proclaimed socialists like Babu also rejected racial nationalism in favor of a materialist doctrine that promoted class identities over those of race. Babu and other ZNP socialists embraced the party's multiracialist stance, while seeking to distance themselves from its cultural chauvinism. Yet as is already clear, Dourado did not consider Marxism a worthy alternative. Babu's worldview was completely at variance with his own, which was that the British had promoted principles of liberal governance and established institutions such as the colonial courts designed to assert and defend such principles. Even if they (or at least some of them) were racists, the British had established instruments of enlightened rule that ought to be preserved after independence. For Dourado, then, revolution—whether inspired by racial or class grievances—posed a dire threat to a system and set of "bourgeois" values that had and would continue to serve islanders well. Despite his anticolonial rhetoric, Ali Muhsin broadly shared such views, earning Dourado's praise.

Unlike Babu, Dourado embraced a concept of civilization that, while rejecting Arab-centrism, located Zanzibar's various communities along a spectrum of relative development and capacities for self-rule, a spectrum in which Goans compared favorably with other communities. And he believed history was on his side. Even with the retreat of colonialism, and the remarkable global advance of socialism after World War II, Dourado felt in a position to help guide Zanzibar in the coming years of independence. He didn't consider politicians such as Karume to be so qualified. Ironically, however, it was Karume—the rough-hewn, charismatic African nationalist and chairman of the ASP—who gave Dourado a chance to rise further within the civil service. Dourado remembers his first encounter with Karume in this way:

> When I was Assistant Administrator General [Karume] came to my office and showed me a piece of paper saying a certain African woman was not being paid [her claim on an inheritance]. I rang a bell to

---

22 See Glassman 2011 and Lofchie 1965: 198ff.

summon my Persian clerk, named Khalil Mirza, and I asked him why had this woman not been paid. He said the money was ready, and I told him to tell the cashier to pay her immediately or else he would go home and not come back, and rightly enough the chap paid her at once. After that I was at my desk and I felt a shadow come over me. I looked up and it was Karume again, who held out a hundred shilling note from his shirt pocket to give to me. I asked him what it was for and he said in Swahili, "You helped us, and now we will help you." I told him this was exactly what the British were saying about us: that when we got power we would accept bribes. "So please," I said, "I get my salary and that's enough for me." And then later on he came back and said to me, "When I take over this government, and I will, I will make you my Attorney General." And that is what eventually happened.[23]

Revolution

In December 1963, only a month before the onset of revolution, Zanzibar celebrated its independence from colonial rule. Dourado remembers the event with vividness and clarity:

> By then I was the Attorney General as well as Principal Secretary for the Ministry of External Affairs and Trade, so I had the honor of escorting Indira Gandhi to the pavilion—she and her two brats, Sonjai and Rajib. I received a position of privilege at the ceremony, seated next to the Duke of Edinburgh. The sultan sat to my right. I had my wig and gown on, and I cried because if this was what we were waiting for, would it be worth it? I didn't know the answer then. I was a true Zanzibari nationalist to the core.
>
> The ceremony was at the Cooper's Ground, near Mnazi Mmoja. The pavilion where I was standing with all the other dignitaries was all lit up, but everyone else was in darkness. At the stroke of midnight beams of light focused on two masts, the Union Jack coming down on one and the Zanzibari flag coming up on the other. The people celebrated when

---

23 Dourado's recollections of Karume accord with other sources that suggest the future president of Zanzibar was something of a populist figure. See, for example, Mwanjisi 1967. Karume's favorable opinion of Dourado may also have stemmed from his role as state prosecutor in colonial Zanzibar's most famous and consequential political trial. Following the June 1961 election riots, in which over 60 islanders lost their lives, nearly all of them Arab members of the ZNP, Babu accused the British government of whitewashing the violence in its official commission report. He claimed the ASP, whose members were responsible for nearly all the deaths, had not been properly singled out for blame. Convinced Babu was an irritating agitator and dangerous communist, the British sought to remove him from the political scene. They accused him of sedition and asked Dourado to serve as state prosecutor. He consented, and he won the case, though its outcome was never really in doubt. From Karume's perspective, Dourado's role in securing Babu's detention served as further evidence of Dourado's impartiality: Babu was secretary general of the ZNP, the party to which a vast majority of Goans and other residents of Stone Town gave their emphatic support. For the June 1961 election riots, see Glassman 2011: 237–63.

our new flag went up. My shirtsleeves were wet from wiping away the tears; there was no time to get out my handkerchief. Later that night we went to the All Races Club for dancing and drinking, a building now occupied by the House of Representatives. The various [ethnic] clubs also held dances in their own buildings.

Yet there was a conspicuous absence of blacks at the ceremony. Most who attended were Arabs, Indians, and Goans, and only a sprinkling of Africans. We should have seen then that we in the government were not much liked.

Dourado's memories of the bloody deposition of the sultan and the ZNP/ZPPP coalition government are in some respects representative of those of many Stone Town residents who heard gunfire on the night of 11–12 January 1964 and who in the days afterwards stayed indoors as much as possible, spending hour after hour listening to the radio. After police recruits loyal to the government retreated from Malindi police station, Stone Town was open to advancing groups of revolutionaries—ASP supporters armed with weapons seized from government arsenals at Mtoni and Ziwani.[24] As Dourado recalls:

> The revolutionaries came through the streets and we peeped through the shutters, and some of those who looked out the windows were shot. The revolutionaries were Africans and Shirazi, all from Zanzibar. The million-dollar question now is the number of deaths in the revolution. I guesstimate around 4,000 died, but others go higher than that. And thousands more left immediately following the revolution. I was very sad to see them go but I kept on saying, "I will die with my boots on here."...
>
> During the killing I did not step outside for three or four days, and then I rang Karume, who sent a car to take me to Raha Leo, where he was broadcasting every day on the radio. He said to me I had nothing to worry about, that he wanted me to serve as Attorney General. And I agreed immediately; I had already agreed that time when he offered me 100 shillings. I was not a revolutionary, but I thought this would be one way of helping the people. It would be my contribution toward moderating the revolution.

Dourado remembers his life from this moment until the end of the 1970s as a time when he sought to reduce the excesses of the revolution. This meant persuading Karume in January 1964 to release his Goan friends from detention at Raha Leo. It meant delivering food to the wife

---

24 Multiple accounts of what happened in the opening days of the revolution have tended to obscure more than they reveal. Sources that allege John Okello conceived, organized, and executed the toppling of the ZNP government include Lofchie 1972; Petterson 2002; and Clayton 1981: 55ff. For another version of events, see Burgess 2010: 429–50.

and children of Ali Muhsin, whom the new regime detained before his eventual transfer to a prison in mainland Tanzania, where he remained for the next ten years.[25] It also meant standing up to John Okello, the self-proclaimed field marshal of the revolution:

> He ordered me to arrest a certain person and put him in jail and I said I wouldn't do that; I said people should be sent to court and receive a sentence. Okello was all bluff, because he would buckle up when I screamed at him. Yvonne would get mad at me for screaming at the revolutionaries with guns, because she thought they would shoot me outright, but I would say, "If it is God's will, so be it." I felt I had to do the right thing. You only have one life to lose, and I've not yet lost it. I found, actually, that if I screamed at them they would get scared, and buckle up. And anyway John Okello was a joke, and we eventually booted him out. He went to Kenya where he was deported, and then on to Uganda.

There is a certain amount of swagger in these memories; Dourado presents himself as "the mouse that roared," yet it undoubtedly required courage to defy as cruel and whimsical a figure as Okello.[26] For weeks following the seizure of power Okello terrorized the islands with his radio broadcasts; he toured the countryside with his band of armed supporters, administering summary racial "justice."[27] Dourado claims to have also defied Karume on multiple occasions. In consideration of the fact that four of the nine earliest cabinet ministers serving Karume in the 1960s were executed, such defiance would have also possessed an element of courage.[28] As Dourado recollected:

> Karume in general hated educated people, except for Wolfango Dourado, whom he liked. I was always honest with him and told him bluntly what I thought. I used to defy him quite often. One time in 1964 he rounded up all the Indians in town at the People's Palace and, in front of them all, ordered me to have them deported. I said, "I cannot do that; I will get in trouble with Julius Nyerere [president of Tanzania] because deportations are a union matter."

---

25 For his long journey through imprisonment to eventual freedom, see al-Barwani 1997: 219–65.

26 See Okello 1967; see also Ann Lee Grimstad's essay in this volume.

27 In March 1964 Karume managed, with the support of a number of Zanzibari politicians, to arrange for Okello's deportation from Zanzibar. His marauding activities were a serious embarrassment to a new regime intent on gaining diplomatic recognition and asserting centralized state control over the revolutionary process.

28 The four ministers who met violent ends during Karume's time were Othman Shariff Musa, Abdulla Kassim Hanga, Abdul Aziz Twala, and Saleh Saadalla.

Karume said angrily, "Leave that to me!" But all the Indians were laughing because I had stood up to him, like the mouse that roared. So Karume said, "Come with me," and we went to the State House, where he called me up to his verandah. He lifted his hand as if he was about to strike me, but he didn't, saying: "Don't ever do this to me in front of the people again!" That is why people admired me, because they thought I had guts, to speak to Karume like that.[29]

Karume the Terrible

Dourado's general reflections on the revolution are in most cases critical, including his memories of Karume's system of corvée labor, which was meant to provide the new regime at almost no cost the labor necessary for its various public works projects. These included the construction of schools, roads, and public housing, as well as labor on state-owned farms. Corvée labor began in 1964 and continued throughout the Karume years. As time went on, the system was institutionalized and dependent on overt coercion. There were both colonial and pre-colonial precedents in Africa for corvée labor; it was also congruent with Eastern bloc economic strategies that promoted group sacrifice and volunteerism, and production over consumption. As Karume ordered citizens to report for labor in the evenings or on weekends, he could be confident he was in line with development strategies employed elsewhere and with alleged success. This was how "more advanced" nations like China and the Soviet Union had achieved their miracles of nation building. Dourado's personal contribution, however, turned out to be minimal:

> They tried once to have me do forced labor along with everyone else in the country. I went on a Sunday to clear the bush with *pangas* [machetes]. For ten days afterwards I was very stiff and sore, so Karume said, "Ah, this is not for you." I never believed, anyway, that the revolution required sacrifice because I was not a revolutionary as such. Ordinary life requires sacrifice; it is not particular to the revolution. I've had to make many sacrifices, and I am no revolutionary.

Dourado also remembers, starting in 1964, the disappearance of shop inventories and years of rampant shortages of rice and other imported consumer items. Such shortages were due to government ineptitude or the result of state attempts to persuade islanders to be more self-

---

29   While this particular incident is not mentioned in other sources, Karume's anti-Asian antipathies are well known. In September 1971 the Revolutionary Council, at Karume's urging, ordered the deportation of 286 Asian families, which was only the latest of Karume's anti-Asian decrees. See Martin 1978: 69.

sufficient.³⁰ Food shortages were most acute in the late 1960s and early 1970s and were only partially ameliorated when in 1969 the regime established a formal system of rationing not seen in Zanzibar since World War II. The history of food rationing and forced labor in Zanzibar has yet to be written, though both provoked frequent comment by journalists, travelers, and diplomats. The following account, written by Philip Ochieng, appeared in the *Tanzanian Standard* on 3 September 1971:

> The islanders ... are heavily engaged in ... building programmes, despite the hungry stomachs and the scenes of starving children and old people unable to stand in the queue.... It is really alarming and shocking that nothing at all is available in Zanzibar. Everywhere you travelled ... you would see long queues, and for what? The answer is rations. If you are a little late you are a loser.... The most pitiable situation ... is the long queues that take place as early as 4 a.m. for bread. Small children are seen crying in these queues as they are often bullied and pushed around by the elders rushing for bread. (quoted in Martin 1978: 62)

Karume was apparently unconcerned that rations and shortages were causing rumblings of discontent:

> Karume would say: "Since when have the *Waswahili* eaten rice?" If that is not contempt, I don't know what is.... Karume put us all on food rations, yet people who were poor would sell their ration cards for sugar, flour, and rice for the money to buy other things. They would just eat cassava, sweet potatoes, maize, and so on. I don't remember any corruption in the rationing system, however. Everything was fixed.

When asked about Karume's positive accomplishments, Dourado had this to say:

> He restored dignity and confidence to the Africans. They were very down on the ladder and he brought them up. Then he preached unity among the different peoples. He said look at Cuba—there are very many different people, but it is one nation. I also look upon these blocks of flats we built during his time as something good. Many say he shouldn't have built them, since they suffer from a shortage of water and electricity, but they were good for the downtrodden.³¹

---

30 For Karume's autarkic economic policies, see Clayton 1981: 134–42.

31 Dourado refers to East German–designed apartment blocks that were mostly constructed in the capital but also on a smaller scale in a few small towns elsewhere in the islands, such as Wete and Makunduchi. For Karume's attempts to bring "modern" housing to low-income Zanzibaris, see Myers 2003.

Karume also tried to provide free medical care, but soon found out that you cannot give away anything for free. And then he harassed the doctors who remained, so many were forced to leave. He also tried to conduct land redistribution, and allocated three-acre plots to individuals, but not all people were farmers, so a lot of land went to waste. And a lot of corruption began when people began to sell their plots.[32] Karume opened up the schools for all, even though as a result the standard of education went down, which is always the case. If you have a little butter and you have to spread it around, then nobody gets very much at all. So after the revolution the government took over the schools and the quality declined. Ali Sultan Issa, as Minister of Education, was the one most responsible for the decline, because he sacked all the good teachers.[33] Gradually they realized free education was not the answer, so now the children pay fees, but only a small amount.

In no way are these assessments unusual for a person of Dourado's generation and background. Those who reject the revolution remember the later years of Karume's rule as a time of widespread hunger and deprivation. And yet in the midst of such austerity the state managed to construct, with citizens' "donated" labor, a series of apartment housing blocks in Kikwajuni, Kilimani, and Michenzani that now dominate the capital's skyline and serve as visible symbols of a regime that did not set out merely to enrich a very few. For some at least, bitter memories of forced labor have gradually given way to a sense of tangible pride.[34]

A recurrent theme of Dourado's recollections is his desire to use whatever influence he had to "moderate" the revolution. Yet he possessed little real leverage over Karume, who could, for example, alter the islands' justice system according to his will. As attorney general, Dourado was forced to simply go along:

> I was actually in a very difficult position. Karume ruled by decree, and I was in charge of writing his decrees. Practically every decree I wrote I did not want to write. Were there any decrees that I was ever proud

---

32 For Karume-era land redistribution policies, see Shao 1992.

33 Ali Sultan Issa served as minister of education in the mid-1960s, and, as a self-identified Maoist and communist, represented something of a nemesis to the more conservative Dourado. For Issa's life story, see Burgess 2009: 29–167.

34 William Bissell observes that while the state constructed new housing, many older neighborhoods of the capital were allowed to languish and collapse into ruin. Still, for some islanders, the new apartments now evoke a positive image of revolutionary era "stability, broad provisions of social welfare, discipline, and basic rights to housing, health, work and wages" (Bissell 2005: 236–37).

of? No, except maybe one on the equality of the people. The decree was something like, "We will create the equality of the people of Zanzibar." But it is impossible to create equality through the law; it is a myth.

Karume had his impulsive ideas. For example, he said to me once, "You should stop women getting pregnant." I said, "Women get pregnant for so many reasons; what do you want?" He said, "You should stop schoolgirls getting pregnant." So I wrote a decree stating that anyone who impregnates a schoolgirl will go to prison, and the girl herself will go to prison. But there was never any enthusiasm for enforcing this law, because it was a violation of human rights.

Karume changed Zanzibar's entire judicial system. The first thing he did was to abolish defense counsels, saying only the rich could afford them, so out went the defense counsels. I put up some sort of defense, saying, "Look, this won't do; this is a violation of human rights not to have a defense counsel." Yet Ali Sultan Issa was the prime mover in removing defense counsels from the judicial system. He accused me of being "a colonial minded Attorney General." When I was hauled before the Revolutionary Council, I said out of frustration to Ali Sultan: "History has proven that persons who create monsters usually have the monsters turn against them." I was in tears, and it happened to Ali Sultan exactly as I said it would. A few years later he was defending himself in court from the accusation of treason, without a defense counsel.[35]

Later Karume appointed men without legal training as judges; he replaced professional bewigged and begowned judges with ordinary laymen. In these circumstances you are bound to have tragedy, yet Karume argued that administering justice was not a difficult thing. So we carried on like that for quite some time, with a bench of three laymen judges, including a chairman. There were no real judges, and no law reports, and not much justice in those courts. The judges thought they were smart, but they were inflicting injustice on those who were brought before them.

I was involved in these cases, though it caused me pain. I'd act as both the prosecution and the defense, and it isn't hard to see the oddity of one attorney acting both parts. In all these cases justice was not completely served.

I thought my role was to moderate the revolution, yet I didn't see any results. I served as Attorney General from 1964 to 1977: thirteen years of gloom and doom, for myself and for all Zanzibaris. I never had any regrets about overthrowing the Sultan, but in the way we changed our legal system. Many times I asked myself: "What is it I am doing?" And an inner voice said, "It will come, it will come." I am not referring to the Holy Ghost per se, or to spirits from outside, just an inner feeling I

---

35 For Issa's account of his own encounters with Karume's People's Courts, see Burgess 2009: 132–41.

had. And slowly I saw that we were turning the corner: less people were brought to court, the police prepared cases more thoroughly, and proper records were kept of their cases, with a stenographer.[36]

None of Dourado's other memories illustrate so well the ambivalent and agonizing nature of his service to a regime for which he had no respect, and that he had little capacity to reform, other than in an often futile attempt to influence Karume's lay judges to enact justice and to follow proper court procedures. Yet it may be asked, was his despair genuine? And was he concerned with questions of complicity? Charles Swift, an American psychologist, provides a revealing snapshot of Dourado from 1969, just as Karume was rolling out his scheme for "People's Courts." Meeting Dourado during one of his professional visits to Zanzibar from his clinical post in Dar es Salaam, Swift noted that the attorney general spoke English with a British accent and wore a jacket and tie, despite the heat. He appeared worried and depressed. Looking "furtively behind him every few minutes," and with many "long, heavy sighs," Dourado confided in Swift that he was facing intense pressure from his own government to formally approve the creation of Karume's People's Courts.[37] Dourado "refused to sign such an order and told me this demand was completely against his whole British legal training. He simply would not legitimize the People's Courts, regardless of the consequences to him personally." Dourado had offered his resignation, which Karume had refused. "Dourado felt he was being used as window dressing, so Karume could say in effect, 'Look, we have an Indian Attorney General and a Christian at that.' With tears in his eyes Dourado declared he would welcome being placed in detention because his present position had become untenable."[38]

Dourado's unprompted confession suggests that he was fully cognizant of the contradictory nature of his position and that Karume was using him to provide his regime a façade of legitimacy.[39] He also knew he faced

---

36 For a description of Karume's system of People's Courts, see Shivji 2008: 110–12; Martin 1978: 64–65; Clayton 1981: 120–1. For a fictionalized portrayal of Zanzibar's system of justice during Karume's reign, see Gurnah 2001: 209–33.

37 This conversation appears to have taken place in September 1969. British-style courts were formally abolished in Zanzibar effective 1 January 1970 (Martin 1978: 64).

38 Swift also wrote, about the conclusion of his professional trips to Zanzibar: "It was such a relief to be back in Dar after two days in Zanzibar; right away I breathed more easily. The atmosphere had been so heavy with suspicion and apprehension.... About the only people who spoke their minds were the patients at the psychiatric hospital" (Swift 2002: 97–98).

39 Dourado said to me: "I was the only one giving any respectability to his [Karume's] government in front of the world."

a choice between compliance with Karume's demands or detention and possibly worse. Convinced his cause was hopeless, Dourado ultimately gave his signature authorizing the formation of People's Courts. This was the culmination of a process underway since 1964 of empowering members of the Revolutionary Council (RC) to function as a "law unto themselves" (Shivji 2008: 111).[40] As a member of the RC from 1964 to 1972, Ali Sultan Issa recalled:

> We ministers in those days could arrest and imprison anyone we wanted. We were representatives of a revolutionary government, after all, so we even had the power to kill. But I did not kill anyone, and I did not abuse my power. Many members of the RC, however, abused their power by putting husbands inside when they wanted to sleep with their wives. Eventually, Karume said, "You can put them inside, but if you want to release them, I need to give my permission." (Burgess 2009: 121)

If Dourado was appalled by Karume's policies and initiatives, he was in no doubt as to their origin. He looked upon Karume's character with considerable contempt:

> Karume was at first a man of the people, but then later on he became violent. Like Lenin, once he obtained power he spat on the people. But having said that, one had to admit that he had a personality. He had deep muddy brown eyes, and if he wanted to he could be very gentle. In the years I worked for him, Karume didn't drink alcohol, and he didn't socialize with anyone. He was incapable of sensible conversation; his conversation was all gruff order—I never heard him speak sensibly. Karume started off a man of the people but once he got power he held the people in contempt....
>
> Though the Americans claimed in their propaganda that we were communists, Karume was not a communist. He would tell [Julius] Nyerere: "Let socialism stay on the outside; here in Zanzibar we will live our own life." And he lived his own life. He flashed around town like a whiz kid, always in a hurry, and because of the fear he might be shot. He had no illusions about his popularity. He saw himself as an unpopular president, and that's why he introduced hardship and repressive laws so that he could continue in power....
>
> His fondness for women made him look like an idiot. He went for sex with young Arab and Persian women in a big way. He would drive to Kibweni Palace with his official car and would park inside the garage there, and they would stop traffic on the whole road while he was shagging. This took place about twice a week, for several years. He

---

40 Shivji also observes that the three figures in government who most often abused their power, by ordering detentions without trial, were Rashid Abdulla, Ahmed Hassan Diria, and Saidi Washoto.

had amazing lusting power! He had pimps going around town rounding up women for him. Women and girls were afraid of going out; they were model Muslim girls who were fearful of such things. Plus he had a beautiful wife in Fatma Karume, and the other girls he would take as wives. One time he broke the law by having five wives, when four was the limit.

Dourado's memories of Karume are illuminating but not unique. Karume's sexual predations are still fairly well known and something of an open secret—although not so much as in the 1960s and 1970s, when the president, in his 60s at the time, employed a man known as "Foum" to drive around the capital every day in search of women and girls, almost always of Arab or South Asian ancestry. Foum would present these unfortunates to Karume at Kibweni Palace, located on the road north of town, on the way toward Bububu (Burgess 2009: 205–6). The total number of those forced to submit to such sexual exploitation is impossible to determine. Most submitted out of fear that he might harm them or people close to them, such as their fathers, brothers, or husbands.

Dourado also remembers Karume's interest in promoting interracial marriages:

One time Karume asked me, "Why don't you take an African girl as a wife? She will like you, and you will enjoy her." Then he made that certain motion with his arm. He was serious; he wanted me to marry, but I already had a wife, and we Catholics cannot marry again. Karume always promoted mixed marriages, so he asked members of the Revolutionary Council to take Persian brides and marry them by force.

Dourado refers to one of Karume's most notorious initiatives, since these "brides" were married against their will and despite their parents' emotional protests. When four Persian teenage girls were taken from their parents' homes by force in September 1970, the abductions became headlines around the world, causing Nyerere considerable embarrassment (Martin 1978: 69–71; Clayton 1981: 123–4). Although he justified the marriages in the name of building interracial harmony and unity, Karume also sought to reverse a long history in East Africa of Arab men marrying and/or sexually exploiting African women. Karume declared in a speech in June 1970: "In colonial times Arabs took African concubines without bothering to marry them. Now that we are in power the shoe is on the other foot."[41] While that was undoubtedly true, the

---

41 *East African Standard*, 5 June 1970.

forced marriages were also merely the public face of what, in Karume's private life, was a long and sordid career of predatory sex, in which his actions are best described as those of a serial rapist. According to Laura Fair, Karume "and numerous members of the Revolutionary Council ... engaged in rape and advocated 'forced marriage' as one means of 'getting back' at families and individuals they viewed as political adversaries. Women's bodies became objects of revolutionary retribution."[42]

Dourado also related a telling anecdote from this period, involving himself, Karume, and Karume's two sons, Amani and Ali. Karume ordered Ali to marry the daughter of Thabit Kombo—for years the secretary general of the ASP and one of Karume's closest political allies. But Ali resisted, and asked Dourado for his opinion on the matter. Dourado responded:

> "Unless you marry of your own free will there is no marriage." Ali then told his father: "Dourado said forced marriages are not real marriages, and I agree with him because he is more educated than you."
>
> Karume immediately told his guards, "Shoot him!" Ali ran away and the guards shot in the air. Karume said to his guards, "Get Dourado also!" Karume's older son Amani was there, who asked his father, "What does poor Dourado have to do with this?" Karume said to his guards, "Take him away also!" So all three of us congregated at Central Prison. When Amani came into the cell he embraced me, and said, "Now we are really brothers." They flogged me in prison until I went unconscious. Amani and Ali were flogged as well, but it was more difficult to knock them out—they were tough characters! We stayed inside for two nights and then were released together.

It is unsurprising, then, that about Karume's assassination in April 1972 Dourado would have this to say:

> I shed no tears when Karume was killed. But there was a certain amount of sadness when I was with him for so long, and knew his weaknesses. I had heard rumors there was going to be a coup, and at 6 PM or so I heard gunfire, and I thought, "Now it is coming." I was at home at the time, and said to Yvonne, "This is it." I told her I was going to momma to tell her to stay at home, and to tell the others to do the same. So I walked

---

42   Fair 2002: 71. In a January 1984 speech to the National Executive Committee of Chama cha Mapinduzi, Tanzania's ruling party, Nyerere cited, along with Karume's assassinations in the forced marriages as one of the issues that most strained his relations with Karume. He related a private conversation in which Karume strongly defended the marriages, saying: "We should reduce these enemies. If we don't reduce them they'll multiply." When Nyerere continued to disagree, Karume asked him why he "loved these people so much." Nyerere's wry response was that it was Karume who was marrying them, not him; Shivji 2008: 218–19.

towards Creek Road, and on the way I saw Karume's car, without his flag flying, but with him in the backseat, leaning way back, and very bloody. My impression was that he was dying.

Most people in town I knew were relieved that Karume was gone, because of all the bloody messes he created, and because of his brutal regime. The Youth League was the most brutal, led by Seif Bakari and Abdul Said Natepe. Others committed the brutalities and Karume was blamed, but Karume was too clever to order someone's execution. He'd order flogging, like my own, and his sons. When people were executed they were killed by Seif Bakari and his gang, including people like Natepe, and Said Washoto, known as "Sweet Willy," a nickname the Goans gave him.[43]

Jumbe the Disagreeable

Aboud Jumbe, Karume's successor, was a well-respected schoolteacher in Zanzibar before independence; he possessed a degree from Makerere University and was known as an ASP moderate. As president he was able to dismantle Karume's extensive, East German–trained security apparatus and network of paid informants. He eviscerated the Youth League, which under its chairman Seif Bakari had served as the state's thuggish enforcing agency. With Nyerere's connivance, Jumbe transferred Bakari to the Tanzanian mainland to become deputy minister of defense in the union government. In general, Jumbe managed to gradually bring an end to an era of violence, fear, and intimidation in the islands. He also ended Karume's system of forced labor and food rationing (though consumer shortages persisted into the early 1980s). Jumbe recruited into government service a number of relatively educated Zanzibaris, who began to supplant those who had enjoyed Karume's favor because of their personal loyalty or their involvement in the 1964 seizure of power. Finally, as a sign of Jumbe's friendship and partnership with Nyerere, as well as a general trend toward revolutionary moderation, Jumbe in 1977 agreed to the merger of the ASP with TANU, mainland Tanzania's ruling party since independence. Although in the long term the merger served to dramatically lessen Zanzibar's autonomy within the Tanzanian

---

43 Karume's assassination was part of a botched coup attempt organized by former members of the Umma Party, which in early 1964 had been forced to merge with the ASP. Convinced the revolution had gone astray and that Karume had lost his popularity among ordinary Zanzibaris, former Umma members thought it would be a relatively easy operation to seize power. They would capture Karume and force him at gunpoint to abdicate over the radio. When their conspiracy was discovered, they decided at the last minute to eliminate Karume instead. For sources on the conspiracy to kill Karume, see Chase 1976: 15–33; Burgess 2009: 136–7; Clayton 1981: 150–3.

union, it helped Jumbe gradually remove revolutionary hardliners from positions of influence in the islands.[44]

Dourado supported some of Jumbe's initiatives, as told in the following account:

> As president, Jumbe did some very good things. He ended the terror of the Youth League. Jumbe was addressing the crowds at the Golf Club once when my wife Yvonne was slow in standing to show her respect. The Youth League noticed this and rounded her up and took her to the Youth League headquarters, and I had to get her out of there. I told Jumbe what happened and he sacked the people involved.

Most of Dourado's recollections of Jumbe, however, are less flattering. They are not so much comments on the worthiness of his policies as they are offered as insights into the president's personality, which he considers a topic of self-evident historical significance:

> Jumbe was a very difficult person to get on with; no one could get on with him well. Everything Jumbe did included a nook and a cushion, where he could relax and build himself up, without disturbance. But he was not corrupt. I still say this today: he was not corrupt. He was very ambitious; he wanted to be president of Tanzania.
>
> Jumbe was very intelligent, but drinks dimmed his intelligence. He was a heavy drinker even in colonial times. When he was a schoolteacher I used to see him carried to his house dead drunk. His wife would come to the door and take charge. He was a drunkard also as a minister in Karume's government. I would be sitting and drinking in the Starehe Club and he would come over and booze with me for a while and then he would say, "Come to my house for some more drinks," and I had no choice, I had to follow. We did this about once a week, and I would be unsteady for a few days afterwards. But for him, once the fog disappeared and the hangover was over he would be all right.[45]
>
> I didn't mind that he drank, but he used to take my bottles away from me. I would make a lot of noise, insulting and abusing him when he tried to take my drinks, and he would just say, "Come on, you earn enough to afford it." So even though we drank together we were not good friends, because all that existed between us were quarrels and arguments. He would create big rows, and the noise would reach the president's house. Karume would haul us before him, and say to Jumbe: "Stop this childish behavior!" But he let him do what he wanted.

---

44 For accounts of Jumbe's reforms of the mid-1970s, see Shivji 2008: 143–201; Bakari 2001: 112–16.

45 Both Ali Sultan Issa and Seif Sharif Hamad related to me very similar accounts of Jumbe's dependence on alcohol, which he managed to end when assuming the presidency.

Before he was president he was a drunkard and a screwer; after he became president he stopped drinking but he continued to screw. So the common factor was that he was a screwer. Jumbe was arrogant, conceited, and a hell of a drunkard, but now he has given all that up, and is living a life, as he would see it, of piety.

Despite an apparently fraught relationship, Jumbe and Dourado managed to collaborate in the early 1980s on a groundbreaking attempt to restructure Tanzania's union government in order to ensure greater Zanzibari autonomy, an effort that made both men vulnerable to the charge of treason. Jumbe and Dourado hoped to pressure or persuade Nyerere and his many supporters in the ruling party on the mainland to replace the two-government system in place since April 1964 (in which the bureaucracy in Zanzibar retained authority over most domestic matters while conceding sovereignty and control of foreign affairs to a union government, which also governed the mainland) with a three-government system, in which the mainland would obtain its own separate government and the domain of union affairs would be strictly curtailed. In 1983 this was a new and radical idea, worked out between Dourado, Jumbe, and a Ghanaian lawyer named Bashir Swanzy, then serving as attorney general in Zanzibar. Dourado made his views on the union known when he gave a public presentation in Dar es Salaam at the Tanganyika Law Society, in which he reported, among other things, that as Zanzibar's attorney general in 1964, he had oddly been excluded from the drafting of the original union agreement.[46] Then, directing his comments to Nyerere personally, he importuned the president to hear his "earnest, passionate, and sincere appeal" for "an association of equal partners in a Federation" (Peter and Othman 2006: 108).

For Dourado, these were exhilarating times:

> I had a linen shirt once that said "Napoleon" across the chest. It was sky blue, with white letters. I bought the shirt on the street and I had a tailor sew the word "Napoleon" on the front. It was to provoke Nyerere, as a message to him to not interfere in Zanzibar, because Napoleon was here. I wore it many times and people called me "Nap." … People passed me in the street, giving me their support. I had my Napoleon shirt and I flaunted it…. I saw myself to be the savior of Zanzibar.

In recalling his attempts to reshape the Tanzanian union, Dourado's view of history as a drama of personalities comes through loud and clear. Nyerere "was a prize fighter. He never knew he met his match, and

---

46 This paper has been reprinted in Peter and Othman 2006: 73–108.

I took him on!" Jumbe, on the other hand, wouldn't take a public stand in opposition to Nyerere or the union:

> Jumbe would never honestly fight for the truth. He was always in the background. For example, he knew that I was honestly struggling for Zanzibar's autonomy, yet when Nyerere challenged him on this issue he ditched me, as if he knew nothing about our struggle… . I was the only one to tell Nyerere he was the one to be blamed for the problems in our union. Nyerere wanted to swallow Zanzibar, and make it a region of Tanganyika.

When Jumbe was forced in January 1984 to stand trial in front of Tanzania's ruling party's national executive committee, and to answer the charge of treason, one of the allegations against him was that he had done nothing to contain "Dourado's outbursts against the union" (Shivji 2008: 216). Jumbe denied he instigated a plot to undermine the union, yet when presented with overwhelming evidence he was forced to resign from government. Dourado, for his part, was imprisoned for three and a half months.[47]

Needless to say, such activities mark Dourado as a hero to a younger generation of Zanzibari nationalists, who since the 1990s have likewise called for a three-government system. While this essay is not so much about popular memories of Wolfango Dourado as it is his own memories of the revolution, it deserves comment that Dourado's early criticisms of Nyerere and his calls for reform of the Tanzanian union have earned him lasting acclaim, at least in Zanzibar and within the global Goan community.

Soon after Jumbe's forced resignation in 1984 and his own release from prison the same year, Dourado could derive some satisfaction from the disappearance of one component of the revolution after another. Karume's People's Courts were abolished; Zanzibar received a new constitution, and saw the end of shortages of food and other essentials. The 1990s saw significant overseas capitalist investment in the islands' tourist economy and Zanzibar's first (failed) attempts since 1963 to stage free and fair multiparty elections. While Zanzibar's government still celebrated the revolution as the birth of a new and more egalitarian

---

47   The best source on the attempt by Jumbe, Swanzi, and Dourado to reshape the union and Jumbe's subsequent fall from power is Shivji 2008: 205-25. See also Throup 1988: 186-8; Burgess 2009: 232-6. For Jumbe's perspective on the Tanzanian union, see Jumbe 1994.

society, many of Karume's initiatives were all but forgotten, or quietly abandoned.[48]

Dourado could take personal satisfaction in the general exhaustion of revolutionary sensibilities, and—after his elevation to the post of deputy chief justice—in an attempted reform of Zanzibar's justice system to a rough approximation of the procedures and principles he embraced as a law student in London in the 1950s. He could note that he was not such a political dinosaur after all; suddenly, after the end of the Cold War, a new world was speaking the language of human rights, a language he had been uttering all along. Nor did he have to feel so continually compromised by his service to administrations that, while able and willing to steal elections, were far more circumscribed than in the days when Karume ruled by decree. Nor did Dourado's idea of a three-government system die on the vine. After years of debate, Tanzania is now in the process, at the moment of writing, of adopting a new constitution, in which versions of the three-government system are being seriously discussed without the taint of treason.[49]

A dedicated civil servant until the end, Dourado never entered the political fray, and never participated in the islands' public reckoning with its troubled revolutionary past. With Yvonne's assistance he commenced work in 2009 on a memoir, a project that unfortunately remained incomplete at the time of his death in 2012.[50]

Conclusion

Dourado remembered the revolution primarily as a morality tale and drama of personalities. With great vividness he recalled his troubled relations with a cast of powerful figures—deeply flawed men whose vices and impulses often came at the expense of ordinary islanders. Dourado considered Karume as unscrupulous in private as he was in public; his service to the regime therefore represented a conundrum of continual compromise. Emerging from this ordeal was a strong sense of self, in which Dourado was both the *mouse* that roared, and the mouse that *roared*. The question naturally arises of how many other

---

48   Of course Karume has had a lasting legacy, particularly in the realm of housing, land redistribution, and in the Arab and South Asian exodus from the islands.

49   Had Dourado lived only a few years longer, he would have taken great satisfaction in these debates. For a brief memorial, written after Dourado's passing, see http://www.goanvoice.ca/2012/issue07/peopleplacesthings.htm#ppt_3.

50   Given my long-term absences from the islands, I was unable to render any major assistance in this effort.

Zanzibaris found the revolution so formative—how many other selves did it produce?

In constructing his memories of the past, Dourado offered an explicit commentary on the personal qualities of those whom he served and who did so much to shape Zanzibar in its age of revolution. Yet he did not remember the revolution solely in terms of the moral codes, or lack thereof, of the people it empowered. He was a trained lawyer, not a minister, and so his memories also reflect a liberal worldview that he appears to have embraced more or less continuously from the 1950s forward. Thus, in addition to his tales of excess, he also assessed the regime in terms of its adherence to, or violation of, abstract liberal governing principles. While he reflected upon the worthiness of a series of state initiatives of the 1960s and 1970s, he was perhaps most attuned to the revolution's impact on Zanzibar's justice system. This was his realm of professional expertise.

Dourado could not have found life utterly unbearable during the revolution. He was neither poor nor malnourished; and he was Jumbe's reluctant drinking partner, after all. Not personally suffering the worst the regime had to offer, Dourado was able to assess the revolution as an assault not so much on himself or even the Goan community but on the shared values and institutions that, in his eyes, had once made Zanzibar a wonderful place to live. These aspects of Dourado's recollections raise interesting questions: Can liberalism command its own memories? Can it shape perceptions of the past? And, if so, from whence does it come? Was Dourado's liberalism intrinsic to his Goan identity, or did it come from his embrace of a creed aspiring to universalism? Or did it emerge from a relationship between the two?

References

Aminzade, Ronald

2013 *Race, Nation, and Citizenship in Post-Colonial Africa: The Case of Tanzania*. Cambridge: Cambridge University Press.

Bakari, Mohammed

2001 *The Democratisation Process in Zanzibar: A Retarded Transition*. Hamburg: Institut für Afrika-Kunde.

al-Barwani, Ali Muhsin

1997 *Conflicts and Harmony in Zanzibar: Memoirs*. Dubai: n.p.

Bissell, William Cunningham

2011 *Urban Design, Chaos, and Colonial Power in Zanzibar*. Bloomington, Ind.: Indiana University Press.

2005 "Engaging Colonial Nostalgia." *Cultural Anthropology* 20(2): 215–48.

Brennan, James

2012 *Taifa: Making Nation and Race in Urban Tanzania*. Columbus, Ohio: Ohio University Press.

Burgess, G. Thomas

2010 "Memories, Myths, and Meanings of the Zanzibari Revolution." In *War and Peace in Africa: History, Nationalism and the State*, ed. Toyin Falola and Raphael Chijioke Njoku, 429–450, Durham, N.C.: Carolina Academic Press.

2009 *Race, Revolution, and the Struggle for Human Rights in Zanzibar: The Memoirs of Ali Sultan Issa and Seif Sharif Hamad*. Athens, Ohio: Ohio University Press.

Burke, Peter

1989 "History as Social Memory." In *Memory: History, Culture and the Mind*, ed. Thomas Butler, 97–113. Oxford: Basil Blackwell.

Chase, Hank

1976 "The Zanzibar Treason Trial." *Review of African Political Economy* 6, May–August: 14–33.

Clayton, Anthony

1981 *The Zanzibari Revolution and Its Aftermath*. London: C. Hurst & Company.

Fair, Laura

2002 "'It's Just No Fun Anymore': Women's Experiences of Taarab before and after the 1964 Zanzibar Revolution." *International Journal of African Historical Studies* 35(1): 61–81.

Frenz, Margret

2014 *Community, Memory, and Migration in a Globalizing World: The Goan Experience, c. 1890–1980*. New Delhi: Oxford University Press.

Glassman, Jonathon

2011 *War of Words, War of Stones: Racial Thought and Violence in Colonial Zanzibar*. Bloomington, Ind.: Indiana University Press.

Gurnah, Abdulrazak

2005 *Desertion*. New York: Pantheon.

2001 *By the Sea*. New York: The New Press.

Gurnah, Ahmed

1997 "Elvis in Zanzibar." In *The Limits of Globalization: Cases and Arguments*, ed. Alan Scott, 117–19. London: Routledge.

Jumbe, Aboud

1994 *The Partnership: Tanganyika-Zanzibar Union: 30 Turbulent Years*. Dar es Salaam: Amana Publishers.

Lofchie, Michael F.

1972 "Was Okello's Revolution a Conspiracy?" In *Socialism in Tanzania*, vol. 1: *Politics*, ed. Lionel Cliffe and John Saul. Nairobi: East African Publishing House.

1965 *Zanzibar: Background to Revolution*. Princeton, N.J.: Princeton University Press.

Malkki, Liisa

1995 *Purity and Exile: Violence, Memory, and National Cosmology among Hutu Refugees in Tanzania*. Chicago: University of Chicago Press.

Mapuri, Omar R.

1996 *Zanzibar: The 1964 Revolution: Achievements and Prospects*. Dar es Salaam: TEMA Publishers.

Martin, Esmond B.

1978 *Zanzibar: Tradition and Revolution*. London: Hamish Hamilton.

Mwanjisi, R. K.

1967 *Ndugu Abeid Amani Karume*. Nairobi: East African Publishing House.

Myers, Garth A.

2003 *Verandahs of Power: Colonialism and Space in Urban Africa*. Syracuse, N.Y.: Syracuse University Press.

1999 "Colonial Discourse and Africa's Colonized Middle: Ajit Singh's Architecture." *Historical Geography* 27: 27–55.

Okello, John

1967 *Revolution in Zanzibar*. Nairobi: East African Publishing House.

Peter, Chris, and Haroub Othman, eds.

2006 *Zanzibar and the Union Question*. Zanzibar: Zanzibar Legal Services Centre.

Petterson, Don

2002 *Revolution in Zanzibar: An American's Cold War Tale*. Boulder, Colo.: Westview Press.

Prins, A. H. J.

1967 *The Swahili Speaking Peoples of Zanzibar and the East African Coast*. London: International African Institute.

Shao, Ibrahim Fokas

1992 *The Political Economy of Land Reform in Zanzibar*. Dar es Salaam: Dar es Salaam University Press.

Sheriff, Abdul, and Ed Ferguson, eds.

1991 *Zanzibar under Colonial Rule*. London: James Currey.

Shivji, Issa

2008 *Pan-Africanism or Pragmatism? Lessons of Tanganyika-Zanzibar Union*. Dar es Salaam: Mkuki na Nyota.

Swift, Charles

2002 *Dar Days: The Early Years in Tanzania*. New York: University Press of America.

Throup, David

1988 "Zanzibar after Nyerere." In *Tanzania after Nyerere*, ed. Michael Hodd, 186–8. London: Printer Publishers.

Zanzibar Government

1968 *Speeches of Their Excellencies the President of Tanzania and the First Vice-President on the Fourth Anniversary of the Zanzibar Revolution, 12 January 1968*. Zanzibar: Government Printer.

Chapter Five

"For Us It's What Came After": Locating Pemba in Revolutionary Zanzibar

Nathalie Arnold Koenings

With plentiful hilly land perfectly suited to the clove tree, Pemba Island was, from the mid-19th century well into the 20th, the primary source of wealth, first for the Sultanate of Zanzibar and then for the British Protectorate established over "Zanzibar and Pemba" in 1890. Despite being smaller than Zanzibar's other major island (Unguja),[1] Pemba has also historically been home to close to half of the isles' population. Yet in much of the historiography Pemba is rarely mentioned; when the island does appear, it is often as something of a side-note.

With the remarkable exceptions of J. E. E. Craster's detailed and affectionate 1913 book *Pemba: The Spice Island of Zanzibar*, important portions of W. H. Ingrams's work, and Esmond Martin's account of a visit to Pemba in the mid-1970s, Pemba has until recently either been curiously absent from much of the literature or has functioned as something of a question mark.[2] When the island has appeared, it has most often been depicted as a verdant and unruly hinterland populated by willfully conservative, "backward," inward-looking people whose tight-knit communities stubbornly lag behind the (political and cultural) times.[3] Yet political events in 20th and 21st century Zanzibar have repeatedly shown that Pemba and Pembans—and the *idea* of these—have played a significant, and significantly vexed, role both in Zanzibar's recent past and in popular imaginings of its potential future.

---

1   The areas of Unguja and Pemba are, respectively, 642 and 381 square miles.

2   A highly welcome recent work is Elisabeth McMahon's *Slavery and Emancipation in Islamic East Africa: From Honor to Respectability*, a detailed examination of the process of abolition in Pemba, published in 2013.

3   The mid-1980s saw the first return of western researchers to Pemba Island (Linda Giles), a shift that intensified in the 1990s with the work of anthropologists and historians beginning to approach questions of Pemban history and cultural life from a variety of lenses (among others, Adria LaViolette, Helle Goldman, Jeffrey Fleisher, Bruce McKim, myself, Elisabeth McMahon, and Justin Beckham).

This chapter explores the idea that Pembans' relationships to and roles in Zanzibar's recent political history have perhaps until this decade hinged on Pembans' place in and experiences of the Zanzibar revolution of 11–12 January 1964, which was neither initiated nor initially carried out on Pemba. Indeed, the revolution erupted on Unguja, and only when Unguja was secured were its "lessons" brought to the "other" island.

The story of the Zanzibar revolution has in East Africa often been told primarily in official venues, and almost always from the perspective of the revolution's major players or supporters. Official narratives have also, perhaps necessarily, focused primarily on Unguja, understood to be the "fount" of revolution and certainly the site of its initial events. In public contexts in Zanzibar, the official vision of the revolution has since 1964 most often been conveyed as a single, overdetermined narrative with little room for the unpredictable poetics of any one ordinary person's particular experience—let alone for open expressions of ambivalence, loss, or grief.

While in recent decades scholarly and more popular works have begun to reverse this trend (Ghassany 2010; Glassman 2011; Haj 2001), and, in recent years, some contemporary Zanzibari politicians have intentionally set about "reclaiming" the revolution on behalf of all of Zanzibar's diverse constituencies,[4] much remains to be heard and said about how the revolution actually unfolded and what its legacies on the (many) ground(s) have been; this may be particularly the case for Pemba Island, which for many decades afterward (and, in certain contexts, to the present day) continued to occupy its longstanding role of "backwater" or "nether land," despite having become densely militarized and the target of concerted state activity in the wake of the revolution. Pemba today remains a part of the "nation" the particulars of whose 20th-century material conditions and popular imagination(s) have yet to be firmly enfolded into the general, public history of "Zanzibar."

This chapter's ultimate goal is to describe recurring features of Pemban experiences of the revolution and the years that followed it. The topics of analytical concern are these: the revolution's effects on Pemban

---

4   Prominent political figures deploying historical narratives in new ways include the first vice president of Zanzibar, Seif Sharif Hamad; an original Revolutionary Council member and the first minister of education under the Revolutionary Government, Hassan Nassor Moyo; the Stone Town representative to the Zanzibar House of Representatives Ismail Jussa; and the former Kiembe Samaki representative Mansour Yusuf (son of the now-deceased Committee of Fourteen member Yusuf Himid), famously thrown out of the Revolutionary Party (CCM) in August 2013 for supporting constitutional reforms calling for greater autonomy for Zanzibar and detained in August 2014.

adult bodies, pre-revolutionary modes of knowledge and authority, and the Pemban landscape; and the theatrical, performative dimensions of revolutionary "education" as carried out in Pemba. But, first, it is useful to contextualize Pemba both in the administrative entity "Zanzibar" over time and in the historiography, where alternating constructions of Pemba and Pembans as either absent or as fundamentally "other" have been remarkably stable features. As in other contexts where agency, identity, and collective futures are at play, it is grounding to begin with the question of names and naming, since it is naming that brings things into being in both time and space (that is, in "history" and "nation").

Pemba in "Zanzibar"—Named/Not Named, There/Not There

Throughout the variegated histories of the East African coast and the Indian Ocean, the term *Zanzibar* has been a constant. But the specific lands to which the name refers have historically been many and unfixed. *Zanzibar* has at different moments referred to an area stretching from Mogadishu to Sofala, westward well into the Congo, northeast to Oman, and to a coastal littoral encompassing a shifting group of islands whose fortunes fluctuated along with the relations of the many Swahili city-states across the coast to each other and to the Portuguese, Mazrui, Muscatis, and Omanis.

Unguja Island has formally been considered part of the area known as Zanzibar since at least 1698, and what is important for us here is that Pemba came under Busaid rule much later than Unguja. After intermittent periods of Portuguese rule and allegiance to Mombasa, Pemba came under Busaid control only in 1823, just 17 years before Seyyid bin Sultan transferred his court from Muscat to Zanzibar town. Although the area known as the Sultanate of Zanzibar had in the past encompassed major areas of East Africa, under the Heligoland-Zanzibar Treaty of 1890, the British established their authority solely over "Zanzibar and Pemba," with *Zanzibar*, here, referring explicitly to Unguja Island. While the unit was often referred to by civil servants and other residents as "the Zanzibar Protectorate" or "the Protectorate of Zanzibar," the title "the Protectorate of Zanzibar and Pemba" does appear in British reports and in the press of the day as the protectorate's full name.

The distinguishing of, or insistence on, *Pemba* in the appellation "Protectorate of Zanzibar and Pemba" is useful to consider here. The longer name does at least two things. First, it recognizes Pemba's importance as a distinct or distinctive part of the sultanate. Second, it conceptually *separates* Pemba from the entity *Zanzibar*. Although the word *Zanzibar* had originally referred to a much larger territory, including but not synonymous with Unguja, the title "Protectorate of Zanzibar and Pemba"—the pairing of *two units* in the name of a polity now principally composed of *two islands*—effectively laid the groundwork for future bureaucratic and political elision of Unguja with the entity *Zanzibar*, and for the ambiguity of Pemba's place within it. When viewed with 21st-century hindsight, the longer title can give one the impression that, unless specifically identified and insisted upon as part of the larger entity *Zanzibar*, Pemba could, with a nudge, or by being forgotten (or by forgetting itself), somehow slide right off the map.

The independent sultanate that came into being in December 1963 accepted the elision of Unguja with *Zanzibar* (indeed all the trappings of Zanzibari power had been built and concentrated on Unguja) but insisted on the full name: the short-lived state was formally known as the "Sultanate of Zanzibar and Pemba." The 1964 revolution established the People's Republic of Zanzibar and Pemba, but, after the union with Tanganyika, the words *and Pemba* disappeared from common and official parlance, and, over time, popular use of the term *Zanzibar* increasingly tended to equate the new nation in its totality with Unguja Island, with Pemba remaining to the side, as an afterthought or question.

Of course, Pemba was under the new government's jurisdiction. There is no question that the administrative entity *Zanzibar* included both islands (as well as several smaller ones that are part of the archipelago). And, since 1872, when a hurricane decimated clove plantations on Unguja, Pemba has produced by far the great majority of Zanzibar's cloves; even as plantations in the 1970s and 1980s became overgrown and overall less productive, Pemba cloves would continue to supply the bulk of the polity's foreign-exchange earnings until late in the 20th century.[5] In economic terms, Pemba was and would remain essential. But, conceptually, the shift in name—from "Zanzibar and Pemba" to "Zanzibar" alone—signals the drawing of Pemba and its people into a discursive, political, and historical bind: there, and yet not named; deeply affected by the events that brought the new Zanzibar into being, yet most implicated in the nation's origin myth by their very *absence* from its decisive moment.

---

5   This state of affairs has caused considerable rancor among Pembans, many of whom feel that benefits accruing from the sale of Pemban cloves have been unfairly hoarded in Unguja.

Today, the largest and most populous islands in post-revolutionary Zanzibar are still Unguja and Pemba. But Pemba's place in the larger entity *Zanzibar* has continued to be uncertain: in the ordinary speech of East Africans and many Zanzibaris themselves, as well as in much academic and official literature, the terms *Unguja* and *Zanzibar* are often used interchangeably and synonymously, as if Pemba were not there or as if it were not fully part of Zanzibar. Allowing that discursive habits can easily double for a kind of epistemological reckoning—where *Zanzibar* often serves as a synonym for the island of Unguja—a question arises: How, in official narratives and public discourse about *Zanzibar*, are Pemban histories, memories, and collective forms of agency to be located and described?

Intimate, local, regional, and national identities are configured by language and silence both, and these have concrete effects: material corollaries that continually affirm and reinscribe the language that both names and realizes them. Naturally, Pemba's relative absence from much of the literature and, in the long and recent past, from open political discourse, does not mean that Pemba (as place or as idea) has been irrelevant to constructions of Zanzibari identity or to Zanzibar's political history. Rather, as Pemba's peculiarly imagined character (simultaneously present and absent, both marginal and central) demonstrates, absences and silence, together with a certain flattening, can exert important structuring force, both in politics as such and in the daily discursive work of ordinary speakers whose ways of saying and seeing continually serve to bring both themselves and their societies into being. This paper proceeds from an assumption established over my nearly 20 years' ethnographic work in Zanzibar: that because of this "discursive bind," any account of "Pemba" or of "Pembans" as such is in fact unfortunately *politicized* from the outset.

When Pemba's There: Geographic Terms

While it would not be very difficult to emphasize the similarities between the islands of Unguja and Pemba[6], the typical historiographic construction of Pemba Island has been as fundamentally, even as

---

6   One could note, for example, that, even if on Unguja the richest land now sits beneath a sprawling capital city and an attendant dense network of roads, both islands have fertile western sides; or the fact that, until the hurricane of 1872, plantations on Unguja, too, produced a significant share of cloves. Recent government policies have focused on encouraging the planting of new trees all over the islands but with special emphasis on Unguja (*Zanzinews* 2015).

"naturally," different from Unguja. The citing of differences usually begins with a contrast in topography. Overwhelmingly rural, with good soil and well-watered valleys, Pemba was suited to the cultivation of many crops, including, crucially, rice. Throughout the 18th century, Pemba Island was Mombasa's granary. In the 19th century, its agricultural products came to sustain the Omani sultanate whose capital had recently moved to Unguja. In Arabic, Pemba was called *Al Jazeera Al Khadra*: "The Green Island." But the construction of Pemba as distinct from Unguja (and therefore as sometimes even distinct from the entity *Zanzibar*) goes, literally, to the bedrock.

Itself a complex cultural construction, geographic knowledge nonetheless has important political implications. In geological terms, since the turn of the 19th century, Unguja has been thought to have separated from the African mainland in the more recent Pleistocene era, and Pemba millions of years earlier, in Miocene times. The idea— that the very matter underlying Unguja Island was "naturally" and from prehistory linked to the mainland in a way Pemba was not—is powerful; its legacy can be easily be tracked through 20th- and 21st-century imaginings of the islands' respective "places" and the relationships between them.

The 1926 scientific report of government geologist G. M. Stockley doubles, very probably innocently, as both grim history and political foreshadowing. Stockley documents not only Unguja's close geological connection to the African mainland (and Pemba's lack of same) but also the great depth of the waters between Unguja and Pemba Islands, dangerous waters he refers to as "The Pemba Trough." For readers already familiar with Pemba's political fortunes in the late 20th and early 21st centuries, the passage below, worth quoting at length, has a chilling quality:

> At a glance, the isolation of Pemba is apparent. The fifty and one hundred fathom lines leave the coast of East Africa south of Pangani, and enclose Zanzibar [Unguja], returning to the coast near Dar-es-Salaam. Thus by the fifty fathom line *Zanzibar is joined to the coast*. [Whereas] *Pemba and its islets are completely isolated*.... In comparison with the Zanzibar Channel, the Pemba Channel is *a deep gorge with steep sides*.... These facts suggest that at one time Zanzibar Island was *more intimately connected with the mainland than Pemba*. They also suggest *either that Pemba had no connection with East Africa and Zanzibar, or that a separation was brought about by some structural dislocation*. (1–2; emphasis added)

What is important here is that differences between the islands' geological origins, described in 1926, were poised to fortify and later naturalize the political ideas that would emerge in the years leading to independence and that have continued to significantly underwrite political discourse in Zanzibar today. Pemba's original relationship to "Africa" is suspect; it may have geological origins in the "Arabian" peninsula; passage from one island to the other requires crossing a deep "divide;"[7] and Pemba's particular position in relation to the entity "Zanzibar" may be due to some kind of natural "error," a "structural dislocation." Whatever geological events may have brought Pemba into being, it is not too difficult to view certain political actions, such as revolutionary activity on Pemba, and later violence associated with elections and directed with particular intensity at Pembans, as repeated attempts to undo the original "dislocation" – either to "educate" Pembans such that they enter "the fold," or to clearly locate Pembans outside of "Zanzibar" and to "put them in their place" (see Arnold 2003). But environmental determinism as political theory should in all cases be suspect; when juxtaposed with the highly polarizing political discourse of the early 1960s, the construction of Pemba as "naturally" distinct ought to give us pause.

Pemban Social Organization

Although constructed as different in key ways from Unguja, Pemba prior to the revolution was arguably typical of the Swahili communities, as described by scholars, of Mombasa and Lamu and of "the Swahili coast" more generally. On Pemba, the famously "absorptive" qualities of Swahili coastal culture—those of an Indian Ocean society in which a stranger can, through conversion to Islam, the cementing of social ties through collaborative or supplicant labor, marriage, or even outright purchase of a tribal name—are reputed, both in Pemban accounts and in the scholarly literature, to have meaningfully obtained. "Pemba changes you" (*Pemba peremba*), the saying goes, and longtime socially engaged residence on the island was reportedly in reality enough to set some on the path to belonging.

---

7   This last is certainly tragically true. Waves in the Pemba Channel can reach more than ten feet in height, and, as recent ferry sinkings attest, it is likely that, over the years, thousands of people attempting the crossing have drowned. For many today, the passage is marked by fear, and real discomfort at the rough seas; at the critical time, ferry crews pass out plastic bags in case passengers feel—as many do—physically sick. In anthropological terms, the crossing between Unguja and Pemba is one through a dangerous, threatening, liminal space, to an entirely "other" locale or "condition."

In Pemban popular discourse, before the revolution, Pemban communities appear crucially *different* from the more unequal and varied groups then comprising the more obviously mixed and vexed population of Unguja in 1963—where, as many have written, Muscatis supported by the sultanate had violently wrested fertile land from local inhabitants, establishing plantations with slave and later migrant labor, and where the busy harbor trade increasingly relied on the presence of landless urban workers.[8]

In Pemba, it is frequently said (by Pembans and scholars of Zanzibar both) that land was neither stolen nor colonized but *given;* one gets the impression both from popular memory and sociological accounts that land was in fact plentiful (Middleton 1961; Lofchie 1965; Sultan and Sharif in Burgess 2009); and that the production of cloves (with attendant ownership of trees) was carried out by more recent arrivals *as well as* by Pemba's local inhabitants, most of whom owned trees and who themselves (like inhabitants of Unguja) were already of mixed African/ Indian Ocean/Shirazi ancestry. Accounts of Arab arrivals in Pemba feature the gradual, intermittent appearance of individuals—often penniless young Omani men who, one by one, formed relationships with locals, worked the land, and eventually acquired their own property by marrying local women and, through the performance and cementing of shared social, religious, and economic ties, over time became Pemban themselves.

While in Pemba varied axes of identity did of course exist, these operated in some contexts but not in others, and it seems that there really was in Pemba, overall, an often meaningful, functional sense of shared identity; even the most skeptical would be wrong to downplay its significance.[9] The often-made, eventually violently crucial distinction between "Arabs" and "Africans" that was so salient on Unguja was not paralleled in Pemba, where, while certainly people did (and do) actively reckon their own and others' descent, the category "Pemban," often hinging on deep knowledge of the several Pemban variants of spoken

---

8   Adam Shafi Adam's novel *Kuli* effectively dramatizes the important role of dockworkers in spreading class and racial consciousness as well as adult literacy in Unguja.

9   This claim was continually made during my fieldwork in 1995 and 1998–2000. It constituted an orienting assumption, a "given," in Pembans' reflections on their own identity as distinct from their perceptions of people from Unguja. For further discussion of the construction of Pemban identity in Pemba, see Vallborg 1996; Arnold 2003.

Kiswahili and of the Pemban landscape,[10] was often more important than any other. Even in Pemba's occult realm, Gining'i, which both reflects and is coterminous with the ordinary, visible world,[11] people across ethnic categories—"Swahilis," "Shirazis," "WaSharifu," "Arabs," "Asians," and occasionally even the British[12]—were reported to work together to ensure social cohesion and prosperity for Pemba as a whole in the world of "real" affairs.[13] In some ways, then, it is not Pemba that presents a marked contrast to "Zanzibar/Unguja" (these days often understood in the West to represent the epitome of Swahili culture) but rather that Unguja—with its history of violent land-grabs by newcomers, ostentatious displays of presumed superiority by a highly visible elite surrounding the royal court, a growing concentration of ex-slaves and migrant laborers, and, overall, a population increasingly attuned to the language of labor, race, and originary Africanity—was perhaps a special case.

The Time of Satiety "Before": Pemba in the 1950s

In popular oral histories, Pembans in the 1950s are generally described as industrious, prosperous people, passionately engaged in silviculture, animal husbandry, farming, fishing, hunting, and a range of highly developed leisure activities. Despite the lingering effects and only recent passing of the rationing and Plant More Food campaigns that had come with World War II, the Pemba of the 1950s is presented in diverse residents' accounts as a providentially prosperous place. Brought about by a rise in the world price of cloves, Pemba's wealth at the time was enviable. In one season, famously known as *mwaka wa kilo* ("the year

---

10   For a detailed discussion of the kinds of geographic/environmental and linguistic knowledge required for a "respectable" claim to "Pemban-ness," see Arnold 2003.

11   Gining'i, located in Chambaani in southern Pemba, is the headquarters of occult activity on the island; it is thus the "capital city" of an important Pemban realm—the invisible world, which, just like its visible counterpart, thrums with life, alliances and competition, labor, conflict and celebration, as well as with the tedious minutiae of accounting and the payment of dues. In Gining'i, qualified Pembans—adults whose senses are especially keen, and who are well versed in the Pemban occult arts—make deals and decisions that have effects on the visible world and its ordinary inhabitants. Arguably like Freemasons, Pemban occult experts belong to a secret, highly ritualized fraternity whose members, in the visible world, often occupy positions of authority. For more on these issues, see Arnold 2003.

12   W. H. Ingrams provided a detailed account of his own initiation into the occult organization. See Ingrams 1931: 467–468.

13   People said or known to be descended from slaves also participated in Gining'i's affairs. Admittedly, however, I heard of no clearly mainland-associated "Wanyamwezi" involvement in this specifically "Pemban" world.

of the kilo"), a common rural hyperbole from people across ethnic and occupational categories was, "We had so much cash that season that we used bills to wipe our sweat." (More cosmopolitan versions of the saying were: we "lit our cigarettes" or "wiped the *halua*[14] from our fingers" with it.)

Pembans from both rural and urban areas recall the island in those days as a thoroughly "modern" place, and themselves as "moving with the times"—an impression that in the 1990s remained bright in elders' minds. The landscape was at last significantly electrified (on Unguja, electricity had been in place since the 1930s) and graced by graded roads; world-renowned musicians such as Umm Kulthum came to perform (not in what are now Pemba's principal towns of Mkoani, Chake Chake, and Wete but in places like Kengeja, which is now clearly "off the beaten path"); once a week, ships from Britain and airplanes from Kenya brought exotic fruits and ice cream; at least one Pemban businessman drove around the island in a Jaguar sports car; in the major towns, several cinemas showed international films to packed houses; Pembans in fashionable hats and gowns spent evenings by the Chake Chake creek dancing to big band music[15]; and, during the clove season, all manner of goods, including French perfume and Scottish shortbread, could be found in even the smallest and most remote of places. Clove-owning and clove-trading families sent their children to study abroad; maulids and traditional dance events were elaborate and could last for days; intellectual and creative life was rich; and all kinds of spiritual and occult activity (which naturally require funds) were thriving. Much of the decade leading up to Independence was, by most accounts, marked by generalized, providentially sanctioned abundance and satiety.

The rural Pemban concept of "satiety" is *shibe* (from the month of *Shabaan*; also in the verb *ku-shiba*, "to be satisfied/well-filled"), and since for many Pembans the revolution ushered in a period that for decades epitomized the precise opposite of *shibe* (see below), the concept is worth describing here.[16] In a time of *shibe*, people have everything

---

14   *Halua* is an expensive local delicacy associated with religious events and times of celebration and plenty.

15   I thank Bruce McKim for a vivid, very useful discussion of his own fieldwork in Chake Chake.

16   The word *neema* (goodness) is sometimes used interchangeably with the term *shibe*, particularly in Pemba's larger towns. And, in my experience, where Pembans would use *"shibe,"* people on Unguja are more likely to say *"neema." Shibe* is a particularly *rural* or particularly "Pemban" term, and while *paired* with *neema*, it is not an exact synonym for it. Tellingly, *shibe* contains the idea that goodness depends essentially on and is reflected immediately in the condition of human bodies, i.e., whether people have enough to eat.

they need and are "equal" to their and their dependents' desires (*watu huwa wanajiweza*); they can materially provide for themselves and for others; they are in full control of their faculties and are able to make effective, meaningful decisions.[17] The atmosphere is cheerful. With *shibe*, anything is possible. *Shibe's* ascendance is sanctioned by God, who brings the blessing (*barka*) attendant to it. But *shibe* and *barka* originate primarily in the quality of human relations, which has a direct impact on, and is reflected in, the landscape. The following, from a Shirazi man now in his seventies, is representative of Pemban discussions of *shibe* and its reflection in the land:

> Blessedness in agriculture comes because the soil is good. And, sure, the soil is good first of all if it's just good soil. But it *remains* good soil if the people who use it are good, very gentle and kind. If the people understand each other. This blessedness comes from purity of heart. If people love each other, there is blessing, goodness. If there's hatred, there's no blessing. *And the soil will show it.*[18]

Certainly not all Pembans had access to the resources that would meet their basic needs, and future research would do well to focus specifically on the experiences of Pemba's marginalized communities, particularly in the less fertile north and east (for example, see Goldman 1996). But a complex and longstanding system of patronage meant that, particularly

---

17   The Kiswahili verb I have translated as "being equal to" is *ku-jiweza*, a reflexive form of the verb *ku-weza*, "to be able" (to do something). *Kujiweza* is something to which everyone aspires. It means to be equal to whatever challenge arises from one's own desire, to be able to provide for oneself, to have access to the things one wants and needs, to express oneself effectively, and it can also mean, at its most mechanical, to be conscious and in control of one's own body. In Pemban discussions of personal and communal agency, *kujiweza* is a key concept. When the verb has another person as its object, as in *kumweza mtu*, it means to be able to outsmart or dominate someone, or to make them act as you wish them to. The abstract noun associated with the verb is *uwezo*, "access to material resources" and/or "effectiveness."

18   Interview, Mkoani, May 2000. Note: The interviews from which extracts appear in this paper were about social geography, cosmology, the occult, and local conceptions of agency. While many conversations featured incidental or structuring comments related to distinct time-periods, including the revolution, the revolution as such was not our primary topic of discussion. Although many of the people who spoke with me have now passed away, to protect the safety and privacy of others, interviewees and interlocutors are not cited either by name, pseudonym, or initials – actual or altered – in this article. As people spoke willingly with me about a wide range of mundane things and their own lives as they knew them, using the term "Anonymous" to designate a source in what is now a fraught context risks generating the false impression that our rather natural conversations were in some way improper or carried out in secrecy. That was not the case. Throughout the paper, when drawing on specific interviews, I have provided the month and year, and the general – regional or district – location of the conversation. Scholars or researchers wanting to know more are welcome to contact me with questions or comments about this choice.

in clove-growing areas, benefits could often "trickle down," or "over" (Sultan and Sharif in Burgess 2009; Glassman 2011; Lofchie 1965; Middleton 1961). A southern Pemban woman from a historically very poor family expressed what in 1999 was a common refrain in this way: "Before [the revolution], if you were poor, someone who wasn't would take care of you. Rich people could help us and they did. What can we do now when our rich people don't have any money?"[19]

Another important element in rural Pemban life at the time—one frequently mentioned in protectorate documents and a key element in popular historical accounts—was the power and authority of local elders, known as *wazee wa mji* or *watu wazima* (respectively, town elders, and "completely matured, fully formed"[20] people), whose grasp of "the facts" is acute and who have the wherewithal to protect themselves and their dependents). At this chapter's outset, I noted that Pembans have long been represented as "inward-looking" people thought to be willful and stubborn. A Pemba-centric way of putting it is that people in Pemba were insistently "taking care of themselves," quite literally "minding their own business," and investing effectively in their own communities. One saying common on Unguja was "what a Pemban wants, will be" (*Mpemba atakalo litakuwa*). Although often imagined as principally rural and apparently "backward," Pembans were also thought to be particularly able to execute projects of their own design and stick to their own plans, and, importantly, to each other.[21] In rural Pemban views, this controlled, cohesive state of affairs was ensured by the knowledge and direction of Pemban elders.

According to many rural Pembans, prior to the revolution, a town's or village's elders knew everything about their communities and exerted crucial control over them, resolving disputes locally and discreetly,

---

19   Interview, Mkoani, January 1998.

20   Another term used in characterizing "complete people" (*watu wazima*) is "ripeness" (*upevu*, from the verb *ku-iva*). The development and expansion of a person's being, particularly of their powers of perception, is often rendered in Pemba through an analogy to fruit, from unripeness through the stages of ripening, and eventually into flower. People whose skills and knowledge have "ripened" perfectly have become as complete and full (*-zima*) as a human being can be.

21   This perception of Pemban "togetherness" obtains today also among people from Unguja, who often say, "In Unguja, you could be starving and your neighbor wouldn't help you; but if you're Pemban, no matter where you are, you are not alone." As for Pembans' "sticking together," people on Unguja have also often called Pembans *vibua*, a species of big-eyed fish that always travel in close schools. The "big-eyed-ness" is, from an Ungujan viewpoint, a sign of the Pemban *vibuas*' "country-bumpkin" identity and their presumed ignorance of city ways.

approving the schedule of rituals and celebrations, and determining how (or whether) their community would respond to government demands. Authority was insistently local, and the most respected elders faced the task of not only leading their own communities but also of protecting these from interference by the government. In the 19th and early 20th centuries, Pemban elders had a marked reputation among protectorate officials for being stubborn and often heedless of British decrees. Getting community representatives to attend monthly district meetings or to ensure that their dependents participated in public-works details, for example, was a problem; officials in Pemba noted repeatedly that community leaders' failure to attend mandated events impeded the course of (protectorate-driven) justice, overall making Pemba difficult to govern.[22]

In addition, elders not only knew the people in their places and the multilayered relationships between them, but also (consequently) could be relied upon to ensure *shibe,* for *shibe* also depends on right relations between leaders and their subjects. In Pemba, that meant right relations among local people and between them and their local leaders, their own *wazee wa mji.* The vision of right leadership in Pemba unfolds in a small setting, in a family or bounded (and protected) community or town. This, from a "Swahili" man who made a living baking and selling "Persian" bread:

> If a leader has the trust of his people, and his soul is good, and the hearts of the people are good, then things will go well. There is divine goodness/ blessedness (*neema*). Even you, ... if you reward your children, there will be blessedness.... if leaders are good, then families are good, and the land is good. The whole area *(nchi*[23]*)* will be good. There's *shibe.* We had this here, once [i.e., before 1964].[24]

Pembans have sometimes been portrayed as being nostalgic for the protectorate and sultanate periods; in my reading, any nostalgia for these

---

22 District Officer's Report, June 1917 and "Note to Acting Chief Secretary of Zanzibar," n.d., both in Zanzibar National Archives AB/31/20 (Witchcraft in Pemba); personal communication, Hamad Hassan Omar; interview, Korosini, 1999; interview, Mkoani, May 2000; interview, Mkoani, June 2000.

23 *Nchi* does not always mean "country" in the sense of a "nation" or "state." Pemba is said to have many *nchi,* indicating the autonomy and distinctiveness of regions as well as hamlets and villages, such that the *nchi* of Ndagoni in central Pemba has a very different character from the *nchi* of Kojani in the north or of Mwambe in the west.

24 Interview, Mkoani, May 1999.

is not for either the British or the sultanate per se but for the significant *autonomy* Pemban communities enjoyed prior to the revolution.[25]

Elders' caretaking of *shibe* was also carried out through religious and occult means, and many respected elders mediated between humans and the spirits whose goodwill could ensure the soil's fertility and enhance human prosperity. In the 1950s, the landscape bore clear signs of abundance, and Pemban communities and the elders who led them are remembered as being strong and well.

Clearly, such power vested in elders could leave young people at a disadvantage. G. Thomas Burgess (2002) has already demonstrated the importance of generational tensions in revolutionary Unguja, and as one Pemban who was in his twenties in the 1960s recalled, "You couldn't do anything without the *wazee* approving what you did. I made so much money harvesting cloves one year I was ready to put a tin roof on my house. But that looked like too much bragging to them and they ordered me to stop. In everything, the *wazee* were in charge."[26] Tensions between youth and elders notwithstanding, a recurring feature of Pemban perceptions of the 1950s is that Pembans "took care of each other," that elders were able to provide amply for their children's and grandchildren's education, marriages, and general well-being, and that, whatever the genealogical differences, most longtime residents who had married into Pemban society (mostly men) "belonged" there.

Pemban visions of the 1950s feature peaceful and well-integrated communities under the knowledgeable leadership and protection of locally chosen elders. Reflecting these right relations between people, the Pemban landscape itself—with its busy-ness, visibly abundant land, and well-kept shining clove trees, and the relative wealth these supported—presented to many who remember it a near-perfect image of *shibe*. The political changes brought by the 1960s would have dramatic effects on the distribution of Pemba's relative wealth, on its elders and their delicately balanced webs of allies and dependents, and on the Pemban landscape, where, for many, signs of *shibe* would be hard to find.

It Didn't Happen Here: 1961, 1964

In considering the role of Pemba in revolutionary Zanzibar, we start out with a fundamental observation. If by "Zanzibar revolution" we

---

25 For a discussion of a similar posture in Unguja, see Bissell 2005.

26 Interview, Chake Chake, April 1999. For a deeper discussion of the role of elders prior to the revolution, see Arnold 2006.

mean to designate the vividly documented events of 11–12 January 1964 on Unguja and of the week or so that followed, then the Zanzibar revolution did not take place on Pemba. This rather obvious statement nonetheless bears repeating: a crucial aspect of recent Pemban history is the fact that the events most defining of modern Zanzibar's emergence—those that "make" the national story—happened elsewhere. The elections of June 1961 provide a useful backdrop for what might be seen as the "reprise" of 1963.

As it did for everyone in Zanzibar in 1957, the emergence of political parties marked an important moment in Pemban reckonings of time. During the period referred to in rural Pemba as *wakati wa siasa* ("time of politics"), adults were naturally aware of mounting tensions between Arabs, Shirazis, ex-slaves, and mainlanders on Unguja, and they too participated in and experienced these at home, though on a less systemic, thoroughgoing scale. While Zanzibaris everywhere were at times actively political, popular accounts by Pembans today yield a vision of Pembans in the 1950s and early 1960s as overall *less* politically involved during *wakati wa siasa* than people on Unguja. In many Pembans' current estimations, Pembans were at the time more concerned with the health of their individual rural communities and lands than with political doings in the capital.[27] The violence that erupted on Unguja shortly after the general elections of June 1961 was in their opinion fundamentally foreign to Pembans and their island.[28] Violence, they said, originated elsewhere.

When people in Pemba voted in June 1961, they, like people on Unguja, came to vote for both the Afro-Shirazi Party (ASP) and the Zanzibar Nationalist Party/Zanzibar and Pemba People's Party (ZNP/ZPPP) alliance. On Unguja, however, the ZNP's acquisition of a seat-majority despite the ASP's capture of the popular vote led, as Jonathon Glassman has documented in detail (2011), to racialized and distinctly racializing violence—an outbreak known as *vita vya mawe*, or the "war of stones." This war, in which 68 Arabs, principally poor and rural, were killed on Unguja, was naturally well known to Pembans. And certainly the June elections had effects on Pemba, too, with party affiliation for a time determining to which weddings and funerals one might go and where one might shop and souring relations between landlords and

---

27 Interviews, Mkoani, 2000.

28 Pembans who spoke to me about this topic often said, *Siye hatukuwa na mambo hayo; kupigana hatujui* ("We ourselves didn't have those [violent] things; we don't know how to fight").

tenants (see also Glassman 2011). But the turmoil that emerged in public and social spheres on Pemba—so much more integrated than those on Unguja—can in no way compare to the violence and loss of life that took place on the larger island.

The 1961 war of stones is often a starting, or bursting, point in Pemban accounts of Zanzibar's modern political history, arguably even more so than the inception of *wakati wa siasa* in 1957. And, like the revolution three years later, the war of stones is recognized as not having happened on Pemba itself. The following observation, from a fourth-generation "Omani" clove-farmer in his eighties in 1998 (now deceased), in an area whose support had gone without fuss to the ZNP/ZPPP, is representative of accounts from similar areas in south-central and northern Pemba from people across categories of identity:

> Ah! In 1961, there was killing. They killed people in Unguja. Many Arabs died. *Here? In Pemba? Not one person died.* Just hatred [*chuki*]. There was hatred. It was—funerals, weddings. They didn't go. You didn't go. *But here, not one person died. That happened on Unguja, just as it would later on* [in 1964].[29]

The comparative absence of explosive originary violence on Pemba in 1961 was repeated at an exponentially higher and ideologically crucial register in January 1964. Despite sizeable support on Pemba for the Afro-Shirazi Party (44 percent) in the elections of July 1963 (a significant percentage that is often ignored or forgotten today), the revolution was not carried out on the island. It was brought there nearly two weeks later; when it came, as many put it, Pembans, as a group, surrendered (*walisalimu amri*).

Latecomers to Revolution: "You Didn't Wield the *Panga*"

Primarily linked to Unguja via radio, Pembans in the second week of 1964 were keenly alert to the happenings in Zanzibar city and the Ungujan countryside. Some people in Pemba—across all parties' memberships—had long believed or feared that tensions on Unguja could result in violence, and even in the government's overthrow (Ghassany 2010).[30] But to many, news of the revolution came as a shocking and complete surprise. From Pemba, events unfolding in the other island's center, over 60 miles away from Pemba's southern harbor

---

29 Interview, Korosini, May 1998.

30 Interviews, Mkoani, 1999; interview, Mkoani, June 2000.

across the redoubtable Pemba Trough, the "beginning" was experienced very differently.

In those first days, as John Okello's outlandish, theatrical radio broadcasts communicated the violent texture of events unfolding on Unguja, a delegation of landowners and community leaders from all over Pemba reportedly traveled to Wete for an urgent meeting at the home of the *liwali*[31], where they discussed the possibility of resistance, in the end deciding that the island's people should yield completely to the ASP.[32] Seventeen days later, on 29 January, Okello arrived in Pemba with revolutionary forces, and Pemban experiences of revolution began. What happened in Pemba then, in part by virtue of its not being "revolution proper" and in part for its long-term effects (relevant to more recent Zanzibari politics), is worth exploring in detail.

On Unguja, ASP supporters were in a clear majority. ZNP supporters were a well-known, highly visible minority. In Pemba, popular support for the ZNP and ZPPP (56 percent) was higher than for the ASP. In the 1963 elections, the ASP secured only two seats in Pemba: Mkoani in the far south and Wingwi in the remote northeast. The remaining 12 Pemban seats went handily, in sixes, to the ZNP and ZPPP. Both in terms of seats and of the popular vote (though, again, emphatically *not* as widely as contemporary political imaginings of Pemba might suggest), the majority of Pembans did support the ZNP and/or ZPPP. An instructive sign of Pemba's cultural and political difference from Unguja is that, as the revolution began on 12 January, ZNP supporters on Unguja briefly but seriously considered sending the young sultan to Pemba for his safety.[33] How to enfold such a place and people into a developing narrative of class- and racially based revolution in which 11 and 12 January would become absolutely key? As one Pemban intellectual told me in 2013, reflecting a sentiment that is widely shared, "For us, what's important is not the revolution itself. For us, *it's what came after.*"[34] As in official narratives, for many Pembans, Pemba has no role in the initial revolutionary story. In 1964, it was (again) "behind the times" and "lagging."

---

31   *Liwali* is often translated as "governor" or "headman." Originally it described a government representative or deputy appointed by the sultan and acting as his representative at a distance, typically operating at a regional level. *Liwalis* were typically learned men of prestige, and the office was continued under British colonial rule at a local level.

32   Interview, Unguja, July 2000; interview, Chake Chake, June 2000.

33   Interview, Unguja, January 2014.

34   Personal communication, USA, October 2013.

Consistently recalled by many older Pembans I knew in the 1990s (many of whom have since died) were two expressions directed at them by revolutionaries in 1964 and in the years following the revolution. These pointed words are still directed at Pembans today: "You didn't wield the *panga!*" (*Hamkushika ndu!*[35]) and, "You don't know what revolution is; today you'll get a taste!" (*Mapinduzi hamyajui niye; leo mutayaonja!*). The assumption on the revolutionaries' part was that Pembans, by virtue of their location in space *and* their "different" identity (on Unguja, "Pemban" was increasingly elided with "Arab," regardless of a person's apparent or actual ancestry), did not know what revolution "meant" and thus needed to be taught. On Pemba, from late January 1964 onward, both in the time called *Mapinduzi moto-moto* ("hot-hot," full-on revolution) and afterward, revolutionary policies were dramatically and idiosyncratically applied. As Ali Sultan Issa, appointed district commissioner of Chake Chake Region in February 1964 and tasked with teaching Pembans the meaning of "revolution," explained to Burgess, on Pemba, "[t]here was a spirit of revenge" (Burgess 2009: 91). In an important conceptual register, Pembans became traitors overnight.

Stories from Clove Lands

Most of the accounts informing this paper, drawn from 150 formal interviews and many more informal conversations carried out over two years of intensive participant-observation in the late 1990s and early 2000s and from continued visits to Zanzibar since then, were gathered[36] in distinctly rural clove-growing areas where the ZNP and ZPPP were popular in the 1960s and where the Civic United Front (CUF) opposition party was at the time (as it now is everywhere in Pemba) already firmly

---

35 The combination of Kiswahili as spoken on Unguja (*hamkushika*) and Pemba (*ndu*) in this expression may be due to informants' assessment of my linguistic abilities. Classical Pemban Kiswahili would show *hamweshika ndu*, to Unguja's *hamkushika panga*. People may have assumed that Ungujan verb forms were simpler for me, but that I might be counted on to know the Pemban word *ndu*. Nonetheless, this particular formulation offers up a salient diagnosis. It accused Pembans not only of having failed to take up arms—with the verb, or impulse for action, stemming from Unguja—but of having failed to take up the particularly Pemban form of this ordinary weapon. The implication is that the *panga* (Ungujan) was a revolutionary tool, and the *ndu* (Pemban) by nature, was not.

36 Accounts of the revolution were given in the context of my inquiries into the relationship between occult powers and the island's landscape/lived environment. I was not intentionally or actively eliciting stories about the revolution and would especially not have done so in the late 1990s. Given the fact that the revolution came up—often obliquely or to give temporal context—in many accounts of occult history in Pemba, it is clear both that occult powers were a key part of how agency was nourished, and that the revolution had an impact on every sphere of life and, in particular, on memory and reckonings of time.

entrenched. I cannot describe the experiences of families whose elders from the beginning supported the ASP, nor can I discuss current Chama cha Mapinduzi (CCM, "Revolutionary Party") members' visions of the past. Future research of this kind will be important. And, again, the views I do discuss should be understood as particularly *rural*. Accounts from Chake Chake and Wete towns would surely differ both in emphasis and texture. But the people I talked with came from varied cultural and economic backgrounds and situations, including the very poor, the newly landed, and the lately impoverished, as well as the historically more well-resourced.

For Pemban adults I spoke with, the revolution's official arrival initiated what was understood as a total cosmic rupture: a "cracking" of both time and space. This violent rupture demarcated the period "before" from what still felt to some in the 1990s like an eternal and unchanging "after," transforming the lived environment—the social geography—itself. In other words, the revolution abruptly ushered in the end of a period of satiety (*shibe*) and the beginning of a seemingly endless time of hunger (*njaa*) and of generalized, total suffering (*dhiki tupu*) whose signs would be, in Pemban perceptions and experience, written on Pemban bodies and on the land itself. Many would know the Zanzibar revolution—and still know it today—as *Mapinduzi ya Unguja* (the Ungujan revolution), and despite Pembans' overwhelming compliance with it, for many (until possibly quite recently) the revolution would not fully "take."

In general, memories of the revolution in rural Pemba featured forced participation in public-works details and agriculture, often at cane- or gun-point; the transformation of property rights, especially the nationalization of the clove trade, after which the government assumed the right to purchase all cloves at prices far below those fetched on the world market (the smuggling of cloves to the mainland, especially for sale in Kenya, was punishable by death, and the waters around Pemba were energetically patrolled); forced attendance and participation at political rallies, sometimes to witness the humiliation of elders (here notably in the guise of an enthusiastic "anti-witchcraft" campaign aimed at disempowering the elders who had for so long maintained particularly Pemban forms of agency[37]); and, less often spoken but still vivid in people's minds, the abduction and sexual abuse of girls and women. There was, too, the ceasing of nearly all literary and openly intellectual activity and the criminalization and collapse of most occult

---

37   See Arnold 2006.

or spirit-related activity on the island. While for a time Pemba's Asian residents were allowed to leave the island (in exchange for giving up their property) and others with the means to do so found ways of escaping north to the Kenya coast, independent travel from the island was soon totally prohibited, as was the delivery of imports to private individuals. (In 1971, leading into the period known as "the time of hunger" or "the famine" [*wakati wa njaa*], no imports would be allowed at all; see below). A once-prosperous island that had for decades been a thriving part of diverse Indian Ocean commercial and cultural networks was suddenly totally cut off from the outside world.

Overall, oral accounts convey a clear sense of the complete transformation of daily life and of the physical environment itself. But for many older men and women, a recurrent topic was the frequency of beatings and petty humiliations they or their neighbors and relatives received at the hands of revolutionary supporters. Pemba's regional and district commissioners, installed on 4 February (less than two weeks after Okello's arrival on Pemba), personally oversaw both the dispensing of punishment and the implementation of new rules, and they were renowned for their enthusiasm and stamina. Regional Commissioner Rashid Abdalla's proclivities quickly earned him the name "Crocodile" (*Mamba*), for "he could consume a whole person in one bite." Abdalla was also known for telling his targets that he was punishing them for their own good and that he (shedding "crocodile tears") didn't like to cause them pain. Abdalla was followed by Abdulrazak Musa, who famously trumpeted to the people of Chambaani in southern Pemba his aspiration to be even harsher, saying, "If Rashid Abdalla was a crocodile, then I am a human god (*mungu-mtu*)."[38]

The Entire Place a Prison: "Days of Caning"

The militarization of Pemba in the wake of the revolution was rapid and dramatic. In the first few months of 1964, the Revolutionary Government established an army camp and two new Field Force Unit (FFU) enclaves on Pemba (where there had been none in the past), at the same time significantly increasing the police presence. Writers of the 1966 government booklet *The Progress Obtained on Pemba Island from 1964–1966* considered that Pembans in the past had had little respect for the police and that, even with the marked strategic increase, the number of police officers on Pemba was still nowhere near enough; the

---

38 Interviews, Mkoani, October 1999; interviews, Mkoani, June 2000.

report expresses the government's intention to continue sending more (Government of the United Republic of Tanzania and Zanzibar 1966: 29). And yet Pembans were not imprisoned in large numbers.

While certainly some Pembans in Pemba were detained—famously taken to one of the three military camps, where some were made to dig the holes in which they would be buried up to their necks then beaten about the head, while others had salt and chili pepper rubbed into their wounds[39]—detentions were reportedly far less frequent than on Unguja. Early on, the People's Republic of Zanzibar and Pemba's first president, Abeid Amani Karume, decided that, rather than be sent to prison, suspect Pembans would instead be beaten and let go. As Ali Sultan Issa recalled in 2009:

> [A] decision came from Zanzibar Town that was sent to the regional commissioner in Pemba, Rashid Abdalla. Instead of putting people in jail, all offenders were to be flogged and then released. That was the decision. I thought it was better than sending them to prison, because if you send a bread earner to prison, you ruin the whole family. When he is gone, the family invariably disintegrates. When the man is "inside," people can do anything to his family, like rape his wife and plunder his goods (quoted in Burgess 2009: 91; see also Walsh 2010).

And, as one thoughtful commentator put it, "Why put people in jail, when you can make the entire place a prison?"[40] The first revolutionary period in Pemba, lasting in various accounts until 1967 or 1968, is famously known as "the days of caning" (*siku za bakora*). It is named for the revolutionaries' weapon of choice, the *bakora* wooden stick that had for generations in Pemba been carried by respected adult men—schoolteachers, imams, intellectuals, cultured businessmen, and traditional healers—who used it primarily as a walking stick and reportedly occasionally to keep children in line. Using this symbol of local authority (or a stick or club that shared the name *bakora*) as a weapon against Pemban adults lent a particular "taste" to what became an atmosphere of generalized, unpredictable violence, symbolically and actually inverting the social order by infantilizing Pemban men.

While the Revolutionary Government articulated plans in 1966 for a prison labor camp (where prisoners could grow their own food, learn a trade, and thus be "self-reliant") that was later built at Tungamaa/Machengwe (Government of the United Republic of Tanzania 1966:

---

39   Interviews, Mkoani, July 2000; interview, Mkoani, May 2000.
40   Interview, Unguja, January 2014.

52), by February 1964, Pemba Island, cut off from all contact with the outside world, had itself effectively become one big detention site. Whatever the purported benefits to families and women of not widely imprisoning Pemban men and publicly humiliating them instead, the decision contributed to people's sense that every aspect of life had been transformed, and this with a particular vengeance directed toward Pembans *as* Pembans. If Pembans did not have entirely shared experiences of belonging prior to the revolution, they certainly did *afterward*. No matter what an individual's political views were, the very fact of being Pemban was enough to make them potential "traitors," and, with few exceptions,[41] the new regulations, accompanied by rampant unregulated pettiness and cruelty, could be directed on Pemba at any time to anyone at all.

Given the period's popular name, it is not surprising that the nature, frequency, and threat of beatings were a frequent topic. In the 1990s in central Pemba, vivid images still rose up of scenes witnessed in the revolution's early years: close friends forced to slap one another in public for hours; elders lined up to be shaved with broken glass bottles in village squares; fathers, uncles, cousins, and siblings made to lie down on the road or in the market while revolutionary supporters beat their legs and feet; and adults made to hop about like frogs while calling out revolutionary slogans. One man still bore on his back a scar in the shape of a clothing iron, for he'd been "ironed like a suit."[42] Others had been whipped with stingrays' poisonous tails.

Less idiosyncratic violations, too, deployed a perverted, eerie local grammar—one in place before the revolution and still in use today. A beating was "an education" (*kufunzwa*) or "being made to dance" (*walitupigia ngoma*). In a disgendering, sexualized violence that continues in prisons today, wounds inflicted on the soles of men's feet were referred to as "henna patterns," which are, in peaceful, ordinary circumstances, lovingly painted by women on the feet of brides in anticipation of the transition to "full womanhood" on the wedding night.[43]

Few people died in Pemba during the revolution proper, and few people (even in later years when military presence seemed to Pembans

---

41   Personal communication, Justin Beckham.

42   Interview, Mkoani, February 1999.

43   See also Human Rights Watch 2002.

to be "everywhere") were killed outright.[44] But many older Pembans felt in the 1990s that the "days of caning," purported by Karume to be "kinder" than imprisonment, were a sort of general "death sentence" for the island. Some returned from detention so psychically and physically ruined that their health never returned; some died quickly after.[45]

Ali Sultan Issa admits that "[t]here were excesses" committed on Pemba. Suggesting that some events might have been "too much" even for his hardy spirit, he goes on to say, "Actually, I thank God I did not stay longer in Pemba because I do not know what kind of cases I would have had to face later on" (Burgess 2009: 92). It is sobering to consider the possibility that much of the "oppositional" character Pemba has had in recent politics may not so much predate the revolution as be one of its hardiest and most important *products*.

Revolution as Theater

An important aspect of revolutionary education, as it is all over the world, is political theater. Without fail, accounts of the revolutionary period cite the mandatory attendance of all islanders at long (to many, seemingly interminable) political rallies and at yearly revolutionary celebrations. Pembans endured forced long-distance marches that sometimes took up to eight hours to attend and perform in these daylong public spectacles. ASP (and later CCM) agents (or members of the youth wing, known as Volunteers, and later as Green Guards), patrolled people's homes to make sure everyone attended, making exceptions only for women who were or who successfully claimed to be breastfeeding.[46] People found hiding in the bushes or in fields were apprehended and made to join the march, again at cane- or gun-point.

At many of these meetings (two of which were addressed by Tanzanian President Julius K. Nyerere himself in 1966), Pembans, despite their public compliance with revolutionary policy, were often likened to animals (here, Pembans were "dogs" or "little goats"[47]) or decried as "sultan-loving" idlers and dandies. And Pemban cultural practices—especially traditional healing and forecasting, which partook

---

44   One famous case of someone killed at Vitongoji is that of Said Khamis Udende, killed by a shot to the head while buried in the ground up to his neck. See Arnold 2003.

45   Interview, Chake Chake, May 2000.

46   Interview, Wete, May 2000.

47   *Vibuzi marika*: a small kind of goat mainly found in the south of Pemba. A dismissive expression used to mean a person who struts about very proudly but in fact has nothing of value to contribute.

of both the occult and religion and which had for so long ensured adults' local agency and provided a meaningful way of being in the world—were decried as *ujinga* (ignorance), their criminalization celebrated as a definite sign of progress.

Accounts of attendance at rallies, particularly from older women, often also touched on the particular humiliation of being forced to sing.[48] For women I knew, forced singing of such songs had kept the revolution alive in a painfully intimate way and was experienced as a petty humiliation—an insult added to a litany of injuries. Through such song, what was to them a distorted vision of a history that either did not include them or negated their experience issued from their own mouths, which in public also no longer belonged to them. One song was written to convince Pembans in particular of the revolution's value. The chorus (*kipokeo*) is telling:

> The Ungujan revolution is worthwhile,
>
> If it were not worthwhile, would you [Pembans] be seeing all this progress?
>
> *Mapinduzi ya Unguja, yana maana,*
>
> *Yasingekuwa na maana, maendeleo kuyaona?*[49]

Having sung for me, the singer said bitterly, "We were lining up for food that wasn't there; we barely had anything to wear; we had rocks piled on our heads! What progress did we see!?"

Another song was specifically written to celebrate the imprisonment and torture of elders accused of being "witches" (that is, the *watu wazima* and *wazee wa mji* who had for most of the 19th and early 20th centuries been respected Pemban community leaders). With this song, which people were forced to sing while ruling party members presented humiliated elders to the captive crowd, audience members were asked to implicate themselves in and celebrate the preferred method of punishing Pemban elders thought to be occult experts:

> Let me dig a hole and bury you, as you are a witch,
>
> Let me beat you with a *bakora*, by the grace of God, stay down/away.
>
> If you fool [with me], I'll split you like a coconut,
>
> Let me beat you with a *bakora*, by the grace of God, stay down/away.

---

48 It is instructive to consider song as a phenomenological bearer of shame and disembodiment, and I imagine that further research into revolutionary songs and their performance would bear rich fruit.

49 Interview, Wete, April 1999.

Nikuchimbie shimo, nikuzike kwa kuwa mchawi,
Nikupige kwa bakora, wallahi kwako kaae,
Usifanye masikhara, takuvunja kama nazi,
Nikupige kwa bakora, wallahi kwako kaae.[50]

Several women recalling this song said they felt ashamed for having sung. One said, "Those old men had been so badly beaten already. We knew them all. They had nothing left, and there we were singing at them." The order to "stay down" or "away" was particularly ironic, since the elders had often already been severely beaten and were unlikely to protest or rise up. "But there wasn't any choice. If you didn't sing, *you'd* get the *bakora*, too."[51]

For some adults, a particularly painful aspect of these public performances was that their young children naturally found the singing and participation in organized parades exciting and fun. For children, the rallies, in preparation for which they were given new uniforms and shoes, constituted a special, wonderful "day out."[52] Children of both sexes participated in the athletic demonstrations and educational games that marked the yearly revolutionary celebrations (during which any particularly oppositional Pemban adults were arrested and kept "safe," usually returning home, beaten and injured, after a few weeks in prison[53]). One striking photograph in the Revolutionary Government's 1966 report shows a unit of young girls in neat blouses and skirts wielding wooden rifles and performing a military drill (Government of the United Republic of Tanzania 1966: 17). Another shows girls in short white dresses excitedly playing tug of war (ibid: 23). For many young people, this excitement came with the feeling that the revolution was truly historic, an important global event that was ushering in a new progressive future.[54]

While in some families oppositional discourse did thrive, for many others this difference between the experiences of adults and their children oriented the generations differently toward history and their

---

50   Interview, Wete, June 2000.

51   Interview, Wete, June 2000.

52   Personal communications, USA, October 2014; interviews, Unguja, January 2014; interview, Dar es Salaam, January 2014.

53   Interview, Wete, January 2014; personal communication, K.S., November 2014.

54   Interview, Mkoani, August 1999; interview, Chake Chake, September 1999; interview, Unguja, January 2014; personal communication, USA, November 2013.

experience of the present. Even with intimates, discussion of the revolution was fraught with fear of surveillance and potential betrayal; many parents were unable to easily provide their children an alternate understanding of the world in which they were growing up.[55] In many Pemban families, it is only in this century that those elders who are still alive have begun to talk openly about what happened after 1964. Others, indicating that the memories are still vivid and too painful, continue to refuse.

The Curtailing of Intellectual Life: "Foreign" and "Traditional" Knowledge

Many sources attest to Karume's disdain for highly educated people. Under his presidency, many forms of learning and the possession of books, notebooks, and papers in any language other than Kiswahili came to represent pretension, otherness, and an attachment to unapproved influences emanating from beyond Zanzibar's tightly monitored borders. Two forms of education came under pointed attack. The first was any learning associated with European or Islamic sources; the second was local—the deep, longstanding forms of complex traditional knowledge and practice known as *uganga* and/or *uchawi*, which, while also part of life on Unguja, had historically been strongest on Pemba.

In the Western historiographic and sociological literature, Pemba is not often represented as a fount of literary or intellectual activity, but in fact many Pembans in the 19th and early 20th centuries were highly educated. Pemba was also renowned across the Swahili world for its poetry, particularly by the famed turn-of-the-20th-century poets Kamange and Sarahani, whose rivalry was legendary and inspired dozens of others to emulate their work (Alawy and El-Maawy 2011).

In 1957, writer Abdurrahman Saggaf Alawy, visiting Pemba from Mombasa, was deeply impressed by the many personal literary collections shown to him (Alawy and El-Maawy 2011: 2). In early 1964, the mere ownership of books became a serious crime. Many Pembans hid or destroyed any English- or Arabic-language books they owned. Revolutionaries went from house to house, seizing what books they found and burning these. One religious scholar in Chake Chake was forced to order his students to dig the fire-pit in which his vast collection was to be destroyed (and to watch as the books burned).[56]

---

55   Interviews, Dar es Salaam, January 2014; interview, Unguja, January 2014.

56   Personal communication, USA, March 2014.

When in 1964 Alawy met with Pembans who had fled to the Kenya coast, Ali Abdalla El-Maawy writes, "he heard them weeping awfully" (ibid: 2) as they mourned their lost collections, which for them had been concrete proof of their rightful participation in regional and international literary and critical traditions. Today, in the storage areas of many old homes in Pemba there remain intriguing piles of severely damaged books accidentally discovered in the ground or rescued from the rafters, where many had been hidden. These unwieldy objects have deteriorated well beyond repair and, in the post-revolutionary absence of a nationally supported and diverse reading culture,[57] have for the most part not garnered the interest of the first owners' descendants—many of whom in any case are now seeking their livelihoods in Dar es Salaam and elsewhere.[58]

Just as "foreign" knowledge and contingent, unpredictable local literary activity became dangerous and suspect, so too did more clearly local forms of intellectual practice aimed at understanding and controlling the invisible forces that had been so intimately involved in traditional Pemban life (Giles 1989; Goldman 1996; Arnold 2003). The land in Pemba and the ocean surrounding it are populated by spirits (*majini*) whose invisible lives mimic those of humans. King Solomon is reported to have banished a huge number of spirits from the Middle East to Pemba, and in some traditional thought the *majini* live in cities and villages beneath the sea that look very much like the cities and hamlets of Pemba. (In 1998, some said that a parallel revolution had also happened *there*; under the sea were the same blocks of Soviet-style apartments—known on land as revolutionary housing [*nyumba za mapinduzi*]—that had come to mark the skyline in each of Pemba's three large towns.[59])

Dealing with spirits required the expertise of Pemba's traditional leaders. The spirits were powerful and walked freely among humans, sometimes interacting with them. But human Pembans, too, advised by expert elders, often sought spirits out themselves and entered into contracts with them, with the understanding that the spirits would protect and enhance a family's security. Contracts with spirits were maintained by regular offerings, depending on the spirit's favorite foods, and by the

---

57 In this respect recent efforts by writers across genres to start a yearly Zanzibar Literary Festival are an encouraging sign of change and renewal.

58 On a more modest but also telling note, European board games, too, were banned in 1964; Monopoly, with its bald-faced celebration of predatory capitalism, was particularly objectionable, and Pembans scrambled to destroy these as well.

59 Interview, Makoongwe, 1998.

regular sacrifice of chickens, goats, or cows. As revolutionary policies nationalized and redistributed wealth (the government implementing a draconian monopoly on cloves and splitting up large holdings into three-acre plots allocated to the poor), as food became scarce, and as soldiers freely and unpredictably took possession of Pembans' livestock, the contracts with family spirits—though forever binding—became a challenge to maintain.

The tending of spirits is inherited. A spirit initially attached to one person will, at that person's death, identify a descendant with whom to continue the relationship, and that descendant becomes responsible for ensuring that regular payments are made. The widespread inability of people to provide the gifts required by spirits had painful consequences for many, as the angered spirits visited a range of illnesses on the descendants of the families they had once guarded. Each village I visited had one or two residents whose strange or reduced mental conditions were understood to be the result of spirit illness specifically visited on the sufferer because their parents had been unable to uphold their end of a bargain after the revolution. Worldly debt had been wiped out, but debts to the spirits remained. Again, all forms of traditional healing had been outlawed as *ujinga* (foolishness, stupidity), and many of the people who might have renegotiated the deals and brought relief to the ailing were, until a slight easing came about in the 1980s, monitored by the state and terrified of practicing their craft.[60]

In January 1964, as the revolution approached, many Pembans had buried their savings underground, setting the family spirits to watch over the funds. But here, too, it became impossible for many people to make regular payments to the spirits in return for their protection. With the lifting of certain restrictions on the ownership of property and the movement of capital in the 1980s and 1990s, people began to make concerted efforts to retrieve the buried assets, but the spirits, upset by the missed payments, would not soften the earth above the pots so that these could be uncovered; where the original owners were deceased, spirits refused to reveal to children the location of the funds buried by their parents. Many people in rural Pemba had the sense that the landscape itself—transformed here particularly by the disappointment and rancor of the spirits who had once helped to ensure the island's well-being (again, *shibe*)—was refusing to yield up the wealth that had once

---

[60] Interview, Mkoani, January 2013; interview, Mkoani, May 2000; interview, Mkoani, June 2000; interview, Mkoani, May 2000; interview, Wete, July 2000.

been generated by the goodness of the earth and which the inhabitants had placed into its care.

The Pemba Famine: *Njaa* Established in the Land

As noted above, *shibe* (providential abundance and generalized satiety) in Pemba had long been a sign that relationships between humans (including parents and children, and leaders and their subjects) were considerate, respectful and mutually beneficial. The existing degree of *shibe* was most obviously apparent in the quality of the soil (and by extension in the quality and abundance of fruits and vegetables and other crops, including cloves), in a sense of social harmony, and in the generous meeting of human needs. As the precise opposite of *shibe* is *njaa* (hunger), it is also important to examine Pemban accounts of the period that is known specifically as *wakati wa njaa* ("the time of hunger," or "the famine"), which reached a keening point in 1971.

After the revolution, all economic activity, including the importing of goods to Zanzibar, had been closely monitored, but in 1971 imports ceased completely. A drought in Pemba exacerbated the shortages there, which, in Martin's assessment (instantiating the common usage of *Zanzibar* as synonymous with Unguja), "were much more acute than any suffered on Zanzibar" (1978: 116). Despite Karume's attempts to keep foreign journalists out of Zanzibar,[61] people in Pemba recalled that news of their plight reached the international community. Foreign governments sent ships loaded with supplies, they said, but Karume refused to let the ships land. One man recalled the agony of seeing the ships themselves and knowing that the food would not reach the hungry:

> There were ships out there in the water. We could see them. Full of sugar, we heard. But Karume turned them around and came to us saying, "Self-reliance! Self-reliance!"[62]

In Pemba, people foraged for what food they could find. Women looked for wild tubers (*bie, chelema, togonya*), many of them poisonous and only rendered edible through a laborious, time-consuming procedure. Others sought tiny, hard-to-find *wanga* roots, normally used as an unguent in the production of specialty sweetmeats but during the "time of hunger" painstakingly pounded to make a thin porridge (also see Walsh 2009). Women reported concealing the whereabouts of *wanga*

---

61 One European radio journalist who traveled to Pemba was reportedly forced to witness and record the screams of people being publically beaten. Interview, Unguja, January 2013.

62 Interview, Mkoani, May 2000.

patches from their friends and relatives ("I couldn't even tell my sister where I was going," one said. "I was afraid she'd get there first."[63]) People cheated each other out of places in line at the government shops, where what food there was was closely rationed and there was no guarantee that everyone would receive a share. In many Pembans' view, not only had the soured relations between rulers and the ruled put *shibe* at serious risk, but, as hunger and penury increased, relations between subjects themselves were ruined, too. Slyness, duplicity, and ungenerousness had become survival strategies. The *njaa* initiated by the revolution had brought a full-blown drought *(ukame)* that, culminating in famine, was as much spiritual and social as political and environmental.

In the logic of *shibe*, which links the nature of human leadership to the physical health of land and of the people on it, Karume's death in 1972 brought relief to the lived world. Although on Unguja, Pembans were still underrepresented in government, and the perception of Pembans as ungovernable, traitorous, and undeserving was still firmly in place, Pembans' daily lives improved in small ways. More food was brought to the island, and the period known as *wakati wa njaa* was over. Public humiliations abated. But the atmosphere remained one of deep distrust, surveillance, and widespread physical and economic hardship. In the mid-1970s, Martin saw many people on the island "dressed in meagre rags," and "barefoot," and the whole place seemed to him dismal and asleep. Martin's view was that the government was "rather embarrassed by Pemba and wary of the resentment still harbored by people there" (1978: 117).

In 1980s, the Revolutionary Government undertook modest economic reforms that allowed certain kinds of imports and greater individual freedoms. One widely remembered sign of change (and, conversely, a comment on the hardship that had come before) was that, in the 1980s, "some of us bought bicycles." Better-resourced people acquired reconditioned vehicles from Japan, which were turned into open-cab "taxis" that enabled people who could afford the fare to travel with a bit more ease (although Pemban roads had long been and were in increasing disrepair; the main arteries, in some places for miles, featured enormous craters that were dangerous to engage). In the 1990s, foodstuffs came in more freely, and those who could opened up their own shops. But the common refrain among adults in Pemba was "there's no Pemba anymore" (*Pemba hakuna tena*) or "Pemba's totally dead"

---

63 Interview, Mkoani, June 2000.

(*Pemba imekufa kabisa*). Most people I spoke with concurred that there was no *shibe* and none of the "goodness" (*neema*) that is both a sign and a cause of generalized satiety. Pemba cloves continued to produce the bulk of Zanzibar's foreign exchange, but the wealth these generated was used principally on Unguja. Pembans' sense of injustice about this issue was (and until very recently remained) keen.

In the 1990s, the effects of decades of repression and systematic neglect were still reflected in the island's deeply rural, underdeveloped environments. This was particularly clear in the condition of Pemba's once legendary clove plantations: overgrown, old trees producing less and less, and, because of the poor return on harvests, people in general unwilling to expend precious energy on maintaining the trees. At the start of the 21st century, impassable roads, broken telephone boxes, the ruins of old dispensaries, and defunct, denuded petrol stations still dotted the Pemban landscape; electricity was either nonexistent or extremely unreliable; and piped water flowed only sporadically a few hours a week in the homes of a handful of relatively well-appointed houses in the larger towns. What is today a 20-minute drive from Mkoani to Chake Chake in the 1990s and early 2000s took an hour and a half. Government hospitals in the principal towns frequently lacked malaria medication and even simple painkillers like Panadol. Executing the smallest bureaucratic task could take weeks or months. Despite the revolutionary promise of progress and self-improvement, in the four decades afterward the Pemban landscape relentlessly offered up a story of sudden interruption and an ensuing (at that time apparently permanent) decline.

On Elections: Where Do Pembans Belong?

As has been widely documented by journalists and election observers since the inception of multipartyism in Tanzania (including Zanzibar) in 1992, Pembans have been particularly vulnerable to state-supported harassment and violence during and in relation to elections.[64] In 1995, 2000, and 2005, Pembans on Unguja—where many had come to seek a livelihood, feeling that remaining in Pemba held no economic hope—

---

64 The singling out of Pembans in Unguja during election time did not begin in the 1990s. Now middle-aged Pembans who were studying in Unguja in the 1980s recalled beatings of Pembans and the looting of Pemban homes in Zanzibar whenever an election took place. The violence attendant to multiparty elections has garnered far more news coverage and attention, but the thread of anti-Pemban violence, as this paper shows, predates the 1990s. Interviews, Wete and Unguja, January 2014.

were a particular target of army, police, and the ruling party's youth wings. Homes were looted and some razed completely; Pembans were beaten and detained, and the chant of "Pembans go home" could be heard at ruling party rallies as well as in the streets and neighborhoods.[65] (Pembans' repeated reply of "We *are* home, here on Unguja. All of us are Zanzibari! Zanzibar for all!" attempts to redefine the meaning of "Zanzibar," but necessarily draws, as always, on the initial discursive bind.[66]). At Unguja's harbor, Pembans awaiting ferries to Mkoani in southern Pemba were stripped of their possessions and beaten by police and Green Guards.[67] Scores of Pembans who worked in government offices were fired without cause.[68] For many Pembans, Unguja felt unsafe, and Pemba, too, once again took on the aura of a highly militarized "camp." There, among other increases in surveillance, the establishment of curfews that coincided with men leaving the mosque after evening prayers created an opportunity for Green Guards and police to punish adult men for "breaking curfew."

Again, "irregularities" and the attendant eruptions of state-supported violence have been characteristic of Zanzibar's elections since 1995. In the context of this essay, it is particularly important to note that, in January 2001, in a state-supported, systematic campaign of punishment, upwards of 40 opposition supporters on Pemba were killed by security forces during peaceful demonstrations; more than 400 were wounded; women were sexually abused; homes were looted; and over a thousand Pembans fled to Kenya, where until just a few years ago, some number still languished in refugee camps along the Somali border.[69]

With Pembans' long history of dissent and the longstanding discourse of difference about them, it was easy in the 1990s and early 2000s for membership in CUF to be elided in Zanzibari official (and in the Tanzanian national) discourse with "Pemban-ness"—whether or not a particular opposition supporter had any concrete or personal association with the island. Being a member or supporter of the

---

65 Witnessed by the author.

66 Also see Arnold 2002.

67 Witnessed by the author.

68 Interviews, Unguja, December 1995; interview, Wete, 1995; interview, Mkoani 1995.

69 On Unguja, too, several people were killed by police and army, and fear was serious and widespread. But many Pembans understood the violence to be aimed directly at them, and at what they and their island had come to signify in political speech and action. See Human Rights Watch 2002.

opposition meant being associated with CUF; and the idea of CUF came to be tightly connected, and in some contexts synonymous with, the idea of Pemba. The question of Pemba's place, role, and history in "Zanzibar"—as well as the oppositional posture it had come to signify in the popular imagination—became steadily more acute, even as the place of "Zanzibar" itself, in the context of the republic, increasingly came into question. In some ways, then, as opposition to the ruling party grew among people in Unguja, the ranks of "Pembans" swelled.

Revolution for All?

Although many Pembans continue to seek their livelihoods on Unguja, in Dar es Salaam, and elsewhere, the formation of the Government of National Unity (GNU) in 2010 improved the quality of life of those remaining on the island. With the GNU's 2011 decree that clove growers should receive 80 percent of the world market price per kilo, growers were paid many times as much as they had been in the 1990s, when the price offered through the Zanzibar State Trading Company (ZSTC)'s clove monopoly was dismally low. In response to the increased price, people weeded previously neglected clove areas and many planted new trees (34,000 in 2012; Mussa 2012). In early 2014 at harvest's end, there seemed to be more cash on hand than at that time in previous years. At least along the main roads (repairs to which had made travel much more comfortable and faster), Pemba appeared "built up," with improvements made to houses, and, in many places, new schools and mosques under construction.

With electricity brought via an underwater cable from Tanga on the Tanzanian mainland, the ubiquitous and often extended power outages became a thing of the past, with many more homes electrified.[70] Although the benefits and cultural effects of tourism are, appropriately, up for debate, beach resorts in Pemba—where for years there were in operation only a handful of guesthouses (three of them government-owned and run)—multiplied. The increased presence of Pembans in government and the apparent easing of restrictions on public speech, together with the notable economic changes, were, for some Pembans, a sign that *shibe* might come back to the island (and to Zanzibar as a whole). Their enthusiasm, however, remained tempered by the memory of the failed peace accords of 2001 and 2008, both of which appeared to redouble the police and military presence on Pemba—readily harkening

---

70 See Winther 2008.

back, for many adults, to 2005, 2001, 2000, 1995, and, for the oldest among them, to the "days of caning" that began in 1964.

Prior to the elections of 2015, despite the continued holding of the Reconciliation (*maridhiano*) instituted in 2010, a constitutional crisis continued to exacerbate tensions between and among Zanzibaris and between Zanzibar and the Tanzanian mainland. Discord was ongoing over the allocation of rights to and profits from the oil that had been discovered in the archipelago. And, given the occasional but recurring arrests of prominent opposition leaders[71] (*Mazrui Media* 2014; BBC 2012), most Zanzibaris were prepared to recalibrate their expectations at short notice.[72] Nonetheless, there seemed to be some hope that the upcoming elections might unfold peacefully, their results announced legitimately and efficiently in a civil atmosphere. However, before an official announcement of the presidential results could be made, the October 2015 elections were annulled by the chair of the Zanzibar Electoral Commission; the rerun elections of March 2016, after which Ali Mohamed Shein remained President of Zanzibar, were boycotted by the opposition.

The delicately balanced anticipation of fall 2015 ceded in 2016 to widespread uncertainty and turbulence in which, as with any political conflict, ideas about identity and belonging played orienting and potentially dangerous roles. As scholars have long noted, when tensions rise in Zanzibar, the narrative that has tended to come to the fore is one in which "Africans" and "Arabs" are locked in endless and unchanging conflict.[73] At times, it can seem to Zanzibaris and outside observers that the political currency of the now familiar dualities (Unguja/Pemba; African/Arab; union/autonomy; revolutionary/resistant; CCM/CUF; ASP/ZNP-ZPPP[74]) is unending, and that the relationships suggested at

---

71 2012 saw the detention of a number of Uamsho members, including Uamsho leader Sheikh Farid Haji Ahmed. In early August 2014, Mansour Yusuf Himid was detained and charged with the illegal possession of arms.

72 In early 2014, staunch "old-guard" CCM members were said to be swearing oaths on the Qur'an to protect the union at all costs.

73 See Larsen 2004.

74 For a discussion of the opposed terms *Wazanzibari* (supporters of increased autonomy for the islands) and *Wazanzibara* (supporters of close relations with the mainland [*bara*]), see Cameron 2004. The term *machotara* (used to describe spotted and mottled livestock, and, increasingly, to identify people of apparently "Arab" and "mixed" descent) has also come into reinvigorated currency. At the time of writing, a tight equivalence of *Wazanzibari* to *machotara* does not seem to be in place, but an ellision in CCM discourse of *machotara* to "Pembans" *has* been noted and described (see Ghassani 2016).

regular intervals by this enduring conceptual structure may never be significantly transformed.

Much has been written specifically about the highly complex and sometimes dangerous interplay between concepts of identity and embodied experience in Zanzibar; I will not review it here.[75] But it may be useful to note that in the larger field of Swahili studies, of which Zanzibar scholarship is a part, it is broadly held that identities on the East African coast have historically been fluid, contingent, shifting, surprising, and experientially complex (Mazrui and Shariff 1994; Caplan 2004). Recent Zanzibar scholarship has convincingly shown that constructing identities and implementing notions of belonging is difficult and time-consuming work; it takes diligence, perspicacity, and will, and, more often than official political discourse admits, requires inventiveness and courage (Fair 2001; Larsen 2004; McMahon 2015; Stockreiter 2015). The substance of ideas can change, and while official discourses have often been hermetic, these, too, can sometimes be pried open. In terms of what Pemba or "being Pemban" means, in 2014, some small but notable discursive developments took place that may in the future come to affect how Pembans' relationships to the past are viewed by others, and how they view themselves.

The formation of the GNU ushered in a distinctly strategic shift in the content of oppositional history-telling; it suggests that, despite continued tension and recurrences of violence in Pemba, the tight conceptual equivalence between the concept of "Pemba," "opposition," and "anti-revolutionary sentiment" may one day come loose. The shift involves the representation of the late Abeid Karume, who has long been resented especially keenly in Pemba.

In 2010, statements made by Zanzibar's first president began to appear with increasing frequency in CUF calls for Zanzibar's increased political and cultural autonomy—a potential future path that many Pembans *do* support. The apparent aim was to transform the target of opposition from the Revolutionary Government *as such* (an opposition which, again, has long been easily equated with "Pemban-ness" alone) to, instead, the union with Tanganyika (which Karume himself—undoubtedly a revolutionary—opposed). The extract below, exemplifying what then became par for the course in CUF presentations, comes from a 2010 election speech by the former first vice president, Seif Sharif Hamad:

---

75   See Lofchie 1965; Larsen 2008; Burgess 2009; and Glassman 2011.

In brief, our intention is to build a new Zanzibar that will *realize the aims of the first president of the People's Republic of Zanzibar,* the late Mzee Abeid Amani Karume, who wanted every Zanzibari to feel *authentically included in* and represented by it [*kujinasibu*], for that was the purpose of the independence our elders fought for. In the ASP's 1961 Election Notice, Mzee Karume described this vision of Zanzibar like so: "Independence [*Uhuru*] is our party's foundation. [The party] naturally aims to abolish the Colonial Government, *and to end all rule from without.* Likewise, *Uhuru* replaces petty grievance and ignorance with an exuberant, welcoming goodwill [*ukunjufu*]. [It insists upon] [t]he freedom of each person to have access to the resources to do as he needs to; to delight in being human; and to live with dignity in *our country.*" (Hamad 2010; translation and emphases mine)

Declarations of admiration for Karume in opposition circles (together with an insistence on Karume's reported affection for *all* "Zanzibaris") created an opening for Zanzibaris who had long felt excluded by traditional revolutionary narratives to retroactively find that they, in agreement with many things Karume did say, had perhaps been "revolutionaries" all along. There now appeared to be a new "Karume for all." Here, CUF's leaders laid claim to the revolution, presenting themselves and their party as revolutionaries, true patriots in support of what they termed the revolution's "real" (as yet unachieved) goals: Zanzibari autonomy and self-determination. The previous interchangeability of "opposition" and "anti-revolutionary sentiment," and of both of these with "CUF" and "Pemban-ness" was no longer so simple. Certainly, allying themselves with this invigorated, welcoming image of Karume was, for many Pembans, a fresh and startling proposition. The shift also represented an effort to build a more polyphonic platform on which Zanzibaris across political parties might be united by a vision of "Zanzibari" nationhood. So, not only might Pembans find themselves to be "revolutionary," but others, too, might find themselves newly allied with an anti–status quo position that had for decades been too neatly linked in official narratives with a flattened vision of what "opposition" meant.

CCM members ambivalent about the union also found in Karume's speeches and writings a way to link themselves to a thrust of revolutionary desire that had arguably been cut short and eclipsed by the union. Supporting Zanzibari autonomy, it was now possible for them to be viewed as originary nationalists and "keepers of the flame."[76] Among these, the highly respected and powerful Mzee Hassan Nassor Moyo was instrumental in creating and supporting this new discursive space. During his long career—initially as trade unionist and member of the ASP and the Revolutionary Council, and later as a prominent CCM member and minister—Moyo was privy to many of Zanzibar's most confidential and controversial political affairs, including the formation of the union. As chairman of the GNU-supported Reconciliation Committee,[77] Moyo repeatedly insisted that Karume "didn't want discrimination.... [He] didn't want people to say, 'this one is from this place,' 'this one is from that place' .... [H]e wanted the people of Zanzibar to be *one thing*."[78] It should be noted that the "discrimination" to which Moyo referred was understood by Pembans to be discrimination by Ungujans and by CCM against *them*. Reference to "this place" and "that place" needing to "be one thing" was construed as a much-needed comment on the costly habit of discursively and politically severing Pemba from Unguja and questioning its place in *Zanzibar*.[79] Moyo publically and forcefully argued for Zanzibaris to come together regardless of old differences. In 2014, many Pembans spoke of him with respect, and he had grown especially popular among the young. While Moyo was expelled from CCM in April 2015, the support he continued to enjoy—in no small part based on his repeated insistence that old divisions be set aside in favor of autonomy for Zanzibar—suggested that this new discursive space had found meaningful favor among people eager for new language about what being Zanzibari can entail. And it raised a relatively new question: When the term "oppositional" could so publically and conclusively be used by the CCM government to refer to a stalwart party member with impeccable revolutionary credentials, what would happen to perceptions

---

76 CCM members rejecting the idea that the Union might be reformed or challenged may find themselves reevaluating their place in the story, too.

77 In conservative CCM circles the Reconciliation Committee engendered significant ambivalence, with President Ali Mohamed Shein insisting in 2013 that he did not recognize it (Sadallah 2013).

78 Address by Mzee Nassor Hassan Moyo to the Zanzibar House of Representatives, 24 September 2012. "Muungano naujua kama jina langu." From Seminar Kuhusu Mafunzo ya Elimu ya Katiba ya Jamhuri ya Muungano wa Tanzania, https://www.youtube.com/watch?v=2CyfPjoTWek, accessed 1 July 2016.

79 For a discussion of the ways that exhortations to unspecified "others" from unnamed places have figured in identity politics and the construction of Pemban-ness in particular, see Arnold 2002.

of "Pemban" identity, which, historically overdetermined, had long been exclusively synonymous with single-minded hostility to government?[80]

On 12 January 2014, the newspaper article "Let's Not Be Fooled: Pembans Did Participate in the Revolution" appeared online in *Zanzibar Daima,* generating a good deal of forwarding and discussion among those (mainly the young or especially politically active) who had access to the Internet. The unidentified writer interviewed Zanzibar National Archives staff in Chake Chake in Central Pemba. Showing an archivist a photograph of the Committee of 14, he asked how one might explain the absence of Pembans in it. The answer: "It's true that those fourteen people are said to be the ones who overthrew the government. But in fact and actually, no revolution in any country is achieved by only fourteen people. That's totally impossible." Another subject recalled Karume's many visits to close friends in Wawi, Pemba prior to the revolution. "[T]hey planned things together, were his confidantes, and they saw each other all the time. So how could Pembans have nothing to do with the revolution?" In conclusion, the author wrote, there is also the fact—only infrequently mentioned, if at all, by people I have known, but in 2014 coming into currency at least in explicitly political discourse—that, before Field Marshal John Okello became one of the revolution's most iconic figures, he had worked in a Pemban quarry. "He didn't have Pemban blood. But he left from Pemba to go overthrow the government in Unguja. How can he have been the only one to have gone to Unguja from here?"

Taking up again the locally powerful idea that "Pemba changes you," it was suddenly not impossible to imagine a future narrative in which Okello's revolutionary ideas could be said to have been crucially *shaped* by his time on the island, in whose earth the roots of revolution might eventually be found. The discursive resources for transforming the way history is told and perhaps even remembered had become publically available; the question now was, and remains, which resources will be taken up, and whether, and how. Whether or not Pembans did participate

---

80 As Salim Said Salim has noted, the expulsion of long-standing, apparently staunch and irreproachable party members from the ASP and CCM is a regular feature of Zanzibari (and mainland) politics. Moyo's expulsion (and, before him, of Mansour Yusuf Himid) should not be viewed in isolation. These came, however, at a particularly effervescent time in Zanzibari politics, where the emergence of new political parties, social movements, and sometimes surprising cross-constituency alliances considerably complicated the scene, and where the airless equivalence of "opposition" and "Pemban" seemed no longer so tight (Salim 2015).

significantly in the revolution of 1964, the fact that the question had, in print, received other than a conclusive "no" does matter.[81]

Still, just as it has been for a long time, a key question in Zanzibari political discourse continues to be, "Who belongs?" One answer often quoted by opposition leaders, and those CCM (or former CCM) members who favor greater autonomy for Zanzibar, was first phrased by the first president, Abeid Karume, in a speech given in the late 1960s, directed to the youth of "Zanzibar":

> You have the right to communicate with your government about your development. That's what it means to be a human being. You can't just huddle together like chickens in the rain. No. This government belongs to *all* the people. Today we have reached the stage of having our own government, our own wealth, and we owe nothing to anyone. This is an independent government.... [A]nd it will be run by its citizens. *And what do you have to know in order to be a citizen? You have to feel anguish and deep pain for your country.* Once you've known anguish for your country, that's when you'll be a real citizen. And how can you know this deep pain? You can't stay by yourself ... [u]nless you want only one perspective, [but] that would run counter to your duty. You've got to exchange views with other people. *Your own context and contributions, as well as those of others. That will be your education.* (translation and emphases mine)[82]

That Karume had in mind at the time a decided polyphony in the public interpretation of history is unlikely. But it seems appropriate to end a discussion of the complexities of memory with this extracted piece of historical material, which has so successfully been repurposed.[83] The use of this speech by contemporary politicians has given this arguably retrojected Karume a new profile, turning his words to a new situation in an effort to demonstrate that "opposition" and multiplicity are part and parcel of the "revolutionary spirit," and that to deny the importance

---

81 On 11 January 2014, the launch of Javed Jafferji's volume of photographs documenting the revolution—interwoven with accounts of the accomplishments of famous Zanzibaris, including author Mohammed Said Abdalla and singer Siti bint Saad—was addressed both by former president (and Abeid Karume's son) Amani Abeid Karume and by Seif Sharif Hamad, who each contributed an introductory chapter to the book. Hamad reminded all Zanzibaris to honor the legacy of the islands' first president; Amani Karume insisted that all Zanzibaris are, properly speaking, revolutionaries (*wanamapinduzi*). For a photo of the book launch, please see page 361, top. Notable as it is, this very public shift in who can claim to be a revolutionary is certainly incomplete and actively contested (see Ghassani 2016 and Makame 2014).

82 Video of Karume's speech, "Huwezi Ukaujua Uchungu wa Nchi Yako Mpaka Uwe Mwananchi." https://www.youtube.com/watch?v=fMaOcqIr1n8, accessed 25 September 2014.

83 See *Zanzibar Media Trust* 2013.

of diversity to successful revolution is, itself, anti-revolutionary. It may well be that peace and unity in Zanzibar's future will require a vision of Zanzibar that accepts multiplicity and contradiction, one that explicitly features the histories of all the islands – not only Pemba and Unguja, but Tumbatu and the others, whose histories have also been eclipsed by the familiar binaries and a too-long-standing elision of "Zanzibar" with the island of Unguja.

Although Zanzibaris disagree amongst themselves about who has truly felt "anguish and deep pain for their country" (*uchungu wa nchi yao*), and what such anguish should look like,[84] the question itself is a potentially very rich one that – perhaps more than previous questions about what people did or didn't do – could yield textured answers whose accumulation might complicate the terms of old debates. It may become necessary, too, for all the islands' inhabitants to revisit the importance of the kind of revolutionary "education" Karume once exhorted them to seek: recognizing and even embracing a full range of sometimes mutually exclusive experiences and views as part of the unique "national story," whether that story unfolds in a two- or three-government system, and whether it unfolds within, or without, the union with the mainland. As Pembans continue to live, work, and raise families on both islands, *Zanzibar* as a whole may come to include Pemban histories and lives as a matter of course rather than as an aside. If it does, the question of what, who, and, importantly, *where* "Pemba" and "Pembans" are may also generate increasingly fine-grained, multiple, coexisting answers that will (eventually "naturally," one hopes) be both timely and welcome.

---

84 See Makame 2014.

References

Alawy, Abdurrahman Sagaf, and Ali Abdalla El-Maawy
2011 *Kale ya Washairi wa Pemba: Kamange na Sarhani.* Dar es Salaam: Mkuki na Nyota.

Arnold, Nathalie
2006 "With 'Ripe' Eyes You Will See: Occult Conflicts in Pemba's Days of Caning, Zanzibar 1964–1968." In *Studies in Witchcraft, Magic, War and Peace in Africa: Nineteenth and Twentieth Centuries*, ed. Beatrice Nicolini, 215–26. New York: Edwin Mellen Press.
2003 "Wazee Wakijua Mambo!/Elders Used to Know Things!: Occult Powers and Revolutionary History in Pemba, Zanzibar." Ph.D. diss., Indiana University, Bloomington.
2002 "Placing the Shameless: Approaching Poetry and the Politics of Pemban-ness in Zanzibar, 1995–2001." *Research in African Literatures* 33(3): 140–68.

Askew, Kelly
2002 *Performing the Nation: Swahili Music and Cultural Politics in Tanzania.* Chicago: University of Chicago Press.

BBC
2012 "Zanzibar Clashes over Missing Cleric: Sheikh Farid Hadi." 18 October. bbc.com/news/world-africa-19997774, accessed 30 June 2016.

Biersteker, Ann
1996 *Kujibizana: Questions of Language and Power in Nineteenth and Twentieth Century Poetry in Kiswahili.* East Lansing, Mich.: Michigan University Press.

Bissell, William Cunningham
2005 "Engaging Colonial Nostalgia." *Cultural Anthropology* 20(2): 215–48.

Burgess, G. Thomas
2009 *Race, Revolution, and the Struggle for Human Rights in Zanzibar: The Memoirs of Ali Sultan Issa and Seif Sharif Hamad.* Athens, Ohio: Ohio University Press.

2002 "Cinema, Bell Bottoms and Miniskirts: Struggles over Youth and Citizenship in Revolutionary Zanzibar." *International Journal of African Historical Studies* 35(2/3): 287–313.

Cameron, Greg

2004. "Political Violence, Ethnicity and the Agrarian Question in Zanzibar." In *Swahili Modernities: Culture, Politics, and Identity on the East Coast of Africa*, ed. Pat Caplan and Farouk Topan, 103–20. Trenton: Africa World Press.

Caplan, Pat

2004 "Introduction." In *Swahili Modernities: Culture, Politics, and Identity on the East Coast of Africa*, eds. Pat Caplan and Farouk Topan. Trenton: Africa World Press.

Craster, J. E. E.

1913 *Pemba: The Spice Island of Zanzibar*. London: T. Fisher Unwin.

Fair, Laura

2001 *Pastimes and Politics: Culture, Community and Identity in Post-abolition Urban Zanzibar, 1980–1945*. Athens: Ohio University Press.

Ghassani, Mohammed

2016 "CCM Haina la Kuomba Radhi kwa Siasa za Uchotara." January 13. *Zanzibar Daima (Kalamu ya Ghassani)*, https://zanzibardaima.net/2016/01/13/ccm-haina-la-kuomba-radhi-kwa-siasa-za-uchotara/, accessed 30 June 2016.

Ghassany, Harith

2010 *Kwaheri Ukoloni, Kwaheri Uhuru! Zanzibar na Mapinduzi ya Afrabia* [Goodbye Colonialism, Goodbye Independence! Zanzibar and the Revolution of Afrabia]. Self published, https://kwaheri.files.wordpress.com/2010/05/kwaheri-ukoloni-kwaheri-uhuru.pdf, accessed 18 July 2016.

Giles, Linda

1989 "Spirit Possession on the Swahili Coast: Peripheral Cult or Primary Text." PhD. diss., University of Texas at Austin.

Glassman, Jonathon

2011 *War of Words, War of Stones: Racial Thought and Violence in Colonial Zanzibar*. Bloomington, Ind.: Indiana University Press.

Government of the United Republic of Tanzania

1966 *Maendeleo Yaliyopatikana Katika Mkoa wa Pemba Tokea Mapinduzi ya Tarehe 12 Januari, 1964–1966.* Zanzibar: Government Printers.

Haj, Maulid M.

2001 *Sowing the Wind: Zanzibar and Pemba before the Revolution.* Zanzibar: Gallery Publications.

Hamad, Seif Sharif

2010 "Tutaijenga Zanzibar Mpya." *Haki na Umma (CUF).* 29 June. hakinaumma.wordpress.com/2010/06/29/tutaijenga-zanzibar-mpya-maalim-seif/, accessed 30 June 2016.

Human Rights Watch

2002 *Bullets Were Raining: The January 2001 Attack on Peaceful Demonstrators in Zanzibar.* New York: Human Rights Watch.

Ingrams, William Harold

1931 *Zanzibar: Its History and Its People.* London: Taylor & Francis.

Jafferji, Javed

2014 *Kitabu cha Picha ya Miaka Hamsini ya Mapinduzi Zanzibar.* Zanzibar: Gallery Publications.

Larscn, Kjcrsti

2008 *Where Humans and Spirits Meet: The Politics of Rituals and Identified Spirits in Zanzibar.* New York: Berghahn.

2004 "Change, Continuity and Contestation: The Politics of Modern Identities in Zanzibar." In *Swahili Modernities: Culture, Politics and Identity on the East Coast of Africa,* eds. Pat Caplan and Farouk Topan, 121–43. Trenton: Africa World Press.

Lofchie, Michael F.

1965 *Zanzibar: Background to Revolution.* Princeton, N.J.: Princeton University Press.

Makame, Asha Bakari

2014. Speech to Tanzanian Parliament, April 23 (Asha Bakari Akiufyatua Bungeni). https://www.youtube.com/watch?v=nQW3VP1W5hU, accessed 30 June 2016.

Martin, Esmond B.

1978 *Zanzibar: Tradition and Revolution.* London: Hamish Hamilton.

Mazrui, Ali, and Ibrahim Noor Shariff

1994 *The Swahili: Idiom and Identity of an African People.* Trenton: Africa World Press.

Mazrui Media

2014 "Hatimaye Mansour Yusuf Himid Apata Dhamana." 19 August. zanzibariyetu.wordpress.com/2014/08/19/hatimaye-mansour-yusuf-himid-apata-dhamana/, accessed 30 June 2016.

McMahon, Elisabeth

2013 *Slavery and Emancipation in Islamic East Africa: From Honor to Respectability.* Cambridge: Cambridge University Press.

Middleton, John

1961 *Land Tenure in Zanzibar.* London: Her Majesty's Stationery Office.

Mussa, Bakar

2012 "Miche ya Mikarafuu 34,000 Yapandwa Pemba." *Zanzinews,* 30 January. zanzinews.com/2012/01/miche-ya-mikarafuu-34000-yapandwa-pemba.html, accessed 30 June 2016.

Sadallah, Mwinyi

2013 "Dr Shein: I Don't Recognize Reconciliation Committee." *IPP Media.* 8 June. http://zanzibarnikwetu.blogspot.com/2013/06/dr-shein-i-dont-recognize.html, accessed 30 June 2016.

Salim, Said Salim

2015 "Expelling Moyo from CCM Is Wrong." *The Citizen,* April 26. www.thecitizen.co.tz/News/national/Expelling-Moyo-from-CCM-is-wrong/-/1840392/2697710/-/6m2c3iz/-/index.html, accessed 30 June 2016.

Shariff, Ibrahim Noor

1988 *Tungo Zetu: Msingi wa Mashairi na Tungo Nyinginezo.* Trenton, N.J.: Red Sea Press.

Stockley, G. M.

1928 *Report on the Geology of the Zanzibar Protectorate.* Zanzibar: Government Printers.

Stockreiter, Elke
2015 *Islamic Law, Gender, and Social Change in Post-abolition Zanzibar.* Iowa City: University of Iowa Press.

Goldman, Helle
1996 "A Comparative Study of Swahili in Two Rural Communities in Pemba, Zanzibar." Ph.D. diss., New York University.

Walsh, Martin
2010 "Ali Sultan and the Days of the Cane." *East African Notes and Records.* 10 October. notesandrecords.blogspot.com/2010/10/ali-sultan-issa-and-days-of-cane.html, accessed 30 June 2016.
2009 "The Use of Wild and Cultivated Plants as Famine Foods on Pemba Island, Zanzibar." *Études Océan Indien, Plantes et Sociétés* 42/43: 217–41.

Winther, Tanja
2008 *The Impact of Electricity: Development, Desires, and Dilemmas.* New York: Berghahn Books.

Zanzibar Daima
2014 "Tusidanganywe: WaPemba Walishiriki Mapinduzi." 12 January. http://zanzibarelite.blogspot.com.tr/2014/01/tusidanganywe-wapemba-walishiriki.html, accessed 30 June 2016.

Zanzibar Media Trust
2013 *Kwa Nini Tusirejeshe Jamhuri ya Watu wa Zanzibar?* (film). Zanzibar Media Trust: Zanzibar city, Zanzibar.

Zanzinews
2015 "Shirika la Taifa la Biashara Zanzibar (ZSTC) Yatoa Vifaa kwa Wakulima wa Karafuu Mkoa wa Kaskazini Unguja." 31 March. zanzinews.com/2015/03/shirika-la-taifa-la-biashara-zanzibar.html, accessed 30 June 2016.

Chapter Six

Uncommon Misery, Relegated to the Margins: Tumbatu and Fifty Years of the Zanzibar Revolution

Makame Ali Muhajir and Garth Andrew Myers

The village muezzin was about to call for the dawn prayers in early January 1969. Juma's father, Mbaruk, was secretly preparing to flee the village, accompanied by a few others.[1] A naval special force was already anchored at Jongowe, a fishing port in southern Tumbatu island, preparing to launch a military search of the settlement. An angry voice was heard throughout the village, issuing from the navy boat's loudspeakers: "Ali Saleh, Chairman of Tumbatu Jongowe, you are required to surrender voluntarily for your own safety at this moment, by the end of this announcement. Your village is under security watch. All villagers should remain calm inside their homes ... on the mission commander's instructions." Obeying this call, Saleh, the local ruling party chair, ran from his house, painfully confused, toward the village's harbor in response to the loudspeaker's command. Within a few hours, the village was under the first of several curfews declared during the last half-century. Six other young Jongowe villagers were later seized and taken on board the navy boat. They disappeared on it down the Tumbatu Channel toward Zanzibar city, where they would join other suspects on a journey from which they would never return. After being accused of sedition and detained without trial, the villagers were ultimately executed; Mbaruk managed to escape this fate by hiding and going into exile.[2]

This vignette epitomizes the menace that transpired in Tumbatu during the early, bloody years of Zanzibar's revolutionary era. Although it was certainly not alone in this regard among other communities in rural Zanzibar (in both Unguja and Pemba), Tumbatu's Jongowe

---

1   For this and all oral interview sources in the chapter, pseudonyms are used to protect the anonymity of the respondents.

2   Interview, "Mbaruk," 18 December 2012, Tumbatu.

community experienced collective trauma in the early revolutionary period from which it has yet to recover. Other communities that fall on this list on Unguja island would include Bumbwini, Nungwi, Uzi, Limbani-Kizimkazi, Bweleo and Fumba—villages in the northern, central, southern, and western districts of Zanzibar, respectively. Many communities on Pemba Island have a comparably negative experience of the revolution and its aftermath. But Tumbatu's indigenous antiquity and prestige in the medieval history of Zanzibar have factored into its particular political significance. If we consider, for example, the claim of Francis B. Pearce (1920: 251) that "the islanders of Tumbatu ... are the most unaltered representatives of the original island stock," then this indigenous character warrants focused attention to Tumbatu's relationship to the revolution.

Fifty years on from the 1964 revolution, the revolutionary government of Zanzibar went on a spending spree to commemorate its Silver Jubilee in 2014 (Feinstein 2014; Oke 2014). The public prominence of the revolutionary government's memorial celebrations of the revolt—particularly at the 25th, 30th, 40th, and, most recently, 50th anniversaries—contrasts sharply with the hidden transcripts of other memories, of what Chris Oke (2014) calls the "forgotten genocide" of the revolution. Beyond the official revolutionary celebrations lies a vast array of memories of repressive military and intelligence deployments that generated simmering community anger around the isles well after that forgotten genocide. These memories of secretive actions and their aftermath are the subject of this chapter, which includes a case study of Jongowe village on Tumbatu. We use interviews, focus-group discussions, life histories, and both archival and secondary sources from research conducted between 1995 and 2013. We document the harsh experiences in Jongowe in Zanzibar's revolutionary and post-revolutionary era and trace the largely hidden narrative of attacks on ordinary community members that largely negated the revolution's promises or desires for settlements like Jongowe. The perspective we adopt and our sense of the hidden narrative are based on the veiled and unveiled threats and then the excessive use of force many interviewees spoke privately about experiencing. This experience of oppression and repression has, we argue, outstripped the capacity to recognize individual community interests, such as those of Tumbatu people even in the allegedly open democratic system of 1995 onward.

Tumbatu memories of the 1964 Zanzibar revolution and its aftermath are refracted through the distorted lens through which Tumbatu islanders and other Zanzibaris view each other. One can only approach what distinguishes Tumbatu Jongowe memories of the revolution after contextualizing those memories within the frame of that distorted lens. Therefore, after situating the case study and providing some contextual understanding of everyday life in Jongowe, we contrast how Tumbatu cultural identity has appeared in the representations of outsiders with how Tumbatu islanders perceive their ties with other Zanzibaris and with mainland Tanzanians. We then detail the key events of the revolution—and of the revolutionary era of 1964–2014—in relation to Jongowe, highlighting several particular memories of the revolution and the early revolutionary era in the settlement. Ultimately, this discussion helps to uncover what we see as a revealing underside of the Zanzibar revolution for marginalized rural settlements such as Jongowe that were, in many respects, communities in need of genuine liberation that did not really happen. It also shows the long-lasting impact of geographic and ethnic stereotypes that mark places like Tumbatu as backward, in both the colonial and postcolonial eras.

Situating Tumbatu and Jongowe

Tumbatu is the largest offshore islet in Zanzibar in both size and population (see Figure 1, page 221). The island had a population of 12,388 in the 2012 Tanzania census, divided between the *shehia* (locations) of Gomani (4990), Uvivini (4136), and Jongowe (3262) (see Table 1, page 219). Although there is some diversity among Tumbatu self-perceptions, most Tumbatu islanders see themselves as humble people, and they often appear to outsiders as people who resist change. Their life even before the revolution was extremely basic in terms of possessions, economic privileges, and access to technological advancement: They are at heart people of the coast and sea, fisherfolk and cooperative small farmers. The island's environment is rocky, and farming produces subsistence crops like pigeon peas, red beans, cassava, maize, and cowpeas. It is common for Jongowe children to help their parents in subsistence activities, including farming, fishing, and small businesses. Unlike most Zanzibaris on Unguja and Pemba, they still transport their goods by dhows and small sailing vessels, and they find pride in depicting themselves as a traditional community, claiming that "in how we live together in the neighborhoods we have not changed much."[3] For Jongowe people, a combination of annual traditional

---

3 Interview, "Issa," 6 July 2000, Tumbatu.

rituals, regular daily prayers, and *Maulidi* (celebrations of the birthday of the Prophet Muhammad) still remain as residents' foundations in life, reproducing the community.

Tumbatu islanders' food is the traditional sustenance with limited exceptions, and a significant degree of malnutrition exists in everyday life. A combination of factors led to malnutrition's persistence, including the island's generally poor soils, poor connectivity with markets, lack of technology or development inputs, and state indifference. Tumbatu fishing still involves the use of basket traps, simple single-hook lines, and *jarife* nets. Women and children, especially, also fish by wading in the foreshore in the afternoon, using methods like *kuchokoa* and *kutanda*,[4] looking for small shellfish, sea snails, oysters, eels, lobsters, octopi, and smelts. When men go at night for open-ocean fishing, they use nets that are laid on the sea floor; for near-shore fishing (for sardines and cuttlefish or squid) they might use kerosene lanterns and thatched *myenge*.[5] Tumbatu islanders' customary practice is to establish fishing camps, where they fish various areas along the East African coast from Lamu in northern Kenya down to Sofala in Mozambique (Sheriff 2010: 33). Jongowe residents say that their yields from the sea and the fields were very good long ago but that these days their resource base has dwindled, with overfishing and a decrease in land available for farming. The surrounding ocean has suffered from illegal fishing, which has exploded all over Zanzibar's waters since the beginning of the modern tourist economy. Tourism is not yet accepted on Tumbatu because of its perceived environmental, religious, and cultural problems.

The village area of Jongowe is 970 hectares, of which 584 are used for rotational bush fallowing agriculture and 135 are the village's protected forest. Many homes are of basic wood and thatch materials and are simply built on the ground. These are being replaced by simple concrete-block structures, with some slight recent growth of the village economy (largely due to income returned to the village from Zanzibar city and elsewhere). As in most areas of Zanzibar, the village is confronted with many environmental problems. Its natural resources are over-harvested, with neither orderly harvesting nor keen local awareness of the impact of population growth, as the birth rate in the village is very

---

4   *Kuchokoa* means "scoop-out" fishing (for shellfish or oysters); *kutanda* designates fishing by a group of women who spread (*-tanda*) very fine nets, then gather the nets, usually for catching smelts.

5   Fish traps.

high (Muhammed 2014). The population of Tumbatu's two settlements has grown since 1988, but the standard of living and quality of life have declined overall. As one resident, "Hassan," put it, "poverty is our biggest problem. We have social unity, water supply—sometimes—and electricity [sometimes], but none of that matters to a child who hasn't eaten all day."[6] Tumbatu today is an out-of-the-way place: A marginalized rural space with a small number of people living in an environment characterized by extreme poverty. Yet it has not always been so, as we discuss in the following section.

Historical Memories and Colonial Misrepresentation

The Jongowe area on southern Tumbatu has been inhabited in some fashion for at least 2,000 years. This southern area of Tumbatu island was home to arguably the largest city of the Zanzibar islands during the medieval era (see Figure 2, page 219). From the Arab geographer Yaqut's frequently cited and prominent reference to "Tumbat" in the 13th century, through the 1989 recovery of a "Shirazi" inscription from an early 12th-century *qibla,* to the recognition that the occupying Portuguese established administrative centers in the 16th century at Limbani in the present Jongowe village and on Unguja itself at Fukucheni directly opposite the Tumbatu city site, there is ample evidence of the city's medieval significance (Pearce 1920; Ingrams 1931; Sutton 1990; Horton 1996; Horton and Middleton 2000; Trimingham 1975). The ruins of medieval Tumbatu have been a source of substantial local pride for Tumbatu Jongowe residents.

Tumbatu was one of the main culture hearths of Swahili civilization from at least the early 12th through the early 16th centuries ce, when the island and its city dominated the northern half of Unguja island. The island lent its name to the culture group that predominates in what is today's Unguja-Kaskazini Region of Tanzania. Tumbatu's Swahili culture has material evidence of the island's long arc of global connectivity: its dhows, fishing boats, and *ngalawa* evolved from different societal traditions beyond Africa, as Tumbatu peoples mingled with and borrowed from ancient and medieval Arab, Axumite, Indian, Persian, and Polynesian (Malagasy) traders or travelers (Gray 1963). All Swahili communities in East Africa share a long history of such connections, but Tumbatu culture has numerous features that distinguish it. Perhaps most notably, Tumbatu has a long tradition of choosing women leaders,

---

6   Interview, "Hassan," 29 December 1999.

such as the medieval queen Mwana wa Mwana and her daughter, Fatuma—a tradition that continues with the current *sheha* of Jongowe village, Miza Sharif.

By the time the seat of Omani control over the islands shifted to Zanzibar city in the 1690s, though, Jongowe was clearly in decline—even if Jongowe's indigenous historians make the case that it was their queen who ceded the land to the Omanis for their new seat of government (al-Barwani 1997). Under Omani rule, Tumbatu remained the seat of regional governance for northern Unguja, but when Britain took over in 1890, it lost even this modest role (Myers 2005). And in many historians' accounts, particularly for those who wrote during the colonial era, there is a disconnect between the contemporary inhabitants of Tumbatu and any evocations of a glorious past: The "backward" people of the islands in the 20th century could not, to these historians, be the descendants of those who made Tumbatu so prominent in the medieval golden age (Kirkman 1964).

Tumbatu island's history and its people have been misapprehended, manipulated, and shrouded in mystery from a time well before the 1964 revolution. Tumbatu's story illustrates well the "anachronistic space" (McClintock 1995) into which colonial discourse sought to cast many of rural Africa's indigenous peoples—a timeless, primeval place, without history or significance. In many colonial settings, such discourse was often paired with claims that Africa's rural people were illogically resistant to change, and particularly to the changes—such as western notions of "welfare," "modernity" and "development"—that colonial regimes sought to impose. Discourses of anachronistic space and of "othering" colonized people often served the dual purpose of justifying colonial rule over distant territories and reinforcing colonizers' sense of their own superiority (Blaut 1993; Said 1993; Slater 2004). Colonialism's discursive tactics in these matters often resonated with post-colonial elites of racial or ethnic heritage different from the most marginalized groups, leading to situations where African nationalist leaders disparaged their own people's backwardness as one of the "pitfalls of a national consciousness" in the post-independence eras (Fanon 1963). Such marginalization often reflects back upon marginalized societies in their cautious regard for outsider authorities. In the Tumbatu example, we see that the misunderstandings, ignorance, and sometimes outright bigotry with which outsiders have viewed Tumbatu have cast a long shadow upon the caution with which islanders view outsiders, whether British,

Zanzibari, Tanzanian, or otherwise. This history of misapprehension colors memories of the revolution for Tumbatu island peoples.

For instance, British colonial officials and early 20th-century historians of the East African coast found only backhanded means for recognizing Tumbatu's medieval importance, while expressing derision toward its contemporary population. In most of what was written about Jongowe or Tumbatu before 1964, Jongowe's underdevelopment and isolation are portrayed as being its own fault. Colonial writers constructed an idea of Tumbatu islanders as backward, suspicious, and isolated people, in a manner paralleling colonialist writings about many other African peoples, and particularly the continent's most marginalized peoples. Colonial scholarship repeatedly drove home the separateness, aloofness, and hostility of Tumbatu islanders to various inroads of progress (Myers 2005; North 2010). The archeologist James Kirkman (1964: 174) wrote that Tumbatu's inhabitants were "a determinedly suspicious people [who] prefer to have as little to do as possible with foreigners, by whom they mean everyone not a Tumbatu." William Ingrams (1931: 146) argued that in Tumbatu "the natives" were "very exclusive people" who "dislike interference, thus, unfortunately, they are largely inbred." British resident Francis Pearce (1920: 251) claimed that Tumbatu's people were "of a characteristically suspicious and retiring disposition." This disposition, Pearce (1920: 144-45) wrote, went together with "a reputation for aloofness and individuality, coupled with an addiction to witchcraft and the black arts." This sort of portrayal parallels historians' relative neglect or disdain toward the medieval Tumbatu queens of Zanzibar, in comparison to the southern Unguja polity of the (male) *Mwinyi Mkuu,* or Great Lord (Nicholls 1971: 72-73). By contrast, Kirkman (1964: 174) claimed, dismissively, that "there seems to have been an independent ruler in the north at Tumbatu but he [sic] succeeded in avoiding the interest of history."

Official colonial documents show that these derogatory ideas had enduring practical consequences for Jongowe. After a rare visit to Tumbatu in 1952, the British resident menacingly informed his chief secretary that the islanders had "acquired some reputation for noncooperation with the Government.... We must bring it home to the islanders that if they fail to co-operate in Government measures for their own benefit the result will be that *much greater attention is paid to them*" (Zanzibar National Archives, 1952; emphasis ours). For the British colonial regime, Tumbatu came to mean a place of resistance, perversity, fear, and magic. Tumbatu's people—who, it needs reiterating, traveled widely and lived all along the East African coast in seasonal fishing camps—could not help but become conscious of the stigma attached to them and to their place. Their identities and the identity of the place became intertwined with this imaginary rendition of them in ways that have resurfaced time and again (Myers 2005).

More recent outsider perspectives have begun to recognize Tumbatu's historic significance, albeit still without much discussion of any threads tying the contemporary Tumbatu islanders to their historic past. Outsider (i.e., non-Tumbatu) researchers have provided more substantial and sensitive archeological, linguistic, and archival evidence of the importance of the medieval city of Tumbatu and of religious and cultural influences of the island on Zanzibari and Swahili society (Sutton 2000; Horton 1996; Horton and Middleton 2000; Pouwels 1987, 1999, 2000; Sheriff 2010; Chami 2009). Yet within Zanzibar itself, there remains an uncomfortable separation of Tumbatu from the rest of Zanzibar and an alienation of contemporary Jongowe from the significant role it has played in defining Zanzibari identity, culture, society, and politics over the course of a millennium.

In party politics as played out from the waning days of colonialism until now, Tumbatu and northernmost Unguja have comprised the political middle ground in Zanzibar. In the "time of politics" (1957–1964), Tumbatu voters in the three pre-independence elections were evenly split between the three political parties of the time, the Afro-Shirazi Party (ASP), Zanzibar National Party (ZNP), and Zanzibar and Pemba People's Party (ZPPP). Crucially, the smallest of the three parties, the ZPPP, won the Tumbatu island constituency in the last pre-independence poll. The British granted independence to Zanzibar in December 1963, handing over power to a ZNP/ZPPP coalition that had earned a combined 37 percent of the popular vote but held 18 of 31 constituencies because of the way the British had drawn constituency boundaries (Mosare 1969; Lofchie 1965). A month after independence, on 12 January 1964, ASP-led revolutionaries overthrew the minority coalition government. Months of turmoil, violence, and retributive killings followed. Tumbatu islanders who supported ZPPP or ZNP paid a heavy price, in properties destroyed, physical harm, and loss of life.

For our purposes, it is useful to contemplate the collective social memories of Tumbatu islanders not just of the Zanzibar revolution itself in January 1964, but of the entire half-century of the revolutionary era since then. Collective social memories are of course very complicated to tease out, and their deployment in academic scholarship, particularly in social and political history, has been a subject of long and deep controversy (Fair 2001). Notably, in the Zanzibar case, Jonathon Glassman (2011) has chastised many historians of Zanzibar—indeed, nearly all of us—for reliance on what he takes as dodgy oral testimonies from interviews that are highly skewed, shaped by ideological arguments and designed to manipulate interviewers. He contends that the collective social memories expressed in these interviews fit into an easy framework that blames British colonialism, in kneejerk fashion, for the racial tensions that led to violence and ultimately the deadly slaughter that followed the revolution (Myers 2012).

It is not our intention to review the vast literature on the question of collective social memories, nor do we wish to reopen the wounds of the debate on Glassman's work. We do not dispute that both collective social memories and oral data can be deeply problematic to work with, epistemologically and methodologically (Fair 2013). However, in our case, there are several crucial facts that reinforce our argument that collective social memories obtained in interviews and focus groups are highly informative and valuable for understanding Tumbatu's relationship to the revolution itself and to the conceptual and symbolic realm in which the revolution lives on. First, many of the written, archival records relating to Tumbatu were burned in public by the revolutionary regime after the 1969 coup attempt, making a paper trail or the sort of methodological claims for rigor Glassman makes virtually impossible for a Tumbatu revolution or post-revolution narrative. Second, Tumbatu Jongowe's customary practice of marriage across close extended-family lines (second-cousin marriages are very common) make it a community with, literally, very intimate interconnections. Undoubtedly, there are differences of opinion, disputes over memories, and ideological forces shaping and manipulating any public statements of memories by Tumbatu Jongowe people, and we have certainly been witness to these. However, when one hears the same or very similar accounts, sentiments, emotions, and recollections from an overwhelming number of respondents, without significant counterarguments, it seems thoroughly legitimate to us to call this a "collective social memory" held by the vast majority of Tumbatu Jongowe people.

In this way, it can thus be said that the scars of the revolutionary era run deep in Tumbatu Jongowe particularly. Before examining this in detail, though, it is important to delineate the more contemporary political context of tension and turmoil in Zanzibar, which has also fostered further alienation of Tumbatu Jongowe from both revolutionary Zanzibar and from the United Republic of Tanzania.

Zanzibar's Revolutionary Era

Undoubtedly, desire for the overthrow of the Omani-dominated sultanate government and an ethnic/party-based rebalancing of power were primary causes of Zanzibar's revolution. However, tensions between underprivileged indigenous and poverty-stricken immigrant communities within both Zanzibar's urban and rural settlements were also key dynamics of the revolutionary era. As Buhaug and Rød (2006: 319) put it, "[P]overty and wealth are spatially clustered within countries: even in societies with low levels of inequalities, some regions are more prosperous than others." But we contend that ethnic community groups in underprivileged rural areas such as in Tumbatu Jongowe might just as easily take a different tack from other underprivileged groups in a revolutionary moment regardless of the inequality, injustice, and poverty they suffer.

It was mostly urbanized African people and those from the city periphery who, with mainland African support, led the revolution, and rose against their own fellow Zanzibaris—many of whom came from cultural communities with a longer settlement background on the islands, such as Tumbatu and Pemba peoples. Led by the ASP's Abeid Amani Karume, the Committee of 14 of the early revolutionary era created a socialist hue to Zanzibar's politics that has endured for more than 50 years despite the return of multiparty politics and opening of the economy (Clayton 1981: 79; Myers and Muhajir 2013). The aftermath of the revolution has been bitter for communities that were targeted as opponents to the revolution or deemed sympathizers with the deposed sultanate. The African revolutionaries began their coup with thousands of killings, by machete or by rifle, of members and followers of the sultan's regime and the ZNP/ZPPP (Petterson 2002; al-Barwani 1997; Glassman 2011). The killings brought shock after shock in many city neighborhoods and, crucially, across rural villages sympathetic to the deposed regime, among them Jongowe. Since 1964, the Revolutionary Government of Zanzibar has had sour relations with indigenous communities like Jongowe, and the atrocities of the early revolutionary era are the fundamental—but usually unspoken—cause of these difficult relations.

After the revolution, the ASP regime quickly united with Tanganyika (on 26 April 1964) to form Tanzania, and the union had a role in quelling the outright slaughter of opponents of the revolution. But the union's focus on the African majority turned it against certain indigenous communities in the islands who appeared less willing to be conceived of as "African," while political power more broadly steadily shifted to the mainland (Muhajir 2011: 144; al-Barwani 1997). When Aboud Jumbe took over the Zanzibar presidency following Karume's assassination in 1972, he came with a new political agenda for reforms that looked to strengthen his own political ambitions under the umbrella of the union (Jumbe 1994). Jumbe favored a federation of Tanzania with three, rather than the existing two, governments, in order to let Tanganyika have its own government. He also opposed the merger of the ASP with TANU (Tanganyika African National Union) to form the Chama cha Mapinduzi (CCM) in 1977, which "seriously eroded Zanzibar's autonomy" (Bakari 2001: 114). Yet Jumbe is also remembered for achieving some other goals. While his so-called "flea revolution" failed, he made gradual strides towards Zanzibar's democratization process. As Makame Muhajir (2011: 147) put it, "[H]is gradualist approach began to abate the power of the revolutionary council (the Zanzibar President's cabinet of ministers) hitherto a powerful and union controlled political body." Jumbe also produced a new constitution for Zanzibar, introducing a legislative House of Representatives that in turn further reduced the power of the revolutionary council.

By 1990, the then president, Salmin Amour, initiated Zanzibar's political reorientation toward a multiparty democracy and a freewheeling economy, beginning officially in July 1992. Zanzibar experienced a tumultuous political tug of war between CCM and the new opposition party, Civic United Front (CUF), through the Amour years (1990–2000) and most of the two terms of his successor, Amani Karume (2000–2010). Following the 1995 and 2000 multiparty electoral tensions, there were two failed peace agreements, the first between CUF and the Amour regime, the second between CUF and Karume. The ruling party's intolerance of people in the opposition—including Jongowe people, who overwhelmingly supported CUF—was the root cause of much of the tumult and rancor. CUF refused to recognize the results of the 1995, 2000, and 2005 elections; they accepted those of 2010 following the ruling regime's agreement with the leader of the CUF opposition, Seif Sharif Hamad, for the formation of the Government of National Unity (GNU), regardless of the election outcome (Myers and Muhajir 2013). Despite some appreciation for apparent achievements under this third peace agreement between CCM and CUF, there have been countercurrents that have run much deeper than the superficial reconciliation. Notably, some of CCM's ruling ideologues viewed the rapprochement between Karume and Hamad with suspicion, fearing that it would jeopardize the legacy of the revolution. Their anxieties echo the words of an anonymous CCM politician who told us in 2008, "We won't give our revolutionary achievement away.... [E]veryone should understand that this revolution is forever."[7]

The current Zanzibari regime, led by Ali Mohamed Shein (2010–), begrudgingly included the opposition in its cabinet from 2010–15, but with very limited responsibilities, and CUF's leader, Zanzibar's first vice president Seif Sharif Hamad, had the role of tamping down his own restive opposition followers. Nevertheless, clear political changes occurred after the secret deal was reached between Hamad and Amani Karume (Myers and Muhajir 2013). A popular referendum on 31 July 2010 paved the path to power-sharing through the GNU. Some 66 percent of the Zanzibaris who voted actually voted in its favor. With this referendum came a constitutional dilemma, too. Zanzibar's House of Representatives went on to amend the islands' constitution, redefining the islands as an *nchi* (country or state) within the United Republic of Tanzania, a move that reignited controversy over the future of the union and a movement to redo the union's constitution (James and Kagashe 2010; Myers and Muhajir 2013).

Chaired by Joseph Warioba (Julius K. Nyerere's prime minister and former chief justice), the 2013 Constitutional Review Commission (CRC) then emerged with the same three-tier federal government framework amid the reinstatement of the government of Tanganyika as proposed long ago by Jumbe (*The Citizen* 2013). This new proposal for a revised union structure aimed "to create a federation of three governments that equates the status of the mainland vis-a-vis Zanzibar, which should operate under an autonomous government status" (Enonchong 2012: 3). As this insurgent constitutional movement created headaches at the highest political levels, leaders from local villages, including those from Tumbatu island, struggled to figure out what path to take in their quest for daily community survival and stability, navigating away from the political risks that they experienced in most of the revolutionary era. Then the results of the October 2015 elections were annulled after the partial announcement of vote counts that suggested an overwhelming CUF victory, leading to a highly faulted March 2016 re-run that CUF boycotted. This most recent election has only further alienated rural communities like Jongowe from the CCM's highly dubious post-2016 regime in Zanzibar.

---

7   Interview, Anonymous, 8 July 2008, Zanzibar.

Outcomes of the Revolutionary Era in Jongowe

With the first president Karume's death in Zanzibar in 1972, the notorious initial phase of the revolution seemed to be over. But the Jongowe community had suffered deeply, in silence, under Karume's regime, particularly following the alleged coup attempt of 1969. Table 2 presents a timeline chart of the key revolutionary events in Tumbatu/Jongowe since 1964 (see page 219–220). As the timeline shows, the village was faced with difficult circumstances from 1964 on. In this section, we use the recollections of one Jongowe family in particular, individuals whom we call Juma, Mbaruk, and Rehema, to illustrate the misery the village has endured. The village's nexus of marginalization, underdevelopment, and repression is not only part of a narrative that has parallels in many rural regions of Sub-Saharan Africa in the era of the post-colonial hangover; it is also a node that highlights one of the most deeply ironic legacies of the revolution. That is this: The revolutionaries continue to portray the revolution and all that followed it as "the logical outcome of centuries of oppression and subjugation" (Mapuri 1996: 1) for the marginalized poor of Zanzibar like those of Tumbatu Jongowe, and yet, for many poor residents of places like Jongowe, the revolutionary party's regime has been seen, in many respects, as only reinforcing the oppression and subjugation.

Juma is a middle-aged man whose father, Mbaruk, was implicated in counter-revolutionary activities in 1969. As a child in a divorced family of five at the time of the naval action against Jongowe in that year (see the introductory section of this chapter), he lived in makeshift desperation in a broken and thatched sticks-and-stones house with his grandmother when his father was forced into exile. Everyone knew about the poor state of their living environment, he says, adding that even moderate rain showers would cause water to drain into the house and flood rooms. Juma's mother, Rehema, was deeply affected by the events in Tumbatu, initially by the departure of her husband, Mbaruk, and later by their divorce and other personal misfortunes, which she associated with the revolutionary era. Rehema's tireless efforts on behalf of her children came with her fervent belief that the revolutionary witch-hunt that had exiled her husband and destroyed many other lives was a mistake.[8]

In spite of great hardship, Rehema sent Juma to school, which fostered his hope for career success and his commitment to mend his family situation. In Jongowe, though, many local politicians, such as Mbaruk, were strong sympathizers of the ZNP who had stood against the 1964

---

8   Interview, "Rehema," 24 June 2006, Tumbatu.

Zanzibar revolution and the ASP. The ideological differences of colonial times were magnified and refracted in the revolutionary politics of Zanzibar, which had ominous implications for Jongowe's position in Tanzania's political affairs. Juma recounts:

> I was about nine years of age in third grade, when I experienced riotous incidents that were harmful to both myself, my village, and my family in Jongowe. Those incidences included my father's displacement to the mainland, harassments, detentions, and political assassinations of my fellow villagers. The first curfew occurred during my childhood in 1969, which paralyzed the whole village and stopped us from going to school for weeks, as I recall. Including this curfew, we have been ambushed, tormented, and politically harmed in Jongowe under three state-organized attacks by the Tanzanian military, Zanzibar marines, and intelligence forces. Nine villagers, including my father, were falsely accused of treasonable offences against the state in 1969. It was alleged by the intelligence forces that Jongowe people were suspected to have collaborated with Arab mercenaries from Mombasa, Kenya, in their failed coup attempt against the revolutionary regime. Six of these young people disappeared from the village and were then killed by a firing squad in one of the naval barracks in the city. Another village ambush was carried out in 1972 following the assassination of the first Zanzibar president Abeid Karume when Jongowe people were again falsely blamed. Following the 1995 election, the state intelligence forces attacked, and again after the 2000 elections, through their militia called Janjaweed, who organized an attack in the village, which had voted for CUF.[9]

Treason accusations have been leveled at Jongowe people after each major political incident since the 1960s. Several of these incidents happened while Juma was still young. Mbaruk endured seven years in exile, working in fishing camps in remote coastal Tanzanian and Kenyan locations during Juma's childhood years in the 1960s and 1970s. As he was in the nine-man group of village-mates accused of treason, Mbaruk sought to escape detention or execution at the hands of the Zanzibar authorities. For Juma, Mbaruk's absence foisted

> the caring role of us four children to our mother and our grandmother in miserable life conditions that depended on subsistence cultivation in a very stony village environment to support us for nearly all that childhood period. As I recall, I could not easily recognize my father when he returned while I was in about seventh grade. It was my uncle, his elder brother, who first took me to school. In my father's absence

---

9   Interview, "Juma," 27 June 2006, Tumbatu.

during my childhood period, I had to learn the hard way how to be the firstborn, trying to support my family while going to school at the same time. From time to time, authorities kept on arresting suspected opposition followers; no one from the ruling party ever gets arrested. The state authorities did not bother to report much of the issues of concern from my remotely located hometown.[10]

The one exception to this, according to Juma, came when "our own native leaders appealed to the then Zanzibar president, Aboud Jumbe, for his help in our village education."[11]

Contrary to the revolutionary promises to provide educational and social development for the poor and underdeveloped majority of the islands, Tumbatu Jongowe was denied a school by the Zanzibar authorities for more than ten years after the 1964 revolution. The village children had to go to the nearest school in Gomani for their primary-school years, as Tumbatu had no kindergarten or preschool system. A primary school was finally established in 1975 in Jongowe; this was the year when Mbaruk for the first time returned temporarily to the village from his involuntary exile, while his son Juma left the community for his junior high and high school education in the city. It seems to most Jongowe people that this denial of a school was purposely done as punishment by the authorities because of their perceived opposition to the 1964 revolution. Juma was in the "first batch of 14" students sent to the Tumbatu school located at Gomani village, built some three years after the revolution to benefit Tumbatu's other, larger village—which had, to a great extent, collaborated with the revolutionaries. It emerged later from our village interviews that most of the "first batch" of Jongowe students became dropouts, due to what they saw as oppressive treatment by the state, among other hardships.

Still, at least a whiff of community progress was felt when the school was built in Tumbatu Gomani in 1966, and then a school in Jongowe in 1975. Since then, no fewer than 80 percent of Tumbatu island's young people have gone to school, and about three-fourths of the graduates have afterward become important generators of income for their families. As one indigenous leader put it to us in an interview in 2000, "[W]e got left behind in education and development. They made us into slaves, servants, porters, you see? So we tried to liberate ourselves.... The key to our liberation is education.... We are too small and powerless

---

10   Interview, "Juma," 27 June 2006, Tumbatu.

11   Interview, "Juma," 27 June 2006, Tumbatu.

to liberate ourselves with weapons. Instead, we liberate ourselves with education, little by little."[12]

However, most Jongowe residents are compelled to eke out a living from subsistence agriculture and artisanal fishing. The limited incomes available on the island force many Tumbatu to migrate elsewhere to seek employment; this typically entails migrating to the city, as it has since at least the 1940s (by which time the Tumbatu had gained a reputation as reliable porters in the city port, meager employment that remains a niche for many Tumbatu today). The reality still obtains that most employment opportunities in Zanzibar hinge on the question of political affiliation. Consequently, for most Jongowe people, each political opportunity revives associations with the village's longstanding political reputation, especially when that opportunity represents a high-profile position. And when a government civil servant, such as teacher or a nurse, who is not native to the islet is posted to work in Tumbatu, he or she is either being punished, sent for intelligence purposes, or given the job for some other hidden political purpose. Juma relates that the petition of the villagers for a school in Jongowe was initially denied. After the minister of education (ironically, at the time this was Seif Sharif Hamad of today's CUF leadership) turned down their request,

> the elders of the village struggled mightily before finally getting the president's approval to build our school. Its first building was only finished due to the efforts of the villagers themselves, while the buildings which followed it came about from various forms of assistance and sponsors who valued the efforts of the villagers. This characteristic of self-supported collaboration with one another has endured as a part of the spirit of this village.[13]

The group that included Mbaruk, who disappeared to escape the 1969 security sweep, boarded a boat, and set off across the channel to go into hiding. "Being very active fishing folk, the only places we could think to hide were in the mainland and Kenya coastal villages. We, young fathers, left behind cracked families and deprived our children of the childhood happiness expected at their ages," in Mbaruk's words.[14] Juma's innocent youthful trust in the revolutionary government eroded as he experienced the deprivation of the first curfew and the school closure that accompanied it. Across the village, he found a dejected

---

12 Interview, "Mohammed," 2 July 2000, Tumbatu.

13 Interview, "Juma," 7 August 2003, Tumbatu.

14 Interview, "Mbaruk," 29 December 2012, Tumbatu.

scene dominated by patrolling security guards, where he feared for his parents' lives and his own chance of ever going back to school.

Mbaruk, who was about 80 years old in 2014, detailed his life story during our series of research visits in the village from 1999 to 2013. He recited for us his male lineage, stretching back for 17 generations, and he had knowledgeable stories about many of the personalities in his patriarchal and matriarchal lines.[15] Mbaruk is a descendant of the Ahdali sharifate, whose establishment at Jongowe predated the "Shirazi" rulers of the medieval city, whom he referred to as "latecomers" to Tumbatu (Pouwels 2000; Sheriff 2010). "We must wage a war against discrimination and isolation," he said in one of our many interviews with him, "and our young people, including my kids and grandkids, must be ready to change their attitudes for their community to progress through trust and the teachings of their faith."[16] Mbaruk has never gone to school, but he knows how to read and write. He is a self-made "organic" or "peasant" intellectual (Feierman 1990; Gramsci 1971). His life is defined by his early involvement in social and political affairs; in his younger years, he chaired the now-defunct *Hiyari ya Moyo* music troupe in the village. He was a member of an ad hoc village committee that asked the government for a dispensary and a school. They were able to get a dispensary in the last years of the sultanate, and then the primary school, in Gomani, after the revolution but before his exile. In his many years of exile, Mbaruk became known in the Kunduchi suburb of Dar es Salaam for his fishing prowess. During Jumbe's regime, he was encouraged to return from the mainland. He was even able to teach Islamic studies as a government employee at Jongowe school from 1976 until his retirement.

Mbaruk has powerful speaking abilities and commands great respect in Tumbatu, as seen during various public gatherings. His depth of knowledge and nuanced understanding of Tumbatu island, Islam, and both Zanzibari and Swahili customs more broadly have led to his serving as an invaluable informant in three major international research projects in Jongowe since his return from exile (Horton 1996; Pouwels 1987; Myers 2005).

Mbaruk took the bold step of joining CUF when multiparty democracy returned to Tanzania in 1992. For a time, he was a member of the party's central committee. Following the last CUF defeat in

---

15   Interview, "Mbaruk," 21 July 1999.

16   Interview, "Mbaruk," 21 July 1999.

Zanzibar's 2010 election, though, Mbaruk began to back away from active Zanzibari politics, leaving it to young people "to keep the wheels rolling."[17] However, in 2010 he stated that he did not believe in the success of the newly formed GNU, because of the greed and selfish behavior in each political party: "I do not believe that this is the ultimate solution for Zanzibar's political problems, because of the very polarized nature of its leaders."[18]

Mbaruk winced with a heartsick face when he discussed the initial curfew years and his exile. "Before the execution of my colleagues," he said, "a huge government rally was organized to draw public support for their execution with other alleged mercenaries who collaborated with those people. Young school children were forced to attend these rallies."[19] His son, Juma, interrupted at this point to say: "There was one rally song and banner which directly supported their execution; it read: *Chinja chinja, chinja, mahaini wote, chinja. Chinja chinja, chinja. Watumbatu wote, chinja. Chinja chinja, chinja. Na mabwana zao, chinja* [Slaughter, slaughter, slaughter all the traitors. Slaughter, slaughter, slaughter all the Tumbatu and their leaders]. Imagine me, forced to attend this rally, chanting along with a banner urging that my father and all my village's leaders be slaughtered."[20]

It was during Jumbe's presidency that Tumbatu people got their first piped water supply, sourced from Mkokotoni, three miles across the Tumbatu channel. Juma, like many in Jongowe, remembers Jumbe somewhat positively because of his investment in the water supply and in the Jongowe school. But the village gained precious little else from the revolution over its first three decades. It cannot have been surprising that when the multiparty era began Jongowe came to support the CUF overwhelmingly.

Zanzibaris represent a mixture of political, ethnic, and national identities that have not necessarily intermingled. The revolutionary regime under the first president Karume orchestrated several efforts to force this intermingling and to forge a national, African identity. Most notoriously, the first Karume's regime (1964–1972) introduced forced interracial marriage, in which higher-ranking members of the government allocated to each other girls and young women of

---

17 Interview, "Mbaruk," 29 December 2012.
18 Interview, "Mbaruk," 17 July 2010.
19 Interview, "Mbaruk," 17 July 2010.
20 Interview, "Juma," 17 July 2010.

Arab and Persian ancestry, many of them under the age of consent (Shivji 2008). But a broader, longer-lasting and more subtle effort has endured to unify Zanzibar under the flag of the United Republic of Tanzania, under African nationalism, and even under pan-Africanism (Myers 2013; Mapuri 1996; Cameron 2009; Larsen 2009). This effort to Africanize Zanzibar, or to make it appear, as the ZNP's leader Ali Muhsin (al-Barwani 1997: 127) put it, that "Bantuism" is the "Sheet-Anchor of Nationalism," led the United Republic to claim both Zanzibar's revolution and its nationhood for Tanzania. This discursive drive has met with resistance in Zanzibari society, most openly in its diaspora, directed particularly toward both Karume and Nyerere (al-Barwani 1997; Joseph 2002; Fouéré 2014), whom Ali Muhsin (al-Barwani, 1997: 162) called the "Destroyer" and "Invader" of Zanzibar. The many disparate strategies begun under both Karume and Nyerere to force-feed national unity and support for the union still suffer from the weight of the racial politics, oppression, regionalism, and ethnic divides of the past.

Said one villager in a focus group with us in 2008,

> It is regrettable that the villagers still continue to be trapped and misconstrued by the revolutionary government because of the oppositional stance of so many of them.... I remember JOBMAS club [Jongowe Blue Magic Squad, a youth environmental community-based organization] applied for US $16,000 in aid from the European Economic Community [EEC] in 1990 in order to start projects for fishing, animal husbandry, and afforestation to reduce the problem of youth unemployment (for young people who were unable to continue to secondary school) in our village. With the procedure for this aid we were required to have the ministry of finance receive the funds and to open a bank account, which in those days we still did not have. To make a long story short, just a bit after meeting with those concerned, we were given only half of the funds that the EEC had awarded us, $8,000. After a lot of complaining and showing the evidence of the exact amount named in the award letter from the EEC, we were told that the funds were not all ours because our fellow islanders in the other settlements [Gomani and Uroa, which supported CCM] deserved to benefit from this aid.[21]

There are many examples like this of Jongowe's development needs being bypassed. Jongowe once was promised sustained support from the end of the 1970s through the early 1990s due to its performance in agricultural competitions, but only twice was it able to get anything substantial—the use of a tractor in the Jumbe years and an earth-moving truck in the time of Salmin Amour. Jongowe also has had its

---

21   Interview, "Salim," 26 July 2000, Tumbatu.

students deliberately failed en masse several times in national exams, once because the students had demanded they be given their own secondary school classrooms in order to lower the costs associated with attending secondary school in the city (Issa 2007). There have been other development projects that don't touch Jongowe because of its political history (see Table 2, page 221–222). As one village leader put it to us in 2008, "Unfortunately, this is just how things are. And the island's political problems and its crises have been coming back around every electoral season since 1992 following the start of the post-independence multi-party democracy. It is hard to win in a situation like this unless one is able to navigate around Zanzibar's sort of revolutionary democracy in a fortunate manner just to achieve survival."[22]

One could possibly disassociate these instances of denial of development aid or educational assistance for Jongowe from the 1964 revolution itself. After all, many of these examples date from the post-colonial/post-revolutionary period of multiparty politics, and so Jongowe could be seen—since it is a CUF stronghold—as just suffering the consequences of not voting for the CCM in these recent elections. No one we have interviewed or spoken with in 20 years of research on Tumbatu, however, including the heads of CCM in the village, has ever disassociated Jongowe's marginalization at the hands of the CCM government's development agenda from the much longer arc of the village's history with the revolution. The names of the villagers who disappeared and were murdered in the Karume regime's 1969 military action were inscribed on the inside wall of the town hall at the center of the settlement until remodeling in the 2000s (when the names were removed on the advice of Jongowe's small CCM contingent, as a means of reducing any continued backlash). Those villagers not old enough to have experienced the revolution and then the 1969 assault—a large majority of the village, it must be said—are nonetheless told stories like Juma's blood-curdling narrative of watching his grandfather butchered before his very eyes. The connection between the Revolutionary Party (CCM's English name) and the revolution itself might be one created out of Nyerere's reach for semantic and symbolic power in the unification of the ASP and TANU in 1977, and the distance grows daily between that party and any "revolutionary" politics. But for most Jongowe residents, the *Revolutionary Party* and the 1964 *revolution* are inseparable and seemlessly tied to memories of the violence and repression.

---

22 Interview, "Hassan," 15 July 2008, Tumbatu.

Conclusion

As shown by the case of Tumbatu, Zanzibar is still haunted by its revolutionary past and its still-menacing intelligence service. It might be claimed that in the 2000s or 2010s Tanzania and Zanzibar turned a corner away from the repressive years. The Ministry of Foreign Affairs of Finland took the hopeful but ludicrous leap in 2003 of claiming that "democracy ha[d] come to Zanzibar in a pervasive manner"—despite the appalling state-orchestrated violence that followed the flawed 2000 elections (and that was to recur during the elections of 2005). Certainly, the multiparty context has brought new challenges, and new power games have entered into the political sphere. After all, as recently as December 2014, Tumbatu Jongowe hosted an open rally for CUF, with throngs of Seif Sharif Hamad supporters ringing the village; in the era of the Government of National Unity in Zanzibar (2010–15), the village was unlikely to suffer any open consequences at the hands of CCM for hosting this rally. But Jongowe residents, like many estranged rural village opponents of the revolution and the CCM, have yet to shake free of the palpable sense that past traumas might one day return, and the absurd annulment of the October 2015 election results only reinforced Jongowe's peoples' fears for that return to trauma.

Tanzanians as a whole, on the mainland and in Zanzibar, who oppose the regime continue to suffer political oppression and disrespect of their human rights (Legal and Human Rights Centre 2013). Despite surface appearances and the veneer of competitive politics, powers of state remain heavily centralized, and the political system remains a controlled one, especially for the islands (Kamata 2010; Idrissa 2010). The CCM-dominated Zanzibar state, even in the era of the GNU but now forthrightly since the collapse of the GNU in 2015, remains reluctant to wholeheartedly recognize the principles of political rights characterized by respect for individual dignity, civilized society, and a transparent democratic way of life. The government's revolutionary leadership countenances a lack of both social equity and freedom of expression (Makulilo 2011).

Watumbatu in Jongowe experienced substantial misfortunes under both imperial and colonial (Portuguese, Omani, and British) regimes in Zanzibar, but they became even more politically isolated after the revolution, given their strong support for the Zanzibar and Pemba People's Party in the pre-revolutionary "time of politics." This isolation escalated at the end of the 1960s, when they were falsely accused of associating with Arab mercenaries and their collaborators who wanted to topple the revolutionary government of Zanzibar. Because of this history and Tumbatu's frequent, continued connection to oppositional politics in Zanzibar, the people of Tumbatu Jongowe are still painted with a broad brush as the regime's political enemy. This history keeps resurfacing in Jongowe village, as in many other native communities of the islands, where since the return of the multiparty democratic system in 1995, its social, economic, and political destiny hinges on the question of support for CCM. We have argued that, for a great many Tumbatu Jongowe people, CCM continues to manifest an association with what they see as a failed revolution and decades of repression.

Because of this sort of history in many parts of Zanzibar (and even on the mainland), it is stunning that Tanzania is frequently named among the countries that have worked the hardest to achieve social unity amid ethnic, cultural, and religious diversity. In our 20 years of collaborative research on different projects, we have yet to see the ethnic, cultural, social, and religious unity in Zanzibar promised by its successive ASP and CCM governments. We have yet to see research that seriously analyzes and explores what Zanzibar has gotten from the revolution of 1964. Its people still discriminate against one another, saying who a person is and what he or she should be able to do based on where he or she comes from, and they still assess one another based on stereotyped notions of their origins and their politics—not in relation to the quest for unity within the isles, let alone across the union. Where would Jongowe's people be in a new, reimagined, genuinely post-revolutionary politics? This chapter helps to provide new insights into understanding both Jongowe village's postcolonial experience and its resilient survival. By highlighting these marginalized perspectives, this chapter is a fundamental first step toward understanding the quest of this village to move beyond the suffering it has endured in the last 50-plus years of the Zanzibar revolution.

References

Bakari, Mohammed
2001 *The Democratisation Process in Zanzibar: A Retarded Transition.* Hamburg: Institut für Afrika-Kunde.

al-Barwani, Ali Muhsin
1997 *Conflicts and Harmony in Zanzibar: Memoirs.* Dubai: n.p.

Blaut, James
1993 *The Colonizer's Model of the World: Geographical Diffusionism and Eurocentric Theory.* New York: Guilford Press.

Buhaug, Halvard, and Jan Ketil Rød
2006 "Local Determinants of African Civil Wars, 1970–2001." *Political Geography* 25(3): 315–35.

Cameron, Greg
2009 "Narratives of Democracy and Dominance in Zanzibar." In *Knowledge, Renewal and Religion: Repositioning and Changing Ideological and Material Circumstances among the Swahili on the East African Coast*, ed. Kjersti Larsen, 151–76. Uppsala: Nordic Africa Institute.

The Citizen [Tanzania] Correspondent
2013 "Warioba Defends Katiba Commission." www.thecitizen.co.tz/News/Warioba+defends+Katiba+commission+/-/1840392/1958126/-/tcsqfqz/-/index.html, accessed 18 August 2013.

Chami, Felix
2009 "Kilwa and the Swahili Towns: Reflections from an Archeological Perspective." In *Knowledge, Renewal and Religion: Repositioning and Changing Ideological and Material Circumstances among the Swahili on the East African Coast*, ed. Kjersti Larsen, 38–56. Uppsala: Nordic Africa Institute.

Clayton, Anthony
1981 *The Zanzibari Revolution and Its Aftermath.* London: C. Hurst & Company.

Coupland, Reginald

1938 *East Africa and Its Invaders, From the Earliest Times to the Death of Seyyid Said in 1856.* Oxford: Clarendon Press.

Enonchong, Nelson

2012 "Tanzania's Constitutional Review: A New Era for the Union." www.comparativeconstitutions.org/2012/07/tanzanias-constitutional-review-new-era.html, accessed 28 January 2014.

Fair, Laura

2013 *Historia ya Jamii ya Zanzibar na Nyimbo za Siti Binti Saad.* Nairobi: Twaweza Communications.

2001 *Pastimes and Politics: Culture, Community and Identity in Post-abolition Urban Zanzibar, 1980–1945.* Athens: Ohio University Press.

Fanon, Frantz

1963 *The Wretched of the Earth.* New York: Grove Press.

Feierman, Steven

1990 *Peasant Intellectuals: Anthropology and History in Tanzania.* Madison, Wis.: University of Wisconsin Press.

Feinstein, Eran

2014 "Zanzibar Celebrates Revolution Day 50th Anniversary." 3gdirectpay.com/blog/zanzibar-celebrates-revolution-day-50th-anniversary/, posted on 13 January 2014.

Fouéré, Marie-Aude

2014 "Recasting Julius Nyerere in Zanzibar: The Revolution, the Union and the Enemy of the Nation." *Journal of Eastern Africa Studies* 8(3): 478–96.

Glassman, Jonathon

2011 *War of Words, War of Stones: Racial Thought and Violence in Colonial Zanzibar.* Bloomington, Ind.: Indiana University Press.

Gramsci, Antonio

1971 *Selections from the Prison Notebook.* New York: International Publishers.

Gray, John

1963 "Zanzibar and the Coastal Belt, 1840–1884." In *History of East Africa*, vol. 1, ed. Roland Oliver and Gervase Mathew, 212-28. Oxford: Clarendon Press.

Horton, Mark

1996 *Shanga: The Archaeology of a Muslim Trading Community on the Coast of East Africa*. London: British Institute in Eastern Africa.

Horton, Mark, and John Middleton

2000 *The Swahili: The Social Landscape of a Mercantile Society*. Oxford: Blackwell.

Idrissa, Jabir

2010 "ZEC Kweli Imedhamiria Kufanya Chaguzi Huru na Haki?" [Is the Zanzibar Electoral Commission Really Committed to Conducting Free and Fair Elections?]. *Mwanahalisi* online. 16 October.

Ingrams, William Harold

1931 *Zanzibar: Its History and Its People*. London: Taylor & Francis.

James, Bernard, and Beatus Kagashe

2010 "Tanzania: After Zanzibar Referendum Comes Constitution Dilemma." *The Citizen* (Tanzania), 10 August. http://allafrica.com/stories/201008110188.html, accessed on 24 March 2016.

Joseph, May

1999 *Nomadic Identities: The Performance of Citizenship*. Minneapolis: University of Minnesota Press.

Jumbe, Aboud

1994 *The Partnership: Tanganyika-Zanzibar Union: 30 Turbulent Years*. Dar es Salaam: Amana Publishers.

Kamata, Ng'wanza

2010 "Jeshi Letu ni la Kulinda Wananchi, si Watawala" [Our Army Is to Defend Citizens, Not to Rule Them]. Blog entry, 13 October, http://www.raiamwema.co.tz/jeshi-letu-ni-la-kulinda-wananchi-si-watawala, accessed 13 October 2010.

Kirkman, James

1964 *Men and Monuments on the East African Coast*. New York: Praeger.

Larsen, Kjersti

2009 "Introduction." In *Knowledge, Renewal and Religion: Repositioning and Changing Ideological and Material Circumstances among the Swahili on the East African Coast*, ed. Kjersti Larsen, 11–37. Uppsala: Nordic Africa Institute.

Legal and Human Rights Centre

2013 *Tanzania Human Rights Report 2013*. Dar es Salaam and Zanzibar: Legal and Human Rights Centre and Zanzibar Legal Services Centre.

Lofchie, Michael F.

1965 *Zanzibar: Background to Revolution*. Princeton, N.J.: Princeton University Press.

Makulilo, Alexander B.

2011 "The Zanzibar Electoral Commission and its Feckless Independence." *Journal of Third World Studies* 28(1): 263–83.

Mapuri, Omar R.

1996 *Zanzibar: The 1964 Revolution: Achievements and Prospects*. Dar es Salaam: TEMA Publishers.

McClintock, Anne

1995 *Imperial Leather: Race, Gender and Sexuality in the Colonial Contest*. London: Routledge.

Mosare, Jonathan

1969 "Background to the Revolution in Zanzibar." In *A History of Tanzania*, ed. Isaria N. Kimambo and A. J. Temu, 214–38. Nairobi: East Africa Publishing House.

Muhajir, Makame

2013 "From Dar es Salaam to Zanzibar and Back: My Tanzanian Trip in Perspective." Minerva Fellow Discussion Paper, U.S. Military Academy, West Point. N.Y.

2011 "How Planning Works in the Age of Reforms: Land, Sustainability and Housing Traditions in Zanzibar." Ph.D. diss., University of Kansas.

Muhammed, Muhammed, M.

2014 *Ripoti ya Hali ya Mazingira ya Jongowe* [Report on the State of Jongowe's Environment]. Zanzibar: privately published.

Myers, Garth A.

2013 Commentary on Joanne Sharp's "Geopolitics at the Margins? Reconsidering Genealogies of Critical Geopolitics." *Political Geography* 37: 33–5.

2012 Review essay on "From 'Us-For-Us' to 'Us-For-Everyone': Zanzibari History Comes of Age." *Journal of Historical Geography* 38(1): 92–5.

2005 "Place and Humanistic African Cultural Geography: A Tanzanian Case." *Journal of Cultural Geography* 22(2): 1–26.

2000 "Narrative Representations of Revolutionary Zanzibar." *Journal of Historical Geography* 26(3): 429–48.

Myers, Garth A., and Makame Muhajir

2013 "'Wiped from the Map of the World'? Zanzibar, Critical Geopolitics and Language." *Geopolitics* 18(3): 663–81.

Nicholls, Christine S.

1971 *The Swahili Coast: Politics, Diplomacy and Trade on the East African Littoral, 1798–1856*. London: Allen and Unwin.

North, Graham

2010 "The Aloof Island." *Mambo Magazine*. www.mambomagazine.com/in-deep/places/the-aloof-island, accessed 17 January 2014.

Oke, Chris

2014 "The Forgotten Genocide of the Zanzibar Revolution." *Speak* (online magazine). speakjhr.com/2014/01/forgotten-genocide-zanzibar-revolution/, posted on 12 January 2014.

Pearce, Francis Barrow

1920 *Zanzibar: The Island Metropolis of Eastern Africa*. New York: E.P Dutton.

Petterson, Don

2002 *Revolution in Zanzibar: An American's Cold War Tale*. Boulder, Colo.: Westview Press.

Pouwels, Randall

2000 "The East African Coast, c. 780–1900 CE." In *The History of Islam in Africa*, ed. Nehemia Levtzion and Randall Pouwels, 252–71. Athens, Ohio: Ohio University Press.

1999 Review article: "East African Coastal History." *Journal of African History* 40: 285–96.

1987 *Horn and Crescent: Cultural Change and Traditional Islam on the East African Coast, 800–1900*. Cambridge, U.K.: Cambridge University Press.

Said, Edward

1993 *Culture and Imperialism*. New York: Harper & Row.

Sheriff, Abdul

2010 *Dhow Cultures of the Indian Ocean: Cosmopolitanism, Commerce and Islam*. London: Hurst.

Shivji, Issa

2008 *Pan-Africanism or Pragmatism? Lessons of Tanganyika-Zanzibar Union*. Dar es Salaam: Mkuki na Nyota.

Sirve, H.

2003 "Program Preparation Phase, Suggested Outline for the Inception Report." Presented to the Planning Workshop for Sustainable Management of Land and Environment (SMOLE) program, 29–30 October 2003, Bwawani Hotel, Zanzibar.

Slater, David

2004 *Geopolitics and the Postcolonial: Rethinking North-South Relations*. Malden, Mass.: Blackwell.

Sutton, John

1990 *A Thousand Years of East Africa*. Nairobi: British Institute in Eastern Africa.

Trimingham, J. Spencer

1975 "The Arab Geographers and the East African Coast." In *East Africa and the Orient: Cultural Syntheses in Pre-Colonial Times*, ed. H. Neville Chittick and Robert Rotberg, 115–46. New York and London: Africana Publishing Co.

Zanzibar National Archives

1952 Correspondence of British Resident with Chief Secretary. 11 August. File AB 8/81: Tumbatu Administration.

Table 1: Tumbatu Island Population by *Shehia*/Village

	Jongowe	Uvivini	Gomani
Population	3,262	4,136	4,990
Male	1,842	2,015	2,412
Female	1,780	2,121	2,578
Household Size	4.6	4.6	4.6
Area/Square Km	8.4	1.1	7.6

Source: Census of the United Republic of Tanzania 2012, at: http://www.meac.go.tz/sites/default/files/Statistics/Tanzania%20Population%20Census%202012.pdf; accessed 27 January 2014.

Table 2: Key Revolutionary and Political Events in Tumbatu, Zanzibar (1964-2010)

Year	Events
1964	• Zanzibar Revolution: 11-12 January
	• First revolutionary attack: Jongowe villagers butchered (12 wounded, three killed)
1966	• Tumbatu Primary School introduced in Gomani village (32 Gomani students joined by 14 Jongowe students to establish the school)
1967	• Karume's Tumbatu visit: Official inauguration of first school building (three miles from Jongowe, one mile from Gomani, though technically at the border of the two villages)
1969	• Terrifying Jongowe village ambush conducted and curfew imposed by heavily armed special navy force
	• Eight villagers (including the ruling party chair) taken onboard the navy boat for questioning
	• Six villagers accused of sedition, detained without trial and tortured
	• Huge rally organized in Zanzibar city to support action against accused traitors; Jongowe village heavily guarded
	• Detained "traitors" and collaborators secretly executed before a firing squad in Zanzibar city
1972	• President Abeid Karume assassinated
	• Village ambush; numerous people tortured; five questioned but released
1975	• Jongowe Primary School introduced

Year	Events
1979	• Tumbatu gets its own piped water supply (from Mkokotoni)
1983	• President Jumbe's "flea revolution" aborted; aimed to introduce three-tier government system in Tanzania
	• Jumbe's forced resignation; placed under house arrest
1984	• Jongowe students systematically failed due to village demand for secondary school
1995	• First post-independence multiparty election in Tanzania, including Zanzibar
	• Vote cheating and theft dominated the election
	• Political dispute erupted in Tumbatu; 35 arrested in Jongowe
2000	• More than 600 people from Tumbatu displaced in post-election violence; seek refuge in nearby Nungwi Village
	• People attacked by government-supported Janjaweed militia
2005	• Series of village attacks; questioning by police force
	People wounded and displaced; some homes demolished
2010	• The first calm round of elections experienced
	• Political agreement made to form GNU between CCM and CUF

Source: Compiled by the authors, 2014

Figure 1: Jongowe and Environs

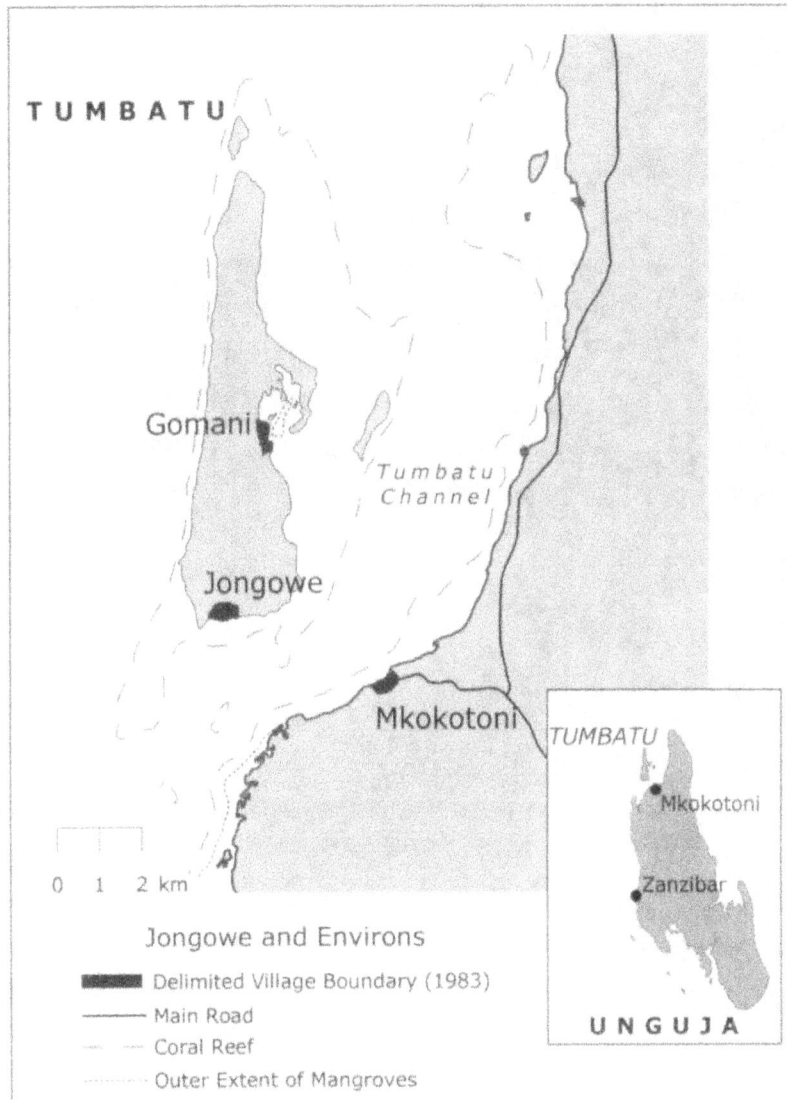

Source: Garth Andrew Myers. The map has previously appeared in Garth Myers (2005), "Place and Humanistic African Cultural Geography: A Tanzanian Case," *Journal of Cultural Geography* 22(2), p. 7.

Figure 2: Ruins of the 12th-Century Friday Mosque in the City of Tumbatu

Source: Myers 2005.

Chapter Seven

"Glittering Skin": Race, Rectitude, and Wrongdoing in Zanzibar

Gavin Macarthur

The islands of Zanzibar are imagined in multiple cultured modes, recombining diverse cultural resources to continuously resituate the isles in differential relations with the Tanzanian mainland and other places around the globe.[1] People bring these alternating cultural imaginaries of Zanzibar into play during informal social performances of "Zanzibariness," allowing them to address the question of who belongs in Zanzibar in a culturally appropriate manner. Even so, in an archipelago that is itself plurally imagined, Zanzibariness cannot be an immutable property or quality of a clearly defined group of island-dwellers. Social performances of Zanzibariness mostly revolve around expressions of differing moral frameworks and notions of sociality,[2] yielding a Zanzibari rectitude that is also plural, ephemeral, perspectival, contingent, and strategic. In practice, social performances of Zanzibari rectitude are channels through which the past is performatively brought to bear on the present, as well as channels by which the politics of the present inform reworkings of the past.

There are also many risks and hazards for those who engage with the performance of Zanzibariness, however. For example, successful claims of Zanzibariness can negate the same claims made by others but that are grounded upon other cultural imaginaries of what it means to be and act as a Zanzibari. Social performances of Zanzibari rectitude can go so far as to become strategic expressions of local and extra-local discourses of racial difference, enabling or even actively constituting violence against those whose claims have failed and who, by virtue of their perceived lack of Zanzibari rectitude, are imagined to belong elsewhere (Arnold 2002). Understanding "race" as a mode of thought in constant interplay with social structures and political processes,

---

1   The United Republic of Tanzania is formed of the union of the mainland/*bara* (formerly Tanganyika) and the Zanzibar archipelago, also known as the isles/*visiwani*.

2   For instance, the ideas of Zanzibari morality and sociality that Mohammed Saleh (2004) has described as "traditional."

Jonathon Glassman (2004, 2011) treats "racial thought" as a general set of assumptions that humankind is divided among constituent categories that are distinguished by inherited traits and characteristics. Glassman's formulation provides a useful theoretical platform from which to consider how the type of racial thought that emerged during the Zanzibar revolution has been adapted and redeployed within at least some contemporary cultural imaginaries of Zanzibar.

During the first "time of politics," from 1957 to 1964, the prevailing cultural imaginary posited an "exceptionalist"[3] Zanzibar (Mbogoni 2012), where Zanzibaris knew their places in an Arabocentric social hierarchy based on inequitable forms of land ownership and resource distribution under the Omani sultanate. In this conception of Zanzibariness, providers of vital cheap labor for this plantation economy, all migrant workers from Tanganyika, were regarded as carriers of alien, even socially destructive mainlander culture. By January 1964, however, this racially exclusionary cultural imaginary of Zanzibariness was violently overwritten by a reactionary cultural imaginary of Zanzibar as an "African" homeland to be reclaimed from venal, brutal, and oppressive Arab colonizers (Maliyamkono 2000; Mapuri 1996). Claiming the right to act on their perception of a shift in the racial thought of the African majority in Zanzibar, agents of this emerging order "enacted" the massacres of Arabs and South Asians, who embodied the inequitable and exploitative old order under the Omani sultanate. While Glassman agrees with Abdul Sheriff's observation that racial identities are mere "images people have of themselves and others" (Sheriff 1991), the Zanzibar revolution bears performative testimony to the impact such images had on people's thoughts and actions over those days of violence and social upheaval. Subjects of continual adaptation and modification, racializing images of "the other" remain central to all post-independence cultural imaginaries of Zanzibari belonging (Bromber 2006; Burgess 2009).

What happens when the culture and history of a given society are themselves plural and perspectival—vague yet visceral and continuously subjected to imaginative reworking through the power of performance? What historical order can tolerate multiple and coexisting schemes of things (Sahlins 1985), structures of experience, and, by extension,

---

3   Zanzibari exceptionalist thought maintains the idea that "true" Zanzibaris are racially distinct from "mainland" Africans, even though this distinction is most often expressed in terms of cultural difference. See Glassman (2004, 2011) for more detailed discussions of the historical roots of Zanzibari exceptionalist thought.

ontological bases and categories of reality, when all are continually subject to the multifarious imaginings that constitute and condition daily life in Zanzibar? Further, what of historical interpretive frameworks that limit understandings of particular modes of thought, such as race (Glassman 2011)? The ethnographic cases in this essay describe contexts in which successive nationalist cultural imaginaries of Zanzibar have been performatively posited, contested, or even displaced, suggesting how shifting racial thought has figured over the course of several distinct periods in Zanzibar's history: the "time of politics" from 1957 until 1963; the 1964 revolution and the union with Tanganyika; the period of single-party state socialism that ended with structural adjustment and market liberalization; the introduction of multiparty politics, resulting in economic, social and political upheaval that persists into the present. Constituting a contingent and often contradictory social ethic, Zanzibari rectitude—a social ethic that interacts with shifting local racial thought—exists as hard images and defined protocols that figure in each cultural imaginary; yet it is also a diffuse set of notions that apply across multiple imagined life-worlds, providing a useful touchstone with which to reconsider extant historical, political, and sociocultural accounts of the Isles.

To better understand the ontological status of the life-worlds created and sustained through social performances of cultural imaginaries of Zanzibar (Gruber 1995),[4] my research addresses several related questions: What agencies create and who—if anyone—has "control" over particular cultural imaginaries? From what common "stuff," both conceptual and material, are they fabricated? What sources and processes provide their power, and where and for what purposes is this power channeled? Who benefits or suffers from their operations and when? Providing a novel perspective on the complex relationships between the isles, the Tanzanian mainland, and elsewhere, my ethnography also reflects upon the positions that Zanzibar occupies in transnational cultural imaginaries of the putative western and Muslim worlds. Further, the performative operations—ideation, contrivance, assertion, propagation, differentiation, and adaptation—that sustain specific cultural imaginaries continually submit identity categories and sense of belonging (Zanzibariness in particular) to "empirical risk" (Sahlins 1985), refashioning them in ways that require analysis. As my ethnographic cases underline, however,

---

4 In artificial intelligence, an ontology is the specification of the concepts and relationships that can exist for an agent or a community of agents. The concepts—such as things, events, and relations—are specified in some way (such as specific natural language) in order to create an agreed-upon vocabulary for exchanging information (see Gruber 1995).

people are not completely free to perform in accordance with whichever cultural imaginary they might deem appropriate to a particular context. Rather, one's ability to perform any of Zanzibar's cultural imaginaries very much depends upon how such a performance is perceived through the matrix of local racial thought.

In an island context that reflects the protean qualities of cultural imaginaries and the shifting racial thought to which they give expression, social performances are complex events in which people engage and rework concepts and materials of all kinds in order to accomplish many tasks. For instance, solo or group social performances might include, exclude, or antagonize others; subvert historical, socioeconomic, or cultural orders; or enable the navigation of otherwise intolerable circumstances or contradictions. Social performances in Zanzibar are also opportunities to showcase the performer's repertoire, including his or her awareness of context and ability to manage several tasks simultaneously: performing to adapt to the microsociology of specific interpersonal exchanges (Giddens 1984); performing to reflect the experiences of self and others—whether personal and unmediated or collective, mediated, even channeled experiences—of Zanzibar(s) past; performing to demonstrate an ability to adapt successfully to Zanzibar's continuously shifting social, cultural, and political landscape. This workload is considerable but necessary, as all three domains are key to the operations of each cultural imaginary of Zanzibar. In an oft-cited example of the way in which Zanzibariness is multiple and negotiated, shifting both in terms of historical time and social context, the numbers claiming "Arab" status rose in Zanzibar during the British colonial period, when it was legally and economically advantageous to be classed as a "non-native." In the aftermath of the Zanzibar revolution, however, the numbers claiming non-native status dropped rapidly (Caplan and Topan 2004: 7–13) as the explicitly anti-foreigner nationalist Afro-Shirazi Party (ASP) took power. The elite Arabs who led the ostensibly "multiracial" Zanzibar National Party (ZNP) did not accept the ASP narrative of centuries of Arab oppression. Even so, the ZNP leaders did share a similar historical vision of the entrenchment and longevity of Zanzibar's racial divisions. This indicates that primordialist explanations of Zanzibar's racial divisions had been ubiquitous among the islands' political thinkers from both sides before the revolution. Yet conceptions about clear, fixed, and deeply rooted divisions between Arab and African do not fully comprehend identity as a social practice in this part of East Africa, where the specific emphasis an individual gives to his or her racial identity can shift according to situation and generation (Glassman 2011: 4–5).

The Revolution: Righting Wrongs and Punishing Wrongdoers

Zanzibar is often described as a multifaceted life-world, where people emphasize their Zanzibariness with reference to their particular way of being in that world: hospitality, friendliness, etiquette, aesthetics, the Kiswahili language, and, for the majority of the population, their shared Muslim faith, rather than stressing the importance of all being from the same locality. Within limits, this may well be how Zanzibar is for some, but not for all who live in life-worlds that are imagined, performed, and informed by racial thought. Even though the majority of Asian Zanzibaris share the identity of "Muslim" and "Zanzibari" with the rest of the local population, such commonalities have become secondary to matters of race (Keshodkar 2004). R. G. Gregory sheds some light on the possible reasons for this state of affairs, describing how migrants from India acted to strengthen their communal ties in order to preserve their cultural identities in East Africa (Gregory 1993b), distancing themselves in social terms from the rest of the local population (Gregory 1993a). The anthropologist Kjersti Larsen finds that this tendency has not been appreciated by members of other communities in Zanzibar, leading them to categorize all Asians as selfish and greedy, and committed only to their own individual and communal needs (2004: 134). Targeted for their lack of rectitude by the revolutionaries in much the same way as their Muslim Arab and South Asian compatriots, the "Goan Indians" who described for me the violence they witnessed and suffered during Zanzibar's revolutionary period were in no doubt about the part that racial thought played in shaping their experiences of and responses to such violent social performances.

Sitting in the Zanzibar Gymkhana Club with a number of middle-aged Goan Indian men one evening during my fieldwork in 2004, the conversation came around to their recollections of the revolution in Zanzibar. "Martin," who would have been a very young man at the time, recounted what had happened to him and his family during the first days of the revolution, when those who were perceived to be "legitimate" targets were robbed, arrested, and detained; some of those were subsequently beaten, raped, or even killed.[5] Along with many other Goans, Martin and his family were dragged from their home and marched to Raha Leo, a large tract of open land where Zanzibar city's fairground and recreation areas were located. When they arrived at Raha Leo, they joined a rapidly growing crowd of Arabs, Africans,

---

5   The names of all my informants have been changed to protect their identities.

and South Asians who had also been marked for detention by agents of the emerging revolutionary government. All stood in fear while armed revolutionaries passed among them, grabbing and beating anyone who stood accused of offenses against true, "African" Zanzibaris. Others were forcibly separated from their families and taken away for further punishment or to be killed.

Martin, his family, and many of his friends had to endure for days out in the open air without food or water, yet they were fortunate enough to survive. After he and his family were finally released, Martin discovered that one of his relatives had been shot dead several days before, during the widespread looting and pillaging in the streets of Zanzibar city. When I questioned the motives of those who felt entitled to treat Martin and his family in this fashion, Martin explained that, regardless of whether they were Christian or Muslim, everyone who had been rounded up for processing in Raha Leo had one thing in common—the revolutionaries saw them as non-Africans who no longer belonged in Zanzibar. While most of Zanzibar's Goan Indians managed to avoid the full extent of the revolutionaries' summary justice, many felt compelled to leave a tense and hostile Zanzibar at the earliest opportunity. Martin also explained that younger, unmarried Goan women faced the threat of being forced to "marry" senior revolutionaries, giving their families reason enough to attempt to flee the isles by any means available, even making use of the dhows of local fishermen. Not all of these attempts were successful, but no one of the company was willing to tell me what happened to those who were caught in the act of escape.

Largely unheard narrative accounts like this one are evidence that Zanzibaris of South Asian descent have occupied a difficult and sometimes dangerous position in their homeland since the revolution. Much scholarship of the revolution agrees that the violence my informants spoke of was the result of their African compatriots' desire to exact retribution for the preferential treatment of Arabs and South Asians under the Omani sultanate, both as an independent Arab state and as a British Protectorate (Gregory 1993a, 1993b; Keshodkar 2004; Mbogoni 2005; Sumich 2002). Martin's account of the detention and violent treatment of "non-African" Zanzibaris by "African" revolutionaries suggests that Arab and Asian bodies became dangerously out of place in the new Africanist Zanzibar that was born in January 1964. Deep-rooted resentment of the prevalent scheme of things in the time of the sultan or the time of the British became the driving force behind the violent events that "turned upside down" the social orders associated with those times.

In the course of this collective imagining and performance of the new scheme of things, Arabs and South Asians were seized, transported out of Stone Town, and detained in a space reserved for pleasure and recreation under the old order. Immobilized in Raha Leo, they became embodied symbols of a cultural order that had once expressed its power by enslaving African bodies from the mainland and transporting them to Zanzibar.

The symbolic ramifications of the act of forcibly mobilising "foreign bodies" for detention and processing—for whatever reason—must have been clear to victims and perpetrators alike. G. Thomas Burgess lends weight to this argument in his discussion of visual spectacles, parading, and regimentation in Zanzibar, when he suggests that the origins of the practices he identifies are found in the treatment of people considered inimical to the objectives of the new regime in the early days of the revolution (2005). People like Zanzibar's *Wagoa* (Goans) were subjected to a set of practices that quickly became routine performances of the emerging African state's ideology of public displays of submission to the regime. The acts of violence against perceived transgressors—*Wagoa* included—were social performances in which the ideals, methods, and social objectives of the new regime were first rehearsed on the bodies of those who had come to be seen as either enemies of the state or members of racial categories that had not yet been reincorporated following the revolution's upheaval of Zanzibar's old social order.

Racial Thought and Being in the Wrong in Zanzibar

Questioning the assumption that race in the nonwestern world arises only from imported western scientific doctrines, Glassman cautions against an understanding of colonial history in which Europeans are the only actors, inventing and imposing identities as prompted by administrative needs (Mamdani 2001). Interpretations of this kind apply "the logic of the trial" to identify "victims and culprits," overlooking the varied and often nonracial, nonscientific sources of racial scientific thought in the historical literature on the topic (Glassman 2011: 9).[6] In colonial Zanzibar, the attachments of blood and tradition and the creation of a locally hegemonic discourse of racial difference were largely the work of indigenous intellectuals at the forefront of mainstream nationalism rather than the result of Europeans' efforts to define and divide their subjects by race and ethnicity (Glassman 2011: 7). Shifting local racial thought—and the variant notions of rectitude that mirror such shifts—

---

6   For a similar approach but through a broader perspective, see Stocking 1982.

comes to function as a "boundary object" (Star and Griesemer 1989) operating both within and between the cultural imaginaries of my analysis: remaining plastic enough to allow different interpretations across "racial" groups, life-worlds and times, as such things are multifariously ordered by different schemes, while holding enough immutable content to maintain its integrity.[7] The most apposite example of racial thought-as-boundary-object is the antipathy and resentment toward South Asian Zanzibaris of all creeds that has persisted in one form or another in successive cultural imaginaries of Zanzibar since the time of the sultanate.

Some have traced the roots of this antipathy and resentment back to the late 19th century, when the Busaid sultanate of Oman transferred its seat of power to Zanzibar (Pearson 1998), expanding its slavery-based economy through the long-distance caravan trade in east Africa to supply a global demand for cloves and ivory. The numerical superiority of the African population notwithstanding (Sheriff and Ferguson 1991), Omanis and South Asians were the politically and economically dominant groups in Zanzibar—on their own before 1890 and with British complicity afterward (Myers 2000). Sheriff claims that these racial categories—Arab, Indian, and African—were largely ideological constructions of British colonialism (1994: 149), while Garth Myers contends that interrelationships among Africans, Arabs, and Indians were more fluid in pre-colonial Zanzibar, especially since the overwhelming majority were Muslims. In his opinion, colonialism compounded ethnicity by separating out migrants from the African mainland; previously, they had been absorbed into local identities even in the years of slavery—particularly when mainlanders converted to Islam (Myers 1995). J. E. Flint suggests that the British colonial authorities even went so far as to attach function and status to ethnicity: Thus Arabs were landowners, Indians were merchants, and the Africans were the downtrodden (1965: 651). Lawrence E. Y. Mbogoni is even more pointed in his description of "the Indians" as "a well-organised

---

[7] "Boundary objects are objects which are both plastic enough to adapt to local needs and the constraints of the several parties employing them, yet robust enough to maintain a common identity across sites. They are weakly structured in common use, and become strongly structured in individual-site use. These objects may be abstract or concrete. They have different meanings in different social worlds but their structure is common enough to more than one world to make them recognizable, a means of translation. The creation and management of boundary objects is a key process in developing and maintaining coherence across intersecting social worlds" (Star and Griesemer 1989: 393).

group of merchant profiteers and moneylenders with a firm grip on Zanzibar's economy" (2005: 202).

The literature I cite above might describe the socioeconomic status and mercantile activities of at least some South Asians under the Zanzibar sultanate, but it also indicates that generalizing notions and stereotyping images of Zanzibar's racialized socioeconomic order can be mistaken for social fact. In the 1950s, dangerous images of wealthy, avaricious, and antisocial "Indians" and privileged, spendthrift, and exploitative Arabs were circulating freely, forming the core of the racial thought of the revolutionaries and justifying violent social performances of the emerging African nationalist cultural imaginary during the days of revolution. Popular recollections of the past "transgressions" of Indians against Africans continue to contour racial thought in Zanzibar in the present. As a case in point, the term *kishuka* ("bird shit") is used by ("African") workers in Zanzibar's informal tourism sector to refer to South Asians, who are despised for their reputation for cheapness and hard bargaining (Sumich 2002: 41). Jason Sumich records the hostility of his African Zanzibari friend toward a family of Indian tourists who were shopping at his stand; the bargaining was loud and angry, with both sides repeatedly walking away in disgust before finally reaching a deal. In the aftermath, Sumich was surprised to hear what his informant had to say:

> That man is bastard, he has no respect, he does not know the business or how to act. You see this is what Indians are like, they will not let a black man have business, they want everything so cheap that it is for free, I hate them. Fucking *kishuka*. . . . All Indians are *kishuka*, all they do is bargain and they treat us with no respect. (2002: 41)

In Zanzibar, social performances like this one often turn on politically inflected and culturally chauvinist notions of rectitude. Drawing their power from reinvocations and redeployments of group memories, experiences, and/or imagination of "racial antecedents" who have been wronged in multiple pasts that are also as much imagined as recollected, such notions continue to inform and deform society, politics, and governance in Zanzibar. In the moment, claims of rectitude—like the one above—are made on the strength of popular notions of the innate wrongness and egregious wrongdoings of South Asians, but such claims can only be made by those who perceive themselves as "entitled" to make them—that is, following an African nationalist cultural imaginary according to which entitlement comes with being the right "race" (i.e., "African"). Those claims that succeed, even if only temporarily, become anchors for fresh enactments of the cultural imaginaries from which they derive. So the past is channeled into and reified in the present by means of a performative process of social inscription (Howe 2000), which, for whatever length of time this new inscription can prevail, overwrites whatever a priori reality might have existed. In effect, the present becomes a palimpsest upon which are performatively inscribed multiple cultural imaginaries of multiple pasts that may also have been subject to the same processes in time.

Imagining Life-Worlds, Performing Racial Thought

As with other nations and nationalisms, Zanzibar's claims for nationhood are established and enforced by invoking particular kinds of imaginaries (Askew 2002: 14). Kelly M. Askew uses the term "national imaginary" to convey the sense that issues around nationality are bound up with other explicitly cultural concerns that condition relations between Zanzibar and the former Tanganyika, its mainland partner in the United Republic of Tanzania (2002: 273). Given that the process of imagination is always subject to interruption and on-the-spot reconfiguration (2002: 160–1), and in order to avoid privileging dominant national imaginaries at the expense of other, subaltern imaginaries, my research data focuses on specific social performances that embody, express, negotiate, and transform at least some of these imaginaries and the life-worlds they create. Each cultural imaginary is simultaneously a differently configured field for, and differentiated product of, ongoing individual and collective deployments of racial thought to establish claims upon rectitude—however these might be formulated—and consequent rights to belong. To better understand how indigenous racial thought shapes the cultural imaginaries and social performances of Zanzibariness that my research data describes, I want to develop a better sense of what "the imaginary" might mean.

Proposed to counter the charges of stasis, coherence, and boundedness leveled against the "culture" concept (Abu-Lughod 1997; Appadurai 1991), the "imaginary" is social practice, forming perceptions of and encounters with "reality" (Appadurai 1991: 198). And yet while "imaginaries" may well be substantial and "real," certain realities are more visceral—even more violent—than others (Weiss 2002: 99). Brad Weiss questions James Ferguson's claim that the "inertia" of tradition and habitus has given way to the "innovation" of fantasy as appropriations of a globalized order of signs and values in the new "deterritorialized ecumene" (Ferguson 1999). As Weiss has it, such a division runs the risk of distinguishing between "closed" and "open" societies arranged as distinct historical moments, rather than as contemporaneous and divergent worldviews (2002: 97). With reference to the worldview of contemporary Tanzanians, Weiss suggests how ubiquitous forms of globalized imagery are engaged through acts of imagination grounded in the specific forms, times, and places through which people project their lives, concluding that fantasy is never the appropriation of external signs according to fixed and transcendent categories. Rather, the horizon of a given imaginary both incorporates distant persons, values, and events and encompasses the real here and now (2002: 93-94). This "global connectivity" is a circuit of imagery, promoting and sustaining itself by transformations in consciousness among people who comprehend and enact themselves with reference to people living elsewhere (2002: 95-6).

An important component of this circuit of imagery took place on April 26, 1964, when Tanganyikans and Zanzibaris were proclaimed citizens of a bifurcated nation-state comprising Tanzania *bara* (mainland) and *visiwani* (isles), with Julius K. Nyerere (the Tanganyikan incumbent) as president and Abeid Amani Karume (the Zanzibar incumbent) as vice president of the new union (Askew 2002: 6-7). In acknowledgment of the fact that the union constitution was never ratified, alongside the pressing need to involve the national populace in deciding the issues involved, the parliament of Tanzania passed the Constitutional Review Act of 2011. It established the Tanzanian Constitutional Review Commission to garner public opinion on the review and validation by referendum of the constitution of Tanzania. As this national state of affairs suggests, many Tanzanians are unsatisfied with the Tanzanian union constitution. Media engagements with this issue tend to revolve around the question of "who belongs where" in Tanzania, reflecting a long-running preoccupation both of official Tanzanian historical discourses of nationhood (Maliyamkono 2000; Mapuri 1996) and of academic treatments of Zanzibar's history, society, and culture (Freeman-Grenville 1998; Middleton 1992; Nurse and Spear 1985; Pearson 1998; Pouwels 1999; Prins 1961; Swartz 1997; Temu 1969). The points and protests of academics, intellectuals, and journalists notwithstanding, racial identities have persisted in shaping political behavior in post-colonial Zanzibar.

According to Mohammed Ali Bakari, voters are polarized along two axes. One axis is ethnic (serving as a good example of racial thought), with Zanzibaris of "Arab origin" overwhelmingly voting for Civic United Front (CUF) while Zanzibaris of mainland origin favor Chama cha

Mapinduzi (CCM).[8] The other axis is regional, dividing Shirazi in Pemba, who give strong support to CUF, from Shirazi in Unguja, who lean toward CCM (Bakari 2001: 237). So during the fraught registration process for the 2005 election, CCM thugs intimidated Pembans living in Unguja; in Pemba, their CUF counterparts targeted mainlanders. CCM speakers have repeatedly accused their opponents of representing the interests of "Arabs" who want to restore the sultanate, institute an Islamic republic, and expel all mainlanders, depicting Pemban opposition supporters as particularly tainted in that regard. CUF speakers respond by characterising CCM politicians as the agents of mainland Christians. Glassman notes how such patterns and the rhetoric that sustains them are similar to those that prevailed in the first *zama za siasa* ("time of politics") between 1957 and 1964, when Arab voters supported one side, mainlanders the other, and the Shirazi were split between those in Pemba who leaned toward the ZNP and their Shirazi nativist Zanzibar and Pemba People's Party (ZPPP) allies and those in Unguja who favored the ASP (2011: 285).

Zanzibar's present political polarization is often simply explained as a continuation of old loyalties from the 1960s that were driven underground during the period of single-party rule. And yet this cannot explain CCM's sharp decline in support, particularly in Pemba, relative to the support the ASP enjoyed in the 1960s (Bakari 2001; Cameron 2004). Further, the opposition's core leaders are too young to have belonged to the ZNP or ZPPP; most in fact were the children of ASP members or had been ASP members themselves. Bakari observes that voters on both sides are motivated by a variety of factors. For example, some CUF members do sympathize with the ZNP government that was overthrown in 1964, while others defend the revolution, which they believe the CCM has betrayed. What unites the disparate opposition is not a shared racial animus or any other single ideological position but simply dissatisfaction with the ruling party's record of mismanagement, corruption, and civil rights abuses. However, the fact that so many understand current divisions in terms of the old conflicts indicates less the persistence of fixed ideas than it does the role that historical memories play in Zanzibaris' current projects of imagining the political sphere. Today's discourses of ethnicized politics are new creations crafted by political thinkers who draw from a repertoire of images and fears—core components of all nationalist cultural imaginaries of

---

8   The nominally socialist "Party of the Revolution" formed out of the merger between Zanzibar's ASP and the TANU party of the mainland in 1977.

Zanzibar—recalled from the first "time of politics." They are the products of ongoing political discussions that do not replay old tensions so much as they seek to address newer ones, the most obvious of which are those generated by the post-revolutionary regime's systematic privileging of "African" racial identity and its simultaneous denigration of Middle Eastern racial markers (Glassman 2011: 288).

Skin that Glitters: Racial Thought in the Aftermath of the Zanzibar Revolution

Public discussions of the Tanzanian union in Zanzibar tend to revolve around partisan recollections of the Zanzibar revolution, an event that is remembered by Tanzanian nationalists in official discourses as the moment when Africans reclaimed their homeland from brutal and oppressive Arab colonizers (Maliyamkono 2000; Mapuri 1996). The racial thought that permeates this version of events deletes the experiences of many older Zanzibaris, whether nominally African, Arab, or South Asian, for whom the revolution and its aftermath have been brutal and oppressive in turn (Arnold 2006; Burgess 2009). Others, who are too young to have witnessed the violent birth of the nation firsthand, are nevertheless living in a society shaped by an African nationalist cultural imaginary that has largely—but not exclusively—conditioned life in the isles since the revolution.

In February 2004, I was sitting in the shade to avoid the enervating heat in Unguja's Stone Town. Keeping me company was "Ronaldo," one of my Goan friends, who was telling me stories about growing up among Muslims in Unguja. His parents had emigrated from Goa under Portuguese passports in the mid-1950s, traveling to what was then the British Protectorate of Zanzibar to join a prosperous Roman Catholic Goan Indian community that numbered in the thousands. However, following the Zanzibar revolution in 1964, the Goan community rapidly dwindled to a few hundred people, as many of its members felt they would be better off—and safer—living elsewhere. "Why did so many Goan people move away?" I asked. "Many decided to leave because of the revolutionaries. Zanzibar quickly became a place where life was not so easy for many people," he replied. To give me an example, Ronaldo told me of his encounter with a local policeman in the 1970s, when he was a schoolboy:

> I was cycling home from school on my bicycle, and I passed down a one-way street. I thought that it was okay, because there was one other man on a bicycle who was also passing the same way as me—that other man

was an African. But when I got to the end of the street, this policeman came—he was African—he came out on the road and stopped me. He said, "Do you know that you have passed a one-way street?" I said, "Yes, but so did this other one. Why do you not stop him as well?" But the policeman told me that he did not see him, this other one. He only saw me. When I heard him say this, I said, "Oh, I must have *ngozi inayong'ara*, I must have—what do you call it when your skin shines?— skin that glitters, if you can see me but cannot see him. You saw me only because my skin looks different to that man's, that African man's."[9]

Ignoring Ronaldo's complaint, the policeman demanded that he pay a "fine" of 700 shillings, roughly equivalent to $20 US, which was a lot of money at the time. Even though he was only a child, Ronaldo knew that the policeman was not authorized to impose and collect such a fine, but he also knew that the policeman could make trouble for him and his family should he refuse to pay. So Ronaldo went home and, without telling his father what had happened, took 700 shillings of his own and sneaked back out to pay off the policeman. "You know, until this day, this policeman, I know him, and he cannot look me in the eye, because he knows he cheated me, and I was only a child. I still see him around, but he can no longer see me now." Ronaldo never told his father about his experience, because it would have been only one more example of the kind of unequal treatment that his family and other Goans dealt with after Zanzibar's independence. Powerless to do anything in the face of this pervasive animosity, his father would only have become angry with Ronaldo for drawing attention to himself in the first place.

Glassman notes that race continues to be distinguished from other ways of categorizing difference, such as ethnicity or autochthony, by the central conceit that cultural identities, and hence cultural boundaries, are fixed in the body or the blood. This thinking is based on the assumption that humanity consists of a discontinuous series of authentic cultural wholes, each internally homogenous, the creation and property of a distinct people linked together by the metaphor of consanguinity and descent. While the concept of race places more explicit emphasis on this metaphor of descent—on the conviction that the "blood relationship" is more than mere metaphor—than does the concept of ethnicity, they both operate on a single continuum that is entirely colored by the "aura of descent" (Glassman 2004: 726–7; 2011: 11). In the present, shifts in indigenous racial thought are once again evident

---

9   Extracted from field notes taken after an informal discussion with "Ronaldo," Stone Town, 21 February 2004.

in a Zanzibar nationalist cultural imaginary that both emerges and diverges from these earlier imaginaries, recombining aspects of their respective schemes of things (Sahlins 1985) with globalized religious and cultural symbols in pursuit of an independent Zanzibar. As before, true Zanzibaris can be recognized for their rectitude in thought and action, unless, of course, their thoughts, actions, and racial types do not conform with the expectations of those doing the imagining. Conflating racial thought with religious and political objectives, this cultural imaginary resents "western" influence upon local culture and politics, engendering hostility against western visitors as well as any locals or mainlanders associated with Christianity and the west.

Zanzibari Purity, Worldly Pollution

Concepts that are core components of an emerging anti-western cultural imaginary of Zanzibar also figured in a conversation I had with the head of a middle-class Zanzibari household one sweltering afternoon in early 2005. I was visiting this household in the company of a friend who had lived there for three months during the previous year while studying at the Kiswahili language institute in Stone Town. The household patriarch, Mzee Saidi,[10] was a senior civil servant, a staunch supporter of the CCM government and a devout Muslim worthy of the title *mheshimiwa* ("respected one"), meaning a man of high status and a pillar of the community. Noting that I had been careful to greet him properly in Kiswahili, Mzee Saidi asked (in Kiswahili) why I was taking the time to learn the language. I explained that I was a doctoral student with an interest in researching the matter of who might rightly claim to belong in Zanzibar. Presented with this ethnographic research opportunity, I invited my host to tell me his own thoughts on the issue. Switching to English (for some reason), Mzee Saidi observed that local culture was being destroyed by foreigners, specifically "white people"[11] from the United States, the United Kingdom, and other European countries, who come to Zanzibar without knowing how to behave properly in public.[12] Under the influence of these foreigners, young Zanzibaris are dressing in inappropriate western clothing, smoking and drinking alcohol, speaking in English and slang Kiswahili instead of

---

10 The honorific *Mzee* is often used for an elder, indicating someone who is venerable, respected, a gentleman.

11 Mzee Saidi used the term "white people," giving expression to the racial thought that informed his discourse.

12 See Parkin 2006: 94 for a discussion of how tourism is seen to be tainting the morality of young Muslims in Zanzibar.

true, "traditional" Kiswahili, and turning to crime rather than working for a living like respectable Zanzibaris.[13]

Listening to my host's arguments for the need to preserve Zanzibar's sociocultural "purity," I was acutely aware of the irony of our discourse: Here I was, the guest of a Zanzibari cultural conservative who chose to tell me—in English—that he did not like the presence and influence of foreigners and foreign languages in Zanzibar, in the knowledge that he could have told me so in Kiswahili. I had also noticed that the women of the household were all in traditional dress, while Mzee Saidi was dressed in a western-style shirt and a pair of slacks.[14] Wondering why he was so forthcoming with me, I supposed that he was giving me the opportunity to present myself to him in the proper manner, to differentiate myself from other, less acculturated visitors to the islands. With this insight in mind, I formed the impression that his conversation was not so much a sustained critique of western culture as a performative "point of entry" or cue for me to show myself in a good light, if only I might have the wit and skill to take full advantage. By this point in my fieldwork, invitations to fully participate in the social performance of Zanzibariness were becoming more recognizable. In the course of a normal day, people nearly always took the time to find out as much as they could about me—the length of time I had been living in Zanzibar, whom I knew and how I knew them, where I had been, and what kind of activities I had engaged in—before deciding how to interact with me. By "performing" as much like a local as I was able, I was learning how to claim my rights and entitlements, as well as how to honor my obligations, positioning me somewhere between the status of *mwenyeji* ("native") and *mgeni* ("guest") (Arnold 2002: 154). This tenuous status was, however, always subject to review and contestation, emerging as it did or, indeed, did not, during performative interactions with Zanzibaris. Above all, my presence always gave the Zanzibaris with whom I interacted the opportunity to perform the cultural imaginaries from which they drew their own senses of Zanzibariness. Even so, Mzee Saidi's negative perception of western visitors to Zanzibar is not unusual. Noting the 348-percent increase in tourist arrivals between 1985 and 1999, Sumich observes that, in the eyes of many of his Zanzibari informants at least, tourism has come to mean cultural "pollution" (2002: 39).

---

13   See Saleh 2004: 145–153, Swartz 1991, and Swartz 1997 for detailed discussions of Swahili norms and values.

14   See Fair 2001 for an anthropological review of traditional dress in Zanzibar.

Gesturing with his hand in the general direction of the Tanzanian mainland Mzee Saidi continued with his educational diatribe, telling me that "true" Zanzibaris also consider *wabara* ("mainlanders") to be foreigners in the isles. According to this perspective, mainlanders are either lazy, untrustworthy Christians or bad Muslims who are unwilling to learn the proper social forms and personal conduct that are vital for good social relations in Zanzibar.[15] Referring to them as *washenzi* (barbarians or uncivilized people),[16] Mzee Saidi complained that mainlanders also try to involve themselves in island politics despite having no "right" to do so.[17] Describing his mainlander compatriots in the union as uncivilized, Mzee Saidi was marking them as inimical to his imaginary of an urbane, sophisticated, and civilized Zanzibar, where the natives have remained "African"—in accordance with CCM conceptions of Africanness—while benefiting from a "high Islamic" cultural heritage with its roots in the time of the Omani Arab sultanate. His insular chauvinism did not, however, extend to all natives of Zanzibar's islands. If Zanzibar city is the economic, political, and cultural center of Unguja, the most important of Zanzibar's islands, then natives of Pemba, who are supporters of the reviled opposition CUF, are, to him, no more than political and economic saboteurs who do not belong in Unguja.

Mzee Saidi's discourse on Zanzibari belonging was categorical: The islands of Zanzibar were cast as culturally distinct and separate from the mainland, regardless of the ruling CCM party's pan-Africanist politics and the union between the isles and the mainland. At the same time and in an overtly contradictory fashion, civilized Zanzibaris are supposed to support CCM Zanzibar, while mainlanders or Pembans—who in his view most likely support CUF—join western foreigners in acting as agents of cultural pollution and social dissolution. Christians of all stripes—including Zanzibar's Goan community—have no place in this ethnic nationalist scheme of religious and political chauvinism. However, Mzee Saidi's nativist and proto-Islamist discourse turned ironic in light of his decision to hang two readily recognizable portraits in the room where we sat. Emulating an iconographic practice that normally applies by law to all places of business in Tanzania, the first

---

15 See Parkin 2006: 97 for an account of Zanzibari notions of the anti-sociality and immorality of mainland Africans.

16 See Bromber 2006: 67–81 for an interesting discussion of the development of the Swahili concept of *ustaarabu* ("civilization") in 1920s Tanganyikan newspaper discourse.

17 See Glassman 2011: 191–2 for a discussion of the pejorative use of the term *mainlander* in political discourse in Zanzibar.

was of the first president of the United Republic of Tanzania, *Mwalimu* (Teacher) and *Baba wa Taifa* (Father of the Nation) Julius Nyerere, a pan-Africanist mainlander and Christian, also cofounder of the ruling party. The second portrait was of the incumbent president of Zanzibar, Amani Karume, the CCM-Zanzibar party leader and son of Abeid Karume, Zanzibar's first president following the revolution. I had to wonder how Mzee Saidi's racializing, political separatist, and religiously chauvinist ideas about Zanzibari belonging might agree with the CCM party's unionist and Africanist politics. In the eyes of Mzee Saidi, the question of who might belong in Zanzibar can sometimes be a function of one's political allegiance, which in turn determines one's position within a racially oriented ranking scheme, but even this insight was not enough to interpret the multiple meanings he attached to the various cultural categories that refused to hold their positions in his discourse. Evidently, these categories were being subjected to worldly risk (Sahlins 1985) and, as such, were not the product of a unified and totalizing individual perspective or collective purview.

To better understand how difference is structured in Zanzibar, Nathalie Arnold attends very closely to the ways in which state-initiated processes are apprehended through, and given phenomenological force by, local idioms of appropriateness, difference, and incommensurableness (2002: 154–5). Focusing on the ways in which the Swahili concept of *haya* (a sense of shame) informs the politics of status and reputation that characterize social interactions in Swahili societies, Arnold remarks that those who act without a sense of shame bring shame itself, *aibu*, into being and are seen as thoroughly, disgracefully bad (2002: 151–2). In addition, shame is highly contagious. If one member of a group can be shown to be shameless, his or her fellows are necessarily implicated. Yet the very act of designating a particular group as shameless has an interesting effect on the speaker, who involves himself or herself in the performance in ways that have consequences. As M. J. Swartz observes, "a reluctance to view others as having failed to behave properly is part of the valued haya" (1991: 172). Thus, the racial thought that permeates CCM discourse renders opposition members as "Arabs and colonists who have exploited us and are not Zanzibaris." Ironically, the CUF response sometimes mimics the CCM argument, implying that CCM supporters are a population of "foreigners" who do not belong in Zanzibar, namely, people of mainland origin, for many of whom Zanzibar is simply another part of Tanzania rather than a distinct cultural and historical entity. This logic is employed by members of both parties to discuss different populations: Popular CUF rhetoric tends to press for a control of the presence of mainlanders on Zanzibar, pointing out the damage being done to "traditional" forms of Zanzibari morality and sociality (Saleh 2004). CCM discourse retorts with an assertion of "commensurableness" between mainlanders and islanders, signaling the party's commitment to its African geographic and political identity (Arnold 2002: 150).

Considered in light of Arnold's recapitulation of politically—and therefore ethnically—partisan statements in Zanzibar, Mzee Saidi's attitudes and perspectives underline the idea that the components of cultural imaginaries are prone to reconfiguration in the politically contingent act of performance, and that cultural imaginaries all draw upon and rework shared cultural resources. Indeed, if we attend to local voices like that of Mzee Saidi, we might find that members of host societies are involved in their own politics of accommodation with or resistance to transnational forces and processes of all kinds. In effect, they might interpret the consequences of encounters with whatever comes from elsewhere in "their own" terms, which are likely to reflect previous acts of accommodation and resistance to other forms of western incursion; they might act, too, according to those interpretations, even if such actions might prove ineffectual or even counterproductive (Bowman 1996). Following Marshall Sahlins's argument (1985) that meaning is always at risk in action, I suggest that the new meanings so produced could themselves be "risky" for those persons who work them into shape, as well as for those to whom the new meanings apply. If imaginaries are plays for power over the meanings of cultural categories, then the "things" (following Sahlins) that acquire different connotations are at once the basis of the act (performance) and its corollary imaginary and, at the same time, might well be beyond the control of those who set their meanings at risk. Simply put, any cultural category put at empirical risk through action-as-performance in the service of a particular imaginary can produce a risky reality, not only in recollections of the past but in the present and future, too. Such categories may also have multiple and potentially risky valuations that exist in several cultural imaginaries simultaneously. Sahlins's point about the diversity of local responses to the "world system"—problematic as that pre-globalization notion might be—suggests that we must also take account of those things from elsewhere that get harnessed to the reproduction and creative transformation of cultural imaginaries of Zanzibar.

Conclusion: Power, Racial Thought, and Performance

Focusing specifically on "forms of speech," Achille Mbembe notes that the project of democratization in contemporary Africa depends not upon the application of a western model of power to African realities but instead upon the cultivation in Africa of "other languages of power" that express emergent African political ethics (2005: 2). These languages, Mbembe asserts, "must emerge from the daily life of the people, [and] address everyday fears and nightmares, and the images with which people express or dream them" (quoted in Geschiere 1997: 7). Harry West warns that so long as policymakers and citizens speak mutually unintelligible languages of power, the project of democracy is impossible. Describing Muedan sorcery discourse to be one such language of power, and emphasizing the importance of *uwavi* (sorcery) to the conception and operation of power on the Mueda plateau of Mozambique, West notes the irony in the way that the interconnectedness of our world renders more challenging Mbembe's mandate to cultivate other languages of power. This is because many Muedans are conversant in multiple languages of power, having gained various degrees of fluency in the languages introduced to them over the years, including the language of the slave trade, the language of Portuguese colonialism, the language of revolutionary nationalism, the language of scientific socialism, and, finally, the language of neoliberal democracy (2005: 3).

Developing upon West's argument, I suggest that the imaginary may very well constitute a theoretical and experiential space for the expression, comprehension, and manipulation of multiple languages of power. Indeed, the imaginary may constitute a language of power in its own right. The anthropological sense of the imaginary that I develop enables an integration and analysis of the various languages of power that have figured in Tanzania's history. It is vital, however, to remember that each of these languages of power is both an agent and subject of history, emerging at different points from the stream of "global interconnectedness" that destabilizes the linguistic and symbolic bases of any worldviews and schemes of things that might be in play. With this point in mind, the ethnographic cases that I set out here suggest how particular highly politicized imaginaries of Zanzibar are invoked, substantiated, modified, or dispersed through the strategic deployment of racial thought, a language of power in its own right. This is a highly performative political process, as it creates the conditions within which particular plays for power that people direct at each other are witnessed, given recognition, and, as a consequence, made more "real." I assert that every performance of Zanzibariness owes more to the particulars of a given politicized cultural imaginary, and to the performativity of the events in question, than to the ostensibly fixed ideas of race and the state.

Critically, my data records that the enduring fantasy of Asians and other ethnic groups as exploitative interlopers has become social fact for many in Zanzibar, producing a concrete reality of social practices that continues to hold real dangers for members of such groups and rendering them as targets for ongoing negative stereotypes and violent acts. For Ronaldo and Martin, the past continues to form and inform the older Africanist and emerging Islamic nationalist cultural imaginaries with which they must contend on a daily basis. For them, the revolution has been internalized and the internment endures.

Burgess's discussion of discipline and the visual spectacle or ritual of parading and regimentation in Zanzibar supports the argument that the origins of the practices he identifies are found in the treatment of people considered inimical to the objectives of the new regime in the early days of the revolution (2005: 3–29). People like Zanzibari's Goans, notably, were subjected to a set of practices that fed into the emerging African state's ideology of public displays of submission to the regime. The detention, beatings, and killings were a very public performance in which the ideals, methods, and objectives of the new regime were worked out on the bodies of those who had come to be seen as either enemies of the state or as members of racial categories that had not yet been reincorporated following the upheaval of the social order in the revolution.

While the treatment of Asians, Arabs, and unfavored Africans at the time of the revolution was not imagined, the "cultural revolution" continues (Askew 2002) under the aegis of a racialized and discriminatory cultural imaginary, authorized by the Zanzibari state, which harnesses the imagery of the past to prejudiced and bigoted actions and performances in the present. For Ronaldo and Martin, their senses of being-in-the-world in Zanzibar are conditioned by a past that is imaginary for many but all too real for them. Components of cultural imaginaries, such as ideas of race, ethnicity, religion, and history, exist in the world of lived experience where they are made meaningful in cultured performances. As the case in point, I suggest that Zanzibar is a place where local categories of ethnicity and race are being submitted to worldly risks, reconstruing their going values—and relative inequalities in particular—in keeping with intelligent, highly creative, and potentially destructive interactions between emerging imaginaries and history.

References

Abu-Lughod, Lila

1997 "The Interpretation of Cultures after Television." *Representations* 59: 109–34.

Anderson, Benedict

1983 *Imagined Communities: Reflections on the Origin and Spread of Nationalism*. London and New York: Verso.

Appadurai, Arjun

1991 "Global Ethnoscapes: Notes and Queries for a Transnational Anthropology." In *Recapturing Anthropology: Working in the Present*, ed. Richard G. Fox, 191–210. Santa Fe, N.M.: SAR Press.

Arnold, Nathalie

2006 "With 'Ripe' Eyes You Will See: Occult Conflicts in Pemba's Days of Caning, Zanzibar 1964–1968." In *Studies in Witchcraft, Magic, War and Peace in Africa: Nineteenth and Twentieth Centuries*, ed. Beatrice Nicolini, 215–26. New York: Edwin Mellen Press.

2002 "Placing the Shameless: Approaching Poetry and the Politics of Pemban-ness in Zanzibar, 1995–2001." *Research in African Literatures* 33(3): 140–68.

Askew, Kelly

2002 *Performing the Nation: Swahili Music and Cultural Politics in Tanzania*. Chicago: University of Chicago Press.

Bakari, Mohammed

2001 *The Democratisation Process in Zanzibar: A Retarded Transition*. Hamburg: Institut für Afrika-Kunde.

1996 "Passion, Power and Politics in a Palestinian Tourist Market." In *The Tourist Image: Myths and Myth Making in Tourism*, ed. Tom Selwyn, 83–103. New York and London: John Wiley & Sons.

Bromber, Katrin

2006 "Ustaraabu: A Conceptual Change in Tanganyikan Newspaper Discourse." In *The Global Worlds of the Swahili*, ed. Roman Loimeier and Rudiger Seeseman, 67–82. Berlin: LIT Verlag.

Burgess, G. Thomas

2009 *Race, Revolution, and the Struggle for Human Rights in Zanzibar: The Memoirs of Ali Sultan Issa and Seif Sharif Hamad*. Athens, Ohio: Ohio University Press.

2005 "The Young Pioneers and the Rituals of Citizenship in Revolutionary Zanzibar." *Africa Today* 51(3): 3–29.

Butler, Judith

1997 *Excitable Speech: A Politic of the Performative*. New York: Routledge.

Cameron, Greg

2004 "Political Violence, Ethnicity and the Agrarian Question in Zanzibar." In *Swahili Modernities: Culture, Politics, and Identity on the East Coast of Africa*, ed. Pat Caplan and Farouk Topan, 103–20. Trenton, N.J.: Africa World Press.

Caplan, Pat

2004 "Introduction." In *Swahili Modernities: Culture, Politics, and Identity on the East Coast of Africa*, ed. Pat Caplan and Farouk Topan, 1–18. Trenton, N.J.: Africa World Press.

Ferguson, James

1999 *Expectations of Modernity: Myths and Meanings of Urban Life on the Zambian Copperbelt*. Berkeley, Cal.: University of California Press.

Flint, J. E.

1965 "Zanzibar, 1890–1950." In *History of East Africa*, vol. 2, ed. Vincent Harlow and E. M. Chilver, 641–71. Oxford: Clarendon Press.

Freeman-Grenville, G. S. P.

1998 *The Swahili Coast, 2nd to 19th Centuries: Christianity, Islam and Commerce in Eastern Africa*. London: Variorum Reprints.

Geschiere, Peter

1997 *The Modernity of Witchcraft: Politics and the Occult in Postcolonial Africa*. Charlottesville: University Press of Virginia.

1992 "Kinship, Witchcraft and 'The Market.'" In *Contesting Markets: Analyses of Ideology, Discourse and Practice*, ed. R. Dilley, 159–79. Edinburgh: Edinburgh University Press.

Giddens, Anthony

1984 *The Constitution of Society: Outline of the Theory of Structuration*. Berkeley, Cal.: University of California Press.

Glassman, Jonathon

2011 *War of Words, War of Stones: Racial Thought and Violence in Colonial Zanzibar*. Bloomington, Ind.: Indiana University Press.

2004 "Slower than a Massacre: The Multiple Sources of Racial Thought in Colonial Africa." *American Historical Review* 109(3): 720–54.

2000 "Sorting Out the Tribes: The Creation of Racial Identities in Colonial Zanzibar's Newspaper Wars." *Journal of African History* 41: 395–428.

1995 *Feasts and Riot: Revelry, Rebellion, and Popular Consciousness on the Swahili Coast, 1856–1888*. London: James Currey.

Goffman, Erving

1985 *The Presentation of Self in Everyday Life*. Garden City, N.Y.: Doubleday.

Gregory, R. G.

1993a *South Asians in East Africa: An Economic and Social History, 1890–1980*. Oxford: Westview.

1993b *Quest for Equality: Asian Politics in East Africa, 1900–1967*. London: Sangam Books.

Gruber, Tom R.

1995 "Toward Principles for the Design of Ontologies Used for Knowledge Sharing." *International Journal of Human-Computer Studies* 43(4/5): 907–28.

Howe, Leo

2000 "Risk, Ritual and Performance." *Journal of the Royal Anthropological Institute* New Series 6: 63–79.

Keshodkar, Akbar

2004 "The Politics of Localization: Controlling Movement in the Field." *Anthropology Matters* 6(2): 1–9.

Larsen, Kjersti

2004 "Change, Continuity and Contestation: The Politics of Modern Identities in Zanzibar." In *Swahili Modernities: Culture, Politics, and Identity on the East Coast of Africa*, ed. Pat Caplan and Farouk Topan, 121–43. Trenton, N.J.: Africa World Press.

1998 "Spirit Possession as Historical Narrative." In *Locality and Belonging*, ed. Nadia Lovell, 125–46. London: Routledge.

Lévi-Strauss, Claude
1966 *The Savage Mind*. Chicago: University of Chicago Press.

Maliyamkono, T. L.
2000 *The Political Plight of Zanzibar*. Dar es Salaam: TEMA Publishers.

Mamdani, Mahmood
2001 *When Victims Become Killers: Colonialism, Nativism and the Genocide in Rwanda*. Princeton, N.J.: Princeton University Press.

Mapuri, Omar R.
1996 *Zanzibar: The 1964 Revolution: Achievements and Prospects*. Dar es Salaam: TEMA Publishers.

Mbogoni, Lawrence E. Y.
2012 *Aspects of Colonial Tanzania History*. Dar es Salaam: Mkuki na Nyota.
2005 "Censoring the Press in Colonial Zanzibar." In *In Search of a Nation*, ed. Gregory H. Maddox and James L. Giblin, 198–215. Oxford: James Currey.

Middleton, John
1992 *The World of the Swahili: An African Mercantile Civilization*. New Haven, Conn.: Yale University Press.

Myers, Garth A.
2000 "Narrative Representations of Revolutionary Zanzibar." *Journal of Historical Geography* 26(3): 429–48.
1995 "The Early History of the 'Other Side' of Zanzibar Town." In *The History and Conservation of Zanzibar Stone Town*, ed. Abdul Sheriff, 30–45. London: James Currey.

Nurse, Derek, and Thomas Spear
1985 "The Origins and Development of Swahili: Reconstructing the History of an African Language and People." *Mankind Quarterly* 25(4): 353–71.

Parkin, David
2006 "Art That Dances and Art That Patrols." In *The Global Worlds of the Swahili*, ed. Roman Loimeier and Rudiger Seeseman, 83–110. Berlin: LIT Verlag.

Pearson, Michael N.

1998 *Port Cities and Intruders: The Swahili Coast, India, and Portugal in the Early Modern Era*. Baltimore and London: Johns Hopkins University Press.

Pouwels, Randall

1999 Review article: "East African Coastal History." *Journal of African History* 40: 285–96.

1987 *Horn and Crescent: Cultural Change and Traditional Islam on the East African Coast, 800–1900*. Cambridge, U.K: Cambridge University Press.

Prins, A. H. J.

1967 *The Swahili Speaking Peoples of Zanzibar and the East African Coast*. London: International African Institute.

Sahlins, Marshall

1985 *Islands of History*. Chicago: University of Chicago Press.

Saleh, Mohammed Ahmed

2004 "'Going with the Times': Conflicting Swahili Norms and Values Today." In *Swahili Modernities: Culture, Politics, and Identity on the East Coast of Africa*, ed. Pat Caplan and Farouk Topan, 145–53. Trenton, N.J.: Africa World Press.

Sheriff, Abdul

1994 "The Union and the Struggle for Democracy in Zanzibar." In *Liberalization and Politics: The 1990 Election in Tanzania*, ed. Rwekaza Sympho Mukandala and Haroub Othman. Dar es Salaam: Dar es Salaam University Press.

1991 "A Materialist Approach to Zanzibar's History." In *Zanzibar under Colonial Rule*, ed. Abdul Sheriff and Ed Ferguson. London: James Currey.

1987 *Slaves, Spices and Ivory in Zanzibar: Integration of an East African Commercial Empire into the World Economy, 1770–1873*. London: James Currey.

Sheriff, Abdul, and Ed Ferguson, eds.

1991 *Zanzibar under Colonial Rule*. London: James Currey.

Star, Susan Leigh, and James R. Griesemer

1989 "Institutional Ecology, 'Translations' and Boundary Objects: Amateurs and Professionals in Berkeley's Museum of Vertebrate Zoology, 1907–39." *Social Studies of Science* 19(3): 387–420.

Stocking, George W.
1982 *Race, Culture, and Evolution*. Chicago: University of Chicago Press.

Sumich, Jason
2002 "Looking for the 'Other': Tourism, Power, and Identity in Zanzibar." *Anthropology Southern Africa* 25(1/2): 39–45.

Swartz, Marc J.
1997 "Illness and Morality in the Mombasa Swahili Community: A Metaphorical Model in an Islamic Culture." *Culture, Medicine and Psychiatry* 21(1): 89–114.

1991 *The Way the World Is: Cultural Processes and Social Relationships among the Mombasa Swahili*. Berkeley, Cal.: University of California Press.

Temu, A. J.
1969 "The Rise and Triumph of Nationalism." In *A History of Tanzania*, ed. Isaria N. Kimambo and A. J. Temu, 189–213. Nairobi: East African Publishing House.

Weiss, Brad
2002 "Thug Realism: Inhabiting Fantasy in Urban Tanzania." *Cultural Anthropology* 17(1): 93–124.

West, Harry G.
2005 *Kupilikula: Governance and the Invisible Realm in Mozambique*. Chicago and London: University of Chicago Press.

Chapter Eight

Silenced Voices, Recaptured Memories: Historical Imprints within a Zanzibari Life-World

Kjersti Larsen

Memory believes before knowing remembers. Believes more than recollects, more than even knowing wonders.

— WILLIAM FAULKNER, *Light in August*

The value of a certain kind of memory [...] is that it can denaturalize the everyday and render it visible, disrupting the illusion of the timeless routine and connecting it again with historical processes.

— JOE MORAN, "History, Memory and the Everyday"

This chapter explores the ways in which the 1964 revolution continues to affect social relationships in Zanzibar city.[1] This examination of social memory and the role it plays in everyday life has been inspired by the "loud silence" that, until recently, enclosed the ongoing impact of this event in people's lives. The violent insurrection occurred on the night of 11–12 January and lasted until 3 February, when Abeid Amani Karume was acknowledged as president by the Revolutionary Council (Shivji 2008: 58–59). Yet the struggle to politically consolidate the revolution was ultimately resolved by the union declaration in 26 April 1964 (ibid: 83; Myers 2003: 106). The revolution led to the overthrow of the sultan of Zanzibar and his government, mainly composed of men of Arab descent, by those who subsequently have been represented as African revolutionaries in the national political history. Many land and property owners, mostly of Arab origin but also of South Asian and Comorian descent were either killed or forced to leave the islands—that is, Unguja and Pemba. Actual estimates of the number of deaths vary greatly, from "hundreds" up to 20,000. The rebellion has been depicted as a struggle between proprietors and non-proprietors (Lofchie 1970; Sheriff 1987)— a distinction that has never been well defined.

---

1   Complying with the editorial style I have accepted the formulation "Zanzibar city" when referring to the place usually called Zanzibar Town. In line with my ethnographic and anthropological approach I would, however, have preferred to apply Zanzibar Town when referring to the capital city of Zanzibar.

One may thus wonder how far the recollections of the revolution remain interpretations influenced by a vision of society as it was before and to what extent the revolution actually transformed the imagining of this post-revolutionary society. For these reasons, I contend that a focus on social memory can provide access to conceptions of society and of how social relations as well as identities and belonging are understood to have been modified or transformed. A focus on memory may further engender perceptions of what the revolution actually distorted in terms of identity formations, social uncertainty, and cultural dynamics more generally. My interest here is therefore to discuss the place of personal and collective memory in practical action and the manner in which "memories implicitly may affect what people do" (Bloch 1996: 231). I am also concerned with the role explicit and implicit memories play in identity construction. Interestingly, social memory—personal and collective—conveys the ways in which the imaginary is both engendered by and proceeds from what I would call a "social inarticulate," nonreflexive, but precisely the seat of an implicit and recurrent imaginary (see Castoriadis 1975). What is referred to here as the social inarticulate should be understood as a mental and practical competence that becomes internalized and embodied through socialization and within a specific sociocultural environment. It constitutes a fundamental dimension of social personhood in articulation with the imaginary. The imaginary should thus not be understood as a fiction or as the product of mere fantasy but rather as that ceaseless creation of signs, figures, and forms that shape perceptions about identity and belonging within a social realm. In distinction from its common meaning, the imaginary is not a potential to subtract or withdraw from the real but rather the capacity to provide it with a shape—a process involving cognitive and practical experience constitutive of the dynamics of remembering and forgetting. Hence, memory is embedded in the imaginary and is thus selective. The imaginary is creative and implicit and may be articulated through particular remembrances of the past and understandings of the future. It is part of social relationships; it is produced by and reacts to a particular sociocultural configuration. Incorporated in the social inarticulate, the imaginary provides direction for how the past is memorized and the future envisioned. It imprints on how past events, like the revolution and what preceded and followed it, are recollected. Therefore, one may ask how and to what extent recollections of the revolution, the period that preceded it, and its outcome fashion and reconstitute ideas of "how it used to be." In a similar vein, one may question how memory could be revived in the present so as to reconstruct social relationships encapsulated by discourses emphasizing both cultural differentiation and incorporation.

A body of literature (Lofchie 1970; Bennett 1978; Cooper 1980; Babu 1991; Fair 2001; Shivji 2008; Bissell 2011; Glassman 2011) has already discussed the political upheavals that preceded and followed the 1964 revolution, with its manifold social, political, and economic consequences. My aim here is not to rehash this history but rather to focus on the ways the revolution continues to be remembered and reverberate in everyday life in Zanzibar. Generally, history as a discipline is perceived as a kind of intellectual and objective approach to analysis and criticism of the past (see Nora 1989; Moran 2010). Usually, it is, if not antithetical, at least, critical to spontaneous memory accounts.[2] In contrast, ethnography and an anthropological attention to the embodied dynamics of memory may not only record social history as it unfolds but also reveal recollections of the past as these emerge in the context of everyday life. My approach to memory, in this case focusing on social history and recollections of the past that are voiced in various daily life contexts, implies that the memories evoked are often fragmentary, indistinct, and, at times, highly selective (see Moran 2010).

Spoken Imprints of the Revolution

Zanzibaris who experienced the 1964 revolution still find it difficult to talk about what precisely happened. This, I suggest, is largely because they have wished, if not to forget, at least to keep at a distance their personal memories and the emotions these may evoke. In the face of this reticence, it is often the children and grandchildren of those who lived through the revolution who speak up about their understanding of how the uprising and its aftermath affected their families' lives. Such openness is partly due to the more liberal political atmosphere that followed the introduction of the "multiparty system" in 1992, but it is also due to the fact that younger generations only have reference to what they have heard narrated and not any actual experience of revolutionary trauma, immediate loss, or dislocation. This does not necessarily mean that they are less emotionally affected than those who experienced the revolution, but rather that they do not, in the same way, try to keep an emotional distance.

---

2   "Historical consciousness, by its nature, focuses on the historicity of events—that they took place then and not now, that they grew out of circumstances different from those that now obtain. Memory, by contrast, has no sense of the passage of time; it denies the 'pastness' of its objects and insists on their continuing presence" (Novic 1999: 4).

With regard to memory, I have previously discussed how in socially and politically contested situations emotions such as fear, anxiety, and distrust are transferred through bodily, emotional, and aesthetic idioms as well as by means of narratives (Larsen 2004). It is only recently that I, while conducting research in Zanzibar, have heard women and men explicitly and in everyday situations refer to episodes they themselves encountered or witnessed during and just after the insurrection.[3] For a variety of reasons, they had until recently left their memories unuttered. This silence was undoubtedly prompted by fear created by the system of denunciation established by the state after the revolution, whereby critics or perceived opponents would be accused and punished. At the same time, the reluctance to speak was also spurred by the desire to forget—linked ultimately to the notion that "speaking of memories" would prevent a wished-for reconstruction of social harmony and propitiation of the past. Allow me to illustrate this point with an ethnographic example:

In the past, when I had mentioned the revolution to Ma Aisha, a woman in her mid-70s, of Comorian origin (*Mngazija*), whom I have known since 1985, she would usually reply, "It was horrible [*mbaya sana*]. People were killed for nothing," and then shift to another topic. The same occurred whenever I raised the issue with other women and men in her age group. We had discussed changes in social, political, and economic conditions as well as morality, but we had never explicitly talked about the days of the revolution. Then, in January 2013, the day of the celebration of the revolution's 49th anniversary, I happened to visit Ma Aisha while she was watching the coverage of the anniversary on TVZ (Television Zanzibar) together with two of her grandchildren.[4] In this context, I asked her whether people felt like celebrating this event. "Some cry while others celebrate," she said, continuing: "They who celebrate are those who could steal from others and who afterwards got what they wanted. They who lost their beloved, they cry. Many will dress

---

[3] Memory also plays a role for anthropologists conducting ethnographic research, especially in terms of what Simon Ottenberg (1990) calls "headnotes." Although, such notes (a conscious and intentional tool for fieldwork) are significant in the formation of ethnographic understanding and refer to information stored in our "heads," such recollections are obviously different from what is defined as "collective" or "social" memory in social sciences.

[4] Apart from Zanzibar, which had state-run broadcasting from 1973 on, TV broadcasting was a late development in Tanzania, relative to other African nation states. State TV was officially launched on the mainland in 2001, several years after the first private TV station went on the air in 1994. The first private broadcasters on the islands were established around 2002. Recently, the video has been replaced by satellite and cable TV.

in black or they will tie a black thread around their wrist, or a small piece of black fabric that they would stick to their clothes with a pin. If you see such things, you know that they lost somebody during the revolution."

Her response illuminates the way in which collective memories provide cultural frameworks that can be drawn upon in order to comprehend unprecedented events (see Larsen 2004). Although as collective memory the 1964 revolution produced a common frame of reference, as Ma Aisha clearly expressed, the way in which it has been remembered, in terms of individual memory, depends upon how people at the time were positioned in society regarding both identity and socioeconomic position. Memories are certainly not documentaries but rather retrospective interpretations of events and experiences, and they are socially mediated and structured. Individual memory is always an aspect of social memory. There could be no individual memory without the framework, or, as I would contend, "the imaginary," provided by collective memories, to which individual recollections of the past can conform (see Halbwachs 1992). Ma Aisha's recollection, referred to above, depicts the manner in which the individual and the collective intertwine.[5]

Following up on this observation, I then asked Ma Aisha whether she had been afraid during those days. She responded, "I was alone in the house together with the children. Suddenly somebody knocked on the door and I was told to come out. The men asked about my husband. He was not home, neither [was] my oldest son. All those days, I did not know where my son was. Afterwards he told me that he had been hiding in the attic of a house belonging to an Indian family." Ma Aisha further described how her family was taken, together with others who were not killed on the spot, to the internment camp at Raha Leo, an area that was then on the outskirts of town, where they were kept for some days before they again were allowed to return home:

> On the way to Raha Leo, we had to step over corpses, some without a head, some with bodies opened with knives. It was terrible. Some were even put on fire and thrown into wells, especially Arabs. We were very scared. When we heard steps or voices outside, we knew "they" were coming. I was even afraid to look through the window, in case I would see "them" beat or kill someone. When "they" knocked on the door one had

---

5   Individual memory refers to the meaning of the past for individuals—how they recollect and make sense of social relationships and life trajectories. Collective or social memory denotes more or less shared and discursive recollections of the past with an explicit reference to social, economic, and political circumstances (Halbwachs 1992; Climo and Cattell 2002).

to open. "They" would enter only to destroy and steal. "They" looked for men. If "they" found them "they" took them away even if only dressed in their underwear. The men were tied together with ropes, and you never saw them again. Many disappeared. Afterwards, survivors whose family members had been killed sold their houses and left. For them, it became impossible to stay on. Many of "those" who violated and killed people were Kikuyu from Kenya. "They" killed many, and we were so afraid.

The manner in which Ma Aisha narrated made it difficult to say what represented a collective memory and what belonged to her immediate individual recollection. No doubt, the two dimensions of "social memory" interrelate in her "spoken" memories from those days.

This was the first explicit conversation I had had with Ma Aisha about her own experiences during the revolution. She might have spoken up because her memories were sparked by watching the official celebrations on TV, but I had recently also noticed that Zanzibaris had begun referring to the revolution more frequently, especially during multiparty election periods. Publicly, it seemed that the revolution was now regarded as more a formal historical event than a dangerous source of political confrontation policed by an active regime of repression. Thus, regarding Ma Aisha's generation, both time and symbolic distance had played a role, and the revolution had, to a certain extent, become an event of the past. From her point of view, what she would now "speak" could no longer harm her family, neighbors, or friends. Yet attention should be directed to the way she still represented the perceived perpetrators of revolutionary violence as "foreigners." It was as if she sensed that to include them as being part of Zanzibari society would mean that "evil" could still be produced from within, as something internal to and inherent in Zanzibari society. Such an understanding, where "evil"—in this case the perpetrators—would be located within society as such and among the local population, could easily produce a reality where trust would become absent in any social relations beyond the immediate household. Thus, in light of Maurice Bloch's argument regarding how "ordinary people's knowledge is a complex mixture of implicit and explicit knowledge" (Bloch 1996: 219), it is interesting to note how Ma Aisha in her recollection systematically referred to the perpetrators as "they." In the end, she even indicated that these men could behave as they did because they were *not* Zanzibaris but foreigners: Kikuyu from Kenya. Her choice of formulation revealed a desire to externalize the "enemy" as an Other, alien to her own social world. In this context, she not only emphasized cultural difference or "tribe" (*kabila*) but also divergent national origins—which, given the revolutionary ideology, is a meaningful detail.

In terms of a political strategy, the Africanization or nationalization process in the wake of the revolution aimed at eradicating any form of distinction linked to *makabila* (sing., *kabila*)—a term applied in everyday life as a categorical distinction about themselves, on so-called ethnic lines.[6] According to revolutionary ideology, racial and "tribal" identities were colonial impositions and had to be abolished as the new regime sought to forge a collective sense of identity.[7] From the beginning, the main targets of the revolution were political opponents within the Zanzibar Nationalist Party (ZNP) and the Zanzibar and Pemba People's Party (ZPPP), many of whom were identified, for instance, as *Waarabu* (Arabs) and *Wahindi* (South Asians or Indians). Subsequently, ordinary Zanzibaris of more multifaceted social identities became identified as being predominantly either Arabs (*Waarabu*), South Asians (*Wahindi*), or Comorians (*Wangazija*) and were equally targeted. Families of Comorian and South Asian origin may have suffered less than people of Arab origin in the sense that only a relatively small number among them were killed. Still, their life situation was far from easy (Petterson 2002: 191; Loimeier 2009), a subject I shall return to below. According to G. Thomas Burgess, the revolution was "a revolt against racial injustice.... [I]t was for a new discipline in citizens' habits of work and consumption" (2002: 290). The aim was to create an atmosphere of sameness and a common identity contrary to an established order of diversity. Still, the upheaval had created fear and distrust, individually as well as socially. Also, those who were not directly impacted knew of others who had been killed or suffered beatings, rape, disappearance, or imprisonment. This awareness created fear compounded by the uncertainty of not knowing who was in control while facing the impact of a repressive security apparatus. Besides the fear and unpredictability, people also experienced profound economic disruption as well as social dislocation

---

6   The term *makabila* refers to places of origin beyond Zanzibar and implies that their ancestors came from other places. The prefix *wa-* or *ma-* meaning people (of) or *m-* meaning person (of) is added to the name of the place of origin, as in *Waarabu* (people from Arabia). "Tribe" tends to be seen as a colonial-rooted term. The vernacular term does not necessarily imply a political system of "tribalism" or a political process based on ethnic groups and explicitly formulated group interests.

7   When Zanzibar gained independence from Britain in December 1963, the sultan remained the constitutional monarch of Zanzibar. Independence did not represent an institutional change (Bennett 1978; Lofchie 1970), nor did it transform Zanzibar into a more African state.

due to the revolutionary project. Before elaborating further, I will briefly comment upon the revolution and its aftermath.

Social Reorganization: Revolutionary Policy and the Suppression of Difference

The revolution significantly changed the composition of Zanzibar's population and initiated a reorganization of society. One of the main aims of the first post-revolution government was, as mentioned above, to turn Zanzibar into an African state where the inhabitants should all be Afro-Shirazi, with no other "tribal" (*kabila*) or cultural distinctions.[8] Identity was to be cast in new ways. The nation-building project addressed not only socioeconomic and political structures but included state control of access to information, clothing styles and forms of adornment, and religious interpretations and practices. The project was inspired by an official development discourse claiming that society was to be rebuilt upon local understandings of what constituted African, Islamic, and socialist discipline (Burgess 2002).[9] Most of the steps taken were implemented by use of force. In order to integrate the various categories of the population, for instance, the Forced Marriage Act was introduced in 1970–71. The decree, according to elderly people with whom I have discussed the matter, implied that men of African descent had the right to marry unmarried women of Arab or South Asian descent, even when the families and the women themselves protested (Larsen 2008).[10] Obviously, the act created suffering in the lives of individuals and until today the consequences form part of their lives (McGruder 1999; Keshodkar 2010).[11] Regarding the political and economic aspects of society, a quota system was introduced to regulate

---

8   The term was meant to indicate that all Zanzibaris were of mixed African and Persian origin. Thus, ironically, the new policies became one of ethnicity, and Comorians were declared noncitizens in 1967 (Loimeier 2009). Some would argue that "racism" entered social and political life with the revolution (G. Hadjivayanis, personal communication 2010; see also Fouéré 2009).

9   In the late 1960s and 1970s people faced chronic shortages of basic household commodities. In the early 1970s the government organized food rationing of flour, sugar, and rice. Elderly people I have known from 1984 onward recollect this period with dismay.

10 The Forced Marriage Act was abolished after the death of the first president, Abeid Amani Karume, in 1972.

11 Memory, whether one's own or mediated by others, may also be manifested in tension that still exists in relation to questions of *makabila*. Occasionally, people who consider themselves not to be of African descent express a genuine mistrust of people of so-called African descent, while the latter refer to the history of slavery in order to express their mistrust of people of non-African origin.

the number of students of African, Arab, South Asian, and Comorian origin who would gain access to higher education, privileging students of so-called African origin. Moreover, a decree was issued giving the government power to confiscate all immovable property without compensation. The Africanization of the civil service hit the South Asians particularly hard, costing many their jobs. All owners of private enterprises, regardless of size, were forced to take an "African" partner; in 1971 owners classified as "non-African" did not get their business licenses renewed. As this implies, economic indigenization measures played a key role (see also Fouéré 2009).[12] Even today, elderly people recall the system of denunciation that was established after the revolution, where neighbors, even family members, informed on each other. Such a system of "daily-life surveillance" served to create additional anxiety and self-censoring—all adding to an atmosphere of restricted social, economic, and intellectual candor. Years later, in the mid-1980s, the Revolutionary Government adopted economic and political liberalization within the terms of what became known as the Structural Adjustment Programme, including a multiparty system and free elections. Access to information and political debate seemed, especially among the young, gradually to neutralize a previous system of fear and suspicion. Economic liberalization accelerated from about 1989, turning Zanzibar once again into a trade and tourism center (see also Cameron 2009; Caplan 2009). In this period, several families of South Asian descent managed to establish international business enterprises through their trade networks outside Zanzibar, based on social relationships established before the revolution, especially in the Arabian Peninsula (Bissell 1999; Keshodkar 2010). Given the historically grounded association between socioeconomic strata and aesthetics, a rather sudden change regarding economic position seemed, at least for some, to have engendered motivations for "new" expressions of social and cultural distinctions. Political and economic liberalization created an atmosphere that facilitated public markings of difference and cultural distinctions through means of aesthetics and adornment in the same way socioeconomic and political differentiation historically had been visualized in Zanzibari society. The "aesthetics" I refer to include clothing styles, architectural designs, jewelry, and musical genres (Larsen 1998, 2008). A marking of diversity of descent and thus of

---

12 During the 1990s a "politics of belonging" linked to economic indigenization measures, also known as "economic preference," was introduced into Tanzanian politics (Fouéré 2009).

identity configurations, which had been politically suppressed since the revolution, was once more made possible because of political changes, which facilitated an opening of the islands to broader global connections, as well as the return of Zanzibaris who were exiled or had migrated. As I shall illustrate below, memory provided access to recollections as well as new ideas of "how it used to be" in the past, before and just after the revolution. Whether individual or collective, "memory is constructed and reconstructed by the dialectics of remembering and forgetting, shaped by semantic and interpretative frames and subject to distortions" (Cattell and Climo 2002: 1). Once again, Zanzibari society resumed a certain form of public marking of difference with regard to identity and socioeconomic standing. Objects and artifacts that were needed to mark difference in aesthetically distinct ways were again available, and, it seemed, appreciated. Obviously, bodily presentation is important in marking identity and thus in the social boundaries that keep people apart or together (Bourdieu 1977). Still, important questions arise concerning how identity is motivated and aesthetically cast within such a context: What sources are drawn upon? To what extent does "memory" over time affect practices as well as identity formations? Below, I shall explore the theme by focusing on one among several milieus of *Wahindi* in Zanzibar city—that is, those whose ancestors are from South Asia. The term *Wahindi* may refer to a variety of milieus including Hindus, Christians, and Muslims belonging to different socio-cultural and economic strata. Despite their diverse identities, social locations, and experiences, however, *Wahindi* all share, along with other Zanzibaris, a collective memory of the events of the 1964 revolution as well as of the impact of the Africanization and nationalization policies that followed.

Reconstructing Notions of Indian-ness under New Conditions

Currently the majority of *Wahindi* in Zanzibar are Muslim, with Shia Muslims more numerous than Sunni.[13] In East Africa, South Asians generally have been often associated with economic wealth and socially segregated lives. In popular opinion, *Wahindi* are commonly said to live in urban settings, to be involved in trade and other kinds

---

13 Akbar Keshodkar refers to a survey conducted in 2001, and verified in 2004, which states that there are "about 2000 South Asians in Zanzibar: 600 Shia Ithna'asharis, 500 Shia Bohoras, 120 Shia Ismailis, 200 Sunni Memons and other Sunni Muslims, 300 Lohana Hindu, less than 100 Baniya Hindu and 100 Goan Christians, and the rest of other South Asian backgrounds, such as Brahmin Hindus, Bhatia Hindus, lower caste Hindus, Jain and Sikh" (2010: 226–7).

of business, and to be socially and culturally segregated. Yet according to Georgios Hadjivayanis (personal communication 2010), before the 1964 revolution Zanzibaris of South Asian origin—considered poor by local standards—were not referred to as *Wahindi*. I wish to draw attention here to the terminology because there are currently shifts in identity representations and in how these affect social relationships. The milieu I refer to below would precisely be composed of Zanzibaris of South Asian descent who, prior to the revolution, were usually not referred to as being *Wahindi*. They claim their place of origin is the Kutch region of India. Historically, in contrast to other *Wahindi* communities, they tended to settle in rural areas such as Chwaka, Makunduchi, and Kizimkazi in the east and southern parts of Unguja, where they mainly managed small shops and engaged in transport services. Still, some families claim to always have lived in the city. Like the majority of Zanzibari Muslims, they are Sunni and follow the Shafi'i law. Keeping in mind Hadjivayanis' comment above, they were perceived to be socially and culturally inferior to other *Wahindi* milieus until the 1964 revolution—lacking in wealth and education, living in *ng'ambo* (outskirts of town/environs) and in rural areas, speaking Kiswahili, and interrelating with *Waswahili*, that is, "Africans" or, more generally, "people of the coast" (see Blanchy 1995: 233–4; Blanchy 2008; Adam 2010c: 93). During the revolution many were protected by their "Swahili" neighbors.[14] Afterward, when most urban *Wahindi* had left, been expelled, or been killed, they, along with many others from rural and semirural areas, settled in the city, where they opened small shops and continued to engage in transport.[15] Currently, this particular milieu is socially and economically differentiated, being composed of households from various neighborhoods, and participating in a number of different social networks in Zanzibar, on the mainland, and beyond. Now, I shall briefly describe how videos of Indian films, in a period when markers of identities were still perceived as suspect, contributed to an awakening of recollections, including reconstructions about life before the revolution.[16] Regarding the blending of individual memory

---

14   Several families with "targeted" identities like *Waarabu*, *Wahindi*, and *Wangazija* have narrated how they were rescued by neighbors during the days of violence.

15   Like many others, after the revolution several from this milieu migrated to Dar es Salaam, Arusha, and Morogoro, or to England or Canada.

16   Lila Abu-Lughod argues, "[T]elevision's messages are certainly deflected by the way people frame their television experiences and by the way powerful everyday realities inflect and offset those messages" (2005: 33).

and social memory and the interconnection between recollections of the past and the envisioning of the future, there is "no one way of relating to the past and the future and therefore of being in history" (Bloch 1996: 229).

With respect to the connection between memory and film, I will refer to ethnographic material collected in Zanzibar city mainly from the mid-1980s into the 1990s, before international, satellite, and private TV channels became accessible in the islands. At that time, before the range of available media changed, imported films on videocassettes represented new openings to information and inspiration. My broader analysis draws upon research conducted until the present. My intention is not to argue that memory could be fashioned only with reference to the messages provided by these films or by the media more generally, but rather that the media inform our understanding of the world and how one positions oneself within it. Including Indian movies as part of my analysis, I thus see it as vital to keep a critical mind and not confuse the media with other complex social processes.[17] Nevertheless, "memory is always found in context" (Lambek and Antze 1996: xvii). This implies that memories can be expressed in particular situations either in the form of sudden reactions sparked by everyday happenings or as narratives that come to mind if the context is appropriate, and it allows for what, following Clifford Geertz, can be denoted as "experience-distance" narratives. I thus refer to situations where a third subject-position is brought into the scene, in this case, through the video. This facilitates an externalization of memories through an external figure, either in the form of a film scenario or a certain character represented by an actor, either of which may initiate an aesthetic response that opens up the possibility for a creative reworking of memory. The examples are meant to illustrate ways in which these films not only created openings for people to "speak" about experiences linked to loss and deprivation but also inspired new forms of identity configurations grounded in ideas about life before and after the revolution. The video scripts and how they were put into dramatic form provided grounds for both a reconstruction and an idealization of "Indian-ness," as well as a reconstruction of a "new" identity as Indian and Zanzibari—an identity that had been silenced during the first decades of the revolution.

---

17 Among other more recent studies on how the media may provide access to processes of social change, Abu-Lughod's (2005) research shows in an excellent way how TV and video films, as a form of popular culture, offer insights into the social, cultural, and political dynamics of particular communities.

Indian Films, Fiction, and Re-membering

Indian films were and still are universally appreciated in Zanzibar. In the 1980s and 1990s, the films were also perceived as rich sources of information.[18] They resonated with memories of life before the revolution and influenced interpretations of Indian-ness in post-revolutionary Zanzibar, including a reappropriation of a certain expression of Indian-ness.[19] The scripts recaptured an imaginary, engendered perceptions and practices, and revitalized a former sense of belonging. The films portrayed processes of socioeconomic and cultural change and displayed how these changes impacted on different aspects of Indian society. The scripts—whether romantic, melodramatic, or heroic—depicted costumes and manners and classes and castes as well as oppositional themes such as rural versus urban, poverty versus wealth, and arranged marriages versus love marriages (see also Fuglesang 1994: 168). The period I here refer to was one characterized by socioeconomic change, yet during this time there was no access to the material and ideological resources displayed in the films, nor were the themes the films touched upon perceived to be "voice-able." What made comparison possible between the films' scripts or characters and viewers' own lives was that what people saw bore resemblance to their own realities. The movies "showed them things" (Abu-Lughod 2005: 8). The stories as well as the environment depicted in the films corresponded to aspects of their own society, ideology, notions of family, aesthetics, and love—and articulated the problems, misfortunes, hopes, and happiness they had observed and experienced. The media could then work as a tool for promoting development, becoming a source of information leading to a reappropriation of what was seen as lost knowledge and practices. Furthermore, the films vividly conveyed and made immediate other worlds in rather powerful ways, providing an opening to alternative ways of life and possibilities that might not otherwise have been conceivable. In this sense, the more immediate effect of the films echoes Brian Larkin's (1997) formulation about "the social life of television."

---

18   Women would watch wedding scenes and note the various dances. Afterward, the young would practice these dances. One dance in particular caught attention: women dancing together, beating sticks while turning around each other in circles. Regarding "memory," it is interesting that elderly women argue that they knew such dancing practices from the past (*zamani*). The dance has now been appropriated as part of their cultural heritage.

19   The Indian popular films referred to here were rooted in Indian mythology, epic accounts, and aesthetics (Rao 1988; Valicha 1989). The plots of these films regularly drew upon the characters and structure of mythological epics.

By making this connection I here allude to how the films pertained to silenced memories and the way in which these surfaced and, in certain contexts, were recast *as if* external to the viewers own lives. In certain situations, the viewers actually seemed to project their own memories into various characters in the Indian films—a process that seemed to make it possible for them to talk about painful personal recollections.

The dramas were easily followed and commented upon, even when they were in Hindi. Inspired by the scripts, the viewers would actively craft and narrate their own understandings of what the films conveyed. The themes were indeed open for alternative readings and, as such, created openings for discussions across the generations on topics like marriage and affinal relations. In general, marriage is a subject of interest between generations both because it is through this institution that social links between kin groups are established and because of parents' involvement in arranging suitable relationships. Still, in this particular milieu, marriage was an especially sensitive issue due to several rushed marriage agreements made during the period of the above mentioned Forced Marriage Act, which produced unions that had resulted in divorce. While talking about a drama portraying the tragic outcome of an arranged marriage, elderly women would at times recollect the life stories of Zanzibari women they knew whose lives had taken a miserable turn when their parents made hasty marriage arrangements to protect their daughters from potential forced marriages. These conversations would often end with someone saying, "Only the parent would know what would be best for their children—they only would know them well enough." Sometimes a sentence would be added, emphasizing, "Parents should never force their children to marry; they should consult their daughters or sons before taking any formal move to arrange a marriage." When the problem of divorce was brought up, these women commented that parents had been arranging marriages without carefully considering their children's wishes. The backdrop of these discussions was the Forced Marriage Act, and the utterances must be seen in the context of what took place in these people's own lives during the revolutionary period. As Lila Abu Lughod (2005: 33) has argued, "[T]elevision's messages are certainly deflected by the way people frame their television experiences and by the way powerful everyday realities inflect and offset those messages."

For instance, one evening in the late 1990s, Jamilla and I were discussing a melodrama about a socially impossible love relationship that we had just watched, when she suddenly changed the topic and began to talk about her own life:

> Here in Zanzibar things like this have happened. After the revolution, our parents wanted us to marry very young. It was to prevent that we, their daughters, should be forcefully married to "strangers." Hasty decisions about marriage partners did result in tragedies for many of us. My brother Mohammed and I were at the time seventeen and sixteen years old. Our parents arranged our marriages with cross-cousins from our age group, without consulting us. Mohammed was married to our cousin Fatma and me to her brother Yusuf. It was an exchange of children between our closely related families. However, at the time Mohammed and another of our cousins, Amina, were in love. Not being asked, they could not tell our parents. Amina was married to another cousin. After some years all the three marriages ended in divorce. Yet, all being divorced, we could not be remarried to the one we initially had been in love with because we are all as if [*kama*] sisters and brothers. It would have been a great shame [*aibu sana*] for the families. It would have been as if, for instance, Mohammed divorced one sister so as to marry the other sister and in this way valuing one of them above the other. This would not be possible.[20]

In this context, Jamilla critically commented on her parents' decisions, yet emphasized that what had happened was due to the political situation at the time. Reading between the lines, I understood that she was blaming the revolution for her not being able to marry the way she wanted and have children of her own. Several of the women whose marriages ended in divorce during this period have not remarried, as might otherwise be expected (see also McGruder 1999). Their life situation as divorced and, in many cases, childless women can be seen as a ramification and social imprint of the revolution—part of its ongoing reverberations in social life. Stories such as Jamilla's have often been confided to me by younger siblings explaining why, for instance, an older sister failed to remarry or why an older brother married a woman from another milieu. Yet, sparked by viewings of the Indian videos, such experiences could sometimes be approached as if they were themes external to their own lives. The videos created a context in which the unvoiceable could be voiced, while those involved could, perhaps, take on the position of an "audience" to their own stories. When people watched these particular films, in that particular period, previously "unremembered" experiences, identities, and events

---

20 Cross-cousin marriage is the ideal, while, simultaneously, cousins by extensional definition are considered as sisters and brothers.

became reincorporated, to a degree, into their recollections of the past. Gradually, these "new" recollections also surfaced in a common social discourse portraying their shared experiences in this society both before and after the revolution. Watching videos of Indian films created, for some women as well as men, a context for memory—for remembering, reworking memories, and even for un-remembering. To see memory as a social and moral practice implies "that we think about memory as a human, cultural practice rather than as a natural object or process; and that this kind of practice is to be understood as moral rather than simply technical, intellectual, or instrumental" (Lambek 1996: 235). Seen as a moral practice, memory concerns who you are—your behavior, appearance, and relative position in the social realm.

Exposing Difference—Presuming Belonging

The revolution led to specific policies but also induced an atmosphere where "sameness" or collective cohesion was insisted upon as a response to "a past" where society was seen as structured according to political, economic, and cultural distinctions. Cultural diversity was to be suppressed, and regulations set by the state had to be publicly followed. If not, Zanzibaris risked being denounced as disloyal to the dominant ideology. These attitudes gradually faded away after the late 1980s, when notions of difference were again expressed through, for instance, dress, manners, verbal expressions, and fashion styles. A description of ongoing changes in language use—a form of change that from the beginning was inspired by the Indian films referred to above—will suggest how notions of cultural diversity have reemerged.

Kiswahili is the main language of communication for the community I explore here, although words and sentences in the Kutchi language are sometimes inserted.[21] When watching Indian videos in Hindi during the 1980s and 1990s, only those present who knew Kutchi well—usually elderly people—managed to follow some of the Hindi and thus could translate words and sentences into Kiswahili. Inspired by the films and the kind of recollection of Indian-ness that these played into, some women of the community have gradually learned more Kutchi, and even some Hindi. Occasionally, conversations—especially between women—would start out in Kutchi, but whenever the themes discussed become detailed and engaging, they would switch back to Kiswahili. Despite

---

21   Kiswahili is the official language. It is used in school, including in Qur'an schools, along with Qur'anic Arabic.

the—for them—more recent significance of speaking Kutchi, the people of the milieu I am discussing still consider Kiswahili their main language, although, for some, Kutchi is dominant, especially when addressing young children.[22] The ability to make use of a language beyond Kiswahili resonates with a past where Indian-ness was recognized as part of Zanzibari social and cultural complexity. The remembered use of Kutchi could be seen as one way of insisting on a particular identity anchored in a pre-revolutionary Zanzibar. Language became one ingredient in the process of reappropriation of an "identity distinction," which both during and after the revolution had been "denied" to them within the broader social realm. In this sense, indirect recollections contributed to new forms of identity logics and new perceptions of society.

The use of Kutchi in public became one way of marking their distinctive identity and, thus, a social status previously denied them. This form of identity marking has not been universally appreciated in Zanzibar. When I observed women switching from Kiswahili to Kutchi while shopping, for instance, I frequently overheard comments from passersby claiming that "they are being typical *Wahindi*." Such comments were by no means meant as compliments (see Fouéré 2009). Rather, they imply that *Wahindi* perceive themselves as distinct and wish to mark a distance between themselves and society at large—a stereotypic notion, still prevalent regarding people of South Asian origin, that dates back to the rhetoric applied before, during, and just after the 1964 revolution. Ironically, women from this social milieu were never denoted as *Wahindi* before the revolution. They were instead categorized as *Waswahili* (a generic term for "people from the coast" or, sometimes, "Africans") because they were seen as generally poor and uneducated. It is only recently that the use of Kutchi in public has evoked comments marking its speakers as *Wahindi,* a term that, in turn, places them in a position of Otherness. Such comments insinuate that *Wahindi* do not really belong in Zanzibari society. As already mentioned, the term is mostly applied by others in situations where people of South Asian descent are perceived to make a statement of distinction. Yet the choice to speak Kutchi by those who have reappropriated it, may be inspired by a particular fiction that they once lived a "past" more privileged than the present. Making use of an Indian language

---

22 For children who attend private schools, English is the school language as well as the language they use among themselves. Currently, their command of Kiswahili is poor. Their mothers' English abilities are limited; simple Kutchi and elaborate Kiswahili are their main tools of communication at home.

accentuates their position among Zanzibari *Wahindi*—a position that members of this community were not granted before the revolution. Meanwhile, for their audience, their choice to speak Kutchi invokes associations and thus memories of a "past" characterized by a social system of racial injustice that had been overturned by the revolution. Thus social memories of the revolution are diverse and interlinked with how identity, social relationships, and society were experienced before and after the event. While for some their fiction of the "past" represents a society that provided them with privileges, for others the "before" evokes a vision of a society that dispossessed them of the very same. Still, both positions concern socioeconomic distinctions, forms of belonging, and a particular political fiction based on "them" and "us." As Sinfree Makoni (1989) reminds us, many things of the past can be "un-remembered," that is, actively forgotten—erasing, for instance, the reality that before the revolution there were many Zanzibaris of South Asian descent who were not urban, wealthy, or educated.

Let me give another example confirming how memory processes may equally distort and reinforce imaginings of the past. Nilofa, a woman in her 40s, was born in Zanzibar city. However, her parents grew up in a rural area. Her maternal grandparents, Nilofa told me, fostered an *Mswahili* boy the same age as her mother. The term *Mswahili* when used in this context refers to someone of "African" origin. Nilofa narrated as follows: "The foster brother became like a real brother for my mother and my uncle although he was *Mswahili* and they were *Wahindi*. Until this day they have a close relationship. My uncle has married a *Mswahili* woman from the same village where they grew up. After they divorced, my parents each remarried a *Mswahili*. Among us [*kwetu*] we have always been close to people of different *makabila*. Others hold this against my family. They even claim that we are of mixed origin and thus we are gossiped about [*semwa*]. They say that we are not 'pure Indians' [*Wahindi safi*]."

Regarding the question of memory, this brief recollection reflected both an image of the past as well as a present discourse on the significance of creating a social boundary or distance in order to maintain a certain cultural identity—in this setting, to reassert a form of "Indian-ness" (see also Keshodkar 2010). According to Michael Lambek and Paul Antze, "[A]ny invocation of memory is part of an identity discourse" (1996: xxi). Seen from such a perspective, a reminiscence of a particular way of being "Indian" may have inspired a form of "inclusive process" in order to reestablish an identity within a political environment that since the 1964 revolution, had insisted on one common identity. With reference to a recollected past, memories of the revolution or, rather, of what the revolution distorted, in unexpected ways, seem to have curtailed its very political ideals. Still, while difference was insisted upon in certain contexts, sameness seemed to be emphasized in others, in particular with regard to matters of religion.

Although the majority of the population is Muslim, distinctions regarding cultural and social identity have, over time, affected social relationships in different ways. More recently, shared religious identity seems to be expressed, if not by way of language, at least through dress. This has meant that clothing as a marker of cultural distinction with reference to *kabila*, which became dominant during the 1990s and which certainly was inspired by the Indian films, has currently become less apparent. The previous dress code, emphasizing designs commonly associated with Indian, Arabian, or mainland East African fashion, seems to have been replaced by more universal preference for the *buibui* (a loose black garment worn by women in public, covering them from head to foot) and the *hijab* (a veil worn by women, covering the head and chest, usually worn on top of a full-length robe). This shift may indicate that although difference may still be marked through an idiom such as language use, the significance of inclusion and common belonging are, simultaneously, made apparent through clothing (Larsen 1990, 2008). Such an emphasis on shared identity should not be understood in terms of particularistic cultural distinctions but rather as an acknowledgment of a common religious and moral conviction underpinning what would otherwise be perceived as Zanzibari identity. Obviously, regarding the wearing of *buibui* and *hijab*, fashion trends more generally have played a role. Moreover, in terms of morality, it seemed imperative for those associated with *Wahindi* identity to aesthetically mark a distance from contemporary Hindu modernity as it has more recently been expressed through the very same film industry that previously produced the dramas that were appreciated for reviving "Indian-ness."

Identity, Distinction, and Incorporation

In the shade of the political ideology framing the "Africanization process" during the revolution, it became a disadvantage to be perceived as Arab, South Asian, or Comorian. As I have discussed this issue with a number of women and men, it has become clear that the 1964 revolution created sensitivity about politics, identity, and belonging—as has been amply apparent during multiparty elections as well as in debates about the union. During recent elections (1995, 2000, 2005, and 2010), some families hid together in houses perceived as safe in case of a violent outcome, while others—especially women, children, and elderly—were sent to stay with relatives on the mainland. Businesses were shuttered, and many households hoarded food, gas, and water in their homes. Although no one would explicitly say that they took precautions because of their memories of the 1964 revolution, their anxiety and strategies can only be understood in the context of previous experiences and "inherited" recollections. Already in the early 1990s, when the introduction of the multiparty political system was being debated, many Zanzibaris, including *Wahindi*, expressed their opposition to the reform. In such situations, they would evoke "a historical past" to illuminate contemporary circumstances (Jackson, 2005: 356). "Remember the revolution," they would say, claiming that a "multiparty system would again make us fight each other on the background of *makabila*. Such politics are not appropriate for our society." Moreover, many within this milieu of *Wahindi* were of the opinion that others would easily claim that Zanzibar was not a place where they belonged. During one such discussion, an elderly woman who had experienced the revolution expressed her frustration: "It is true, our place of origin is India [*kwetu India*], but we have never lived there, we have only lived here on Unguja. We have nowhere else and this is where we are born and have lived." Saying this, she voiced precisely the political ambiguities attached to notions of "Asian" origin and *Wahindi* identity. Citizenship and its endurance over time appeared for them to be a question of politics rather than a right.[23]

In general, people still seem to experience and consider the present political situation in Zanzibar as unsettled. Many women and men of different ages in the milieu I have discussed observed, "Being *Wahindi* means that we can never trust that we will be politically and economically protected by our government." Saying this, they were implicitly referring to what they, their parents, or their grandparents experienced during and after the 1964 revolution, including political regulations introduced in 1967, 1970, and 1971, which I have referred to above. Currently, there are, as I have suggested above,

---

23 Historically, the dominant guideline for the colonial administration in Zanzibar was to distribute civic, political, and economic rights according to an identity politics based on the categories "African," "Asian," and "Arab." Today, the same categories are applied politically as means of exclusion and inclusion and are linked to an idea of belongingness where "African" is represented as autochthonous and "Indian" (or "Asian") and "Arab" are depicted as foreign (see Fouéré 2010: 371).

also intensified nativist challenges to their identity, questioning both their belonging and their allegiance as citizens. Whenever potential difficulties appear, the immediate framework for interpretation relates to individual and social memories mediated from older to younger generations (Larsen 2004).

Let me illustrate how a historical past may be brought in to explain contemporary circumstances in such a way that the phenomenon effectively takes on a renewed reality (Jackson 2005: 356). Abdul, a man in his mid-30s, expressed frustration regarding the current political climate, particularly the political relations between Zanzibar and mainland Tanzania:

> Racism has once again entered the political arena. Today these can even be openly uttered by politicians in the parliament. It could become very dangerous even here in Zanzibar. On the mainland it is already dangerous. Terms such as *Wahindi, Waarabu, Wangazija* [Indians, Arabs, Comorians] are applied to describe people who exploit resources and who do not belong. Rumors are saying that many of the new churches that are built are not meant to be houses of worship but to provide housing for young men sent to Zanzibar from the mainland and to shelter guns and machetes, just like they did before the revolution. Remember, most of those who took part in the revolution were mainlanders.[24]

Such immediate or mediated memories have certainly produced a form of insecurity and uncertainty regarding notions of belonging as well as citizenship for many Zanzibaris and Tanzanians of South Asian descent.

A renewed political rhetoric of indigenization, of exclusion and inclusion, has created forms of anxiety that could easily be intensified by implicit or explicit reference to both individual and social memories of the 1964 revolution. As already discussed, the post-revolutionary government imposed the label *Afro-Shirazi*—an identity label created in the 1950s to indicate that all Zanzibaris were to be considered of one common origin, although coastal society has historically recognized a

---

24 Interesting to note is Marie-Aude Fouéré's analysis of "the politics of belonging" and economic indigenization measures appearing in Tanzanian national politics as part of the neoliberal wave. Concerning the relative success of many Tanzanians of Indian origin targeted as "foreigners" according to the above-mentioned ideology, she writes: "*Les hommes d'affaires indiens, certes fragilisés par les mesures économiques de la période socialiste mais qui ont néanmoins conservé les ressources financières et les réseaux familiaux nécessaires à l'entrepreneuriat, ont été la cible privilégiée du mécontentement de ces nouveaux entrepreneurs africains*" (These new African entrepreneurs specifically expressed discontent against Indian businessmen who had maintained the financial resources and family networks required for entrepreneurship in spite of the fact that they had been weakened by the economic policies of socialist times) (2009: 141).

variety of cultural identities. Unlike politics, society is "multicultural" in the sense that it has, over time, succeeded in producing a shared form of social organization, value system, and ideals that seem to accommodate an interpretation of difference from within (Larsen 2009). Increasingly "loud" political debates focus on social boundaries of inclusion and exclusion. Simultaneously, "silent" memories of the execution of such an ideology seem to have ensured a continuous negotiation and incorporation of historically recognized differences through everyday recollections and practices, although not within political arenas.

Conclusion

In addressing the theme of social memories of the revolution, I have chosen to focus on identity discourses and practices and on the way these are affected by both explicit and implicit recollections of the past. Whether personal or collective, such recollections, I have argued, are intertwined with a "social inarticulate" imaginary where lies the capacity to transform embodied imprints into memories through which the past can be recaptured and anticipations for the future voiced. In this attempt, I have in particular explored how Indian-ness has been revitalized in recent years by reference to memories of life before the revolution and to recollections of what the revolution distorted. My attention has concentrated on processes of inclusion and exclusion, aesthetic preferences, and transformations of social relationships. In order to indicate what, at the local level, could be seen as sources of inspiration and motivation to engender such particular processes of remembering, I have emphasized the changing political and economic circumstances as well as the role of the media, such as Indian movies. The latter is due to women and men's apparent appreciation of these films, but also because the films became accessible during a particularly crucial historical period characterized by social and economic change together with limited possibilities for communication with the outside world. The films provided contexts where aspects of a "social inarticulate" (i.e., awareness, not immediately reflexive) could be expressed and enacted in such a manner that it became again part of a social memory, materialized through changing practices and social relationships. To a certain extent, the films provided scripts from which fictions about past identities and practices could be constructed and, in turn, induced processes in which vernacular perceptions of cultural diversity could be simultaneously both "remembered" but also "un-remembered" according to the dominant notions of current identity politics. By focusing on a certain milieu of *Wahindi*, I tried to show, on the one hand, the manner in which broader sociopolitical and economic changes facilitated certain new forms of identity discourses. On the other hand, and simultaneously, I have suggested how the same processes actually facilitated certain reformulations of historically constituted notions associating identity differences with questions of belonging. Within this framework, the revived endeavor to foster "Indian-ness" could, precisely, be seen as a way to insist on ways of belonging in a society historically constituted through cultural diversity. With such an understanding of cultural diversity, an emphasis on, for instance, "Indian-ness" would not in itself negate the fact of being Zanzibari. Still, in the process, those involved may be perceived by others as being less ingrained in society than those associated with different kinds of identity configurations. In this sense, every human society is a system that remains imaginarily constituted; within its own realm each society manufactures and mediates "memories," through material and ideal idioms, ordering practices and relationships grounded in an enduring social inarticulate.

References

Abu-Lughod, Lila

2005 *Dramas of Nationhood: The Politics of Television in Egypt*. Chicago: University of Chicago Press.

Adam, Michel

2010a "Des Indiens des comptoirs aux Indo-Africains." In *L'Afrique indienne. Les minorités d'origine indo-pakistanaise en Afrique orientale*, ed. Michel Adam, 15–78. Paris: Karthala.

2010b "Les Indiens et les autres: des mondes qui s'ignorent. Extraits de dossiers de la presse kenyane." In *L'Afrique indienne. Les minorités d'origine indo-pakistanaise en Afrique orientale*, ed. Michel Adam, 409–22. Paris: Karthala.

2010c "Panorama des communautés socio-religieuses." In *L'Afrique indienne. Les minorités d'origine indo-pakistanaise en Afrique orientale*, ed. Michel Adam, 79–107. Paris: Karthala.

Babu, Abdulrahman Muhammed

1991 "The 1964 Revolution: Lumpen or Vanguard?" In *Zanzibar under Colonial Rule*, ed. Abdul Sheriff and Ed Ferguson, 220–249. London: James Currey.

Bennett, Norman R. A.

1978 *A History of the Arab State of Zanzibar*. London: Methuen & Co.

Bissell, William Cunningham

2011 *Urban Design, Chaos, and Colonial Power in Zanzibar*. Bloomington, Ind.: Indiana University Press.

1999 "City of Stone, Space of Contestation: Urban Conservation and the Colonial Past in Zanzibar." Ph.D. diss., University of Chicago.

Blanchy, Sophie

2008 "The Impact of Political, Economic and Juridical Context: On Identification in Indian Gujarati 'Diaspora': Examples from Western Indian Ocean Islands and France." Presented at the International Conference on Global Gujarat and Its Diaspora, 17–19 January, Hemchandracharya North Gujarat University, Patan, India.

1995 *Karana et Banians. Les communautés commerçantes d'origine indienne à Madagascar.* Paris: L'Harmattan.

Bloch, Maurice

1996 "Internal and External Memory: Different Ways of Being in History." In *Tense Past: Cultural Essays in Trauma and Memory*, ed. Paul Antze and Michael Lambek, 215–34. New York: Routledge.

Bourdieu, Pierre

1977 *Outline of a Theory of Practice*. Cambridge, U.K.: Cambridge University Press.

Burgess, G. Thomas

2002 "Cinema, Bell Bottoms and Miniskirts: Struggles over Youth and Citizenship in Revolutionary Zanzibar." *International Journal of African Historical Studies* 35(2/3): 287–313.

Cameron, Greg

2009 "Narratives of Democracy and Dominance in Zanzibar." In *Knowledge, Renewal and Religion: Repositioning and Changing Ideological and Material Circumstances among the Swahili on the East African Coast*, ed. Kjersti Larsen, 151–76. Uppsala: Nordic Africa Institute.

Caplan, Pat

2009 "Understanding Modernity/ies: The Idea of a Moral Community on Mafia Island, Tanzania." In *Knowledge, Renewal and Religion: Repositioning and Changing Ideological and Material Circumstances among the Swahili on the East African Coast*, ed. Kjersti Larsen, 213–36. Uppsala: Nordic Africa Institute.

Castoriadis, Cornelius

1975 *L'institution imaginaire de la société*. Paris: Éditions du Seuil.

Cattell, Maria G., and Jacob J. Climo

2002 "Introduction. Meaning in Social Memory and History: Anthropological Perspectives." In *Social Memory and History*, ed. Jacob J. Climo and Maria G. Cattell, 1–39. Walnut Creek, Cal.: Altamira Press.

Cooper, Frederick

1980 *From Slaves to Squatters: Plantation Labor and Agriculture in Zanzibar and Coastal Kenya, 1890–1925*. New Haven, Conn.: Yale University Press.

Fair, Laura

2001 *Pastimes and Politics: Culture, Community and Identity in Post-abolition Urban Zanzibar, 1980–1945.* Athens: Ohio University Press.

Fouéré, Marie-Aude

2010 "Les Indiens sont des exploiteurs et les Africaines des paresseux! Production des catégories "raciales" et enjeux socioéconomiques en Tanzanie." In *L'Afrique indienne: Les minorités d'origine indo-pakistanaise en Afrique orientale*, ed. Michel Adam, 371–407. Paris: Karthala.

2009 "La préférence nationale en Tanzanie postsocialiste: Entre citoyenneté, autochtonie et race." *Politique africaine* 115: 137–54.

Fuglesang, Minou

1994 *Veils and Video: Female Youth Culture on the Kenyan Coast.* Stockholm: Stockholm Studies in Social Anthropology.

Glassman, Jonathon

2011 *War of Words, War of Stones: Racial Thought and Violence in Colonial Zanzibar.* Bloomington, Ind.: Indiana University Press.

Halbwachs, Maurice

1992 *On Collective Memory*, ed. and trans. Lewis A. Coser. Chicago: University of Chicago Press.

Jackson, Michael

2005 "Storytelling Events, Violence, and the Appearance of the Past." *Anthropological Quarterly* 78(2): 355–75.

Keshodkar, Akbar

2010 "Marriage as the Means to Preserve 'Asian-ness': The Post-Revolutionary Experience of the Asians of Zanzibar." *Journal of Asian and African Studies* 45: 226–40.

Lambek, Michael

1996 "The Past Imperfect: Remembering as Moral Practice." In *Tense Past: Cultural Essays in Trauma and Memory*, ed. Paul Antze and Michael Lambek, 235–54. New York: Routledge.

Lambek, Michael, and Paul Antze

1996 "Introduction: Forecasting Memory." In *Tense Past: Cultural Essays in Trauma and Memory*, ed. Paul Antze and Michael Lambek, xi–xxxviii. New York: Routledge.

Larkin, Brian

1997 "Indian Films and Nigerian Lovers: Media and the Creation of Parallel Modernities." *Africa* 67(3): 406–40.

Larsen, Kjersti

2009 "Introduction." In *Knowledge, Renewal and Religion: Repositioning and Changing Ideological and Material Circumstances among the Swahili on the East African Coast*, ed. Kjersti Larsen, 11–37. Uppsala: Nordic Africa Institute.

2008 *Where Humans and Spirits Meet. The Politics of Ritual and Identified Spirits in Zanzibar*. Oxford: Berghahn Books.

2004 "Change, Continuity and Contestation: The Politics of Modern Identities in Zanzibar." In *Swahili Modernities: Culture, Politics, and Identity on the East Coast of Africa*, ed. Pat Caplan and Farouk Topan, 121–43. Trenton, N.J.: Africa World Press.

1998 "Spirit Possession as Historical Narrative." In *Locality and Belonging*, ed. Nadia Lovell, 125–46. London: Routledge.

1990 "*Unyago*—Fra jente til kvinne. Utformingen av kvinnelig kjønnsidentitet i lys av initiasjonsritualer religiøsitet og moderniseringsprosesser" [*Unyago*—From Girl to Woman: The Formation of Female Gender Identity in the Light of Initiation Rituals, Religiosity and Processes of Modernization]. *Occasional Papers in Social Anthropology* 22, University of Oslo.

Lofchie, Michael F.

1970 "African Protest in a Racially Plural Society." In *Protest and Power in Black Africa*, ed. Robert Rothberg and Ali Mazrui, 924–27. New York: Oxford University Press.

Loimeier, Roman

2009 *Between Social Skills and Marketable Skills: The Politics of Islamic Education in 20th Century Zanzibar*. Leiden: Brill.

Makoni, Sinfree

1989 "African Languages as European Scripts: The Shaping of Communal Memory." In *Negotiating the Past: The Making of Memory in South Africa*, ed. Sarah Nutall and Carli Coetzee, 242–48. Cape Town, South Africa: Oxford University Press.

McGruder, Julie

1999 "Madness in Zanzibar: 'Schizophrenia' in Three Families in the 'Developing" World." Ph.D. diss., University of Washington.

Moran, Joe

2010 "History, Memory and the Everyday." *Rethinking History: The Journal of Theory and Practice* 8(1): 51–68.

Myers, Garth A.

2003 *Verandahs of Power: Colonialism and Space in Urban Africa.* Syracuse, N.Y.: Syracuse University Press.

Nora, Pierre

1989. "Between Memory and History: Les lieux de mémoire." *Representations* 26: 7–25.

Novic, Peter

1999 *The Holocaust in American Life.* Boston: Houghton Mifflin Company.

Ottenberg, Simon

1990 "Thirty Years of Fieldnotes: Changing Relationships to the Text." In *Fieldnotes: The Making of Anthropology,* ed. Roger Sanjek, 139–60. Ithaca, N.Y.: Cornell University Press.

Petterson, Don

2002 *Revolution in Zanzibar: An American's Cold War Tale.* Boulder, Colo.: Westview Press.

Rao, Leela

1989 "Media and Culture in Indian Society—Conflict or Cooperation?" *Media, Culture and Society* 11(4): 395–413.

Sheriff, Abdul

1987 *Slaves, Spices and Ivory in Zanzibar: Integration of an East African Commercial Empire into the World Economy, 1770–1873.* London: James Currey.

Shivji, Issa

2008 *Pan-Africanism or Pragmatism? Lessons of Tanganyika-Zanzibar Union.* Dar es Salaam: Mkuki na Nyota.

Valicha, Kishore

1988 *The Moving Image—A Study of Indian Cinema.* Bombay: Orient Longmans.

Chapter Nine

Memory, History, and the Nation among the Grieving Cosmopolitans: Omani-Zanzibaris Remember the Zanzibar Revolution, 1964–Present

Nathaniel Mathews

O my brothers, your nobility should not look backward but ahead! Exiles shall you be from all father- and forefather-lands! Your children's land shall you love: this love shall be your new nobility—the undiscovered land in the most distant sea. For that I bid your sails search and search. In your children you shall make up for being the children of your fathers: thus shall you redeem all that is past. This new tablet I place over you.

— FRIEDRICH NIETZSCHE, *Thus Spoke Zarathustra*

This is what I would like to have told my children if I had spoken about that little place. That we all lived together in peace, in a forbearing society built as only Muslims know how, even though among us were people of many religions and races. I would have known no other way of talking about it. I would not have told them about our hatreds.

— ABDULRAZAK GURNAH, *The Last Gift*

Young and old, regardless of age, are encompassed within the same perspective ... so long as certain national, political, or religious situations have not yet realized their full implications. As soon as this task is finished and a new one proposed or imposed, ensuing generations start down a new slope, so to speak.

— MAURICE HALBWACHS, *The Collective Memory*

"We are not Jews, Zanzibar is not Zion."

— OMANI-ZANZIBARI returnee in Muscat

This article is an examination of how the collective memory of violence and the trauma of displacement and exile are remembered, transmitted, and transformed across generations of a diaspora from Zanzibar, as members of the diaspora become citizens of a new nation-state. Taking up Maurice Halbwach's concern with how people articulate the shame, humiliation, and rage of a traumatic event, I explore how these feelings are transmitted to children, friends, and neighbors, are made into narrative history, and are read by those who did not directly experience the events. I argue that this traumatic memory of the old homeland (Zanzibar) takes on new meaning and importance in the new space of the new homeland (Oman) and its constraints. When a former homeland cannot be called to mind, a diaspora by definition ceases to exist. But even when a new homeland replaces the old, which is shrouded in traumatic memory, members of the diaspora may still value their double consciousness (Malkki 1995). The idea of diaspora, as Brent Edwards has argued, allows for bridging gaps in memory and historical experience, and the Zanzibari exiles use a diaspora consciousness of Zanzibar to bridge the gap between the two locales (Edwards 2003). But the Omani context also shapes their consciousness in important ways. Zanzibar is not the homeland it once was; the exiles have transformed themselves into an Omani diaspora who migrated to Zanzibar and "returned" to Oman, a place most had never seen before arriving (Markowitz and Steffanson 2004). They turn the space of Zanzibar into a site of Omani national glory rather than a horizon of political struggle. This process is encouraged by the state, which in the words of Mandana Limbert is "trying to coopt Zanzibar's history without reifying Zanzibaris as a separate entity" (2010). The Omani state is an active, powerful, and recognizable historical center that authorizes new discourses about the past.

But if memory is elicited in the name of a national discourse, it also "reconfigures the nation that wants it" (Creet and Kitzmann 2011). The Omani-Zanzibaris do not fit the mold of de-diasporization that commonly accompanies becoming citizens in a new nation-state (Van Hear 1998). They have not abandoned co-responsibility to Zanzibar; rather, they have transformed their memory of it in a way that echoes the way their grandparents and great-grandparents generations related to it. This transformation has entailed a productive forgetting (Ankersmit 2001) and a shift in the diaspora's horizon, "the spatial edge of longing and the temporal edge of nostalgia and futurity" (Johnson 2007). But the transformation has also entailed an active narrative reshaping of the past by what Derek Peterson and Giacomo Macola (2007) call "homespun historians." Thus, even if a diaspora remains "permanently aware of the social idyllic of the lost worlds it was forced to surrender, and to which it will never be returned" (Ankersmit 2001: 302), it can, through the assumption of a new nation and a new citizenship, transcend the "victimhood nationalism" that is usually nourished by diaspora-nationalism and accompanies victims of political violence and ethnic conflict into exile (Lim 2010). Victimhood is transformed into what Will Hanley calls "grieving cosmopolitanism," a nostalgia for a lost society of civility, order, and refinement (Hanley 2008). Following William Bissell's work conceiving colonial nostalgia as a kind of social imaginary or cultural project, I want to argue that the nostalgia of grieving cosmopolitans (the Omani-Zanzibaris) can work to bridge gaps in memory and historical experience, even in the context of a completely different national project (Bissell 2005).

This essay will focus primarily on the major impact of the revolution on the consciousness of the Omani-Zanzibari community.[1] This community, also referred to in the literature as "Swahili-speaking Omanis," is actually made up of Omanis with roots all over East Africa and diverse routes of return to Oman (al-Rasheed 2005; Hirji 2007; Valeri 2007; Kharusi 2012, 2013; Verne and Müller-Mahn 2006). For reasons I discuss below, the historical experience of those from Zanzibar has taken on a metonymic character for many returnees. It would be presumptuous to assume that all returning Omanis from East Africa share the same historical experience, class, education, and worldview. But I would argue that the Zanzibar revolution and the imagining of an imperial heritage of Oman in Zanzibar are the two major ideas connecting and weaving together the various translocal networks of Arab migrants from East Africa into a coherent community in Oman.

Memory and the Zanzibar Revolution

The momentous events of the revolution in Zanzibar in 1964 led to the overthrow of an independent state and to targeted killings of political opponents and often the forced migration of Zanzibaris of Arab and Indian descent. Those who stayed were subject to harassment and discrimination. The revolution remains controversial and important to this day: controversial for the horrific episodes of violence that followed in its wake, important as the founding event of a new regime in Zanzibar and as the main catalyst of its union with mainland Tanganyika. For many years, communities of Zanzibari exiles in the United Kingdom, the United Arab Emirates, and Oman advocated for the overthrow of

---

1 Another impact was to impress on some exiles the inadequacy and dangers of any kind of nationalist discourse and recourse to easy patriotism. An outstanding example of this viewpoint is captured through fictional characters in the novels of Abdulrazak Gurnah, who move through exile wrestling with identity, history, and belonging—and resisting facile answers to these problems.

the revolutionary regime, which they saw as an illegitimate invasion of a sovereign state (Kharusi 1967; Fairooz 1995; Barwani 1997).

For the generational offspring of these exiles in Oman, especially those born in Zanzibar but who emigrated with their parents at an early age, the revolution of 1964 is being transformed from a collective memory experienced by actual people into a metonym for national belonging and national identity in Oman. In this way, the process of victimhood nationalism, which becomes hereditary by being stabilized in the national historical imagination, is mitigated or cut short. Generational forgetting, prosperity in the new homeland, and the cultural work of homespun historians can mitigate and transform victimhood into a very special kind of history and heritage, infused with nostalgic grieving for a lost past. Zanzibar turns into, in the words of Karen Armstrong, "a mythical place that lacks temporal progression, that remains alive only through memory" (Armstrong 2004). There are two processes at work here. One is the self-idealization of memory experienced by elderly citizens of Oman who experienced decolonization and the events of the Zanzibar revolution. The second is the reshaping of this memory into discursive representations, narratives that make claims of historical authority. As we shall see, discursive historical representations of Zanzibar by the Omani-Zanzibaris portray a highly idealized place, and even Omani-Zanzibaris who return to Zanzibar for visits feel themselves belonging to a "landscape of the past" (Bissell 2005).

Significantly, this transformation of memory into history is also a transformation of Zanzibari history into Omani heritage, with the Zanzibar revolution portrayed as the "overthrow of Omani Arab rule." The Zanzibar revolution is the key fulcrum for the impetus to become Omani citizens, and it also serves as a metonym for the collective Omani Arab experience in East Africa. Depending upon the context in which it is invoked, it can serve to highlight the futile conflict of democratic politics, show the dangers of political militancy, underline the risk of being an ethnic minority, and highlight the progress of contemporary Oman vis-à-vis the backward or underdeveloped condition of Zanzibar.

The Zanzibar revolution was essentially the final blow in a bitter conflict between two political parties, the Afro-Shirazi Party (ASP) and the Zanzibar Nationalist Party (ZNP), but the political dimensions of this conflict were deeply entangled with race and class (Lofchie 1965; Clayton 1981; Bakari 2001; Sheriff 2001; Glassman 2011). The ZNP was composed of a wide swath of Zanzibar's ethnic communities (though its leadership was largely Arab), while the ASP's membership was mostly drawn from the poorer African population. The two parties were drawn into a "war of words" that became increasingly bitter and eventually culminated into violent pogroms (Glassman 2011). These processes of racialization led Zanzibaris to think in terms of exclusionary racial categories of "Arab" and "African," with a substantial population of Zanzibaris who identified as "Shirazi" caught in the middle of a war between two nationalisms. These categories were not innate but imagined, variable, and context specific. They nevertheless took on an urgent valence in the logic of political competition leading up to independence and culminating in the revolution.

The Revolutionary Council and representatives of the ruling ASP—which later combined with the Tanganyika African National Union (TANU) to form the Chama cha Mapinduzi (CCM, the "Party of the Revolution")—view the revolution as an African liberationist triumph over Arab feudalism (Mapuri 1996). Even where they acknowledge the complexity of the events of 1964, they have tended to downplay or whitewash the violence as either incidental or insignificant. One official party history claimed that Arabs simply ran away from the island because they disliked socialism (Afro-Shirazi Party 1973). Since 1995 and the introduction of a multiparty elections, this discourse has become a cynical attempt to hold onto power in Zanzibar against the opposition Civic United Front (CUF), which takes a much more complex stance toward the revolution (Fouéré 2012; Cameron 2010; Burgess 2009).

The first generation of Zanzibari exiles view the revolution as the greatest moral and social catastrophe in their history. As a community, they are primarily constituted as an Arab diaspora from Zanzibar, including forced exiles, escapees, and political refugees. The anti-Arab polemics and pogroms of the early 1960s, culminating in the massacres of 1964, deeply shape their memories and historical consciousness.

In 1964, the Arab exiles from Zanzibar were stateless people and thus uniquely vulnerable to the appeal of ethnic patriotism. Having been singled out for violence and discrimination as Arabs, many were also stamped with a renewed conviction of the importance of "Arabness" to their identity (Kharusi 2013: 433). Such conviction had a long history in Zanzibar and along the east coast of Africa, most strongly symbolized by the idea of *ustaarabu*, a word that equated being refined and civilized with Arab identity (Glassman 2011; Pouwels 2002). But in the period of political competition leading up to independence, many Arab political activists from the ZNP took pains to distance themselves from their Arabness, especially their legacy as a ruling Arab elite.

This distancing, which accompanied political decolonization, contrasts sharply with the urgency many of them now feel about reattaching themselves and their offspring—culturally, ethnically, and linguistically—to the Omani nation. This urgency of associating with Arabism is a new lens through which the Zanzibari exiles–cum–Omani returnees elaborate and refine their collective memory of the revolution. Their sons and daughters, meanwhile, are active in the transformation of their parents' memories into history; the Zanzibar revolution becomes a critical part of Omani national history, and Zanzibar takes its place in a transnational seascape of Omani heritage across the Indian Ocean. Out of this vision, the Omani-Zanzibari returnees and their descendants construct their vision of belonging to the Omani nation.

In the half-century since 1964, discourse on the revolution has been transformed on two levels—the level of collective memory and the level of discursive historical representation. The age of the first generation of returnees, the national context in Oman where they are relatively prosperous and well cared-for, and the lack of a way to publicly memorialize the violence they experienced have encouraged them to frame their memory of the revolution along the lines of an inevitable catastrophe that was God's will. In contrast, the early exiles of the ZNP maintained a horizon of politics that was activist anticolonial, anticommunist, and pro-democracy (Kharusi 1967, 1969, 1971, 1974). Many of these exiles were imprisoned by Tanzanian president Julius K. Nyerere and maintained a deep antipathy toward the Tanzanian government and Nyerere personally (Fouéré 2014). They lived with a conviction that Zanzibar was their nation—the horizon of their political and cultural belonging. This influenced their advocacy for international sanctions, counterrevolution, and political reform in Zanzibar.[2]

Nasser al-Riyami's *Zinjibār: Shaksiyāt wa Ahdāth*

The sons and daughters of these exiled Zanzibaris were mostly educated abroad, in the United Kingdom, Cairo, Baghdad, and the Gulf states. Some were already abroad when the revolution occurred, while others were still children who left Zanzibar with their parents in the late 1960s or 1970s. Their worldview was less concerned with political agitation around Zanzibar and more about acquiring pragmatic and technocratic skills in law, engineering, business, and finance. The most

---

2 See, for instance, old issues of the *Free Zanzibar Voice*, the international newsletter of the Zanzibar Organization, a network of Zanzibari exiles in opposition to the revolution.

popular distillation of this group's moral and historical vision is Nasser al-Riyami's *Zinjibār: Shaksiyāt wa Ahdāth*. First published by Beirut Bookshop in 2009, it sold 5,000 copies in its first week and sold out shortly after publication (Verne and Müller-Mahn 2014). It is now in its third edition, and an English translation, *Zanzibar: Personalities & Events (1828–1972)*, was published in 2012. It can be found in both the original Arabic and in English translation at most supermarkets and bookstores in Muscat. It is a handsome hardback with color photographs and reproductions of important historical documents relating to Zanzibar. Its bibliography alone is an impressive achievement, representing the most comprehensive listing of Arabic language scholarship on the history of Zanzibar and East Africa to date.[3] Al-Riyami was also able to interview a number of notable Zanzibari exiles, including Ali Muhsin al-Barwani, Aman Thani Fairooz, Issa bin Nasser al-Ismaily, and the exiled sultan of Zanzibar, Seyyid Jamshid bin Abdullah. The book is endorsed and has an introduction by fellow Omani returnee (and current mufti of Oman) Sheikh Ahmed al-Khalili, who came to Oman from Zanzibar on a Red Cross ship a few months after the revolution.

In the English version of al-Riyami's book, the first four chapters concern the "time of politics," decolonization, and the Zanzibar revolution (in the Arabic version these are chapters 3 through 6.) These sections of the book are closer in style to a formal work of history (in the sense that al-Riyami advances an interpretation of the past), while the remaining chapters are a composed of biographies of great Arab Zanzibaris. The book is emphatically related to a politics of commemoration and mourning in a context where the Omani state has not formally recognized or memorialized the Zanzibar revolution (Connerton 2011). Al-Riyami's narrative draws deeply from a discursive well of Zanzibari Arab history, and his book can be thought of as an imagination of a possible future for Zanzibari Arabs, shaped by various kinds of mythical reconstructions of Zanzibar's past (Scott 2004).

Al-Riyami was born in Zanzibar ten months after the revolution. He left Zanzibar with his family at the age of five, was educated in Cairo, and grew up in Oman. He returned to Cairo for university and his legal training. The book arose out of conversations with his children, who asked him about the many family pictures he had hung up, including

---

3 For more on the contents of the book, see the comprehensive review by Gerard C. van de Bruinhorst, "Acquisition Highlight: Zanzibar: Personalities & Events (1828–1972)," African Studies Centre Leiden, 10 January 2014, http://www.ascleiden.nl/news/acquisition-highlight-zanzibar-personalities-events-1828-1972.

several with the past sultans of Zanzibar. These conversations led al-Riyami back to Zanzibar, to search the archives and discover the truth about his family's past.

One moral lesson emphasized in al-Riyami's narrative is the need for national belonging, for a return and rediscovery of roots, an understanding of connection to an ancient and authentic genealogy. In this respect al-Riyami's work stands in a tradition of what Peterson and Macola call "homespun historians," who use history to constitute a moral community. As Peterson and Macola write, the texts produced by homespun historians "set an identifiable people on a path and invited them to travel together." History is "a way to hold people accountable, to guard moral community against the rootlessness of ignorance" (2009: 5–9). Al-Riyami lays vigorous claim to a collective identity associated with Islam and Arabism in Zanzibar, an identity of cosmopolitan refinement, Indian Ocean connections, and great civilizational achievements. Al-Riyami's work is thus located within a transnational community of homespun historians in Oman and Zanzibar whose main commonality is emphasizing Zanzibar as an Indian Ocean seascape, as opposed to an African landscape. Al-Riyami, along with Ibrahim Noor al-Bakry, who introduces his volume, sees the Indian Ocean as "a continent in its own right," crisscrossed by merchants and traders and views the movement between Oman and Zanzibar as an "internal migration movement." In one sense, al-Riyami's historical sense is parallel with a growing historical literature on Indian Ocean studies (Pearson 2003; Alpers 2007; Pearson, Hofmeyer, and Gupta 2010; Kresse and Simpson 2011; Sheriff 2011). The Indian Ocean connections and the cosmopolitan ethos they allegedly promote are the root metaphor of the narrative template around which many Zanzibari exiles build their engagements with history, and al-Riyami's work is no exception. His main contribution to broader scholarship is to give East African Arabs agency as an essential piece of East Africa's cosmopolitan history. But, as Jonathon Glassman has warned, this promotion of cosmopolitan oceanic connections can also work to reify a false binary between an Indian Ocean that is fluid, civilized, and open, and a mainland that is ethnic, tribal, and the passive recipient of the gifts of civilization (Glassman 2014).

Exile and the problem of roots and belonging posed the fundamental problem of al-Riyami's generation. As part of a group who articulate what sociologist Karl Mannheim calls a "generational memory," al-Riyami and his peers were disproportionately shaped in their early years by narratives and memories focused on their parents' exile and emigration from Zanzibar (Mannheim 1952: 182; Creet and Kitzmann 2011). They grew up hearing about the events of 1964 without having experienced them directly. According to Mannheim, generations are born from historical disruption. Whereas al-Riyami's parents' generation was shaped as such by being "sucked into the vortex of social change"— the intensely contested "time of politics" in Zanzibar, culminating in the revolution—al-Riyami's generation was molded through the experience of exile and then of becoming Omani national citizens, finding new lives in a new land.

Al-Riyami's book is thus an attempt by a member of this generation to understand the period from 1957 to 1964 in Zanzibar and its broader significance. As Ibrahim Noor al-Bakry writes in his introduction to the English edition, the Zanzibar revolution was "the main impetus that plunged the author into the research endeavor and the writing of the book" (p. 19).[4] Much as postwar German émigré historians were preoccupied by how fascism came to power in Germany, al-Riyami is concerned with how the violence and tragedy of the revolution could have occurred in an allegedly tolerant and cosmopolitan society (Lehmann and Sheehan 2002).[5]

Al-Riyami signals his own interpretation early on, with a dedication to the "countless souls of the martyrs who fell in black January" (p. 7).[6] Al-Riyami goes on to call the Zanzibar revolution an "invasion by foreign elements," a "genocide," and an "ethnic cleansing." (pp. 17–8). In the Arabic edition, the main terms used are *mahzarah* ("slaughter") and *inqilāb* ("coup"). Al-Riyami, like many of the other Omani-Zanzibaris I talked to, sees the events of 1964 as an invasion of Zanzibar by mainlanders directed by Tanganyikan president Nyerere.[7] It is important to note here that, if Harith Ghassany's collection of oral accounts is to be believed, there was a contingent of mainlanders who tried to help ASP party members to swing elections in Zanzibar. These mainland groups, along with islanders, were also participants in various kinds of anti-Arab violence in the Zanzibar countryside during the post-revolution period (Ghassany 2010). But it is also important to note that "invasion"

---

4   All citations are from the English translation of the book unless otherwise noted.

5   Such portrayals draw strongly on a nostalgic view of the alliance between the British and Zanzibar's Arab elite as co-creators of a great civilization, see Bissell 2005.

6   The phrase "black January" originally occurs in Ali Muhsin al-Barwani's memoirs *Conflict and Harmony in Zanzibar* (1997).

7   See Fairooz 1995 and Ghassany 2010. See also old issues of the *Free Zanzibar Voice*, edited by Ahmed Seif Kharusi.

is a discursive gloss on the significance of these events that is just as simplistic as the ASP depiction of the events of 1964 as a revolution against Arab feudalism. It also reproduces an anti-mainlander discourse that has a long political history in Zanzibar and that was used extensively in the pages of pro-ZNP newspapers such as *Mwongozi* (Glassman 2000). The diverse interests of the Umma Party, Abdulrahman Muhammed Babu, the ASP, and other players in the revolution are all collapsed into the fundamentally evil intentions of Nyerere and a cabal of "barbaric" mainlanders. In turn, Nyerere is represented as a tool of anti-Arab and anti-Muslim European imperialists. Educated in Anglican and Catholic schools, he is portrayed as having wholly absorbed the anti-Arab abolitionist discourse of European missionaries; this explains his alleged hatred of Zanzibar (p. 215).

According to al-Riyami, Zanzibar was a society united before the coming of the Europeans, and "even those few [Arabs] who used to perceive themselves as a separate entity from the Africans" only did so as a direct result of "colonial divide and rule policies" (pp. 36–47). Al-Riyami's narrative foregrounds a series of large and evil forces at work to conspire against a small and vulnerable country, as well as the tragedy of a nationalist party that the Zanzibari public was not ready for, due to its "high level of illiteracy" (p. 277). The revolution thus takes on an air of tragic inevitability, the irresistible outcome of evil machinations by outsiders (p. 218).

By labeling the events of 1964 as an invasion, al-Riyami can avoid having to directly address the sensitive question of the participation of islanders in the post-revolutionary violence. Such discursive moves also preclude an in-depth discussion of the various forms of hierarchy and exclusion that obtained under the rule of the sultans of Zanzibar. In Oman, these representations cement the revolution as a terrible tragedy for Arabs. In Zanzibar, this interpretation has the virtue of reinforcing Zanzibari exceptionalism vis-à-vis the mainland and of crystalizing existing grievances about the mainland's hegemony (Burgess 2010). These opposing interpretations also play into impassioned debates about Zanzibari identity, sovereignty, and the union.

One might usefully contrast the dramatic simplicity of al-Riyami's interpretation with that of a ZNP member and fellow Omani returnee, Maulid Mshangama Haj, who was imprisoned for many years after the revolution before settling in Oman. His fictionalized account of nationalist politics in Unguja and Pemba, *Sowing the Wind*, communicates some of the subtle feelings, gaps in miscommunication, and complicated factional splits that led to the revolution. One might also look to Abdulrazak Gurnah's account of the revolution in his classic novel of exile, *By the Sea*. Both these works strongly critique the violence and racism of the revolutionaries while also offering relatively subtle and complex interpretations of why the ZNP failed to win a substantial number of subaltern intellectuals to its side (Haj 2001; Gurnah 2002).

Some of the particularity of al-Riyami's interpretation can be traced to his transmission of the viewpoint of his set of informants, most of them participants in Zanzibar's turbulent decolonization process who were themselves personally victimized by the revolution. They look back on the events with a mixture of fury and resignation. This last sentiment is sometimes entangled with their own position as Omani citizens, no longer in search of a country. For example, the former Zanzibar deputy commissioner of police Sulaiman al-Kharusi, who is now an Omani citizen, tells al-Riyami, "It is Allah's will. Despite this calamity that was followed by division and diaspora, Allah has now bestowed upon us his blessings and bounties that we enjoy today in our ancestors' homeland Oman" (p. 148). In a published history of the Busaid sultans in Zanzibar, the Omani-Zanzibari returnee Ahmed Hamoud al-Maamiry writes, "A revolution had to come in Zanzibar as a matter of Divine Decree" (al-Maamiry 1988: 78). The relative poverty of Zanzibar as compared with Oman is seen as the ultimate judgment on the revolution's legacy. "Roya," one of the returnees from Zanzibar I interviewed, pointed to Abeid Amani Karume's efforts to prevent her family from leaving Zanzibar as one of the proofs of the futility of the revolution: "They needed us; we were the educated ones."[8]

Identity, Language, and Nationalism among the Zanzibaris

Because of its entanglement with Omani nationalism, al-Riyami's emphasis is also slightly different than the original thesis of "revolution as mainlander invasion" that had been floating around since the 1960s (Loimeier 2006; Glassman 2010). Al-Riyami, unlike many of his predecessors, no longer writes from a place of statelessness. While an earlier generation of activists, such as Ahmed Seif Kharusi and other members of the Zanzibar Organization, sought regime change in Zanzibar from exile in the Gulf or the United Kingdom, al-Riyami foregrounds a narrative of belonging to Oman, as a place where the

---

8   Interview with "Roya," Muscat, April 2013. Pseudonyms have been used to protect the identity of my research subjects.

stateless Omani-Zanzibaris became citizens. In spite of his fierce condemnation of the revolution, his book simultaneously strikes a conciliatory tone, going so far as to call the revolution a "cloud with a silver lining." That silver lining was the return of the exiles to their ancestral home of Oman, where, after 1970, they sparked a "renaissance" under Sultan Qaboos. Al-Riyami dedicates his book to "His Majesty Sultan Qaboos bin Said, whose name is synonymous with peace, justice and civilization. He kindly permitted Omanis to return to their ancestors' motherland" (p. 6). The representation of the revolution in al-Riyami's work is thus filtered through a lens of redemption through return to the homeland, and ultimately he does not call for regime change in Zanzibar but for "reconciliation and forgiveness" between Africans and Arabs. In al-Riyami's historical vision, exiled Zanzibari Arabs need to forget the bitter quarrels of anticolonial nationalism and remember their "ancestral root and identity, which had all but disappeared amid the darkness of politics and its games" (p. 220).[9] What are these games precisely? Al-Riyami is most likely implicitly referring to Arabs in Zanzibar who refused to embrace Arab identity as a dominant aspect of their being in the contested political environment of late colonial Zanzibar.[10] In the context of the revolution, the refusal of that identity looks to al-Riyami like a tragic political strategy, tainted by association with communism.[11]

Yet even as al-Riyami and others see themselves as "part of Zanzibar" (Verne and Müller-Mahn 2014), the former homeland is viewed with some ambivalence as a source of cultural degradation, of the forgetting of true identity and language. The marks of diaspora—exile, the hope of return to an ancestral homeland, and the eventual repatriation—also map a route to the purification of the self and its corporate identity (Malkki 1995). The way al-Riyami deals with the relationship between Arabic and Kiswahili can be understood as an expression of this ambivalence, which is also linked to the larger community's anxieties about not belonging properly to Oman (Kharusi 2013). Significantly, al-Riyami's explanation of why the Arabs in Zanzibar lost their Arabic language avoids any mention of intermarriage and local acculturation that made

---

9   In the Arabic version see page 502.

10   Arab identity became a liability for Zanzibari nationalists to the extent that both Ali Muhsin al-Barwani and Abdulrahman Muhammed Babu denied they were Arab before the Foster-Sutton Commission, called to investigate the post-election riots of 1961.

11   See, for instance, al-Riyami's comments on Babu and the Umma Party, 269–71.

Arab Zanzibaris culturally indistinguishable from other Zanzibaris. The ideal of intermarriage and acculturation was absolutely central to the self-conception of Zanzibari nationalists such as Ali Muhsin al-Barwani. Instead, al-Riyami paints a picture of loss of cultural identity through the loss of Arabs' original language, which was itself rooted in a "Bantu invasion."[12]

In al-Riyami's view, "Arabic was the dominant language of the coast until the arrival of the Bantu in the 16th century." Able to smelt iron to make weapons, the Bantus blazed a path of conquest across Central Africa before arriving on the coast. Their arrival in East Africa led to the decline of Arabic language on the coast and "the imposition of much of their language's grammatical structure." This theory, which is unsupported by serious historical and linguistic investigation (Nurse and Spear 1985), can be traced to al-Riyami's interviews with Ibrahim Noor al-Bakry, a notable scholar of Kiswahili literature who became an Omani citizen after teaching at Rutgers University in New Jersey for many years. Al-Bakry has also popularized the idea in Oman that the percentage of Kiswahili that is actually Arabic is as much as 80 or 90 percent. The import of these ideas may not be clear to outsiders, unless one takes into account the Omani context, where speaking Kiswahili has at times been viewed by other Omanis as evidence of insufficient patriotism and an impure identity (Kharusi 2012). If one follows al-Riyami and al-Bakry's logic, Arabs who lost their language in Zanzibar cannot be blamed, for it was but the first of many trespasses on Arab cultural sovereignty by Bantu invaders.[13] Furthermore, if Kiswahili is mostly just Arabic anyway, one can speak Kiswahili without shame in Oman, as an extension of the unquestionably more prestigious Arabic language.

Contrast this view with that of other Omani-Zanzibari scholars, for whom the loss of Arabic language by Arabs in Zanzibar is proof that Omani Arabs in Zanzibar were not imperialists. Ghassany cites the same process of Arabic language loss as evidence not of Bantu hostility but of Omani Arab receptiveness to cross-cultural interaction: "*Si ubeberu wa Kiarabu/Kiislamu, utumwa wa Waarabu, wala kunyanganywa ushindi*

---

12   "Bantu" hostilities also play into the idea of a mainland invasion of Zanzibar, for according to al-Riyami it was "Bantus" from the mainland who destroyed Zanzibari civilization in the violence of 1964.

13   One might also note the indebtedness of al-Riyami and al-Bakry's idea to colonial-era historiography on the Swahili coast, especially to Reginald Coupland's work *East Africa and Its Invaders from the Earliest Times to the Death of Seyyid Said in 1856* (1938).

kwenye chaguzi ndizo sababu kubwa ya Mapinduzi ya Zanzibar. Kama ni ubeberu ilikuwaje Waarabu waliokwenda Afrika Mashariki wakaisahau lugha yao ya Kiarabu na badala yake wakawa wanasema lugha ya Kiswahili?" ("It wasn't Arab or Islamic imperialism, Arab slavery, nor the illegitimate outcome of elections which was the major reason for the Zanzibar revolution. If it was [Arab] imperialism that was the cause of the revolution, how is that those Arabs who went to East Africa then forgot their Arabic language and instead were speaking Kiswahili?") (Ghassany 2010: 303). In Ghassany's vision, knowing Kiswahili makes possible a community of language between Arabs and Africans in Zanzibar. Al-Riyami's conception of a fluid and open Indian Ocean seascape is at uneasy odds with deeper ideas of Arab civilizational exceptionalism and linguistic purity, to which Omani nationalism gives a powerful fillip.

The Bantu invasion thesis also interestingly leads al-Riyami to be wary of calling Zanzibar "the Andalusia of Africa." He writes, "While the Arabs did conquer parts of Spain and subjugated its people, the situation was not the same in the East African coast. Arabs arrived and settled at the coast millenniums before the Bantu African and it was the Arabs' settlements that were invaded by the Bantu; hence the two cases are fundamentally different" (p. 31n4).

One can see echoes in these remarks of earlier debates over indigeneity between Africans and Arabs that characterized the political debates of the mid-20th century in Zanzibar and on the Swahili coast (Glassman 2010). Debates over indigeneity were a way for Zanzibar's Arabs to contest the interpretation of their ancestors' rule on the coast as a colonial venture that enslaved the indigenous inhabitants. If Arabs were indigenous as well, then the disagreement took on the air of a family quarrel, with Arabs as the paternal tutors of the later-arriving Bantus, in al-Riyami's view, rather than as imperialist conquerors. Historian Jonathon Glassman notes a profound shift in this negative emphasis that early Zanzibar nationalists placed on colonization and invasion (Glassman 2014). The horizon of anticolonialism led Zanzibar's early nationalists to craft strategies to show themselves as "sons of the soil" rather than "foreign civilizers." But al-Riyami's rootedness in Oman sits uneasily with the ideal of jus soli that anchored Zanzibari nationalism. We thus also find echoes of a much older discourse, one in which Arabs arrived to the East African coast to civilize the primitive Africans through infusions of language, culture, religion, and blood. Al-Riyami's work sticks closer to this earlier ideal of Arabs as Muslim civilizers of Africa.

Indeed, one can find in his work some of the most stark "civilizationist" rhetoric of any of the anticolonial nationalists of his father's generation, a rhetoric much more reminiscent of an earlier generation of Arab Zanzibaris described by historian Amal Ghazal (2010).

This idealizing vision also pervades al-Riyami's explanation of slavery and squatting in Zanzibar. To al-Riyami, squatting was a form of "Islamic socialism" that was allowed by Arab landowners in order to give Africans sustenance and share their wealth. Similarly, in his eyes slavery was mostly benevolent and even beneficial for the slave, largely because of the salutary role played by Islam in regulating the master-slave relationship (p. 242). Al-Riyami's idealization of Islamic slavery significantly elides the question of the economic importance of slavery to Zanzibar in the 19th century, especially to the prosperity of its elite plantation owners (Sheriff 2001). Ignoring the economic importance of slavery allows al-Riyami to paint Sultan Seyyid Said, the first sultan of Zanzibar and the person most responsible for Zanzibar's commercial expansion, as a progressive abolitionist, when it was clear Said only abolished the slave trade reluctantly under tremendous colonial pressure and to great public outcry from his elite Arab subjects (p. 243). What is particularly striking is the way al-Riyami concedes tremendous agency to Said while denying the same to later Zanzibari leaders, including Karume, Babu, the ASP, and the Umma Party. For if Babu, Karume, and others were mere tools of Nyerere and western powers, why does it not follow that Said was likewise a tool of western powers?

The granting of agency to certain heroic individuals, such as Said, and the presentation of Zanzibar's history in mythical terms serve two important purposes. One has to do with the unhealed wounds of violence in Zanzibar. Vituperative rhetoric by victims of violence is not uncommon as a way of making sense of trauma and displacement. A number of social scientists describe how memories of violence can easily become a part of the historical consciousness of subsequent generations who did not directly experience that violence (Malkki 1995; Das et al. 2000; Alexander et al. 2004). Traumatic events are usually commemorated when the generation that suffered them has the power and psychological distance to engage in commemoration, usually beginning in middle age (Pennebaker and Banasik 1997). The generation directly affected by the violence in Zanzibar, now mostly elderly Omani citizens, is now beginning to publicly pass on these memories through autobiographies (al-Busaidi 2012). But a younger, mostly middle-aged generation, born in Zanzibar but having left it as children, is also entering the field of discursive representation (al-Hinai 2013). In Oman, where most of this narration and discursive production occurs, blaming the violence on mainlanders confirms the nobility and the futility of the Arab project of anticolonial nationalism in Zanzibar while allowing for reflection on the blessings of belonging to a place where they are not an ethnic minority but an integral part of the nation.[14] Omani nationalism is the healing balm that allows these bitter memories to find safe expression.

Zanzibar's more ancient history also serves as a national myth for the returnees. Having been disillusioned by what they see as the distasteful and corrupt vagaries of anticolonial politics, and living in a monarchy still close to its own tribal and dynastic past, the Omani-Zanzibaris needed their own moral and historical genealogy to tie themselves to the nation (Rabi 2006; Valeri 2009: 138).[15] Tarred with various attributes such as not being "real" Omanis (and thus possibly of impure, slave descent), not speaking Arabic, lax piety, and a host of other stereotypes, the Omani-Zanzibaris have felt a strong need to authorize their attachment to the Omani nation in explicit discursive ways, by recasting their Zanzibari heritage, culture, and history in an Omani national mode.

By painting in broad brushstrokes, al-Riyami skillfully addresses this need. It is a view whose horizon is neither a diasporic longing for the tradition of anticolonial Zanzibari nationalism, nor a purely local idea of returning to Omani traditions. Rather it is an imperial idea, the idea that the Zanzibari exiles were subjects of a great Omani empire and civilization that is now lost to history. Their service on the front lines of this great work, as well as the toughness forged by the condition of exile, made them exemplary national citizens.

The Omani Empire in Zanzibar

The sojourn of the Zanzibari exiles in the wilderness of statelessness did not necessarily coexist with a natural idea of Oman as the homeland. Rather, such an idea had to be discursively constructed and naturalized culturally and socially. As al-Riyami astutely observes, "Leaving Zanzibar was for many Arabs a journey into the unknown, regardless of rhetorical and patriotic slogans about going back to ancestors'

---

14 Such critiques had been around since the "time of politics." See comments by Sir Mbarak al-Hinawy in Zulfikar Hirji, *Between Empires, Sheikh-Sir Mbarak al-Hinawy 1896–1959* (2012). See also the advice of Sheikh Hashil bin Rashid al-Maskery to the Arab Association in the early 1960s in al-Riyami, p. 346.

15 Tribal name and membership are mandatory for employment in Oman.

lands" (p. 206). Thus, even though Omani nationalism viewed itself as enfolding its "lost" children in the secure arms of the parent, Sultan Qaboos, the "father" of the Omani nation, returnees from Zanzibar still had to culturally authenticate themselves. They have done this by emphasizing the great imperial glory their ancestors achieved in East Africa. The return to Oman has thus led to a re-embrace of the idea of Omanis as glorious and civilized imperial rulers in Africa. Africa was no longer a place Omanis went to escape the hardships of Oman and to obtain *rizq* ("sustenance"); rather, it was the front line of a courageous crusade to plant Islam and civilization through great personal sacrifice. And the revolution was no longer merely the fall of "an independent Zanzibar" but instead the "overthrow of Arab Omani rule."[16]

Examples can also be drawn from the broader realm of Omani media and Arabic language literature on Zanzibar. Dr. Asya al-Bualy is the daughter of Nasser Seif al-Bualy, an Omani returnee from Tanzania who served in Oman as director-general of the Ministry of Information and aided thousands of Omani-Zanzibaris to return to Oman. Dr. al-Bualy is active in writing about the Omani presence in East Africa. In a scathing and eloquent reply (published in both Arabic and English) to a criticism of Omani-Zanzibaris who speak Kiswahili, she defends the community thusly: "As for those whose citizenship the writer questioned because they speak Swahili, let me tell you that they sacrificed their souls and their wealth for the sake of establishing an Omani empire on the Swahili coast, which dates back to the 16th century."[17] Sheikh Saleh bin Hashil al-Maskery, in an editorial calling for Oman to recognize Omani refugees from East Africa, calls Omanis remaining in East Africa "remnants of the great Omani empire, which carried the light of truth, religion, culture and humanity to the tribes and peoples of East Africa, who knew almost nothing of Allah." Al-Maskery is proud of this imperial heritage: "We continue in the present age to glory in it and in its grandeur."[18] A somewhat altered version of this vision also informs the aforementioned scholarly work of Harith Ghassany, who claims that the first sultan of Zanzibar, Seyyid Said, helped to make East Africa "one nation from Zanzibar to the Congo," which was only later divided by colonialism (Ghassany 2010: 242). It

---

16 See al-Riyami, Arabic edition, p. 500.

17 Asya al-Bualy, "Rud 'ala 'Ain al-watan muwattin," *Shurfāt*, 10 May 2011.

18 Sheikh Saleh bin Hashil al-Maskery, "Alāf min Ahlna Yantazirūn i'tirāfna bihim," *Al-Watan*, 9 May 2013.

is not my goal in this essay to refute this type of thinking, although one might note historian Abdul Sheriff's analysis of Zanzibar and question whether Said's domains constituted an empire or even a nation in the modern sense (Sheriff 2001: 2). Certainly it is clear that Said's government depended greatly on British power and that his transfer of the Omani capital to Zanzibar was not necessarily a reflection of Omani imperial might (Bhacker 1992). For the purposes of this essay, the most important thing I wish to emphasize is that civilizationist thinking and the Omani imperial ideal go hand in hand in contemporary Zanzibari-Omani thought to authorize the returnees as true citizens. The Zanzibar revolution is remembered and commemorated as a trauma signaling the final and irrevocable collapse of this empire. This suggests that Zanzibari-Omanis (contra Valeri 2007) do not constitute in any significant sense a separate ethnicity from the bulk of Oman's Arab population. Certainly they do not perceive themselves as a distinct ethnic group. Rather, they see themselves, at least at the present time, as integrally linked by blood and sacrifice to the Omani nation. Their Arab genealogy, which ZNP activists had tried to play down, is now the basis for a claim to citizenship in Oman. Their own self-conceptions share significant commonalities with the *pied noir* returnees to France from Algeria, who authorized their French citizenship with reference to the sacrifices of blood they made on behalf of the nation and who painted Algeria as a kind of Eldorado, associated only with happy memories (Stora 2005; Horne 1977).

The imperial imagination also plays an important role in knitting together the diverse strands of Omani migration to East Africa under an imperial umbrella. If Oman had an African empire, then all Omanis in Africa were (and are) its subjects, and Zanzibari identity is an expansive one, connecting the Zanzibar-island dwellers to the "Zanzibara"—that is, the Omani diaspora in Tanganyika, Kenya, Burundi, Rwanda, Uganda, and Congo (al-Rasheed 2005: 100). In a 2012 interview I conducted with "Zainab," a returnee originally from Shinyanga in mainland Tanzania, she laughingly related some of the stereotypes perpetuated by some Omanis about the Zanzibari community, following this with an assertion that Omanis from East Africa should not be ashamed of their past because "Oman was an empire, we spread Islam there [Africa] and taught the Africans about religion."[19] Other evidence of this can be found in a letter shared with

---

19 Interview with "Zainab," Muscat, 3 March 2013.

me by "Ali," an Omani returnee from mainland Tanzania, who is also a member of the Omani Majlis al-Shura, a body set up by Sultan Qaboos to consult on matters of state. He described his 2004 visit to Zanzibar as akin to visiting a place "familiar" to him even though he had never been there before; because of the "Omani-ness" of the place, he felt immediately right at home.[20] In this respect, the old proverb "When they pipe in Zanzibar, they dance on the lakes," which originally symbolized the sovereign reach of the Zanzibar sultans to the lakes region of East Africa, takes on a new meaning, as it signifies a shared imperial and diasporic subjectivity for which all Omanis in Africa can been portrayed as having shared and sacrificed for.

The imperial past of Zanzibar is appealing to Omani state authorities for several reasons. First, the imperial past is a domesticated past that can exist in the realm of heritage rather than playing a role in any active political imagination. Oman fought no wars in Zanzibar to end alternate claims on sovereignty, as it did in Jebel Akhdar and Dhofar (Takriti 2013). And it has thoroughly domesticated any irredentist tendencies among the Omani-Zanzibari community while working to develop a strong relationship with the Tanzanian government.[21]

Second, imperial thinking draws a deeper attachment to the idea of Omani national heritage and national history in Zanzibar, thus glorifying Oman's role in human civilization. Stone Town and the bevy of 19th-century palaces and buildings built by Omani sultans in Zanzibar are increasingly being seen as part of Oman's national heritage, and the Omani Ministry of National Heritage has even sent teams to inquire about preserving them. In May 2013, a contingent of ministers from the Ministry of Heritage and Culture, including the director general of archaeology and museums, visited Zanzibar to discuss "the desire of the Ministry to conduct technical studies to restore some of the landmarks in Zanzibar within the framework of the joint efforts between the two countries." The Ministry also expressed interest in obtaining artifacts for the Omani National Museum, currently under construction.[22]

---

20   Interview with "Ali," Muscat, 2012. Also see "Oman Faces and Places: Articles from PDO News Magazine," in which a PDO (Petroleum Development of Oman) employee writes, "The more time I spent in Zanzibar, the more I was struck by the 'Omani-ness' of the place."

21   Tanzanian president Jakaya Kikwete visited Oman in October 2012 in a bid to encourage Omani private and governmental investment in Tanzania. All presidents of Zanzibar after Abeid Karume have visited Oman in both private and public capacities.

22   "Omani Team in Zanzibar for Restoring Heritage Sites," *Times of Oman*, 27 May 2013.

The impact of al-Riyami's work on readers in Zanzibar is hard to gauge. The work was available for a time in Markiti's Masomo Bookshop, but those who engaged with the work most seriously tended to have links to Zanzibar's Arab elite from the older generation.[23] One older Zanzibari, descended from a prominent Omani family requested the book in order to see a picture of one of her relatives, but she denounced al-Riyami's portrayal of the 19th-century Zanzibari caravan leader and adventurer Tippu Tip. "Tippu Tip was a slave trader," she insisted. There is no doubt that Omani families vacationing in Zanzibar during June and July brought copies of the book, but its political impact was muted by its being available in Arabic and English only, and not in Kiswahili.

Memory, Nostalgia, and Reconciliation in Oman and Zanzibar

In spite of some its more incendiary historical rhetoric, al-Riyami makes few political demands. The main one comes at the end of the book, when al-Riyami, discussing reconciliation between Oman and Zanzibar, points to the example of Uganda, where Yoweri Musuveni offered to return properties expropriated from Uganda's Asian community under Idi Amin (p. 215–6). In fact, al-Riyami (along with other Omani Zanzibaris) raised the issue of the return of lands and houses to those who lost them in the revolution at a meeting with Tanzanian president Jakaya Kikwete during his Oman visit in October 2012. Kikwete answered the question by saying it was an issue best taken up with the Zanzibar government directly. In fact, the issue of return of properties has long been the condition of a return of Arab exiles to Zanzibar. In the early 1980s, both Tanzania and Zanzibar made overtures to these exiles to return and invest in the flagging economy, as part of Tanzanian president Ali Hassan Mwinyi's policy of economic liberalization. These talks usually broke down on the issue of guarantees of property return.[24] The issue is significant for both sides: For Zanzibar's government, it would mean an explicit renunciation of the stated goal of the revolution, to combat economic inequality. For the Omani-Zanzibaris, regaining lost property would be an acknowledgment of what they have long maintained—the fundamental illegitimacy of the revolution. In fact

---

23 A copy was obtained there by G. C. van de Bruinhorst. Personal communication, 1 October 2014.

24 See for instance, "When the Snubbing Has to Stop," *Free Zanzibar Voice,* January/February 1986.

the issue may be moot; Omani-Zanzibaris never lost all their family property in Zanzibar and have returned in droves since the 1980s to refurbish old family homes, a process that has proceeded apace with massive investment in the rebranding of Stone Town as a tourist center (Bissell 2005).

At the time of this writing, debates about Zanzibar and mainland Tanzania's political relationship is ongoing.[25] As the revolutionary regime celebrates its 50th year, it seems unlikely that Zanzibar's government will decry its revolutionary past. Nevertheless, Zanzibar is likely to continue to "look east" to Oman and the Gulf for investment and education, although this is likely to take place within the respective hegemonies of the Omani and Tanzanian states. There is shared interest by the Zanzibar and Omani governments in rehabilitating Stone Town; Oman sees it as a piece of its national heritage, while Zanzibar would love to attract the prestige and tourism revenue that comes from having a World Heritage site (Bissell 2005).

Omani visits to Zanzibar are also on the rise, but for many from the exile generation, the Zanzibar these Omanis might return to has changed in ways that make it unrecognizable. In the words of one exile quoted by al-Riyami, in contemporary Zanzibar "Arabism has eroded" to the point where he no longer desires to return (p. 385). Zanzibar is no longer the Zanzibar they remember; it contains only shards of the beautiful landscape they once belonged to. Indeed, al-Riyami concludes the Arabic version of the book with a stark comparison of Zanzibar then and now, which is an ideal way to summarize some of the themes of this essay.[26]

Al-Riyami contrasts the old neighborhood of Forodhani, where the police band used to play classical music and symphonic pieces, with the current Forodhani, whose former prestige and splendor have departed, to be replaced by Maasai and other mainland tribespeople selling their "African idols." Zanzibar, he claims, has gone from a developed nation to an "underdeveloped and impoverished" one, declining from the capital of Seyyid Said bin Sultan's empire to "an obscure country on the world map." After making this comparison, al-Riyami concludes the Arabic edition of the book on a philosophical note: "It is true what is said, for every age there is a country and a people." For many in al-Riyami's generation, Zanzibar has passed from the horizon of political

---

25 The opposition party CUF boycotted the most recent March 2016 election re-run.

26 The English version's conclusion, in contrast, is a summary of major points of each chapter.

struggle into the realm of heritage and memory. Their engagement with Zanzibar is ongoing, but there is (at least publicly) an emphasis by some on moving forward and letting go of the past. But without the ability to commemorate those of their family and neighbors who died in Zanzibar, and without the ability to influence the political situation there, many Omani-Zanzibaris will continue to see Zanzibar as a familiar, not yet alien place, tinged with a great and monumental heritage that is slowly passing away under the influence of the mainland.

As the Omani-Zanzibaris enter ever deeper into the "authorizing center" of Omani national history, their imagination and memory of their own past becomes interwoven with a narrative that privileges the continuity of Omani blood ties across national boundaries and makes past generations of Omanis in Zanzibar into "migrants" instead of "sons of the soil." The Zanzibari exiles become returnees, bruised but strengthened by their sojourn on the frontiers of the former empire, but having acquired valuable knowledge in the process, knowledge they put to use modernizing the Omani nation (Valeri 2007). The collective memory of the revolution is transformed into a historical *fait accompli*, something to be accepted and moved past.

One result of this process has been to domesticate some of the earlier generation's potent desire for regime change. The granting of national citizenship in Oman has allowed for a productive "forgetting" of their lost nation of Zanzibar under the aegis of progress, reconciliation, and forgiveness. Not only that, but the newly-minted Omanis return to Zanzibar for visits from a position of economic and social privilege, which nourishes a renewed sense of paternalism and "there-but-for-the-grace-of-God-go-I" attitudes toward family members and friends who remained behind. The Zanzibari exiles–cum–Omani returnees still critique aspects of state failure (such as the failure of the Zanzibari government to maintain old monuments and buildings that are deemed part of Omani heritage), but they stop short of advocating regime change or interfering in the internal politics of Zanzibar. They come to Zanzibar as a very special kind of visitor—a kind of nostalgic tourist, navigating a landscape of memory. Soud Ahmed al-Busaidi, who served the sultans of Zanzibar as well as the British colonial government and who later settled in Oman, expresses well the new attitude in the introduction to his memoirs: "Those of us who loved Zanzibar did not lose it forever, and the book ends happily with holidays there in a family setting" (2012: 4).

Nostalgia is directed toward a landscape of Zanzibar's past, but its most important function is in Oman. For Omani-Zanzibaris, Zanzibar represents a beautiful past, like the paintings and photos of the green trees and narrow cool lanes of Zanzibar that adorn Omani-Zanzibari homes in Muscat. Zanzibar might be thought of as an oasis in the collective memory of these Omani-Zanzibaris, a well of heritage into which they and the Omani state can dip for access to a glorious ancient and civilized past that the world once admired. The Omani-Zanzibaris thus reconfigure themselves as an Omani rather than a Zanzibari diaspora, while the Omani state gains the prestige and cultural legitimacy that comes with having a national heritage that reaches beyond the nation.

Above, I have tried to accomplish several things. First, I have tried to give an account of how a particular generation of Zanzibari exiles/Omani returnees remembers the Zanzibar revolution. Second, I have tried to show the transformation of collective memory under conditions of migration, displacement, and renationalization, and the simultaneous work of a new generation to represent and reshape these memories into history in the presence of a new authorizing center, a national state. As the events of the revolution recede ever farther from the horizon of the returnee generation's memories, it becomes harder and harder to preserve a sense of the possibility of different futures based on alternate paths the past may have taken, or alternate choices actors may have made to change that past. History comes to seem more and more an inevitable outcome, "the will of God" or the result of some inexorable divine process. Thus, the next generation who absorb the revolution as history (through narration from their parents or grandparents) will tend to see things more and more in the tragic or romantic mode. Memory passed on as historical understanding is often highly idealized, and it is further idealized by the context of being an Omani citizen, where the nation places a high premium on Arabism and Arabic language. When this history in Zanzibar is appropriated as heritage by the Omani state (a process often encouraged by the activities of the homespun historians themselves), there is a strong tendency toward idealization and removal of agency, and toward what Friedrich Nietzsche called antiquarian history (Lowenthal 1998; Nietzsche 1980). Nietzsche both admired and condemned antiquarian history; he thought it admirable to want to look at the past and preserve it, but he also thought it necessary to be critical and to eventually destroy antiquarian history in search of a more critical and holistic outlook on the past.

The inevitable idealization in the antiquarian outlook also reveals the danger of reifying or reducing a complex transoceanic relationship to the achievements of certain ethnic or racial categories. Such categorical thinking is not easily left behind, even by exchanging an African landscape for an Indian Ocean seascape (Becker and Cabrita 2014). Especially in our contemporary era of Westphalian sovereignty, diaspora-thinking can, instead of liberating us from national boundaries, be a racial way of recognizing fellow nationals. (One Omani returnee once informed me that blood descent was the basis for the Omani nation.) Diaspora imaginaries can create strong bonds of affection, but when deployed as a litmus test for finding the nation in distant spaces and times, they often lead to reductive forms of racial thinking.

Ghassany suggests that what is needed by both Omanis and Zanzibaris is a willingness to confront the most fraught parts of a shared history between the two regions without being bound or blinded by the terms of order set by colonial modes of thinking. I would like to add to and amend this argument slightly. What is most needed is attendance to the violence, misunderstandings, assumptions, and power inequalities that characterized pre-colonial relationships as well as those of the colonial period. It is not simply a matter of seeking to "remove colonialism" in order to restore the harmonious mixture of races and relationships that prevailed in the 19th-century sultanate or earlier periods. In seeking a new rapprochement, Zanzibaris and Omanis, while sharing a common heritage and religion, will still have to navigate deeply held ideas about class, race, and civilization, themselves rooted in various and often incommensurable universalist relationships that do not have their horizons or their genealogies in the western political order—even if they are now entangled with it vis-à-vis the Westphalianization of the globe.

References

Alpers, Edward
2007 *East Africa and the Indian Ocean*. Princeton: Markus Wiener.

Ankersmit, F. R.
2001 "The Sublime Dissociation of the Past: Or How to Be(come) What One Is No Longer." *History and Theory* 40, October: 295–323.

Armstrong, Karen
2004 *Remembering Karelia: A Family's Story of Displacement during and after the Finnish Wars*. New York: Berghahn Books.

Bakari, Mohammed
2001 *The Democratisation Process in Zanzibar: A Retarded Transition*. Hamburg: Institut für Afrika-Kunde.

al-Barwani, Ali Muhsin
1997 *Conflicts and Harmony in Zanzibar: Memoirs*. Dubai: n.p.

Becker, Felicitas, and Joel Cabrita
2014 "Introduction: Performing Citizenship and Enacting Exclusion." *Journal of African History* 55(2), July: 161–71.

Bhacker, Reda
1992 *Trade and Empire in Muscat and Zanzibar: Roots of British Domination*. New York: Routledge.

Bissell, William Cunningham
2005 "Engaging Colonial Nostalgia." *Cultural Anthropology* 20(2): 215–48.

Bromber, Katrin
2002 "Who Are the Zanzibari? Newspaper Debates on Difference, 1948–1958." In *Space on the Move: Transformations of the Indian Ocean Seascape in the Nineteenth and Twentieth century*, ed. Brigitte Reinwald and Jan-Georg Deutsch, 21–38. Berlin: Klaus Schwarz.

al-Bualy, Asya
2011 "Rud ala 'Ain al-watan muwattin." *Shurfaat* 10 May.

Burgess, G. Thomas

2010 "Memories, Myths, and Meanings of the Zanzibari Revolution." In *War and Peace in Africa: History, Nationalism and the State*, ed. Toyin Falola and Raphael Chijioke Njoku, 429–450. Durham, N.C.: Carolina Academic Press.

2009 *Race, Revolution, and the Struggle for Human Rights in Zanzibar: The Memoirs of Ali Sultan Issa and Seif Sharif Hamad*. Athens, Ohio: Ohio University Press.

al-Busaidi, Soud Ahmed

2012 *Memoirs of an Omani Gentleman from Zanzibar*. Muscat, Oman: al-Roya Publishing.

Clayton, Anthony

1981 *The Zanzibari Revolution and Its Aftermath*. London: C. Hurst & Company.

Connerton, Paul

2011 *The Spirit of Mourning: History, Memory and the Body*. Cambridge, U.K.: Cambridge University Press.

Cooper, Frederick

1980 *From Slaves to Squatters: Plantation Labor and Agriculture in Zanzibar and Coastal Kenya, 1890–1925*. New Haven, Conn.: Yale University Press.

1977 *Plantation Slavery on the East Coast of Africa*. New Haven, Conn.: Yale University Press.

Coupland, Reginald

1938 *East Africa and Its Invaders, From the Earliest Times to the Death of Seyyid Said in 1856*. Oxford: Clarendon Press.

Creet, Julia, and Andreas Kitzmann

2011 *Memory and Migration: Multidisciplinary Approaches to Memory Studies*. Toronto: University of Toronto.

Edwards, Brent

2003 *The Practice of Diaspora: Literature, Translation and the Rise of Black Internationalism*. Cambridge, Mass.: Harvard University Press.

Fairooz, Aman Thani

1995 *Ukweli ni Huu (Kuusuta Uwongo)*. Dubai: self-published.

Fouéré, Marie-Aude

2014 "Recasting Julius Nyerere in Zanzibar: The Revolution, the Union and the Enemy of the Nation." *Journal of Eastern African Studies* 8(3): 478–96.

2012 "Reinterpreting Revolutionary Zanzibar in the Media Today: The Case of *Dira* Newspaper." *Journal of Eastern African Studies* 6(4): 672–89.

Ghassany, Harith

2010 *Kwaheri Ukoloni, Kwaheri Uhuru! Zanzibar na Mapinduzi ya Afrabia* [Goodbye Colonialism, Goodbye Independence! Zanzibar and the Revolution of Afrabia]. Self published, https://kwaheri.files.wordpress.com/2010/05/kwaheri-ukoloni-kwaheri-uhuru.pdf, accessed 18 July 2016.

Ghazal, Amal

2010 *Islamic Reform and Arab Nationalism: Expanding the Crescent from the Mediterranean to the Indian Ocean (1880s–1930s)*. Abingdon, Oxfordshire, U.K.: Routledge.

al-Ghonaimi, Sheikha

2012 *Zanjibār: Wa Akfān min Rahim Alālam*. Maktaba dāmirī. Muscat, Oman.

Gilbert, Erik

2007 "Oman and Zanzibar: The Historical Roots of a Global Community." In *Cross Currents and Community Networks: The History of the Indian Ocean World*, ed. Himanshu Prabha Ray and Edward A. Alpers, 163–178. Oxford: Oxford University Press.

Glassman, Jonathon

2014 "Creole Nationalists and the Search for Nativist Authenticity in Twentieth-Century Zanzibar: The Limits of Cosmopolitanism." *Journal of African History* 55(2), July: 229–47.

2011 *War of Words, War of Stones: Racial Thought and Violence in Colonial Zanzibar*. Bloomington, Ind.: Indiana University Press.

Gupta, Pamila, Isabel Hofmeyer, and Michael Pearson

2010 *Eyes Across the Water: Navigating the Indian Ocean*. Pretoria, South Africa: Unisa Press.

Haj, Maulid M.

2001 *Sowing the Wind: Zanzibar and Pemba before the Revolution*. Zanzibar: Gallery Publications.

Halbwachs, Maurice

1980 *The Collective Memory*. New York: Harper & Row.

Hanley, Will

2008 "Grieving Cosmopolitanism in Middle East Studies." *History Compass* 6(5), September: 1346–67.

Head Office State Affairs and Workers Rights, ed.

1973 *Afro-Shirazi Party: A Liberation Movement*. Zanzibar: Afro-Shirazi Party.

al-Hinai, Hinai

2013 *Ā'idūn haythu al-hulm, mashāhid wa-zikrayāt 'awdah min Zinjabār wa-al-Jazīrah al-Khadrā' ila 'Uman*. Beirut: Beirut Bookshop.

Hirji, Zulfikar

2012 *Between Empires, Sheikh-Sir Mbarak al-Hinawy 1896–1959*. London: Azimuth Editions.

2007 "Relating Muscat to Mombasa: Spatial Tropes in the Kinship Narratives of an Extended Family Network in Oman." *Anthropology of the Middle East* 2(1), spring: 55–69.

Horne, Alistair

1977 *A Savage War of Peace: Algeria, 1954–1962*. London: Macmillan.

al-Ismaily, Issa bin Nasser

1996 *Uzanzibari na Usultani*. Muscat, Oman: n.p.

Kharusi, Ahmed Seif

1974 *Zanzibar Cries For Help*. Hampshire, U.K.: The Zanzibar Organization.

1971 *Letters Smuggled Out of Zanzibar*. Portsmouth, U.K.: Portsmouth Printers.

1969 *The Agony of Zanzibar: A Victim of the New Colonialism*. Richmond, U.K.: Foreign Affairs Publishing.

1967 *Zanzibar: Africa's First Cuba: A Case Study of the New Colonialism*. Richmond, U.K.: Foreign Affairs Publishing.

Kharusi, Nafla

2013 "Identity and Belonging Among Ethnic Return Migrants of Oman." *Nationalism and Ethnic Politics* 19(4): 424–46.

2012 "The Ethnic Label Zinjibari: Politics and Language Choice Implications among Swahili Speakers in Oman." *Ethnicities* 12(3), June: 335–53.

Kleinman, Arthur, Veena Das, and Margaret Lock, eds.
1997 *Social Suffering*. Berkeley, Cal.: University of California Press.

Kleinman, Arthur, Veena Das, Mamphela Ramphele, Margaret Lock, and Pamela Reynolds
2001 *Remaking a World: Violence, Social Suffering and Recovery*. Berkeley, Cal.: University of California Press.

Kleinman, Arthur, Veena Das, Mamphela Ramphele, and Pamela Reynolds
1997 *Violence and Subjectivity*. Berkeley, Cal.: University of California Press.

Kresse, Kai, and Edward Simpson, eds.
2008 *Struggling with History: Islam and Cosmopolitanism in the Western Indian Ocean*. New York: Columbia University Press.

Lim, J. H.
2010 "Victimhood Nationalism and History Reconciliation in East Asia." *History Compass* 8(1), January: 1–10.

Limbert, Mandana
2010 *In The Time of Oil: Piety, Memory and Social Life in an Omani Town*. Stanford: Stanford University Press.

Lofchie, Michael F.
1965 *Zanzibar: Background to Revolution*. Princeton, N.J.: Princeton University Press.

Loimeier, Roman
2009 *Between Social Skills and Marketable Skills: The Politics of Islamic Education in 20th Century Zanzibar*. Leiden: Brill.

Lowenthal, David
1998 *The Heritage Crusade and the Spoils of History*. Cambridge, U.K.: Cambridge University Press.

al-Maamiry, Ahmed Hamoud
1988 *Omani Sultans in Zanzibar (1832–1964)*. New Delhi: Lancers Books.

Malkki, Liisa
1995 *Purity and Exile: Violence, Memory, and National Cosmology among Hutu Refugees in Tanzania*. Chicago: University of Chicago Press.

Manger, Leif, and Munzoul Assal, eds.

2006 *Diasporas within and without Africa: Dynamism, Heterogeneity and Variation.* Uppsala: Nordic Africa Institute.

Mannheim, Karl

1952 "The Problem of Generations." In *Karl Mannheim: Essays*, ed. Paul Kecskemeti, 276–322. New York: Routledge.

Mapuri, Omar R.

1996 *Zanzibar: The 1964 Revolution: Achievements and Prospects.* Dar es Salaam: TEMA Publishers.

Markowitz, Fran, and Anders H. Steffanson

2004 *Homecomings: Unsettling Paths of Return.* Oxford: Lexington Books.

al-Maskery, Saleh bin Hashil

2013 "Alāf min Ahlna Yantadhirūn I'tirāfna bihim." *Al-Watan.* 9 May.

Nietzsche, Friedrich

1980 *On the Advantage and Disadvantage of History for Life*, trans. Peter Preuss. Indianapolis, Ind.: Hackett Publishing Company.

Olick, Jeffrey

1998 "Memory and the Nation: Continuities, Conflicts, and Transformations." *Social Science History* 22(4): 377–87.

Pearson, Michael

2007 *The Indian Ocean (Seas in History).* New York: Routledge.

Pennebaker, James W., and Becky L. Banasik

1997 "On the Creation and Maintenance of Collective Memories: History as Social Psychology." In *Collective Memory of Political Events: Social Psychological Perspectives*, ed. James W. Pennebaker, Dario Paez, and Bernard Rimé, 3–19. Mahwah, N.J.: Lawrence Erlbaum Associates.

Peterson, Derek, and Giacomo Macola

2009 *Recasting the Past: African History Writing and Political Work in Modern Africa.* Athens, Ohio: Ohio University Press.

Pouwels, Randall

2002 *Horn and Crescent: Cultural Change and Traditional Islam on the East African Coast, 800–1900.* Cambridge, U.K.: Cambridge University Press.

Rabi, Uzi

2006 *The Emergence of States in a Tribal Society: Oman under Sa'id bin Taymur, 1932-1970*. Brighton, U.K.: Sussex Academic Press.

al-Rasheed, Madawi

2005 "Transnational Connections and National Identity: Zanzibari Omanis in Muscat." In *Monarchies and Nations: Globalisation and Identity in the Arab States of the Gulf*, ed. Paul Dresch and James Piscatori, 96-113. London and New York: I. B. Taurus. 96-113.

al-Riyami, Nasser Abdulla

2012 *Zanzibar: Personalities & Events (1828-1972)*, trans. Ali Rashid al-Abri. Cairo: Beirut Bookshop.

2009 *Zinjibār: Shaksiyāt wa Ahadāth*. Cairo: Maktab Beirut.

Scott, David

2004 *Conscripts of Modernity: The Tragedy of Colonial Enlightenment*. Durham, N.C.: Duke University Press.

Sheriff, Abdul

2010 *Dhow Cultures of the Indian Ocean: Cosmopolitanism, Commerce and Islam*. London: Hurst.

1987 *Slaves, Spices and Ivory in Zanzibar: Integration of an East African Commercial Empire into the World Economy, 1770-1873*. London: James Currey.

Sheriff, Abdul, and Ed Ferguson, eds.

1991. *Zanzibar under Colonial Rule*. London: James Currey.

Shyrock, Andrew

1997 *Nationalism and the Genealogical Imagination: Oral History and Textual Authority in Tribal Jordan*. Berkeley, Cal.: University of California Press.

Stora, Benjamin

2005 "The Algerian War in French Memory: Vengeful Memory's Violence." In *Memory and Violence in the Middle East and North Africa*, ed. Usama Makdissi and Paul Silverstein, 151-174. Bloomington, Ind.: Indiana University Press.

Takriti, Abdel Razzaq

2013 *Monsoon Revolution: Republicans, Sultans and Empire in Oman, 1965–1976*. Oxford: Oxford University Press.

Trouillot, Michel-Rolph

1995 *Silencing the Past: Power and the Production of History*. Boston: Beacon Press.

Tsuda, Takeyuki

2009 *Diasporic Homecomings: Ethnic Return Migration in Comparative Perspective*. Palo Alto, Cal.: Stanford University Press.

Valeri, Marc

2009 *Oman: Politics and Society in the Qaboos State*. New York: Columbia University Press.

2007 "Nation-Building and Communities in Oman Since 1970: The Swahili-Speaking Omani in Search of Identity." *African Affairs* 106(424): 479–96.

Van Hear, Nicholas

1998 *New Diasporas: The Mass Exodus, Dispersal and Regrouping of Migrant Communities*. Seattle: University of Washington Press.

Verne, Julia, and Detlef Müller-Mahn

2013 "'We Are Part of Zanzibar'—Translocal Practices and Imaginative Geographies in Contemporary Oman-Zanzibar Relations." In *Regionalizing Oman: Political, Economic and Social Dynamics*, ed. Steffen Wippel, 75–89. New York: Springer.

Chapter Ten

Africa Addio, the Revolution, and the Ambiguities of Remembrance in Contemporary Zanzibar

*Marie-Aude Fouéré**

"Perhaps the most pitiless mass shooting in the entire macabre anthology of death": These words subtitle the twenty or so minutes of rough footage of the mass murders of the revolution of 1964 in Zanzibar that feature in the controversial Italian documentary *Africa Addio* (1966). This sensationalist characterization casts a sinister gloom over the episodes of racial violence that tore apart this Indian Ocean archipelago only one month after it gained independence. Originally conceived and circulated for audiences in the former colonial metropoles, *Africa Addio* shows scenes filmed in the 1960s in several countries of Africa that are "so terrifying and horrific that one at times has to look away from the screen" (Goodall 2006: 93). Produced by two Italian filmmakers, Gualtiero Jacopetti and Franco Prosperi, this disturbing visual document was castigated as an inauthentic and racist movie by film critics and anticolonialist intellectuals after its release in 1966. It was criticized in scathing terms as a retrograde apologia for European colonialism and was lambasted for promoting the view that Africa without the European colonial powers would quickly revert to primitive brutality and bloodshed—hence the title's more lurid translation as *Africa Blood and Guts* in the "truncated and hyper-sensationalist" version released in the United States (ibid: 105).

Yet *Africa Addio* is no longer just a spectacle for colonial sympathizers in the Global North: It has now surprisingly resurfaced in one of the

---

* This chapter is a slightly revised version of an article published in *Social Anthropology/Anthropologie sociale* in 2016 (Fouéré 2016).

ex-colonies allegedly depicted in the film,[1] circulating in new and unexpected contexts. In Zanzibar, the Revolutionary Government banned the film for years in an attempt to control the interpretation of the revolution as well as to deny opponents of the regime any ideological ammunition. But more recently, following political and economic liberalization, the documentary is now easily accessible through the Internet, and the short sequence on the massacres of 1964 has been watched by growing numbers of urban, educated Zanzibaris. This article will show that *Africa Addio*—along with other materials, oral, written, and visual, that circulate in Zanzibar—is increasingly appropriated and debated as archival evidence that ordinary Zanzibaris use to trace the 1964 event and make sense of its significance for the present and in the future. The use of nonconventional pieces of evidence to come to terms with the dark past of the isles has become a commonplace practice, especially among the historically conscious post-1964 generations who did not experience the revolution, as few historical sources are readily available in authorized public records and archives in Zanzibar.

Recent intellectual and political engagement with *Africa Addio* as a potential repository of historical evidence has to do with the central role of the revolution of 1964 in the history of Zanzibar and its enduring legacy in shaping imaginaries of belonging and nationhood. The revolution was cast as the founding myth of the Zanzibari nation by the revolutionaries and their heirs who have wielded power until today, but it is decried by its opponents as the "original sin" (Burgess 2009: 2) that prompted the cultural, economic, and political decline of the archipelago. It provoked a "collective trauma" (Glassman 2011) from which the society has yet to recover 50 years after. Although the official version of the revolution deployed by the state has long held a dominant position in the public sphere, the clandestine transmission of alternative historical narratives, based upon living memories, has always undermined the hegemonic efforts of the revolutionary regime to control the official story. Since the mid-1990s, when political competition was reintroduced and a public sphere reconstituted, the regime's historical interpretations of the revolution have been increasingly challenged (Fouéré 2012a, 2012b). *Africa Addio*, among other nonfiction media, has been appropriated to contest the supposedly clear-cut and unambiguous official version of the past. This explains why watching *Africa Addio* is not just a private

---

1 Zanzibar, a pair of islands situated in the Indian Ocean a couple of miles off the East African coast, was a British protectorate from 1890 to December 1963. It has been part of Tanzania since 26 April 1964, after the passage of a treaty of union with former Tanganyika.

and subjective act by isolated individuals, even though news about the documentary has spread by word of mouth, circulating in informal and dispersed, even secretive ways. Instead, I contend that watching *Africa Addio* is a socially embedded political practice: It prompts real-life enquiries and fuels collective interrogations about the significance of the revolution, its substance and meaning. These interrogations are "collective" not in the sense that they would take place during public and open discussions that would equally involve all segments of Zanzibari society and be widely disseminated by the media; the term here refers to locally situated debates among more or less close friends whom one trusts and acquaintances who one knows have a similar political leaning—mostly, in this case, urban middle-aged men who are sympathizers of the opposition party. Because individuals straddle several circles of sociability, these debates involve, little by little, other segments of the population. This article will show that the documentary does not simply contribute to thinking and talking about power, politics, and belonging in Zanzibar today; it can shape the imagination of a utopian post-revolutionary nonracial polity against deep-rooted racialist narratives about Zanzibariness.

Making *Africa Addio* a Postcolonial Archive

This article is first and foremost a contribution to the debate about the production of historical consciousness and political subjectivities. It focuses on the everyday and mundane processes of sense-making through which such consciousness and subjectivities emerge, rather than on state-led or elite initiatives. *Africa Addio* is used as a gateway into social practices that common people and homespun intellectuals use to investigate and build knowledge of the past, interpret the present situation, and imagine different modalities of social life—in other words, to craft an alternative polity for the future. This study therefore draws upon a Foucauldian approach to subjectivity in order to shed light on the intertwined dynamics that both subject individuals to various kinds of power and allow them to take themselves as the objects of their own action, displaying their agency. Within this theoretical framework, the study of the production, use, and circulation of this documentary archive for historical enquiry, memory work, and political imagination will be examined in depth from the point of view of its contemporary audience.

The notion of archive is not understood in a conventional way as a site and its contents—that is to say as materials abstracted from the "particular relations within which they originate and circulate (family, bureaucracy, religious institutions, etc.)" (Chakrabarty 2009: 67) and stored to be accessible for consultation by an authorized public only, mostly academic historians (Ricoeur 2000: 209-18). Instead, my detailed exploration of debates surrounding the authenticity and authority of *Africa Addio* will show that this process of historical and political sense-making is at the same time a process of archive-making. In other words, the archive is constituted through the collective—yet ordinary—use of documents. In this regard, *Africa Addio* can be conceptualized as an archive not because it has been selected and preserved by the state or any other official institutions but because it is being constructed—or deconstructed—as a container of evidence, signs, and clues for exploring Zanzibari history. It is, in Arjun Appadurai's words, a "collective tool" rather than the product of state policies aimed at converting the archive into "an accessory to policing, surveillance and governmentality"; indeed, "the creation of documents and their aggregation into archives is also a part of everyday life outside the purview of the state" (2003: 16). This reminds us that "archivability" (Mbembe 2002: 19) does not rest in the hands of the state only. *Africa Addio* can all the more be considered a popular tool as it is manipulated by its audience to excavate a past whose living memories have started to crumble in the face of the many politicized historical narratives of the event that now saturate the public sphere—therefore echoing Jacques Derrida's words that the archive is also a product of "the breakdown of memory" (1998: 11). In sum, this article provides a genealogy of an archive in the making, exploring its construction and deconstruction, which, to this day, leave its status undetermined.

This study is inevitably inspired by, and resonates with, conceptions of nationalism and nationhood as an "imagined community" (Anderson 1995). However, it does not simply attribute the building of such an ideational community—and the formation of a public sphere[2]—to the diffusion of the printed word, such as newspapers and novels. On the contrary, it asserts that images (photographs, movies, etc.) and spoken words can also be appropriated to establish such imaginaries and sentiments of collective belonging (Appadurai 2003). It also contends that the formation of a public sphere is in the line of fire of the everyday creation of historical sources as collective tools to reflect upon the past,

---

2   In Zanzibar, the *baraza*, an everyday place of casual talks for men, plays this role of public sphere (Loimeier 2009). As friends and acquaintances gather there, it is a place where discussions about *Africa Addio* take place.

just as the discipline of history has "the utopian ideal of the public sphere written all over it" (Chakrabarty 2009: 67). The archives of the historian were indeed initially aimed at providing "unfettered access to historical information" rather than reserving it to some "privileged" communities (Chakrabarty 2009: 68).

This study is also situated within the field of memory studies focused on loci such as monuments, sites, figures, and rituals in which the past is recast in the present (Halbwachs 1997; Nora 1984–87). The archive is one such locus; its study proves once again that shedding light on how collective memory works and is mediated is deeply relevant if we want to capture the present concerns of a society. Lastly, although acknowledging that Zanzibari society can be imagined in plural modes, according to the social status, ethnic or racial identities, generational belonging, political affiliations and biographical trajectories of the individuals considered, this article relies upon Jonathon Glassman's argument (2011) about the pervasiveness of "racial thought" in Zanzibar, notably since the struggle for independence in the 1950s and early 1960s, which has produced the essentialized categories of "Arabs" and "Africans." This shared discourse explains why today's various "scripts" of the revolution (Myers 2000), including those prompted by the screening of *Africa Addio*, tend to replay the secular and deep-rooted tropes about race and autochthony to define identity and belonging, even though more positive conceptions of Zanzibariness, which recoup the pre-revolutionary past to imagine an ideal postracial society, have emerged more recently.

Mondo Shockumentaries

"Be prepared to be disturbed!" These were the words used to promote a "Mondo film night" organized by Charles Kilgore, an aficionado of the genre, in Washington, D.C., in the mid-1990s (Staples and Kilgore 1995). The warning aptly communicates the "culture-shock treatment" provoked by the screening of a series of sensationalist, extremely violent "documentaries" that in the 1960s were filmed and released for a Western audience. The so-called Mondo film genre, an "ugly bastard child of the documentary and the peepshow" (Kilgore 1988: 2) invented by several Italian filmmakers in the late 1950s, reached its apex with the work of controversial Italian filmmakers Gualtiero Jacopetti and Franco Prosperi. These two high-profile documentarians adopted a primitivist and voyeuristic stance to portray bizarre and exotic customs (or unrestrained cruelty and perverted sexuality) in trash documentaries that constitute the "Mondo cycle," among them

Mondo Cane (1963), *Africa Addio* (1966), and *Addio Zio Tom* (1972). Heir to patently staged, fake travel and exploration films of the 1930s to 1950s, which combined field material with studio-staged scenes, the Mondo films constitute a "cinema of attraction" that blurs fact and fiction and appeals to a "voyeurist pathology" (Goodall 2006). *Africa Addio* is not, however, just another film in the Mondo series: Fans of the genre consider it the greatest Mondo film, as it was the most shocking of all. This "masterpiece" mixes scenes of violence and brutality exerted by Africans against wild animals in game reserves with the footage of Mau Mau rebels in Kenya, mass graves of Arabs in Zanzibar, the first genocides in Rwanda, and mercenary executions in Congo. Some of the film posters added taglines such as these to the title: "Consumed by savagery, conceived in blood," "Savagery! Brutality! Inhumanity! It bathed the world in blood!" and "This is Africa like it is! Where Black is beautiful, Black is ugly, Black is brutal!"

Shortly after *Africa Addio* was released in Europe and the United States, scandalized reviewers condemned the scenes of extreme violence that were so bluntly featured. The renowned film critic Roger Ebert opened one of the first reviews of the film, published 25 April 1967, by stating, "*Africa Addio* is a brutal, dishonest, racist film. It slanders a continent and at the same time diminishes the human spirit. And it does so to entertain us." Ebert strongly objected to the aesthetics adopted by the moviemakers to shock their viewers—which is why these documentaries are called "shockumentaries"—with their "saccharine sound track, arty photography and... authoritative-sounding narration" (Ebert 1967). The pro-colonialist and Afro-pessimist stance of the movie, which the opening sentences abruptly illustrate ("Europe has abandoned her baby just when it needs her the most. Who has taken over, now that the colonialists have left?"), was also severely criticized. The sequence about Zanzibar exemplifies the filmmakers' patronizing and infantilizing attitude. In voiceover, Jacopetti and Prosperi indeed chastise "the colonial powers for abandoning Africa" (Glassman 2011: ix), declaring that they blame the European powers for "hastily abandoning Africa to itself in the false modesty of antique colonialism, authorizing a new Africa flooded with misery and blood." Film critics were not the only ones outraged by the mise-en-scène of Africa in the documentary. In August 1966, German and African students protested the West Berlin premiere of the movie. In the Netherlands, protesters demonstrated with signs saying, "With Africa Addio we are back in Hitler's time." And although it continued to be screened in Italy, where it earned the equivalent of more than $2 million US at the box office, the film was eventually banned in the United States and Great Britain, and blocked in France (Bandel 2005). Five African states requested a ban on *Africa Addio* at the United Nations (Shipka 2007: 72).

Another significant criticism pointed to the fact that many scenes seemed to have been directed or staged by the filmmakers, although the voiceover repeatedly insists that *Africa Addio* is a testimony to the historical realities of decolonization, not a fiction or an artwork. The Zanzibari footage, shot from a plane (or helicopter) that flew over the isles a few days after the revolution occurred, is said to be "the only existing documentation of what happened in Zanzibar between January 18 and 20, 1964," therefore emphasizing its historical truthfulness. Jacopetti and Prosperi have always presented themselves as impartial movie journalists, stating: "We didn't have a political viewpoint. The film was totally objective. We were witnesses to a tragedy, political meaning left aside" (Gregory 2003). However, the authenticity and actual location of the events portrayed in the film have remained a controversial and unresolved issue until today. Because of this epistemological uncertainty, *Africa Addio* has much in common with "the parafictional" category of creative works (Lambert-Beatty 2009), in which not only is the line between the real and the fictional blurred, but "playing with reality" aims at bringing out a truth that may otherwise not be clear. As the Mondo aficionado Kilgore emphasizes, the core of the controversy surrounding *Africa Addio* has ultimately less to do with how Africa is represented than with the lack of ethics by the two filmmakers in the field. "What is the responsibility of journalists who are present in a situation where they may have enough influence to save a life?" (Staples and Kilgore 1995: 119). Jacopetti and Prosperi were accused by an Italian newspaper of orchestrating the executions of some of the people killed instead of trying to save their lives, and much ink was spilled over this moral issue. In spite of recent attempts to rehabilitate the Mondo genre, notably in Goodall's essay (2006), most scholars remain scathing about the ethnocentric slant of *Africa Addio*. Given the ideological leaning and intentions of the filmmakers, the documentary does not constitute an archive from which to extract information about African decolonization; rather, it is an archive of the popular culture and imagination of the 1960s produced by decades of colonialism—a popular imagination that the filmmakers both reflected on the screen and stimulated through their end-of-empire movies.

Yet in Zanzibar, it is neither the pro-colonial and anti-African slant of *Africa Addio* nor questions about the ethics of its makers that fire most local debates, but rather its historical authenticity and, consequently, its potential to be used as an authoritative archive of the 1964 revolution. The question is whether the footage that appears in the film is truthful or fictional. The document notably shows hundreds of dead bodies in mass graves and scattered on beaches that, the filmmakers say, are located in Unguja. Interrogations about the truthfulness or fictiveness of *Africa Addio* are locally crucial because the revolution has not only "left a deep, and so far unhealed wound" (Shivji 2008: 3), but because it has deeply influenced present-day networks of sociability, determining whom Zanzibaris "call their friends, with whom they share a cup of coffee, or whom they welcome to their homes as in-laws" (Burgess 2009: 2). Although Jacopetti and Prosperi's shockumentary remains a troubling document for Zanzibari viewers, as will be shown below, it is also a powerful tool to rethink the revolution and recast conceptions of belonging and nationhood.

The Revolution of 1964

The *revolution* refers, in state discourses and official history, to the overthrow of the first independent government of Zanzibar—a constitutional monarchy under the rule of a sultan and his elected government—on the night of 11–12 January 1964. This armed takeover happened only one month after the archipelago had gained independence from British rule and was conducted by forces that legitimated their action through discourses that conjoined race, belonging, and legitimacy to exercise power. They claimed they had expelled the oppressive rule of an alien Arab minority and given it to the African majority of genuine autochthones, who had been deprived of their natural right to sovereignty on the islands for centuries. This explains why this coup d'état was labeled, in the writings of its supporters, the first "African revolution" in East Africa. Massive violence occurred during the following days, even weeks, targeting people of Arab origin as well as Indians and Comorians considered allies of the "Arab oppressor." They were humiliated, beaten, raped, and killed. Attempts to control or contain the turbulence of the revolution appeared vain in the face of the violence and "terror" (Clayton 1981: 71) that was unleashed for days (see also Lofchie 1963, 1965).

Similar bloody incidents, though on a smaller scale, had occurred before. The population had experienced mob violence and pogroms in June 1961, during and after tense elections, at a time when the competing political parties had engaged in a politics of racial hatred. These killings had deepened the racial divide between "Africans" and "Arabs" and profoundly traumatized a society that, before the 1950s, was characterized by ethnic fluidity, racial indeterminacy, and a cosmopolitan heritage (Glassman 2011: 5, 282) but that also bore the legacy of slavery. Zanzibar had served as the main slave-trading point for East Africa and the Indian Ocean in the 18th and 19th centuries, and its economy flourished on a slave-based plantation system (Cooper 1980; Sheriff 1987). Far from resulting from any spontaneous uprising, the killings rested upon a narrative of reclaimed justice for the Africans after decades of oppression and enslavement. The killings were also deeply tied up with the revolutionaries' political aspirations and social programs for a profound transformation of the isles. During the year that followed the revolution, the Arabs and other minorities who had not been killed or expelled from the archipelago witnessed the confiscation of their lands, shops, and houses and were systematically excluded from government employment.

The revolution, however, has remained an "enigma" (Shivji 2008: 62) for the common citizen as much as for the historian. The identity of the planners of the coup and the scope and scale of the killings remain uncertain, if not unknown. As Glassman notes, "the full story of the revolution has yet to be written" (2011: 284). No systematic historical materials have yet been collected, and at the National Archives of Zanzibar the records of the revolutionary days remain unavailable. Some say that these documents or accounts have been intentionally or carelessly destroyed or assert that many files may still lie hidden away in inaccessible and protected government offices. This suggests that, as with other regimes, the Zanzibari state thought it "could defer the archive's ability to serve as proof of a suspect fragment of life or piece of time" and tried to "shut down the past for once and for all so that [it] could write as if everything was started anew" (Mbembe 2002: 23).

As far as the scale of the killings is concerned, Glassman reminds us that opponents of the revolution tend to inflate the number of deaths while its defenders minimize this figure to less than a hundred (2011: 374n1). The megalomaniac memoir of the self-appointed leader of the insurrection, "Field Marshal" John Okello, which boasts of 7,994 people killed during the very first days and more than 13,000 by the end of the period of uncontrolled violence (1967: 150, 160), can be seen as "apocalyptic fantasies" (Glassman 2011: 374n1). More trustworthy figures estimated by less partisan external observers range between 3,000 and 5,000 deaths, "Africans" included. Anthony Clayton states that "the deaths ran into several thousands" (1981: 81n63), his estimate relying on the overall figure of 8,000 deaths provided by a witness who counted burned-out houses after the violence. He also estimated that the pre-independence Arab population of 50,000 was reduced by 12,000 to 15,000 as a result of the mass murders but also the deportations and the flights during the months that followed the coup. Clayton also mentions that during the revolutionary days, "bodies were buried five to an average-sized grave in some graveyards or pushed down well-holes" (1981: 80). It is because the number of deaths remains so uncertain that local debates about the revolution in Zanzibar focus so much on it—as exemplified in the case of *Africa Addio* discussed below—even though numbers always fail to express the social dislocation and trauma that the massacres brought about.

The "Great Revolution" was turned by the new regime into the foundational narrative of the new Zanzibari nation–that is, a nation in which "Africanness" was made the criterion of belonging and citizenship. Led by a Revolutionary Council, the new regime functioned as an authoritarian state under the personal autocratic rule of Abeid Amani Karume until he was assassinated in 1972. "Revolution Forever" (*Mapinduzi Daima* in Kiswahili) was made the slogan of the single party, the Afro-Shirazi Party (ASP), and repeated over and over during public rallies, in government publications, on buildings, in songs, and so on. The expression is used to the present day by the ruling party, which in 1977 was renamed Chama cha Mapinduzi (CCM, the "Party of the Revolution") after merging with the single party on Tanzania's mainland, the Tanganyika African National Union (TANU). From 1964 to the mid-1980s, the state and its repressive security apparatus controlled most channels of expression, suppressing narratives of the revolution that could compete with the state's official story. Not only was history banned in schools, but several pro-government publications and Kiswahili novels (Myers 2000) were made required readings to impart pupils with a partisan version of history.

The official injunction calling for silence did not, however, induce a forgetting of the past in the isles. The murky period of the revolution could not be referred to in the open, but it was clandestinely talked about within circles of close acquaintances, leading to the transmission of fragments of individual, familial, and community memories within intimate networks. The political democratization in the mid-1990s, however, led to the not-so-secret topic of the revolution being discussed publicly in newspapers, on street corners, and in open forums. Although still addressed with caution, as a consequence of self-censorship adopted in the face of state control, the dark past has resurfaced (Fouéré 2012b). The revolution has been politicized mainly in the political struggle between the incumbent CCM party and the main opposition party, the Civic United Front (CUF). Its opponents connect CUF to the former Zanzibar Nationalist Party (ZNP), overthrown by the revolutionaries, which had the support of most Arabs in pre-revolutionary Zanzibar. CUF is sometimes accused of planning to restore the Omani sultanate and institute an Islamic republic (Glassman 2011: 285) or even of plotting, in case of an electoral victory, the massacre of people of African descent (Bakari 2011: 279).

Africa Addio in Contemporary Zanzibar

In this tense political context, where belonging has been essentialized and equated with binary political loyalties (Arabs versus Africans rhetorically paralleling CCM versus CUF), a new vocabulary has developed within circles of political activists who are heir to the ZNP political party and/or among the victims of the revolution. It qualifies the revolution as an "ethnic cleansing" or "genocide" and defines the overthrow of the regime as an "invasion" of mainlanders. These terms appear in some printed publications about the politics and history of Zanzibar produced since the mid-1990s (Fouéré 2012a). They also appear in the passage from *Africa Addio* featuring the revolution in Zanzibar that was extracted from the original Italian documentary and posted on YouTube in several different edited versions. One such version, put online under the title of *The Untold Massacre* and edited by a production house identified as Sheep 2012 Production,[3] was very likely made by a descendant of a victim of the revolution, as it bears the following notation: "This video is dedicated to my grandfather who managed to escape this bloody massacre." The overdramatic violin orchestra soundtrack of the movie *Requiem for a Dream* (2000) was added to it. Several intertitles with stationary text were inserted into the filmed sequence to add comments that convey palpable emotion: "A horrific event occurred in Zanzibar"; "an ethnic clensing [sic] event that target [sic] Muslims and Arabs"; "Some escaped... Some buried alive...

---

3   http://www.youtube.com/watch?v=4lpY8_mKvjk (posted on 13 August 2008; still accessible on 14 November 2016).

Some raped in front of their husbands... ." One of these title cards takes a position in the debate about the number of deaths, asserting that "over 10,000 Muslims and Arabs" were killed. The last intertitles, presented as the video's epilogue, emphasize the profound sense of grievance felt by the person or people who edited the video. They bitterly condemn the silence that has surrounded these massacres, saying "Have you learnt about this in schools? On TV? In books? No Media Coverage." The international powers are blamed for closing their eyes, and it is even suggested that they were implicated in these events: "No U.N. backed resolution... Where was the United Nations? [...] Why were the war criminals never been brought [sic] to Justice? Why did Britain supply those Africans with weapons?" In another YouTube version, edited as a photomontage,[4] Carl Orff's *Carmina Burana* backs a series of macabre snapshots that concludes with the following comment in Arabic: "After this massacre, Zanzibar has become the poorest country in the world. No money, no freedom, no peace nor justice and democracy; and obscurantism has become pervasive."

The people who mentioned *Africa Addio* to me in 2008 belonged to the urban educated elite I was interviewing during the early steps of my fieldwork on the 1964 revolution. My initial aim was to collect family memories in order to capture variations between communities and generations. The first person to cite the documentary was an educated Zanzibari in his 30s who had worked as a research assistant for various outside researchers, had graduated from university, had traveled abroad, and was a CUF sympathizer (though not an active member of the party). He concluded our discussion by saying, "You really want to know what happened during the revolution? Then I must lend you a copy of this documentary shot from a helicopter and showing Arab mass graves." After this first occurrence, *Africa Addio* was regularly and spontaneously mentioned by people I interviewed. Its centrality in discussions showed that it was impossible to limit research to orally transmitted memories, as oral transmissions clearly intersect with written and visual material in reconstructions of the past. Yet the ethnographic material presented here reflects a specific viewership made up of urban, educated, computer-literate, middle-aged men residing or working in Stone Town and its close vicinity, who constituted my primary interlocutors. Most of them were well disposed to—or even have strong allegiance with—the

---

[4] http://www.youtube.com/watch?v=Ycr3WRelbC8 (posted on 17 February 2010, still accessible on 14 November 2016).

CUF opposition party and are therefore critical of the official story of the revolution promoted by the ruling CCM party. Many brought up the past government restriction on the circulation of *Africa Addio*. As a Zanzibari man of Asian origin in his early 50s put it while looking for a CD of the movie he thought he had kept at home but never managed to retrieve: "I remember seeing it in color, of good quality, not like this YouTube version; there was an Asian guy, he has an Internet café nearby, who kept copies of the documentary. You should try to talk to him, though I doubt he would confirm he had them, because he may think you are a spy of the government." The government restriction on the circulation of the documentary may add to the film's appearance of authenticity: Today, many Zanzibaris see the ban as indicative that the film contains certain truths that the government may prefer to hide. If watching *Africa Addio* is often prompted by curiosity, it generally brings about perplexity, puzzlement, disturbance, or even distress. This emotional entanglement propels some of those who have seen the film to undertake a quest to seek out sources of historical understanding, as the life history of Salim[5] will now illustrate.

Salim and *Africa Addio*

Salim is a married man in his early 40s. He first went to school in Zanzibar and then continued his education on the Tanzanian mainland, where he earned a master's degree. When we met for the first time, he was a government officer. Born right after the revolution to a mother of mixed Afro-Arab descent and an African father, Salim does not have any personal memories of this historical event, but only, as he insisted, a "blurred understanding" built upon accounts of others, mostly within his family. However, neither his father nor his mother ever spoke to him about the events of the revolution. His father was an army soldier whom Salim describes as an austere and inflexible man who rarely recounted his past at home. Salim remembers that when directly faced with his children's questions about the revolutionary times, his father would always remain elusive or simply refuse to answer. Today, Salim suspects this reticence was because his father participated in the revolution and killed people. His mother, only briefly mentioned by Salim, never talked about Zanzibar's dark past at home, apparently because she was afraid of her husband.

---

5   All names used in this paper are pseudonyms.

It was from his light-skinned maternal grandmother, a woman of Arab origin who in early 1964 lived in the city recently occupied by the revolutionaries, that Salim heard about the revolution when he was still a young man. On several occasions, he recounts, she explained to him how she had to hide from the revolutionaries, who were forcing their way into houses in search for people of Arab origin. She only managed to avoid the slaughter because she was a member of the ASP—the party that claimed to have organized the revolution—and could show her party membership card when the revolutionaries gained entrance to her house. But from the top windows of her multistory dwelling, she witnessed the looting of shops and the murder of people in the streets during the most intense days of the revolution. Salim also recalls two of his uncles telling him about the revolution when he was in his teenage years. One of them, a fisherman, recounted several times how he had taken advantage of the general disorder of the revolution to loot shops after the revolutionaries had left the premises. Salim also remembers his other uncle, his father's brother and also an army officer, mocking the revolution, describing it as "just a big mess" but unwilling to go into detail about why he called it so.

Salim insists that, apart from these evasive and fragmentary family testimonies, he does not know much about the history of the isles because history was not taught at school. Official versions of the revolution were pervasive, and everyday discussions were controlled by the state, as explained above. Except from his family, therefore, other channels of historical knowledge were not accessible to Salim. But when he was in his 30s, a friend of his who lived in London recommended that he watch a documentary he had then never heard about, *Africa Addio*. After several months, he managed clandestinely to obtain a DVD copy and watch it. As he tells me, the screening "was a total shock," for he had never heard about the mass killings and mass graves of the revolution. He describes several scenes that left him aghast: long lines of prisoners seemingly walking to their deaths guarded by armed men, mass graves containing dead bodies and even people about to be buried alive, and corpses scattered on the beach after people allegedly tried to escape the islands by boat. After watching the DVD, Salim embarked on an active quest for historical knowledge. He gathered information from the Internet, especially on the different waves of migration to the islands, seeking to cross-check this material with what *Africa Addio*'s images of the revolutionary massacres implied about the intensity of racial divisions. Yet given that (according to him) he could not find any satisfactory and useful data, he decided to confront some members of his family with scenes from *Africa Addio*.

He watched the sequence of the documentary featuring the Zanzibari revolution with his uncle in an attempt to compare it with his uncle's testimony, insisting that, even though his uncle had been an army officer, the trust and mutual appreciation that had developed between them led him to expect some sincere answers. The uncle viewed the documentary with skepticism, quickly asserting that the images did not correspond to anything he had seen or heard about; moreover, he asserted, the scenes featured in the film were unquestionably staged. For instance, the white clothes of the Muslim captives shown walking to their deaths were too clean and white; in actuality, they would have been stained with blood or dirt. Moreover, too many people in the film were portrayed as wearing Muslim dress, whereas in Zanzibar in 1964 such garments were typically only worn on Fridays or special occasions. And all the victims wore Muslim caps on their heads, while most people would have lost them in the jostling and scramble unleashed by the revolutionary uprising. To Salim, the questions raised by a witness to these events did not simply amount to a cross-checking of words and images but also enabled him to look for further evidence and clues that could help him decide how much credit to give to *Africa Addio*—testing the authenticity and authority of the document as an archive on which to found his historical quest.

Investigating the Past?

I have presented the case of Salim's historical quest in detail because it illustrates the searching-for-the-truth motive adopted by many educated urban Zanzibaris challenged by *Africa Addio*. They place at the center of their inquiry historical clues and traces that they think could help discriminate the authentic from the counterfeit and draw the line between the truthful and the fictional, if not between forgery and falsification. Yet, like all my interlocutors, Salim did not reach any satisfactory or definitive conclusion. To him, none of the pieces of evidence scrutinized could testify to the film's authenticity, and Salim eventually admitted that he had to suspend his investigation on the status of the Zanzibari scenes of *Africa Addio* for lack of proof. This difficulty or even failure to authenticate the film echoes the Mondo aficionado Kilgore's remark that sounds like a warning even today: "No one has ever come forth with an article saying this film has been staged, that these events didn't really happen the way they are presented. If they did stage it, they were far more masterful at staging it than anything they staged in the two Mondo Cane films, where a lot of the segments appear staged" (1995: 120).

Undeniably, the *intentio lectoris* of *Africa Addio* among Zanzibaris largely exceeds the *intentio autoris* of the filmmakers. In any intellectual production, the meaning sought by the author indeed never "inscribes itself in an immediate and transparent way, without resistance or deviation in the mind of its readers" (Chartier 1985: 82). Yet beyond the intrinsic multivocal character of any intellectual production, this discrepancy between the production and the reception of the documentary in Zanzibar today is the product of several related factors. On the one hand, Jacopetti and Prosperi did not provide an explicit protocol—whether on or off the screen—that could guide the reading of *Africa Addio*. Contrary to "parafictioneering" artists discussed by Lambert-Beatty (2009), who eventually disclose the parafictional nature of their artwork, *Africa Addio*'s moviemakers always insisted that they were dedicated to the pursuit of historical facts and truth. Also considering that the targeted audience of *Africa Addio*, as of all the Mondo films, was the western public of the 1960s, the visual, aesthetic, and formal codes used in the documentary do not necessarily resound in the same way among an African audience in the 21st century. Moreover, the current circulation of the Zanzibari part of *Africa Addio* through the Internet contributes to the construction of meanings that depart from those projected by the directors. As seen above, the YouTube versions focusing on the Zanzibar revolution have been abstracted from the original documentary and presented as if they can stand on their own; they have been reworked, with dramatic soundtracks and comments added that implicitly validate the authenticity of the images and explicitly aim at directing the viewer's interpretation in a way congruent with oppositional historical scripts of the revolution—unsurprising, given that one may assume that the authors of these reedited versions are those who were themselves dispossessed or dislocated by the revolution or their children.

On the other hand, oral memories or written texts used to engage with *Africa Addio*'s footage of the revolution provide no firm ground to qualify or disqualify the documentary and to determine its archivability, in the sense defined by Achille Mbembe (2002) and by Appadurai (2003). For, as mentioned earlier, there is no consensual and homogeneous memory of the revolution, but rather a collection of fragmented and competing memories that say one thing and its opposite (Loimeier

2000; Myers 2000).⁶ And neither is there any in-depth historiography for building consensus on historical understanding. As historian G. Thomas Burgess reminds us, "No text speaks with an authority to all islanders about their past" (2009: 7). This lack of reliable and readily accessible sources explains why Zanzibaris are eager to delve into their past but quickly realize the difficulty of reaching a full and conclusive understanding of it. Lastly, and as mentioned above, the historical conditions in which this documentary is being circulated today are characterized by the recasting and politicization of essentialized racial categories that profoundly shape today's reception of the film.

In view of the various factors affecting how *Africa Addio* is taken up by its Zanzibari audience, it is not surprising to see people navigate between two extreme positions—one that gives full credit to the film as an original archive to be used to understand the anatomy of atrocity and another that conforms to revisionist narratives that minimize, sometimes even refute, the scope of the massacres. None of those interrogated who discredited the truthfulness of *Africa Addio*, however, ever suggested that a faux or a partly fictionalized document could produce plausibility—as in the case of a parafictional work of art (Lambert-Beatty 2009)—by hinting at the real facts lying behind the images rather than (re)presenting them; when they characterized the documentary as a faux, they rejected it as a lie. Interestingly, how *Africa Addio* is appropriated today by Zanzibaris seems to go against new patterns of disjuncture between location, community, and memory prompted by the new media, whereby, as Appadurai argues, the electronic document "denaturalizes the relationship of memory and the archive." On the contrary, in our case, the media reinforce this link by prompting reflections on the "way in which traces and documents should be formed into archives" (2003: 17). It is instructive, in this regard, to see that a recent publication by a prominent scholar, Ibrahim Noor Shariff, entitled *Tanzania na propaganda za udini* ("Tanzania and Religious Propaganda"), uses some extracts of the movie as historical evidence about the religious and racial divide in Zanzibar (Shariff 2014: 75–81). Written in Kiswahili and available in the main bookshop of

---

6   Only witnesses of or participants in the revolution are able to evaluate *Africa Addio*'s images with reference to their own experiences. Yet when I showed the documentary to a group of revolutionaries, now in their 70s—some of whom had seen it when it was released in the mid-1960s, while others attested they did not know about it—they asserted that they had not seen such mass graves in Zanzibar, or bodies scattered on the beach, during or after the revolution. They characterized the documentary as fake and fictional (23 October 2013).

Stone Town, this book may contribute to the further dissemination of the images of the documentary among the urban literati of Zanzibar by presenting *Africa Addio* as an authentic and legitimate source of historical information.

Utopian Zanzibar

"Africa Addio still exists, it is still relevant today." When Gualtiero Jacopetti uttered these words, he had in mind that the documentary, as a "picture of the agony" of Africa, bespeaks the ugly face of endless conflicts, with their primitive violence, their lawless mercenaries, and their brutal deaths (Goodall 2006: 104). He may not have imagined that *Africa Addio* could radically move beyond the initial intentions of its creators. They aimed to produce a testimony about decolonization that would at the same time constitute evidence of the repetition of a history of violence and death in Africa; yet the film is now being used by the very subjects of the movie to precisely break away from such history, at least intellectually. For, like people elsewhere, Africans "have always sought to master their past, have had their own historic discourses which render and interpret the facts of the past, placing them in an explicative and aesthetic frame producing the sense of their past" (Mudimbe and Jewsiewicki 1993: 3–4).

Yet the homespun use of *Africa Addio* and its constitution or rejection as a heuristic historical device does not look back simply at the past but also at the present and toward the future. In the case of Salim, it is his own family story, his mixed-blood descent, the complicated relationship between his African father, imbued with the revolutionary ideology, and his matrilineal side, with people of Arab origin, that Salim is trying to read again, in order to rethink his identity and position in Zanzibari society. More broadly, it is his conception of what Zanzibari society should be as a moral community that is projected onto his historical inquiry. Salim now defends the idea that the cosmopolitan and creolized identity of the isles should be foregrounded, instead of turning a blind eye to it as the state has been doing for years. Against the aesthetics of hatred and race of *Africa Addio*, he imagines a pacified Zanzibar as a peaceful melting pot of races, where Arabness and Africanness would be subsumed under the common denominator of Zanzibariness. This utopian polity resonates nostalgically with rosy colonial descriptions of Zanzibar as an idyllic archipelago inhabited by people from various horizons peacefully blended (Bissell 2005). Imagined futures emerge out of efforts to forge a historical continuity that erases the revolution as a moment of radical rupture, even though it remains an epochal, politically charged event. Salim's trajectory of historical consciousness and political subjectivity illustrates an emergent trend in the imagination of what today's body politic should ideally be. Ironically, it is this very social utopia that was said to be the driving force under the revolutionary efforts to liberate islanders from a colonial system of class exploitation and establish a "society of tolerance and mutual respect" (Burgess 2009: 3–4).

The introduction of *Africa Addio* into debates about the past and present in Zanzibar is undeniably the result of a certain state of technology characterized by the manipulation and circulation of electronic documents through the Internet. Through websites and storage sites, the archive is indeed expanded and "gradually freed of the orbit of the state and its official network" (Appadurai 2003: 17). Yet, although the material conditions of knowledge are a prerequisite to understanding access to knowledge and its circulation, the centrality of this pseudo-documentary in today's local historical investigation cannot be explained outside of the political realm or without considering broader ongoing discussions about the past, first muffled by the state but coming into the open since the 1990s. *Africa Addio* is therefore appropriated at this specific moment of history because of its availability, but also as one piece of evidence among others, whether first- or secondhand, that Zanzibaris knit together to produce narratives about their past. As Stuart Hall asserts, "Constituting an archive ... occurs at the moment when a relatively random collection of works, whose movement appears to be propelled from one creative production to the next, is at the point of becoming something more ordered and considered: an object of reflection and debate" (2001: 89).

References

Anderson, Benedict
1983 *Imagined Communities: Reflections on the Origin and Spread of Nationalism.* London and New York: Verso.

Appadurai, Arjun
2003 "Archive and Aspiration." In *Information is Alive,* ed. J. Brouwer and A. Mulder, 14–25. Rotterdam: V2_/NAi Publishers.

Bakari, Mohammed
2001 *The Democratisation Process in Zanzibar: A Retarded Transition.* Hamburg: Institut für Afrika-Kunde.

Bandel, F.
2005 "Das Malheur: Kongo-Müller und die Proteste gegen 'Africa Addio,'" *iz3w* 287: 37–41.

Bissell, William Cunningham
2005 "Engaging Colonial Nostalgia." *Cultural Anthropology* 20(2): 215–48.

Burgess, G. Thomas
2009 *Race, Revolution, and the Struggle for Human Rights in Zanzibar: The Memoirs of Ali Sultan Issa and Seif Sharif Hamad.* Athens, Ohio: Ohio University Press.

Chakrabarty, Dipesh
2009 "Bourgeois Categories Made Global: Utopian and Actual Lives of Historical Documents in India." *Economic and Political Weekly* 44(25): 67–75.

Chartier, Roger
1985 *Pratiques de la lecture.* Paris: Payot & Rivages.

Clayton, Anthony
1981 *The Zanzibari Revolution and Its Aftermath.* London: C. Hurst & Company.

Cohen, John
1966 *Africa Addio.* New York: Ballantine.

Derrida, Jacques
1996 *Archive Fever: A Freudian Impression*. Chicago: University of Chicago Press.

Ebert, Roger
1967 Review of *Africa Addio*. *Chicago Sun-Times*, 25 April.

Fouéré, Marie-Aude
2016 "Film as Archive: Africa Addio and the Ambiguities of Remembrance in Zanzibar." *Social Anthropology/Anthropologie Sociale* 24(1): 82–96.
2012a "Remembering the Dark Years (1964–1975) in Zanzibar." *Encounters: The International Journal for the Study of Culture and Society* 5: 113–26.
2012b "Reinterpreting Revolutionary Zanzibar in the Media Today: The Case of *Dira* Newspaper." *Journal of Eastern African Studies* 6(4): 672–89.

Glassman, Jonathon
2011 *War of Words, War of Stones: Racial Thought and Violence in Colonial Zanzibar*. Bloomington, Ind.: Indiana University Press.

Goodall, Mark
2013 "Dolce e Selvaggio: Italian Mondo Documentary Films." In *Popular Italian Cinema*, ed. L. Bayman and S. Rigoletto, 226–39. New York: Palgrave Macmillan.
2006 *Sweet & Savage: The World through the Shockumentary Film Lens*. London: Headpress.

David, Gregory, dir.
2003 *The Godfathers of Mondo*. Blue Underground. 90 min. DVD.

Habermas, Jürgen
1989 *The Structural Transformation of the Public Sphere: An Inquiry into a Category of Bourgeois Society*, trans. T. Burger. Cambridge, Mass.: MIT Press.

Halbwachs, Maurice
1997 *La mémoire collective*. Paris: Albin Michel.

Hall, Stuart
2001 "Constituting an Archive." *Third Text* 15(54): 89–92.

Jacopetti, Gualtiero, and Franco Prosperi, dirs.
1966 *Africa Addio,* prod. Angelo Rizzoli. Italy: Blue Underground. 128 min. DVD.

Kilgore, Charles, ed.
1988 "Mondo Movies." *Ecco: The World of Bizarre Video* 1(2), 3–7.

Lambert-Beatty, Carrie
2009 "Make-Believe: Parafiction and Plausibility." *October* 129: 51–84.

Lofchie, Michael F.
1965 *Zanzibar: Background to Revolution.* Princeton, N.J.: Princeton University Press.

Loimeier, Roman
2007 "Sit Local, Think Global: The Baraza in Zanzibar." *Journal for Islamic Studies* 27: 16–38.
2006 "Memories of Revolution: Zur Deutungsgeschichte einer Revolution (Sansibar 1964)." *Afrika Spectrum* 41(2): 175–97.

Mapuri, Omar R.
1996 *Zanzibar: The 1964 Revolution: Achievements and Prospects.* Dar es Salaam: TEMA Publishers.

Mbembe, Achille
2002 "The Power of the Archive and Its Limits." In *Refiguring the Archive,* ed. Carolyn Hamilton et al., 19–26. Dordrecht: Kluwer.

Mudimbe, V. Y., and B. Jewsiewicki
1993 "Africans' Memories and Contemporary History of Africa." *History and Theory* 32(4): 1–11.

Myers, Garth A.
2000 "Narrative Representations of Revolutionary Zanzibar." *Journal of Historical Geography* 26(3): 429–48.

Nora, Pierre
1984–1987 *Les lieux de mémoire.* Paris: Gallimard.

Okello, John
1967 *Revolution in Zanzibar.* Nairobi: East African Publishing House.

Ricoeur, Paul

2000 *La mémoire, l'histoire, l'oubli.* Paris: Éditions du Seuil.

Shariff, Ibrahim Noor

2014 *Tanzania na propaganda za udini.* N.p.: Self-published.

Shipka, D. G.

2007 "Perverse Titillation: A History of European Exploitation Films 1960–1980." Ph.D. diss., University of Florida.

Shivji, Issa

2008 *Pan-Africanism or Pragmatism? Lessons of Tanganyika-Zanzibar Union.* Dar es Salaam: Mkuki na Nyota.

Staples, Amy J., and Charles Kilgore

1995 "An Interview with Dr. Mondo." *American Anthropologist* New Series 97(1), 110–25.

Chapter Eleven

Healing the Past, Reinventing the Present: From the Revolution to *Maridhiano*

Ahmed Rajab

> But while I own history,
> it owns me; it illumines me.
> But what use is such a light?
> —PIER PAOLO PASOLINI, *The Ashes of Gramsci*

January is a cruel month in Zanzibar. The temperatures are unbearably high, it's muggy, and the humidity too stifling. The elements bog one down, forcing even hyperactive beings to behave as if they are in a drunken stupor. Which is probably what must have happened to some members of Zanzibar's newly independent government on the cusp of the revolution that ousted the sultanate on 12 January 1964.

My day had started slightly late with the cawing of the crows and a distant sound of gunfire. It was at least two or three hours after the first sounds of the neighborhood's strutting cocks.

The momentous events are still etched in my mind, as are two of the previous evening's memorable happenings. One was a society wedding of Tewa Saidi Tewa, a Tanganyikan minister, to a Zanzibari bride. The groom was a member of a government that was hugely sympathetic to the opposition Afro-Shirazi Party (ASP) in Zanzibar while the bride was identified with the ruling circles.

She was a sophisticated British-trained nurse who upon her return to Zanzibar had entered the coterie of Zanzibar's upper class, albeit in its decline. The wedding was much talked about among the Zanzibari beau monde since the bride was a socialite whose reputation of being "too British" intimidated most of her local prospective suitors. Her wedding to an outsider from Tanganyika was, perhaps, the only way for her to escape the quagmire of her constrictive society. The wedding reception was planned to be held at the Karimjee Jivanjee Hall, near Mnazi Mmoja. (The hall housed the House of Representatives, the isles' legislature, until 2012.) The reception went ahead without the groom, who most likely was tipped off about the impending onslaught against the government.

The second event, which turned out to be of more significance, was a fete and dance organized by plebeians in the Raha Leo area, whose habitués were mostly the downtrodden of society. We now know that that particular function was a ruse to divert attention from what would ensue a few hours after midnight. Most of those who attended the event would take up arms against the government later that night. Much of the population was oblivious to the initial salvos—the storming of the police armory in the darkness of the night and the first blows against a government that had only a few hours left of its shelf-life.

And so it was that just before the outbreak of dawn on that muggy Sunday, the first calls of the muezzin were accompanied by a staccato of gunfire. Although it was too early, many of the faithful emerging out of mosques after the *fajr* (dawn) prayers were convinced that the police were at it again—using their guns to cull the growing population of crows, always a troublesome presence in urban Zanzibar.

Those dwelling in urban and peri-urban areas were caught unawares and could not have associated the sound of gunfire with the government's imminent collapse. By daybreak it was clear that the government was already into its long sleep. And if anyone had any doubts, these were dispelled by mid-morning, when a macabre announcement over the government radio station pronounced its death as well as that of the sultanate.

A self-styled "Field Marshal," John Okello, an unknown 27-year-old Ugandan mason, had made the earth-shaking pronouncement in halting Kiswahili over Sauti ya Unguja (The Voice of Zanzibar), the government's radio station. I can still recall how Okello's proclamation and his subsequent tirades, delivered in a gravelly voice, instilled fear in the population. These were reinforced by the grotesque, almost Kafka-esque, announcements of punishments he decreed against supporters of the ousted government, mostly Arabs. Okello's thick, upcountry-accented Kiswahili immediately identified him as an outsider, a non-Zanzibari, which later gave credence to the widely held view that he was a "front" for the Zanzibaris who planned and executed the revolution (Grimstad, this volume; Okello 1967; Lofchie 1967).

The rape and massacre of Zanzibaris of Arab or supposed Arab origin, as well as of those of Asian ancestry, began almost immediately

(Haj 2001). Most of the victims met their fate in the rural areas.[1] Few were killed in the periurban areas of Ng'ambo, and the number of those killed in Stone Town was small. The insurrectionists apparently believed—wrongly it seems—that there was an abundance of arms in Stone Town belonging to wealthy Arabs, some of whom passed their weekends hunting wild pigs. There is no record of anyone being killed in Pemba.[2] However, the exact number of people who were massacred during the first three days of the revolution, when most of the killings took place, remains unknown and is a subject of much controversy.[3]

Not that individual ministers were not apprised that their government would soon come a cropper, because news of the impending revolution had leaked in conformity with the sieve-like nature of Zanzibari society. Indeed, one of the ministers, Maulid Mshangama Haj, recalls in his autographical novel that on the afternoon of 11 January his driver informed him of the rumors about the impending coup (Haj 2001: 9). The ministers, however, dismissed the rumors as far-fetched. "This government is not like a saucer that can be turned over," intoned one.

One cannot say that the former ministers were touched by the sun, but their reaction was indicative of their collective disdain for those most likely to oust their government. But who were the insurrectionists, when did they start plotting, and what drove them to take such a bloody course of action? These are some of the questions that today's generation of Zanzibaris are trying to unravel as they try to make sense of the revolution.

In fact, they are equally vexed about the true nature of the revolution itself—whether it was a classic response by the downtrodden class to

---

1 A few of the Arabs (*Wamanga* as well as *Washihiri*) who were killed were, in fact, members of the ASP, according to "Mzee Selemani," a self-identified participant in the revolution, quoted in Ghassany (2010: 90). Mzee Selemani maintained that Arabs who were ASP members were killed by Makonde tribesmen from Tanganyika who were brought to Zanzibar to participate in the revolution. This was also attested to by another insurrectionist, Mzee Ahmed Othman Aboud (Aboud Mmasai) (Ghassany 2010:158).

2 "The extreme violence following the revolution of 1964 was heavily concentrated on Zanzibar [Unguja], while Arab and Shirazi landowners on Pemba maintained relatively peaceful relationships due to a history of intermarriage and communal relationships" (Mullins 2013).

3 This continues to be one of the problematics of "remembering" the revolution whose resolution is necessary for healing the past. The number varies from 3,000 to a high of 24,000. Abdulrahman Babu, in an interview with the BBC Swahili Service in the 1990s, maintained those killed were fewer than 150. When questioned by this writer, he claimed that he got the figure from the Red Cross in Zanzibar during the first few days of the revolution. He wrote elsewhere that the "real casualty figure was minimal"; see Babu 1991 and also Fairooz 1995.

oppression by a landed class or, rather, an *accidental* revolution brought about by a collision and concoction of random factors. The collision between race and class, tensions between landowners and African mainland laborers, the first post-colonial government's palpable bias against police officers recruited from Tanganyika and Kenya, and the widely held perception among members of the opposition ASP that the government was reinforcing the colonial myth of Zanzibar being an "Arab State" (Bennett 1978)—all these factors conspired toward the revolution (Lofchie 1965; Sheriff 2001; Mullins 2013).

This medley of factors, reported to them by disjointed or contradictory and contested memories, has befuddled the new generation of Zanzibaris. As a result, they cannot make sense of—or they find it difficult to come to terms with—the events of the revolution. Their predicament has been compounded by the myths surrounding the events as well as by the rewriting of Zanzibar's recent history by Tanzania's ruling establishment as well as by opponents of the revolution.[4] The former narratives constitute the victor's history. Although they contain some factual accounts of events, they are not averse to misconceptions, as is likewise the case with the latter narratives.

The past has, thus, become a highly disputed space in which the revolution has been entangled in contested histories and social debates. The new generation of Zanzibaris access the past mostly through the avenue of memories of their elders, but these have oftentimes proved to be conjectural, with varying degrees of unreliability and dubious interpretation. Those who claim to "remember" history cannot agree on even some of the most basic facts about the revolution.

Deconstructing Memories

Some of the new generation, in trying to make sense of what happened, have penned books drawing on oral history based on the memories of participants or witnesses of the revolution or on key episodes of the revolution. Oral narratives may democratize the gathering of history, but oral history has its limitations and inherent weaknesses as a reliable witness to past events (Jeffrey and Edwall 1994). It is so because in oral history one carries too much baggage. One relies on people's memories (which can be selective and faulty) and prejudices not only of ideology but also flaws introduced by the lapse of time. Events or remarks may be misreported, taken out of context, or "remembered" differently

---

[4] Compare, for example, Omar R. Mapuri's *The 1964 Revolution* (1996) with the counter-narratives of Issa Nasser al-Ismaily's *Zanzibar: Kinyang'anyiro na Utumwa* (1999).

by different people. It therefore becomes well nigh impossible to deconstruct those memories and prejudices.[5]

Oral narratives are thus not without blemishes, and those on the Zanzibar revolution have turned out to be galumphing *parti pris*. A recent and good example is Harith Ghassany's *Kwaheri Ukoloni, Kwaheri Uhuru! (Goodbye Colonialism, Goodbye Independence!* 2010), which, according to the author, seeks to refute many of the myths of the revolution. Clearly Ghassany revels in his role as a myth-buster, but his account is handicapped by his reliance on other myths, such as the one that portrays pre-revolution Zanzibari society as an idyllic—indeed paradisiacal—one where people of all races lived together harmoniously without any strife. That surely is a folkloric reading of a society that was racially stratified and in which everyone knew his/her place. The entire relationship between the races was a charade (Glassman 2011).

If it was not a façade of racial bonhomie, how does one explain the latent animus between Zanzibaris who trace their ancestry to South Yemen (the *Washihiri*) and those who trace their lineage to Oman (the *Wamanga*), which erupted into the so-called *vita vya Wamanga na Washihiri* (the war between *Wamanga* and *Washihiri*), which in 1928 pitted Omani Arabs against Hadhramis?[6] Fighting between the *Washihiri* and the *Wamanga* "continued intermittently for four days and four persons were killed and some thirty wounded" (Ingrams 1943: 45).[7] Or how does one explain the rivalry between Omani Arabs and Comorians or the fact that Zanzibaris of Shirazi origin (the so-called *Waswahili*) were at the bottom of the pile, only above recent immigrants from mainland Africa? Or why the 1961 political riots quickly took on racial overtones when supporters of the Afro-Shirazi Party targeted Manga Arabs for attacks (Glassman 2011)? Or indeed why the revolution itself, which, but for the initial few months until the April 1964 union with Tanganyika, had decidedly racist undercurrents?

Zanzibar's much touted racial amity was, in fact, a mythical nonsense. The social structure benefited only a certain strata of the population. Africans were classified and treated as the "Other." To be blunt, African

---

5 For a philosophical meditation on the problems of memory and recollection, see French philosopher Paul Ricoeur in *Memory, History, Forgetting* (2004).

6 Both categories of Arabs were considered immigrants and were a butt of jokes by Zanzibar-born Arabs.

7 The chief ringleader of the *Washihiri*, Nasir bin Abdulla al Kathiri, was deported along with others. He went to Java, Indonesia, and in 1934 returned to the Hadhramaut in Yemen (Ingrams 1943: 45).

nationalists believed that Arabs or Arab-identified individuals controlled things, to the detriment of "Africans." It was not the case, they surmised, that Zanzibaris lived as one happy family or in a civilized cocoon. In this they were partly correct, as Zanzibar was a racially stratified society in which race and class intersected in such a manner that Africans always found themselves at the bottom of the pile.

Pre-revolution Zanzibar was a curious, if not an incongruous, society. It was united by religion, Islam, as much as it was divided by race. Of course, there was no apartheid in Zanzibar as in South Africa, nor did Zanzibar's situation resemble colonial Kenya's racial segregation. Zanzibar was neither racist in structure nor in beliefs. However, racial undercurrents were nevertheless there. These were subtle, almost muted, and were fed on a diet of prejudices. Although Arab men took on African wives, it was extremely rare for an Arab woman to be married to an African, even if the African man was a Muslim. Nor was it easy for a Shirazi woman to be married to a mainlander (Ghassany 2010: 88).

Despite their farcical fixation with their race's supposed supremacy, the so-called Arabs did not engage in a cultural praxis that was singularly or exclusively "Arab," whatever that meant in the Zanzibari context. Only a few of them, for example, could speak Arabic. On the other hand, there were quite a number of non-Arabs whose command of Arabic was flawless, some to the extent of having authored learned religious and literary tomes in Arabic. Most of these were published locally or in Cairo or Beirut.[8]

To compound the complexities of Zanzibar's racial stratification, there were also hierarchies of sorts among the Africans as well as among the Arabs. The landed aristocracy, composed largely of urban-based Arab elites who were connected to the ruling al-Busaidis, were considered, economically and socially, far above the rural-based *Wamanga* and *Washihiri*. The *Washihiri* occupied lowly positions as laborers, coolies, stevedores, private servants, fishermen, small shopkeepers, water carriers, and coffee sellers. Others dealt in the shark and dried-fish products of their native Shihr (Ingrams 1943: 44–5). According to Ingrams, at one time they "owned shambas of cloves and coconuts and much house property in Zanzibar town," but by the 1940s they had lost most of the properties to the Indians (ibid.: 45). Over time, however, the Indian merchants replaced the so-called Arab aristocracy as a dominant

---

8   Two of these are Sheikh Burhan Muhammad Mkelle and Sheikh Hassan bin Ameir bin Mazi bin Haji bin Khatib al Shirazy (1880–1979).

economic force. Indeed, most Arab landowners were indebted to members of the Indian capitalist class (Bader 1991).

Nor did it matter what color or physical features one had, because in Zanzibar's maddening racial mix there are Arabs who look more African and Africans who look more Arab. This is more true on Pemba island, where the population is much more ethnically mixed than on Unguja (Middleton 1961; Mullins 2013: 29). However, Zanzibaris themselves know who is who, despite the mixing of different histories and the so-called "postmodern" attributes of fluid and multiple identities of those who can lay claim to them. This is very much in line with the view that "[i]dentity, tradition and indigenization only make sense contextually" (Robertson 1992: 130).

The nuances of racial stratification and the subtle distinctions between the races in the pecking order were, however demeaning to the victims, as they were to the perpetrators. The so-called Revolutionary Government tried to erase the historical role of the vanquished from its version of history. The participation in the revolution, for example, of those not considered African or "African enough" has been brushed away from the official history. The erasure has continued in the official narrative of the revolution up to the present and is part of the lingering racism of the ruling class. The revolution turned Zanzibar into a country where saying that someone had "Arab" ancestry was akin to a form of slander.

Where one would have expected the fragmentation of identity as a social construct following the revolution—which banned racial associations—"identity" instead metamorphosed into a political construct and has been used by the regime against members of ethnic minorities. The reconstruction was deliberate and systemic, impinging on struggles seeking political recognition and rights, and it explains the marginalization of ethnic minorities in the political sphere. The new rulers fostered the politics of identity and embedded ethnicity in the power structure to buttress their legitimacy and to deny political rights to the minorities.

People of Arab, Comorian, or South Asian ancestry have been routinely excluded from employment in the security apparatuses, for example, as they are viewed as a "security risk."[9] Their inclusion in the upper echelons of government has been minimal.

---

9   A resolution was passed at the first ASP party congress, held in Pemba, following Karume's assassination to exclude minorities from employment in the army and other security organs. This explains why since 1972 no Zanzibaris of Arab origin were employed in the police or the army.

Reinventing the Present

It is hard to correctly remember the revolution because of the counter-discourses that pit the traumatic period against a mythical past, which supposedly ended with the flaring of multiparty politics from the mid-1950s to the early 1960s, the tail-end of the so-called *zama za siasa* ("time of politics"). This sentimental claptrap informs much of the politics of those idealizing the old order, if not the ancien régime.[10]

In fact, opponents of the revolution never fail to recount their bitter experiences during and after the traumatic events. In the process they mourn the loss of a Zanzibar that once was (or the one that refuses to be dislodged from its place in their psyche). They thus run the risk of romanticizing the past since fantasy of memory and of imagination intrudes in their interpretation of history.

It would be foolhardy, however, to dismiss their ruminations as being no more than nostalgia for a lost past. In a very profound sense, the revolution, both as an event and as a process of change over time, remains a part of their lived experience. Precisely because they have never been reconciled to the changes, they use the revolution in an obsessional way as a yardstick for contrasting the present with the past. Most of these microhistorical narratives had been repressed until the mid-1980s as a result of fear and concerns about potential consequences.

However, it would be impossible to unlink from the past without appreciating its socio-historical context. Opponents of the revolution never cease to challenge its political legitimacy and, in the process, to debunk it. This despite the fact that, notwithstanding its microcosmic nature, the 1964 revolution could be compared with other major world events that they would readily endorse, Egypt's Nasserite revolution being a prime example.

"Remembering" the past is not the express preserve only of opponents of the revolution. Almost all Zanzibaris of different political persuasions are fond of remembering it. In fact, they delight in reminiscing about the past. But they all remember differently. Not only do they remember different episodes of the revolution, for example, but they also give different interpretations to even the same episodes. In this sense, it is indeed a pity that the revolution was not televised.[11]

---

10   The word "*siasa*" is borrowed straight from the Arabic "*siyasa*" which in its origins refers to the grooming of horses (Sadiiki 2004).

11   "The Revolution Will Not Be Televised" is one of the best-known recordings of the American jazz and soul poet Gil Scott-Heron (1949–2011).

The Zanzibar revolution, as revolutions are wont to be, was a ragged affair that at times degenerated into settling of scores, paradoxically more personal than political. This, although inexcusable, was hardly surprising, as the dynamics of a revolution can never be coherent or, at times, even logical. However, in the case of the Zanzibar revolution, the trauma that was unleashed by its whimsical rule, which began on that portentous date in January 1964, is far from over and has left its indelible mark on over half a century of Zanzibar's turbulent recent history.

The revolution saw the emergence of an elite that monopolized power without paying any regard to basic democratic principles, which, ironically, the revolution aspired to. High principles of the revolution were betrayed, causing untold miseries and indignities to the people.[12]

This new elite appropriated to itself the "right to rule" through the barrel of the gun and ensured privileged lives for its members, families, and cronies. In a very real way, society was turned upside down. It did not take long for the revolution's declared progressive and revolutionary principles to collapse. The revolution turned racist as the people's fundamental human rights were suppressed unnecessarily.

Extrajudicial killings and disappearances were common during the entire eight-year rule of its first president, Sheikh Abeid Amani Karume, and the main prison at Kiinua Miguu became notorious for torture.[13] One gets uniform responses when one asks people who lived under Karume what they remember of those dark days. They mention "fear of detention without trial," "fear of torture," "members of the dreaded security services," and "long queues" for basic items such as bread, rice, and flour.

Karume's Zanzibar was an island to escape. Zanzibaris, particularly nubile young women scared of forced marriages, risked their lives by escaping in canoes, euphemistically called VC10s after the long-range British airliner of the time.[14] There was no state institution that the

---

12   "The situation was really bad. Karume was killing people, undermining everybody and the economy was in a mess.... The country was ushered into a thirty-year rule of unprecedented brutality and loss of Zanzibari identity." Abdulrahman Babu, quoted in Othman 2001: 49, 77.

13   The situation that prevailed at the time is graphically captured in two novels, Adam Shafi Adam's *Haini* (Traitor) in 2013 and Hashil Seif and Ahmed Faris's *Living under the Shadow of Terror: Zanzibar Caught Off Guard* in 2015. Amnesty International, the human rights organization, issued various statements during the Karume and post-Karume eras cataloguing and condemning detentions without trial, disappearances, and extrajudicial killings in Zanzibar.

14   The incidents were widely reported worldwide. See, for, example, https://www.google.co.tz/?gws_rd=cr,ssl&ei=8eXBVeX4FcW07gbil4qwCQ#q=zanzibar%27s+forced+marriages, accessed 5 September 2016. See also Kjersti Larsen 2008: 29.

people respected or trusted—not the judiciary, not the army, not the police, not the government media. Each was suspected of being biased toward the ruling establishment.

For two decades the number of those who emigrated from Zanzibar exceeded those who ventured to return. In fact, only a handful did return. The route of self-imposed exile led to diverse destinations. Zanzibaris were scattered everywhere, abandoning the place of their identity for the largely unknown.

The victims of the revolution were quick to realize that history can become very cruel out of nothing. Because of the gross human rights violations, terror, economic collapse, and hardships it has become difficult to see history, particularly the revolution, as constant progress.

While even supporters of the regime might, however grudgingly, agree to the list of hardships that the population was subjected to during the revolution, one would not get matching responses from across the political spectrum when one asks about what obtained in the country before the revolution. ASP members remember the pre-revolution days differently from supporters of the fallen regime.

Whether the events of 12 January 1964 qualify to be termed a revolution is a moot point and, in the final analysis, perhaps of lesser importance for the purpose of our discussion. Suffice it to say that we will miss the point if we restrict "revolution" to its outward meaning of "change." The disturbances of the early days of the revolution portended tragedy, as was witnessed in the subsequent societal breakdown in tandem with the physical decay of Stone Town.[15]

Stone Town Memories and National Identity

Zanzibar experienced a swift post-revolution urbanization, as a result of internal migration and natural population-growth rates. Zanzibar city, which traces its origins to the 1690s, had by 1978 a combined urban and peri-urban population of 142,041 people; by 1988, the number was 208,137. According to the 2002 census, 391,000 people were residing in the culturally pluralistic city.

---

15 See the discussion paper by Francesco Siravo, "Zanzibar Stone Town Projects: A Plan for the Historic Stone Town" in which the author writes, "The physical condition of the traditional building stock throughout the town has now reached a critical point, with over eighty-five percent of structures in deteriorating or poor condition. Although these buildings are resilient, their past performance cannot be considered a guarantee of their future endurance." See also *Zanzibar: The Plan for the Historic Stone Town*, published by the Aga Khan Trust for Culture 1996: 97.

The city, which rose into prominence as the "metropolis of the East African coast" following the withdrawal of the Portuguese from the region in the 18th century (Pearce 1920: 181), is divided into two sections: Stone Town, which before the revolution was almost exclusively Arab and Asian,[16] and Ng'ambo (the Other Side), which had an African majority. This division has always reflected Zanzibar city's political divide, with the Ng'ambo area traditionally being a stronghold formerly of the ASP and lately the CCM (Chama cha Mapinduzi).

Zanzibar city's rapid urbanization carried demoralizing consequences. These, coupled with the aftershocks of the post-revolution nationalization of private property, almost all in the Stone Town area, brought their own dynamics of demography and new cultural settings. A massive uprooting of the original or historical Stone Town dwellers happened in tandem with an influx of new residents, mostly from Pemba or from the Ng'ambo area. Five decades after the revolution, with the rehabilitation of old buildings, the return of exiles (albeit in modest numbers), the redesign of the waterfront at Forodhani, and the expansion of the city's limits into new residential neighborhoods, one can say that the city, particularly Stone Town, is in a process of redefining itself, shedding its pre-revolution memories.

Stone Town can now be described only as decidedly Zanzibari. It has shed its former communal memories and moved to embrace a national identity. However, this runs the risk of being diluted by the relative influx of mainlanders, who have set up shops and other businesses in Baghani and Shangani, once the core preserves of the Arab landed aristocracy.[17] The once pluralistic and cosmopolitan part of the city has become relatively more homogeneous, spatially as well as culturally, changing the area's spatio-cultural ecology. Physical and social space has become almost identical. Gone, too, are the streets that were once "inhabited

---

16 At one time, Stone Town was characterized as having a European residential quarter (Pearce 1920: 208).

17 The gradual appearance over the past few decades of Maasai residents and shopkeepers in the once almost exclusively Arab and Asian mansions is derided privately by many with long memories of the social composition of the core areas of Stone Town. They regard the Maasai attire and their presence as being "incongruous" with the decidedly Arab or Asian architecture.

mainly by clock makers, or cobblers or tailors, or hardware merchants"[18] (Ommanney 1955: 41).

It would be interesting to see how far the shift in the population of Stone Town has resulted, if at all, in two dissonant "memories" of the revolution—those of the original inhabitants of Stone Town and those of the post-revolution arrivals. Both sides of the political divide have been using the past selectively and subjectively to promote their own ideological bias. Reinventing the present may necessitate rewriting the past, particularly in the official accounts, by taking a historicized approach to the reconstructions of the past.

Toward *Maridhiano*

Until 2010, Zanzibar was engulfed in a rhythmic but menacing cycle of electoral violence and was veering toward national political paralysis. The idea of reconciliation (*maridhiano*) between CCM and the Civic United Front (CUF), the two major political parties on the isles, was unimaginable. There was no doubt that Zanzibar was in limbo, partly as a result of the contested memories of its inhabitants about the pre-revolution days and what followed. Hitherto, the official CCM line presented pre-revolution Zanzibar as a repressive society in which the Arabs held sway at the expense of the Africans. The CCM narrative wanted people to remember the old Zanzibar as such.

However, there are many in Zanzibar who remember otherwise and who insist that Zanzibar became repressive *after* the revolution. *Maridhiano* offered Zanzibaris the opportunity to confront political orthodoxies of both sides of the political divide. It brought relief as the absence of political bickering was almost palpable. Suddenly, the pre-*maridhiano* tension had dissipated. There prevailed a degree of unity that had not existed since the pre–party politics days of 1957.

The government of national unity that was created under *maridhiano* provided hope to overcome the uncertainty and vulnerability that had threatened Zanzibar's existence as a nation since the promulgation of the union of Tanzania on 26 April 1964. A political modus vivendi of

---

[18] "One whole, gaily coloured little passage is given up to the sale of those brilliant African garments, the printed cotton 'kanga', which the women wear, the more sober 'kikoi', which the men wear like a skirt round the waist, the long white linen 'kanzu' and the round embroidered caps. It is a street of a thousand sewing machines, clicking merrily all day long outside the little shops. In the hardware street venerable old gentlemen, of cunning and Confucian appearance, sit at the entrances to caves which are full, literally, of everything that opens and shuts.... In the street of the clockmakers hundreds of dials proclaim as many different hours" (Ommanney 1955: 41).

sorts was put in place. At last, like a phoenix, Zanzibar had risen from the ashes of its own near-destruction. Or at least it seemed it had. In fact, *maridhiano* has not been able to substantially revise people's views of the revolution, nor has it been able to reconcile the clashing memories. For most part, though, those born after the revolution maintain that since they have no memories of pre-revolution Zanzibar and of the early period of the revolution they simply do not want to be mired in the past.

We have to posit Zanzibari counter-discourses within the space that is occupied by the contrasting poles of politics of identity. This is a space of contestation that bedeviled Zanzibari society from the advent of modern politics in the 1950s and 1960s to the period of multi-party elections before *maridhiano*. The emerging politics of *maridhiano* held the potential of enabling racial identities to be deconstructed and then rebuilt by being fused into a counter-discourse of Zanzibari identity as a homogenized entity. Through this counter-discourse, Zanzibaris, particularly those of the younger generation, could have made the "self" and the "other" indistinguishable. This, however, did not happen. Instead, Zanzibaris have reverted to identifying themselves with their communities, as evidenced by the revival of a number of community associations and of the establishment of tribal associations identified with the mainland.[19]

An opportunity has been missed. Specifically, the authorities could have assisted in the deconstruction of racial identities by, for example, banning racial associations, which could work against the forging of a common Zanzibari identity. In addition, stakeholders, including religious leaders, government authorities, and those involved in the reconciliation process, could have embarked on a robust civic education exercise in reasserting Zanzibari identity. This would not have been a difficult task, because since the adoption of *maridhiano* there has been a serious reassessment by Zanzibaris of their identity as a vehicle for the expression of a truly nonracial and a non-partisan nationalist discourse. This reassessment has become synchronous with a reappraisal of democracy. This, in turn, has already translated into a dynamic of its own: a visceral nationalism that further bonded Zanzibaris together and made them aggressive in asserting their identity. There were signs that their old allegiances to races and political affiliations were at last

---

19 It is common these days to hear death announcements over the Zanzibar Broadcasting Corporation's broadcasts directed to members of particular mainland tribes, such as the Zaramo or Makonde.

beginning to give way to a singular identity more powerful and potent as a force, if not a catalyst, for change.

Consequently, by adopting *maridhiano* the Zanzibari leadership across the political divide, principally former president Amani Abeid Karume and Maalim Seif Sharif Hamad, the CUF secretary-general, tried to "dissolve," as it were, pre- and post-revolution memories. In essence, *maridhiano* sought to resolve longstanding—and seemingly intractable—differences. But how far could *maridhiano*, as an exercise of "forgetting," be used a matrix of reconciliatn in a country that is plagued by internal strife and instability caused by domestic political divisions?

Despite *maridhiano*'s promise, it would be precipitous to suggest that it had finally put to rest Zanzibar's perennial internal problems or that violence would not resurface. The big question is whether Zanzibar can reinvent itself in the face of the onslaught by hardliners on both sides of the political divide who are seemingly keen to continue to use social memory to legitimize their political stances, and for some, even return the isles to the dark days of divisive politics. Hardliners clinging to the nostalgia of pre-revolution Zanzibar deprecate any measures, social or political, taken by the post-revolutionary governments and blame the union government and the ruling CCM for the underdevelopment of the isles. Hardliners within the CCM, on their part, still use social memory to legitimize the revolution and perpetuate the "politics of hate" against those deemed to be "outsiders," which include all Zanzibaris with a non-African ancestry. Images of slavery and of power relations between the Arab landed class and the African farm laborers are invoked to "remind" CCM followers of what necessitated the revolution.[20]

Detractors of the opposition CUF continuously use memory to scare the population by suggesting that CUF has been working for the return of the "Arab" sultan.[21] They also try to scare outsiders, including Christians

---

20 A number of Zanzibari CCM leaders, including Borafya Silima, Baraka Shamte, Seif Idd, Asha Bakari, and indeed Zanzibar's president, Ali Mohamed Shein, have at various times between 2013 and 2015 made public speeches invoking memories of the revolution, which could only be construed as overtly "racist" and as prime examples of hate speeches. Similar statements were made by CCM leaders from the mainland, including Stephen Wasira. This was manifestly evident particularly during the constitutional-making exercise under prime minister and retired judge Joseph Warioba and as the country was nearing the 2015 general elections.

21 During the 2015 electoral campaign, for example, Ambassador Seif Ali Idd, Zanzibar's second vice-president who is considered a hardliner within the CCM, went on record accusing CUF that by demanding full sovereignty for Zanzibar within a union structure they were, in fact, rooting for the return of the sultanate to rule Zanzibar. http://www.zanzinews.com/2015/09/mamlaka-kamili-ni-kumrejesha-sulatn.html#more, accessed 5 September 2016.

in Tanzania, by portraying CUF as an "Islamist" party working for the establishment of an Islamist state in Zanzibar or for the return of the "Arab" sultan or both.[22] Curiously, the identification of CUF with a supposed plan to "bring back the Arabs" finds resonance even among some locals in faraway Kilwa, where CUF is strong (Becker 2007: 285). Its detractors heaped contumely on the CUF for its advocacy of a union that would give back Zanzibar its sovereignty. There was also *froideur* between the CCM/Zanzibar leadership under President Ali Mohamed Shein and the CUF leadership over Tanzania's draft constitution, which was proposed by the Warioba Commission.

That notwithstanding, by a curious trick of fate an interweaving of narratives of political violence and a united stand on the return of Zanzibar's sovereign powers over time bonded ordinary Zanzibaris of different political affiliations. Finally, there was hope for the possible resolution of over half a century of contested history. This found expression even in the decaying physical landscape of Stone Town, where historic buildings were being restored and some nationalized properties reclaimed by their original owners. Urban renewal was underpinned by expectations of deeper social and political changes.

Whither Zanzibar?

In today's Zanzibar, unity, stability, peace and tranquility prevail, but only in relative terms. The high degree of optimism regarding the future of the islands found expression following *maridhiano*. This newfound unity had come quickly, warts and all, simply because many Zanzibaris could no longer accept the high price to be paid if they were to remain disunited. This was happening for the first time since multiparty politics were introduced in 1957, which unleashed a fierce contest between the government and the opposition that continued for decades after. The post-revolution government had treated opposition party members and supporters as enemies of the state. Following the formation of a coalition government, officially the Government of National Unity (GNU), this appeared to have been no longer the case for either the government or the opposition. They had started working together, adopting common policies on major economic and social issues.

---

22 A good example is the 10 September 2015 article by Abdulrahman Kinana, the CCM secretary-general, which appeared in the blog of *The Hill* newspaper in Washington, D.C.: http://thehill.com/blogs/congress-blog/foreign-policy/253142-tanzania-cannot -be-allowed-to-be-the-new-front-for, accessed 5 September 2016.

The ghosts of the past, it was hoped, had at last been put to rest. However, such optimism quickly dissipated following the shenanigans of the October 2015 elections. The brief hiatus in the war of words between the two camps on Zanzibar's political landscape proved to have been a temporary aberration. Zanzibaris remain haunted by jaundiced or bigoted memory. In this case, "memory" was subverted by the ruling elite to perpetuate its hold on power. The islands' political life remains vulnerable to the fragility of memory.

This has found expression in the tussle over the structure of the Union of Tanzania between the two opposing political camps in Zanzibar. According to the Warioba Commission, which collected Tanzanian citizens' opinions about the country's constitution, the majority of Zanzibaris were in favor of a treaty-based union instead of the current institutional arrangement, which makes Zanzibar only a semi-autonomous entity within Tanzania. They regard the idea of introducing a three-government union structure as an outmoded proposal – something that could have been adopted and implemented decades ago. But even those who support a union with three governments (Tanganyika, Zanzibar, and Tanzania) believe that the third union government (Tanzania) should have minimal powers, as they are anxious to ensure that Zanzibar secures much greater autonomy within that system than it enjoys at present. Yet, in the case of Zanzibar, the question is still wide open. Very few Zanzibaris are prepared to accept the continuation of the current system, even if it is artificially tampered with to give an impression of change. They regard it as an existential issue. All indications are that the status quo will almost certainly be rejected at referendum.

Those who participated in the struggle for Africa's independence from colonialism and foreign domination in the 1950s and 1960s hoped that the era of oppression they were struggling against would be replaced by one of justice, harmony, and progress. They hoped that Africans would once again live peacefully and in dignity in their independent countries, fighting the three evils of poverty, ignorance, and disease that were the legacy of colonial rule. The nature of the struggle for independence varied from country to country, depending largely on the response of the colonial powers. For example, in Tanganyika, Britain did not resist the struggle waged by the Tanganyika African National Union (TANU) for independence. However, in Kenya, where there was a large white settler community, the Mau Mau movement had to resort to an armed struggle to win the country's independence. Kenya also had two dominant political parties, the Kenya African National Union (KANU) and the Kenya African Democratic Union (KADU).

In Zanzibar, there was no single dominant party in the mold of TANU in Tanganyika. But Zanzibar had two strong parties, the Zanzibar Nationalist Party (ZNP), led by Sheikh Ali Muhsin al-Barwani, and the Afro-Shirazi Party (ASP) led by Abeid Karume. Whereas the ZNP campaigned for immediate independence, the ASP felt that it was better to postpone independence and give priority to educating the Africans. It took the efforts of the Pan-African Movement for East and Central Africa (PAFMECA), at a meeting held in Mwanza in 1958, to persuade the ASP to accept the slogan of independence so that, as Kwame Nkrumah said, "Seek ye first the political kingdom and all else will follow" under local management and in an air of freedom.

In East Africa and beyond, other countries produced competing political parties in the run-up to independence. Uganda had two parties—the Uganda People's Congress (UPC) under Milton Obote and the Democratic Party (DP) under Benedict Kiwanuka. And elsewhere, as in Zanzibar, once colonized peoples had to resort to armed struggle—in South Africa and the Portuguese colonies of Angola, Cape Verde, Guinea Bissau, and Mozambique. The Portuguese in particular never considered pursuing a policy of independence for their colonies but regarded them as provinces of Portugal and created a local class of *assimilados*. Indeed, other colonialists also created local classes of their stooges who they used to rule the colonies, assisted by the use of force and other forms of intimidation and denial of civil liberties. In West Africa, as indeed in all the remaining parts of Africa (central and southern), there sprung up liberation movements that were led by visionary Africans who made the sacrifice of defying the colonialist powers so as to seek justice for their countries. The result of all this activity was that there were high expectations, at least in our region of Africa, that after independence life would be far better than before. But what has been Zanzibar's experience?

The question of standards is, perhaps, one of the most important aspects of life in Zanzibar today. Those with memories of the 1950s and early 1960s attest to the high standards in education, healthcare, and other social services that Zanzibaris enjoyed during that period. Today, these conditions have stagnated. In general, the majority of Zanzibaris live under harsh economic conditions, with a rising cost of living, a stifling bureaucracy, and endemic corruption. The state of the environment everywhere leaves much to be desired, with people living in unhygienic conditions and lacking a reliable supply of water and electricity, adequate housing, and access to sanitation and waste disposal. Arguably, these inadequate infrastructural issues are widely experienced in other urban African sites, too. But they underlie the need, across the continent, for a more progressive, just, and sustainable set of urban futures.

By Way of Conclusion

Despite the resurgence of racial or community associations in the mid-1980s, the emergent identities in post-revolution Zanzibar are becoming increasingly blurred and are constantly being reconstituted and redefined. Inasmuch as what we remember and what we forget are socially constructed, communal differences in present-day Zanzibar are less polarized as contrasting memories of the revolution are being "rationalized." In this context, the issue of collective memory assumes a critical dimension. How much of the past needs to be remembered? By whom, and for whom? Paul Connerton (1989) argues that collective memory legitimizes a current social order. In Zanzibar, the problem arises with the hardliners, the so-called conservatives in the ruling establishment, who are wont to use "memory" to promote an ideology of enmity so as to exploit racial differences with the ultimate aim of maintaining power.

To Zanzibaris, the future is not yet fully assured, because they are still grappling with the remaining ghosts of the past—conflicting memories and contested histories—and the uncertainties of the present. To paraphrase Jacques Derrida, these ghosts never die, they remain always "to come and to come back" (quoted in Eagleton 1986: 142). Managing the present may prove the deciding factor in ensuring a stable future and may determine the shape of Zanzibari politics in a new arrangement of the structure of the union. That is a history waiting to be born.

References

Adam, Adam Shafi
2003 *Haini* [Traitor]. Nairobi: Longhorn Publishers.

Babu, Abdulrahman Muhammed
1991 "The 1964 Revolution: Lumpen or Vanguard?" In *Zanzibar under Colonial Rule*, ed. Abdul Sheriff and Ed Ferguson, 220–249. London: James Currey.

Bader, Zinnat
1991 "The Contradictions of Merchant Capital 1840–1939." In *Zanzibar under Colonial Rule*, ed. Abdul Sheriff and Ed Ferguson. London: James Currey.

Becker, Felicitas
2008 "Cosmopolitanism beyond the Towns: Rural-Urban Relations on the Southern Swahili Coast in the Twentieth Century." In *Struggling with History: Islam and Cosmopolitanism in the Western Indian Ocean*, ed. Edward Simpson and Kai Kresse, 261–90. New York: Columbia University Press/Hurst.

Bennett, Norman R. A.
1978 *A History of the Arab State of Zanzibar*. London: Methuen & Co.

Connerton, Paul
1989 *How Societies Remember*. Cambridge, U.K.: Cambridge University Press.

Eagleton, Terry
1986 *Against the Grain: Essays 1975–1985*. London: Verso.

Fairooz, Aman Thani
1995 *Ukweli ni Huu (Kuusuta Uwongo)*. Dubai: self-published.

Ghassany, Harith
2010 *Kwaheri Ukoloni, Kwaheri Uhuru! Zanzibar na Mapinduzi ya Afrabia* [Goodbye Colonialism, Goodbye Independence! Zanzibar and the Revolution of Afrabia]. Self-published, https://kwaheri.files.wordpress.com/2010/05/kwaheri-ukoloni-kwaheri-uhuru.pdf, accessed 18 July 2016.

Glassman, Jonathon

2011 *War of Words, War of Stones: Racial Thought and Violence in Colonial Zanzibar*. Bloomington, Ind.: Indiana University Press.

Hashil, Hashil Seif, and Ahmed Faris

2015 *Living under the Shadow of Terror: Zanzibar Caught Off Guard*. CreateSpace Independent Publishing Platform, n.p.

Ingrams, William Harold

1943 *Arabia and the Isles*. London: John Murray.

al-Ismaily, Issa Nasser

1999 *Zanzibar: Kinyang'anyiro na Utumwa* [Zanzibar: The Scramble and Slavery]. Muscat, Oman: n.p.

Jeffrey, Jaclyn, and Glenace Edwall, eds.

1994 *Memory and History: Essays on Recalling and Interpreting Experience*. Lanham, Md.: University Press of America.

Larsen, Kjersti

2008 *Where Humans and Spirits Meet. The Politics of Ritual and Identified Spirits in Zanzibar*. Oxford: Berghahn Books.

Lofchie, Michael F.

1967 "Was Okello's Revolution a Conspiracy?" *Transition* 33, October–November: 36–42.

1965 *Zanzibar: Background to Revolution*. Princeton, N.J.: Princeton University Press.

Mapuri, Omar R.

1996 *Zanzibar: The 1964 Revolution: Achievements and Prospects*. Dar es Salaam: TEMA Publishers.

Middleton, John

1961 *Land Tenure in Zanzibar*. London: Her Majesty's Stationery Office.

Mohan, Jitendra

1967 "Nkrumah and Nkrumahism." In *Socialist Register 1967*, ed. Ralph Miliband and John Saville. London: Merlin Press.

Mullins, A. B.

2013 "The Zanzibar Revolution: The Formation of Racial Group Identity and Class Struggles, 1890–1964." Master's thesis, Graduate Faculty in Liberal Studies, City University of New York.

Okello, John

1967 *Revolution in Zanzibar*. Nairobi: East African Publishing House.

Ommanney, F. D.

1955 *Isle of Cloves*. London: Longmans Green & Co., Ltd.

Othman, Haroub, ed.

2001 *Babu: I Saw the Future and It Works: Essays Celebrating the Life of Comrade Abdulrahman Mohamed Babu, 1924–1996*. Dar es Salaam: E&D Ltd.

Pearce, Francis Barrow

1920 *Zanzibar: The Island Metropolis of Eastern Africa*. New York: E.P. Dutton.

Ricoeur, Paul

2004 *Memory, History, Forgetting*. Chicago: University of Chicago Press.

Robertson, Roland

1992 *Globalization: Social Theory and Global Culture*. London and Delhi: Sage.

Sadiki, Larbi

2004 *The Search for Arab Democracy, Discourses and Counter-Discourses*. New York: Columbia University Press.

Sheriff, Abdul

2001 "Race and Class in the Politics of Zanzibar." *Afrika Spectrum* 3: 301–18.

Chapter Twelve

Capturing the Commemoration: A Documentary Photo Essay on the 50th Anniversary of the Revolution

Ania Gruca

Statue of Abeid Amani Karume, first President of Zanzibar (1964–1972), standing in front of the Chama cha Mapinduzi headquarters building in Zanzibar city, 7th January 2014.

Spectators attending the 47th commemoration of the revolution at Amani Stadium, Zanzibar city, 12th January 2011.

Military troops opening the 50th anniversary ceremony of the revolution at Amani Stadium, Zanzibar city, 11th January 2014.

Children rehearsing before the parade of the 50th anniversary ceremony of the revolution at Amani Stadium, Zanzibar city, 11th January 2014.

Banner highlighting Presidents of Zanzibar since 1964 at Beit Ras Village fair set up for the 50th anniversary of the revolution, 1st January 2014.

Officials, with second Vice-president Seif Ali Idd (center), are looking at a model of the new Kariakoo Amusement Park, Zanzibar city, 7th January 2014.

First Vice-president Seif Sharif Hamad (left) and former President of Zanzibar Amani Abeid Karume (right) are holding the recently published book, "Zanzibar: Photographic Journey 50 Years of the Revolution" at its launch ceremony held at the Peace Memorial Museum, Stone Town, 3rd January 2014.

Visitors looking at historical photographs at an exhibition organized during the 50th anniversary month of the revolution celebrations at the Peace Memorial Museum, Stone Town, 3rd January 2014.

Former presidents and officials receiving medals of honors from the incumbent President of Zanzibar Ali Mohamed Shein (back to camera) during an official ceremony held at the State House, Stone Town, 3rd January 2014.

Group picture gathering the President of Zanzibar, Ali Mohamed Shein (front, center), and the following former Presidents: Ali Hassan Mwinyi (left from President Shein), Amani Abeid Karume (right from the President), Salmin Amour (right from Amani Abeid Karume) as well as first Vice-president Seif Sharif Hamad (right from Salmin Amour), Salim Ahmed Salim (right from Seif Sharif Hamad) and Bi Fatma Karume (third left from President), and state representatives after the Medal of Honors Ceremony held at the State House, Stone Town, 3rd January 2014.

A new memorial project, the Tower of the Revolution (Mnara wa Mapinduzi), is unveiled to the public during an official ceremony on the occasion of the 50th anniversary month of the revolution celebrations, Michenzani, Zanzibar city, 8th January 2014.

Former President of Tanzania, Jakaya Mrisho Kikwete, inaugurates a new hospital in Kibweni, Zanzibar city, 3rd January 2014.

Children and military forces rehearsing for the upcoming celebration of the ceremony of the 50th anniversary of the revolution at Amani Stadium, Zanzibar city, 10th January 2014.

Military parade at Amani Stadium for the 50th anniversary of the revolution, Zanzibar city, 11th January 2014.

Fireworks in honor of the 50th anniversary of the revolution, Mnazi Mmoja, Zanzibar city, 11th January 2014.

Glossary

Baba wa Taifa	Father of the Nation
Adui wa Taifa	Enemy of the Nation
Aibu	Shame
Aliguruma kama simba	He growled like a lion
Baba wa Kanisa	Father of the Church/Church Elder
Bakora	Stick, club, cane
Bara	Mainland
Baraza	Council; discussion group; architectural feature of a building, such as a stoop or outer porch where such groups gather
Baraza la Mapinduzi	Revolutionary Council
Bie, chelema, togonya	Wild tubers
Buibui	A loose black garment worn by women in public, covering them from the neck to foot
Chuki	Hatred
Dhiki tupu	Total suffering
Heka tatu	Three acres
Hamkushika ndu	You didn't wield the panga
Haya	A sense of shame
Hijab	A veil worn by women, covering the head and chest, usually worn on top of a full-length robe
Inqilāb	Coup
Kabila	Tribe
Kali	Severe, fierce, harsh
Ki-mao	Maoist style, as in the uniforms favored by Kaunda and others in the 1960s and 1970s
Kipokeo	Chorus
Kishuka	Bird shit

Kwetu India	Our place of origin is India
Liwali	Governor or headman
Machotara	Term used to identify people of apparently mixed descent
Mahzarah	Slaughter
Majini	Spirits
Makabila	Tribes
Mamba	Crocodile
Mapinduzi daima	Revolution forever
Mapinduzi hamyajui niye; leo mutayaonja	You don't know what revolution is; today you'll get a taste
Mapinduzi moto-moto	Full-on revolution
Mapinduzi ya Unguja	The Ungujan revolution
Maridhiano	Appeasement/Reconciliation
Matunda ya mapinduzi	Fruits of the revolution
Maulidi	Celebrations of the birthday of the Prophet Muhammad
Mbaya sana	It was horrible
Mgeni	Guest
Mheshimiwa	An honorific title used as a sign of respect or higher status
Mnara wa Mapinduzi	Tower of the Revolution
Mngazija	A Comorian
Mpemba atakalo litakuwa	What a Pemban wants, will be
Mtumwa	Slave
Mungu-mtu	A human god
Mwaka wa kilo	The year of the kilo
Mwalimu	Teacher
Mwenyeji	A resident or inhabitant; an indigene
Nchi	Country
Neema	Goodness, blessedness
Ngalawa	Canoe
Ngozi inayong'ara	Skin that glitters
Njaa	Hunger

Nyumba za mapinduzi	Revolutionary housing
Panga	Machete
Pemba hakuna tena	There's no Pemba anymore
Pemba imekufa kabisa	Pemba's totally dead
Pemba peremba	Pemba changes you
Shairi	Poem
Shibe	Satiety
Siku za bakora	The days of caning
Siye hatukuwa na mambo hayo; kupigana hatujui	We ourselves didn't have those violent things; we don't know how to fight
Taarab	A music genre popular in Tanzania and Kenya. It is influenced by the musical traditions of the African Great Lakes, North Africa, the Middle East, and the Indian subcontinent
Ubaguzi	Racism
Ubeberu	Imperialism
Ubepari	Capitalist exploitation
Ubwanyeye	Bourgeois or aristocratic power
Uchawi	Witchcraft
Uchungu	Anguish and deep pain
Uganga	Witchcraft
Uhuru	Freedom, independence
Ujinga	Ignorance, foolishness, stupidity
Ukame	Drought
Ukunjufu	Welcoming goodwill
Upevu	Ripeness
Ustaarabu	Equated with being refined and civilized
Utawala wa kigeni	Foreign rule
Utawala wa kisultani	Sultanate rule
Uwavi	Sorcery
Uwezo	capacity; financial means

Vibua	A species of big-eyed fish that always travels in close schools
Vibuzi marika	A small kind of goat mainly found in the south of Pemba
Visiwani	In the Isles
Waarabu	Arabs
Wabara	Mainlanders
Wagoa	Goans
Wahindi	South Asians or Indians
Wakati wa njaa	The time of hunger
Wakati wa siasa	The time of politics
Walisalimu amri	They surrendered
Wamanga	Used to designate Omanis of poor background
Washenzi	Barbarians or savage people
Washenzi wa bara	Savages of the mainland
Washihiri	Yemenis
Waswahili	A term used for the people of coastal East Africa, often designating Kiswahili speakers of mixed descent who practice Islam and have long roots in the region
Watu wazima	Completely matured, fully formed people, adults
Wazanzibara	A term used for Zanzibaris with ties to the mainland (bara) or who support the union and close links with the mainland
Wazanzibari	A term used for Zanzibaris who are depicted as "authentic" or "genuine" residents of the isles, or those residents who support greater sovereignty and local control
Wazee	Elders
Wazee wa mji	Town elders
Zama za siasa	The time of politics

Index

A

Abdalla, Ali Omar, 79n2, 80, 80n4, 80n6, 88n23, 89n25
Abdalla, Rashid ("Mamba"), 133n40, 164, 165
Abdulrasul, Amirali, 41n6
Abeid, Khamis Hussein, 49
Abu-Lughod, Lila, 261n16, 262n17
Acon, Yoweri, 96
Africa Addio, 20, 311–329
Africa House hotel, in Unguja, 115
African(s), 27, 40, 41, 42n9, 59, 62, 86, 90, 98, 103, 110, 111, 117, 119, 122, 123–124, 126, 129, 224n3, 227, 230, 231, 235, 261, 296, 316, 322, 328, 350, 351
    ancestry/descent/origin, 59, 258–259, 268, 321
    and Arabs, 43, 54, 57, 58, 59, 60, 61, 62, 63, 152, 159, 178, 228, 229, 230, 231, 233–234, 235, 258, 288, 290, 292–293, 315, 319, 321, 339–340, 341, 346, 348
    as essentialized group, 25
    liberation struggle, 11
    nation, 10, 254
    nationalism.
        See nationalism, African
    as population/people, 197, 200, 230, 282–283

African Association, 40n4
African National Congress (ANC), 11
Africanization, 59, 257, 259, 260, 269
Afro-Shirazi Party (ASP), 10, 12, 25, 27, 39–40, 45, 50, 51, 53, 58, 61, 88, 96, 98, 100, 117, 124, 125n23, 167, 178, 180, 181, 198, 200, 204, 212, 226, 234, 282–283, 287, 324, 335, 338, 341n9, 345, 351
    cadres, 48
    commemorations, 3, 4
    histories, official, 10, 100, 101, 288
    leadership/leaders, 10, 64, 89, 293
    merger with TANU, 53, 136–137, 201, 210, 283, 320
    politicians, 16, 40, 81
    secretary general, 135
    supporters, 41, 42, 126, 161, 163, 337n1, 344
Afro-Shirazi Party Youth League (ASPYL), 42, 44, 46, 48, 49, 55, 58, 60–61, 99, 136, 137
Afro-Shirazi Union (ASU), 39–40
Ahdali (sharifate), 207
Ahmed, Sheikh Farid Haji, 178n71
Alawy, Abdurrahman Saggaf, 170–171
Alebtong, in Uganda, 94–95
Aley, Juma, 41n6, 57, 67
Alonso, Ana Maria, 9
Amani, Ibrahim, 99

Amani Stadium, in Unguja, 1–2, 358–359, 364
Ameir, Hamid, 45, 81–82
Ameir, Khamis Abdallah, 49
Amin, Idi. *See* Dada, Idi Amin
Amour, Salmin, 64, 201, 209, 362
Amugu, in Uganda, 95
ANC. *See* African National Congress
Anglican, 90, 288
Angola, 351
Anino, in Uganda, 41
anniversary. *See* revolution, of 1964, in Zanzibar, anniversaries of,
anticolonial/anticolonialism, 10, 11, 23, 84n14, 124, 284, 290, 292–294
anti-imperialism/anti-imperialist, 23
appeasement. *See maridhiano*
Arab-centrism/Arabocentrism, 25, 124, 224
Arabian Peninsula, 6, 151, 259
Arabism, 284, 286, 299, 301
Arabness, 283, 328
Arabic (language), 111, 150, 170, 266n21, 285, 290–291, 294, 295, 299, 301, 322, 340, 342n10
Arab(s), 5, 25, 26, 39, 40, 41, 42, 47, 48, 56, 64, 87, 88, 89, 91, 109, 110, 111, 117, 123, 124, 125n23, 126, 133, 140n48, 152, 153, 159, 160, 195, 204, 212, 227, 234, 240, 243, 255, 261n14, 269, 270n23, 271, 281, 282, 283, 285, 286, 288, 290–291, 292, 293, 294, 295, 316, 318, 322, 336, 337, 339, 345, 349
    and Africans, 43, 54, 57, 58, 59, 60, 61, 62, 63, 152, 159, 178, 228, 229, 230, 231, 233–234, 235, 258, 288, 290, 292-293, 315, 319, 321, 339–340, 341, 346, 348
    ancestry/descent/origin, 22, 27–28, 134, 162, 209, 233–234, 251, 257, 258, 296, 318, 323–324, 328, 341
    colonial rule of, 102, 134, 224, 292
    elite(s), 10, 49, 226, 287n5, 298, 340
    as essentialized group, 5, 25, 315
    as (landed) aristocracy, 57, 62, 63, 340–341, 345

land ownership, 62, 63, 224, 341
nationalism. *See* nationalism, Arab
as population/people, 296, 320
Argwings-Kodhek, C.M.G., 86
army mutiny, in Tanganyika, 92
Arnold (Koenings), Nathalie, 14, 16, 151, 240–241
Asian(s). *See* South Asian(s)
Askew, Kelly M., 232
ASP. *See* Afro-Shirazi Party
ASPYL. *See* Afro-Shirazi Party Youth League
Assmann, Jan, 38, 67
ASU. *See* Afro-Shirazi Union
Atim, Lily, 96
Awilo, Agnes, 96

B

Baalawi, Idarus, 41
Babu, Abdulrahman Muhammed, 10, 12–13, 39, 41, 44, 45, 46, 49, 50, 51, 52n34, 54, 55n39, 56, 59n48, 63n56, 81, 97n43, 98, 122, 123, 124, 125n23, 288, 290n10,11, 293, 337n3, 343n12
Baghani, in Unguja, 345
Baghdad, 284
Bakari, Asha, 348
Bakari, Mohamed Ali, 63, 233–234
Bakari, Seif, 44, 45, 46n20, 48, 49, 55, 60, 99, 136
al-Bakry, Ibrahim Noor, 286, 287, 291
Banda, Hastings Kamuzu, 93–94
Bantu, 291–292
bara. *See* mainland
Baraza la Mapinduzi.
    See Revolutionary Council
Barghash bin Said, Seyyid (sultan), 14, 24
al-Barwani, Ali Muhsin, 25, 39, 41n6, 55n41, 89–90, 98n45, 123, 124, 127, 209, 285, 287n6, 290n10, 291, 351
al-Barwani, Hamud Muhammed, 45
al-Barwani, Muhammad b. Salim b. Hilal, 47
al-Barwani, Muhammad b. Salim "Jinja," 45

INDEX 373

al-Barwani, Muhammed Hamud, 45
Barwani family, 48
Bavuai, Said Iddi, 45, 46, 48, 97
BBC Swahili Service, 337
Beit el Ajaib (House of Wonders), 14, 15–16
Beirut, 340
belonging, 4–5, 12, 14, 29, 151, 178, 179, 225, 252, 255, 259, 263, 266–269
Bissell, William, 24, 122, 130n34, 281, 282
BLFK. *See* British Land Forces in Kenya
Bloch, Maurice, 256
Bohora, 112, 260n13
Bomani headquarters, in Unguja, 42
Britain (Great), 4, 154, 196, 317
British,
  (colonial) rule, 10, 24–25, 58, 62, 87, 226
  secret service, 51
  protectorate, 39, 40, 145, 228, 235, 312
  secret service/intelligence, 46, 51
British High Commission, 40, 52, 58
British Land Forces in Kenya (BLFK), 52
al-Bualy, Asya, 295
al-Bualy, Nasser Seif, 295
Bububu, in Unguja, 47, 134
Bumbwini, in Unguja, 47, 192
Burgess, G. Thomas, 8, 14, 18, 51, 55n39, 66n60, 133, 158, 162, 165, 167, 229, 243, 257, 312, 318, 327, 329
Burundi, 296
al-Busaidi, 24, 48n24, 289, 340
Bwawani hotel, in Unguja, 16, 115
Bweleo, in Unguja, 192

C

Cairo, 284, 285, 340
Canada, 113, 117, 261
Cape Verde, 351
Catholicism, 118, 122, 124,
  Catholic Church, 111

CCM. *See* Chama cha Mapinduzi
Central Africa, 291, 351
Chake Chake, in Pemba, 154, 162, 163, 170, 175, 182
Chama cha Mapinduzi (CCM), 11, 16, 18, 24, 27, 53, 57, 60, 63n56, 64, 65n59, 68, 101n53, 117, 135n42, 163, 167, 178, 180, 181, 182n80, 183, 201, 202, 209, 210, 211, 212, 220, 234, 237, 239, 240, 241, 283, 320, 321, 323, 345, 346, 348, 349, 358
Chambaani, in Pemba, 153, 164
Changu (island), 112
China, People's Republic of, 39n3, 49, 50, 51n33, 53, 60, 61, 98n45, 128
Christian(s), 234, 239, 260, 348–349
Christianity, 112, 118, 237
Chwaka, in Unguja, 261
citizen(s), 2, 3, 4, 5, 11, 18, 19, 28, 109, 242, 257, 279, 280, 282, 296
citizenship, 14, 270, 271, 280, 296, 300, 320
Civic United Front (CUF), 11, 18, 24, 27, 60, 63n56, 64n58, 65n59, 162–163, 176–177, 178–179, 180, 201, 202, 204, 206, 207, 208, 210, 211, 220, 233, 234, 239, 240, 241, 283, 299n25, 321, 322, 323, 346, 348, 349
Clayton, Anthony, 22, 42n10, 47n23, 51–52, 58, 101, 126n24, 132n36, 136n43, 320
Clementis, Vladimír, 12
clove(s), clove trees, 25, 26, 53, 62–63, 111, 145, 148, 152–154, 158, 162–164, 175, 177
Clove Bonus Scheme, 62–63
coastal exceptionalism, 92, 102, 224, 288, 292
Cold War, 6, 140
colonialism, 4, 23, 24, 87, 100n50, 119–122, 124, 196, 198, 199, 230, 242, 295, 302, 311, 316, 317, 350, 351
  See also British, (colonial) rule
colonial nostalgia, 119, 122, 157–158, 281, 300
Comaroff, Jean and John, 21–22

Commanders Committee
  East Africa, 52n34
Committee of 14, 45, 52n34,
  55n40, 81–82, 96, 97, 99,
  100, 103, 146n4, 182, 200
Communism/communists, 43, 46n21,
  52n34, 125n23, 130n33, 133, 290
  See also revolution, of 1964, in
    Zanzibar, socialist support for
Comorian(s), 22, 41n6, 49, 59, 63, 64,
  66, 119, 123, 251, 254, 257, 258, 269,
  271, 318, 339, 341
Congo, 93, 147, 295, 296, 316
Connerton, Paul, 352
Constitutional Review Act of 2011, 233
Constitutional Review Commission
  (CRC), 202, 233, 349, 350
cosmopolitan/cosmopolitanism, 6, 14,
  66, 102, 103, 111, 112, 119, 154,
  279–302, 319, 328, 345
CRC. *See* Constitutional Review
  Commission
Crosthwaith, T. H., 40, 41n6, 43,
  46n21, 58
Cuba, 39, 49, 52, 60, 83, 97, 98, 129
CUF. *See* Civic United Front
Czechoslovakia, 12, 39

D

Dada, Idi Amin, 94, 95
Dar es Salaam, 9, 12, 41, 44, 45, 46,
  48, 50, 52, 55, 56, 92, 93, 99, 116,
  132, 138, 150, 171, 177, 207
Darwesh, Khamis, 45, 81–82
Davis, Nathalie Zemon, 7
Dole, in Unguja, 45
DP. *See* Democratic Party
decolonization, 6, 282, 284, 285, 289,
  317, 328
democracy, 9, 101, 201, 207, 210, 242,
  342, 347
Democratic Party (DP), 351
Derrida, Jacques, 314, 352
development, 2, 11, 17, 53, 56, 60, 61,
  117, 124, 128, 183, 194, 196, 197,
  203, 205, 209, 210, 258, 263, 348

Dhofar, in Oman, 297
diaspora. *See* Omani, diaspora;
  and nationalism, diasporic
Dourado, Wolfango, 6, 14, 48n26,
  109–141
  first encounter with
    Karume, 124–125
  experience as law student in
    London, 120–121, 122–123, 140
  interview method with, 113–114
  "mouse that roared," 114, 127–128,
    140
  "Napoleon," 138
  pride of, 115–116, 140
  restructuring the union, 138–139
  seeking to curb excesses of
    revolution, 56, 116, 126, 130

E

East African Publishing House, 94
East Germany (German Democratic
  Republic), East German, 39, 49, 50,
  55, 60, 61, 136
Egypt, 39, 49, 342
elections, Zanzibari, 27, 40, 45, 50, 54,
  63, 98, 139, 140, 151, 175–176, 198,
  201, 210, 259, 269–270, 283, 287,
  292, 347
  and conflict, 18, 54, 61, 178
  of 1961, 40, 44n16, 159, 318–319
  of 1963, 40, 50, 98, 160, 161, 198
  of 2000, 24, 27, 54, 60, 175, 204, 211
  of 2005, 27, 54, 64–65, 175, 201, 234
  of 2015, 11, 27, 178, 202, 211,
    348n20, 350
elite, 3, 4, 5, 10, 14, 59, 61, 64, 117, 153,
  196, 226, 283, 293, 298, 322, 340
Emergency, the. *See* Mau Mau
epistemic murk, 18–22
ethnic associations, 113, 126
ethnicity, 61, 62, 63, 110n2, 118, 153,
  193, 196, 200, 208, 209, 212,
  229–230, 236, 241, 243, 257, 258n8,
  281, 282, 283, 284, 286, 294, 296,
  301, 315, 319, 341

Etuku, John Gideon, 83
exile(s), 4, 13, 14, 15, 17, 18, 21, 23, 27–28, 54, 65, 191, 203, 204
exploitation, 10, 25, 87, 117, 121, 134, 329

F

Fair, Laura, 135, 238n14
Fairuz (or Fairooz), Amani Thani, 59n49, 285, 287n7
Faki, Ramadhan Haji, 45, 46, 49, 81, 97
Faulkner, William, 29, 251
feudal/feudalism, 10, 53, 58, 117, 283, 288
Field Force Unit (FFU), 164
Finland, 211
Flint, J. E., 230
Forced Marriage Act, 258, 264
Forodhani (gardens), in Unguja, 118, 299, 345
Foster-Sutton Commission, 290
Fouéré, Marie-Aude, 20, 103, 271n24
Freedom Fighters, the, 80
FRELIMO (Frente de Libertação de Moçambique), 11
fruits of the revolution (*matunda ya mapinduzi*), 2, 11, 59
Fukucheni, in Unguja, 195
Fumba, in Unguja, 192

G

genocide, 23, 192, 287, 316, 321
German(s),
 historians, 37, 287
 in Zanzibar, 14, 39, 50
Germany, 287 (*see also* East Germany)
Ghassany, Harith, 37, 287, 292, 295, 302, 339
Gikuyu (or Kikuyu), 83, 256
Gining'i, 153
Glassman, Jonathon, 22, 25, 27, 159, 199, 224, 225, 229, 234, 236, 286, 312, 315–316, 319
GNU. *See* Government of National Unity

Goan(s),
 ancestry/descent/origin, 18, 118, 227–228
 community, 112–113, 118, 121–124, 139, 141, 227–228, 235, 239
 as population/people, 111–113, 116, 118–126
Goan Institute, in Unguja, 112, 113, 118, 120
Goan Sports Club, in Unguja, 112
Goan Union, 112
Gomani, in Tumbatu, 193, 205, 207, 219
Government Central School, 39, 44
Government of National Unity (GNU), 11, 50, 102, 177, 201, 202, 208, 211, 220, 346, 349
Government Primary School, 44
Green Guards, 167, 176
Guevara, Che, 98
Guinea Bissau, 351
Gulf, the, 289, 299
Gulf states, 284
Gulioni, in Unguja, 42
Gurnah, Abdulrazak, 109, 279, 281, 289
Gurnah, Ahmed, 111
Gymkhana Club, in Unguja, 227

H

Hadrami(s), 66
Hadjivayanis, Georgios, 260
Haj, Maulid Mshangama, 288, 337
Haji, Ramadhan, 45, 46, 49, 81, 97
Hamad, Seif Sharif (Maalim), 137, 146, 179–180, 183, 201, 202, 206, 211, 348, 361, 362
Hamadi, Rashid, 41
Hanga, Abdulla Kassim, 44–46, 48n26, 49, 50, 98, 127n28
Harding, Leonard, 37
Harthi family, 48
Havana, 49
hegemony/hegemonic power, 9, 11, 12, 13, 16, 24, 37, 38, 64, 66, 67, 103, 111, 229, 288, 312

Heligoland-Zanzibar Treaty, 147
Hemed, Khamis, 45
heritage,
  cosmopolitan, 319
  cultural, 239, 263
  imperial, 281, 295, 297
  national, 27, 297, 299, 301
  Omani, 281, 282, 284, 297, 300, 301
  racial or ethnic, 196
  World Heritage Site, 299
Himid, Mansour Yusuf, 178, 182
Himid, Yusuf, 45, 46, 47, 146
Hindi, 111, 264, 266
history, 37, 66, 67, 82, 103, 109, 115, 122, 124, 131, 138–139, 146, 168, 169, 177, 182, 183, 192, 195, 196, 197, 212, 224, 225, 229, 242, 253, 261–262, 279–280, 283, 286, 294, 300, 312, 314, 315, 321, 324, 328, 338, 342, 344, 349, 352
  as historical production, 13
  and memory, 6, 7, 28, 282, 284, 300, 301, 338
  official, 16, 18–19, 55n40, 64–65, 68, 96, 97, 101, 197, 318, 320, 341. *See also* Afro-Shirazi Party, histories, official
  of Pemba, 147–164
  of the revolution. *See* revolution, of 1964, in Zanzibar
  of slavery. *See* slavery (and slave trade), history of,
  as "truth," 18–22
  of Tumbatu, 195–202
House of Representatives, in Unguja, 126, 146, 201, 202, 335
human rights, 122, 131, 211, 343, 344
  language of, 117–118, 140
al-Husayni, Muhammad Umar "Lyne," 39

I

Idd, Seif Ali, 11, 348, 360
identity, in Zanzibar, 4, 5, 12, 17, 149, 179, 198, 227, 262, 267, 269, 288, 296, 343, 347

imaginary(ies), 4, 25, 198, 223–226, 230–235, 237–243, 252, 263
imperialism/imperialist, 10, 89, 91, 100, 288, 292
imprisonment, 54, 109, 115, 127, 167, 168, 257
independence, 4, 24, 39, 40–41, 43, 65, 111, 136, 151, 154, 180, 236, 257, 283, 311, 315, 318, 350–351
  See also Zanzibar, independence
India, 113, 227, 261, 270
Indian(s). *See* South Asian(s)
Indian Ocean, 5, 6, 21, 111, 147, 152, 164, 286, 292, 302, 311, 312, 319
Indian-ness, 260–266
Indonesia, 339
infrastructure, 11, 14
Ingen, Absolom Amoi, 45, 49
Ingrams, W. H., 153, 197, 340
intellectual(s), 48, 49, 114, 116, 122, 154, 165, 170–173
intermarriage, 110, 290–291, 337
Internet, 19, 38, 182, 312, 324, 326, 329
invasion, 18, 23, 59, 282, 287, 288, 289, 291, 292, 321
Irish, 112, 122
Islam, 65, 110, 124, 151, 207, 230, 286, 293, 295, 296, 340
isles, 2, 3, 25, 56, 99, 145, 192, 212, 223, 225, 228, 233, 235, 239, 312, 317, 319, 320, 324, 328, 346, 348
Ismaili(s), 112
al-Ismaily, Issa bin Nasser, 27, 285,
Issa, Ali Sultan, 48, 49, 66, 122, 130, 131, 133, 137, 162, 165, 167,
Ithnasheri(a), 47, 112, 119

J

Jafferji, Javed, 183
Jahazi Asili, 63
Jamshid, Sultan, 41
Janjaweed, 65n59, 204, 220
Java, 339
Jaws Corner, in Unguja, 65n59
Jebel Akhdar, in Oman, 297

Jecha, Daudi Mahmoud, 46
Jivanji family, 48
Jongowe, in Tumbatu, 191–195
jubilee, 1, 2, 4, 192
Jumbe, Aboud, 44, 46, 48, 136–140, 201, 205,
Jussa, Ismail, 146n4
justice, 127, 130–132, 157, 175, 290, 319, 322, 350, 351
  notion of, 114
  system, 114, 130, 140, 141

K

kabila (tribe), 256, 257, 258, 268, 269, 270
KADU. *See* Kenya African Democratic Union
KANU. *See* Kenya African National Union
Kang'ore, Abdallah, 47
Karimjee family, 48
Karimjee Jivanjee Hall, in Unguja, 335
Karuma Falls, in Uganda, 95
Karume, Abeid Amani, 10, 39, 44
  accomplishments of, 129–130, 180, 200
  assassination of, in 1972, 45, 113, 135–136, 201, 204, 320, 341n9
  disdain for intellectuals, 48n26, 113, 127, 170
  his regime or system of rule, 52, 64, 112–113, 114, 128, 129, 132, 136, 203, 208–209, 210, 320
  legacy, 15, 140, 202
  mixed marriages and, 134, 208–209, 258
  role in the revolution, 46, 53, 251, 289
  personality, 40, 44, 65, 89, 165, 233
  speeches, 10
Karume, Ali, 135
Karume, Amani Abeid, 64, 135, 183n81, 201–202, 240, 348, 361, 362
Kaujore, Muhammad Abdallah Ameir, 45, 46n20
Kengeja, in Pemba, 154

Kenya African Democratic Union (KADU), 351
Kenya African National Union (KANU), 351
Kenya, Mzee, 45, 49
Kenyatta, Jomo, 92
Keshodkar, Akbar, 227, 228, 258, 259, 260n13, 268
Khamis, Pili, 45, 46
Kharusi, Ahmed Seif, 28, 281–284, 287n7, 290, 291
al-Kharusi, Sulaiman, 289
Khatib, Abadhar Juma, 41
Khatib, Muhammed S., 25
al-Khatiri, Nasir bin Abdulla, 339
Kiembe Samaki, in Unguja, 146n4
Kiinua Miguu (prison), in Unguja, 343
Kikwajuni, in Unguja, 14, 42, 130
Kilimani, in Unguja, 14, 42, 130
killing(s), 22, 42, 47, 54, 55, 95, 126, 160, 198, 200, 243, 281, 319, 324, 337, 343
Kilwa, in mainland Tanzania, 349
Kinana, Abdulrahman, 349
King George School, in Unguja, 44
King's African Rifles, 92
King's College Hospital, 120
Kisasi, Edington, 46
Kisiwandui, in Unguja, 16, 42
Kisumu, in Kenya, 86
Kiswahili (language), 25, 39, 53, 61, 81, 82, 98, 111, 152–153, 155n17, 162n35, 170, 227, 237–238, 261, 266–267, 290, 291, 292, 295, 298, 320, 327–328, 336
Kiwanuka, Benedict, 351
Kizimkazi, in Unguja, 192, 261
Koff, David, 85, 94
Kombo, Salim, 41
Kombo, Thabit, 48, 50, 135
Koselleck, Reinhart, 37
Kutch, 261
Kutchi (language), 266–268
Kwacha, A.S.-R.M., 49
Kyle, Keith, 97, 98, 99

L

Lambek, Michael, 17, 262, 266, 268
Lamki family, 48
Lamu, in Kenya, 151, 194
land, 61, 86, 110, 145, 152, 155, 171, 173–175, 194, 196, 227, 251, 279, 287
  ownership, 62, 63n55, 152, 224
  redistribution, 53, 59, 130, 140n48
Langi, 83, 84, 94
Larkin, Brian, 263
Larsen, Kjersti, 17, 227
Latigo, 95
Legislative Council (LEGCO), 45n18
liberalization, in Zanzibar, 8, 17, 38, 56, 60, 225, 259, 298, 312
Limbani-Kizimkazi, in Unguja, 192
Lira, in Uganda, 95
liwali (governor or headman), 161
Lofchie, Michael F., 22, 62, 63, 100, 101
London, 39, 49, 50, 52, 60, 113, 120, 121, 122, 140, 324
Luo, 83, 86, 88, 100
lumpen, 13, 42, 58
Lumumba, Ali, 100
Lumumba college, in Unguja, 15

M

al-Maamiry, Ahmed Hamoud, 289
Maasai, 299, 345n17
Machakos, in Kenya, 83
Mahfoudh, Ali, 49, 52
mainland, the, or mainland Tanzania (*bara*), 5, 24, 40–42, 45–47, 55, 65, 81, 100, 117, 123, 127, 138, 150, 177, 178, 193, 211, 223, 225, 232, 239, 271, 281, 288, 296–297, 299, 320, 323
mainlanders, 41, 42, 46, 59–60, 81, 123–124, 159, 230, 234, 237, 239, 241, 271, 287, 288, 294, 321, 345
Makame, Hasnu, 44, 46, 50
Makerere University, in Uganda, 44, 94, 96, 136
Makonde, 40, 54, 337, 347
Makunduchi, in Unguja, 45, 129, 261
Makungu, Ibrahim, 45, 48
Malawi, 44, 93, 116
Malindi, in Unguja, 2, 42, 43, 80
Mangapwani, in Unguja, 27
Manyema, 40
Mao Tse Tung stadium, in Unguja, 15
mapinduzi. *See* revolution, of 1964, in Zanzibar
Mapinduzi Daima (Revolution Forever), 1, 11, 28–29, 53, 320
Mapuri, Omar, 55n40, 57, 63, 101, 117n14, 338n4
Mary, Akello Kulusita, 84, 94
maridhiano (reconciliation or appeasement), 11, 24, 178, 346–349
Martin, Esmond Bradley, 101, 115
Maruhubi Palace ruins, in Unguja, 116
Marxism/Marxist, 11, 12–13, 50, 98n45, 122, 124
al-Maskery, Saleh bin Hashil, 294n14, 295
mass graves, 20, 22, 47, 316, 318, 322, 324, 327
massacres, 23, 42, 48, 54, 224, 283, 312, 320, 322, 324, 327
matunda ya mapinduzi. *See* fruits of the revolution
Mau Mau, 81, 83, 87, 91–92, 100, 316, 350
Mazizini police station, in Unguja, 43
Mazrui family, 87
Mbembe, Achille, 242, 314, 319, 326
media, 7–29
  mediation, 7
  memory, 4, 6, 7–9
    collective, 67–68, 82, 95, 199, 252, 255, 256, 260, 279, 282, 284, 300, 301, 315, 352
    "errant," 67
    and history, 6, 7, 28, 282, 284, 300, 301, 338
    individual/personal, 8, 14, 55, 66, 255, 261
    popular, 4, 8, 152

reformulations/transformations/
reworkings of, 28, 66, 223, 233,
272, 273
silenced, 6, 27
social (cultural), 7–9
Mfaranyaki, Muhammad
Abdallah, 45, 46, 47, 49
Michenzani, in Unguja, 2, 14, 16,
130, 363
Mihangwa, Joseph, 98
Misufini, in Unguja, 42
Mkoani, in Pemba, 154, 161, 175
Mkokotoni, in Unguja, 11, 208
Mkunazini slave market, in Unguja, 27
Mlandege, in Unguja, 42
Mnazi Mmoja (grounds), in Unguja, 1, 125, 335
Mogadishu, 147
Mombasa (Kenya), 83, 147, 151, 170, 204
Mondo films, 315–316, 326
Moscow, 50
Moyo, Hassan Nassor, 46, 48, 49, 65, 146, 181
Mozambique, 194, 242, 351
Mnara wa Mapinduzi. See Tower of the Revolution
Mshangana, Maulidi, 194
Mtendeni, in Unguja, 42
Mtoni detention camp, 45
Mtoni police station, in Unguja, 15
Mueda, Mozambique, 194, 242, 351
Mugambwa, Joseph ("Matias Simba"), 45
Mughayri, Ali Sultan, 45
Muhammad, Bibi Titi, 40n4
Muhammad, Mzee, 45, 49
Muhsin, Ali. *See* al-Barwani, Ali Muhsin
multiparty/multipartyism, 11, 18, 24, 54, 56, 101, 139, 175, 200, 201, 207, 208, 210
multiracialism/multiracialist, 123, 124
Musa, Abdulrazak, 164
Musa, Othman Shariff, 44, 127
Museveni, Yoweri, 102n56, 298
Muslim(s), 103, 134, 227, 292, 321–322, 325

identity, 227
faith, 227
Shia, 260
society, 88
Sunni, 260, 261
worlds, 225
Muscat, in Oman, 147, 152, 285, 301
Mwana, Mwana wa, 196
Mwanza (Tanzania), 93, 351
Mwembeladu, in Unguja, 42
Mwembetanga, in Unguja, 42
Mwera, in Unguja, 44n15
Mwinyi, Ali Hassan, 44, 45, 64, 298, 362
Mwinyi Mkuu, 197
Mwita, Hasnu Makame, 44, 46, 50
Myers, Garth A., 5, 15, 17, 112, 116, 230, 315

N

Nairobi (Kenya), 83, 93, 94, 95,
Nairobi African District Congress, 86
Natepe, Abdallah Said, 45, 46, 48, 82, 99
nation, 10
 father of the, 15, 103, 240, 295
 -state, 233, 279, 280
nationalism/nationalist(s), 10, 122–125, 283
 African, 6, 43, 100, 102, 109, 110, 117, 124, 196, 209, 231, 235, 339–340
 anticolonial, 290, 293, 294
 Arab, 124
 diasporic, 281
 Omani, 289, 292, 294, 295
 racial, 124
 revolutionary, 242
 trans-, 6
 victimhood, 280–281, 282
 Zanzibari, 125, 139, 234, 237, 289–294
nationalization, 47, 61, 163, 257, 260, 301, 345
nationhood, 5, 15, 180, 209, 232, 233, 312, 314, 318

New Kings Football Club (also *Wafalme wapya*), 44
newspapers, 25, 27, 65, 82, 92, 96, 98–100, 106–107, 109, 111, 288, 314, 321
Ng'ambo, 42, 43, 261, 337, 345
Nisula, Tapio, 56
Nkrumah, Kwame, 351
nostalgia, 119, 122, 157–158, 280–281, 300–301, 342, 348
Nottingham, John, 94
Nungwi, in Unguja, 47, 192
Nyamwezi, 40n5, 153n13
Nyekyon, Adoko, 94
Nyerere, Julius K., 23, 40n4, 52n34, 93, 100n50, 103, 116, 123, 127, 133, 134, 167, 202, 209, 210, 233, 240, 284, 287, 288, 293
Nyuni, Khamis Hemed, 45, 46

O

Obote, Milton, 92–95, 107, 351
Ojera, Alex, 95
Okello, Akao Erin (Erin), 96
Okello, John ("Field Marshal"), 6, 12, 22, 41, 42, 54, 79–103
 deported from Zanzibar, 47
 early portrayals of, 83
 psychological warfare of, 80
 radio speeches, 12, 42, 43, 79–80, 81, 82, 85, 89–90, 91, 93, 161
 seeking to keep British out of revolution, 80
 threatening voice of revolution, 79–83
Okello, Yeko, 84, 95
Oman, 147, 230, 280–282, 284–292, 294–302, 339
Omani(s), 289, 291
 Arabs, 47, 291, 339
 ancestry/descent/origin, 160, 289
 diaspora, 6, 280, 296
 elite, 282, 284
 exiles, 284, 294
 nationalism. *See* nationalism, Omani
 state, 280, 285

sultanate, 24, 150, 200, 224, 228, 239
 Wamanga, 337n1, 339, 340
 -Zanzibaris, 281, 282, 287, 290–302
Omani-ness, 297
Opio, Jonathan, 80, 94, 95
Otuboi, in Uganda, 86

P

PAFMECA. *See* Pan-African Movement for East and Central Africa
Palace Museum, 15
pan-African/pan-Africanism, 6, 11, 102, 209, 239, 240
Pan-African Movement for East and Central Africa (PAFMECA), 351
pan-Arab/pan-Arabism, 286, 299, 301
Pearce, Francis B., 192
Pemba, 1, 6, 14, 40, 54
 absent from literature, 145
 clove production and, 162–164
 "days of caning" (*siku za bakora*), 14, 164–167, 178
 differences with Unguja, 150
 entire place a prison, 164–167
 famine (*wakati wa njaa*), 164, 173, 174
 geologic and geographical descriptions of, 150–151
 majini, 171
 neglect, impact of, 175
 occupying an uncertain place, 149
 prosperity and modernity in the 1950s, 153–158
 representations of, 193
 social organization in, 151–153
 uganga (*uchawi*), 170
Pemba Channel, 150, 151
Pembans, 145–184
 autonomy of, before the revolution, 158
 associations with CUF, 176, 239
 detentions, 165
 highly educated, 151
 memories of revolution, 163–167
 not "wielding the *panga*," 16, 160–162

INDEX 381

as "others," 147
poverty and wealth, 174
public denigration of, 175–176
shibe, 154–155, 157, 158, 163, 172, 173, 174, 175, 177
shock of revolution, 160
wazee wa mji (watu wazima), 156, 157, 168
People's Courts, 131, 132–133, 139
People's Republic of Zanzibar and Pemba, 47, 148, 165, 180
Pereira, Yvonne, 113, 116, 123, 127, 135, 137, 140
performance(s), 3, 6, 8, 16, 18, 112, 113, 152, 169, 209, 223–226, 229, 231, 232, 238, 240–241
Persian, 125, 133, 195. See also Shirazi(s)
  ancestry/origin, 110n2, 209, 258
  as population, 157, 195
  teenage girls, brides, 134
Petterson, Don, 92, 115
Plant More Food campaign, 153
Police Mobile Force (PMF), 43
Pongwe, in Unguja, 44
Portuguese, 111, 112, 147, 195, 211, 242, 345, 351
postcolonial, 1, 5, 21, 24, 29, 193, 210, 212, 313–315
post-revolution/post-revolutionary, 11, 15, 17, 41, 54, 149, 171, 199, 210, 212, 235, 252, 263, 271, 288, 313, 344–348
power-sharing government, See Government of National Unity
propaganda, 12, 25, 133, 327
protectorate, British. See British, protectorate
Public Record Office (PRO), London, 60

Q

al-Qa'ida, 64
Qaboos bin Said, Sultan, 290
Qullatayn, Ahmad "Badawi" Abubakar, 49
Qur'anic classes, 55

R

race(s), 223–237
  hierarchy of, under colonialism, 62
  racialist paradigm, 61–62
  racial thought, 25, 224–227, 229–237
  in racism, 271, 289, 341
radio, 12, 42, 43, 79–85, 89, 91, 93, 99, 109, 126, 127, 136, 160, 161, 336
Raha Leo, in Unguja, 42, 43, 46, 48, 80, 89, 90, 96, 126, 227, 228, 229, 255, 336
Rajab, Ahmed, 11, 18, 26n5, 98
Rashid, Salim, 49, 80
RC. See Revolutionary Council
Reconciliation, the. See maridhiano
Reconciliation Committee, 181
Red Cross, the, 285, 337
remembrance, 5–9, 17, 18, 21, 252, 311–329
revolution, meaning of term, 4, 37n1
revolution, of 1964, in Zanzibar,
  alternative narratives, 16–18, 19, 38, 312
  anniversaries of, 1, 2n2, 3, 4, 9, 16, 102n56, 254, 357–365
  as anti-imperialist, 10, 58
  British plans for intervention in, 51–52
  as "civil war," 18, 37n1, 59, 60–66, 68
  commemorations of, 1–4, 5, 9, 285, 357–365
  confiscation of property, 48n24, 90, 259, 298–299, 345
  consolidation of regime, 42, 52, 64
  cultural, 167–170, 243, 258
  depicted in racialist terms, 23, 25, 47, 58–59, 61–62
  diverse interpretations of, 4, 6, 56–60, 146, 282
  ethnicity and, 230, 236, 243
  explained in class terms, 11, 124
  first official account of, 1965, 9–10, 56
  first officials appointed, 44–46

as freedom struggle/liberation, 4, 10, 11, 18, 24, 25, 283
histories of, 8, 24, 57, 100–102
initial events of, 42–48, 146, 160–161
international anxieties about, 50
legacy of, xiii, 5, 15–16, 23–28, 53, 54, 56–58, 60, 64n58, 65n59, 68, 129–130, 140n48, 202, 289, 312
mainlanders in fighting force, 42n11, 46–47, 59–60, 81, 123–124, 271, 287, 288, 294, 321
museum displays about, 15–16
as myth, 68
numbers of deaths, debates about, 22–23, 54, 126, 251, 319–320
official stories about, 4, 9–13, 17, 18–20, 341
portrayed as a struggle against "foreign" rule, 4, 10
radical Arab and Comorian elite, 49
security apparatus, 8, 13, 64n58, 109, 136, 257, 320, 341
spatial transformation and, 14–15, 130
socialist support for, 10–11, 53, 61
suppression of press, 109, 241
struggle for hegemony of interpretation, 12, 37–38, 67
three distinct phases of the, 41–53
time of terror, 13, 22, 47, 48, 80, 127, 318, 344
unresolved, 28
"victim" and "victor" perspectives, 57
violence and, 14, 18, 21, 22–23, 54, 200, 243, 318, 320
zones of secrecy/silence, 7, 13, 18–19, 20
Revolutionary Council, 10, 44n17, 45, 46–48, 52n34, 81, 101, 128n29, 131, 133, 134, 135, 146n4, 181, 201, 251, 283, 320
members of, in January 1964, 46
"Revolution forever." *See Mapinduzi Daima*

Revolutionary Government of Zanzibar (RGZ), 19, 46, 79, 192, 200
forced labor and, 128–129, 130, 136
forced marriages and, 135, 208–209
legal decrees, 130–131, 140
liberalization and, 17, 38
militarization in Pemba, 164–167
shortages and rationing, 129, 136
socialist character of, 61
three acres policy (*eka tatu*), 61, 64
rickshaws, 53
riots, 43, 60, 61, 125n23, 290n10, 339
al-Riyami, Nasser Abdulla, 27, 28, 285–295, 298–299
rumor, 6, 19, 21, 38, 83, 135, 271, 337
Russia. *See* Soviet Union
Rwanda, 296, 316

S

Saateni, in Unguja, 42
Said bin Sultan, Seyyid (sultan), 299
Saadalla, Saleh, 44, 45, 46, 50, 127
Sahlins, Marshall, 241
Saleh, Ibuni, 41
Salim, Said Salim, 182
St. Joseph's Catholic Cathedral, in Unguja, 112
St. Joseph's Convent School, in Unguja, 112, 113, 118
Sanger, Clyde, 81
Second Battalion Scots Guards, 52
secrecy/secrets, 6, 18, 19, 20, 155
security apparatus, 8, 13, 64n58, 109, 136, 257, 320, 341
Serikali ya Mapinduzi ya Zanzibar (SMZ). *See* Revolutionary Government of Zanzibar
Seyyid Khalifa, 43
Shafi'i, 261
Shangani, in Unguja, 42, 345
Shamte, Baraka, 348n20
Shamte, Muhammed, 40, 41, 43, 89, 90
Shariff, Othman. *See* Musa, Othman Shariff

Shein, Ali Mohamed, 1, 65, 178, 181, 202, 348n20, 349, 362
Sheriff, Abdul, 37, 48, 59, 60, 224, 296
Shihr, in Yemen, 340
Shinyanga, in mainland Tanzania, 296
Shirazi(s), 40
  ancestry/descent/origin, 41, 42, 152, 195, 207, 339
  as essentialized group, 39, 57, 62, 81, 90, 101, 117, 159, 160, 226, 234, 282, 320, 335
  as population/people, 40, 45, 62, 153, 155, 283, 340
Silima, Borafya, 348
Simba, Matias, 45, 49
SMZ (Serikali ya Mapinduzi ya Zanzibar). *See* Revolutionary Government of Zanzibar
slavery (and slave trade), 10, 111, 230, 348
  Arab, 292
  experience of, 27
  history of, 24–25
  interpretations/narratives of, 25
  Islamic, 293
  legacy of, 23–28, 319
slave(s), 10
  condition of, 10, 25
  masters, 293
slogans, 1, 2, 11, 53, 320
  socialist or revolutionary, 166, 294, 351
social memory. *See* memory, social
Sofala, in Mozambique, 147, 194
Somali, 51, 66, 176
Songea, in mainland Tanzania, 46
Soroti, in Uganda, 86
South Asian(s), 6, 18, 22, 42, 56, 58, 59, 88, 109–113, 116–117, 126, 127, 128, 134, 153, 164, 224, 227–231, 235, 243, 251, 257–261, 267–269, 271, 318, 340
Soviet Union (Union of Soviet Socialist Republics), 50, 60, 61, 128
Starehe Club, in Unguja, 137
Starn, Randolph, 7

Stasi, 45, 53
Stone Town, in Unguja, 1, 2, 14, 15, 27–28, 39, 42, 43, 55, 80, 111, 112, 113, 118, 123, 125, 229, 235, 236, 237, 297, 299, 322, 328, 337, 344–346, 349
Structural Adjustment, 225, 259
Sturken, Marita, 7
subaltern, 5, 6, 112, 232, 289
Sulaiman, Hafidh, 46
Sultan, Ali. *See* Issa, Ali Sultan
sultanate, 14, 24, 27, 39, 40, 58, 145, 147, 148, 150, 152, 157, 158, 200, 207, 224, 228, 230, 231, 234, 239, 302, 321, 335, 336, 348
Sumich, Jason, 231
Swahili, 24, 63
  coast, 147, 151, 291, 292, 295
  culture, 151, 153, 195, 207
  language. *See* Kiswahili
  as population/people, 24, 151, 195, 198, 240
Swanzy, Bashir, 138
Swartz, M. J., 240
Swift, Charles, 132

T

TAA. *See* Tanganyika African Association
Takaungu, in Kenya, 87
Tanganyika, 10, 23, 40, 41, 42, 44, 45, 47, 50, 52, 60, 92, 99, 101, 139, 148, 179, 200, 201, 224, 232, 233, 281, 296, 335, 338, 350
Tanganyika African Association (TAA), 40
Tanganyika African National Union (TANU), 40, 117, 136–137, 201, 283, 320
Tanzanian Constitutional Review Commission, 233
taarab, 16
Teachers Training College, 50
Television Zanzibar (TVZ), 254
terror, 13, 22, 47, 48, 80, 137, 318, 344
Tewa, Tewa Saidi, 335

Third World, 10
"time of politics" (*zama za siasa, wakati wa siasa*), 39, 61, 159, 198, 211, 224, 225, 234, 235, 285, 287, 294, 342
Tip, Tippu, 298
Tito, Ogangi, 85
torture, 54n37, 109, 168, 219, 343
Tower of the Revolution (*Mnara wa Mapinduzi*), 2, 16, 363
Trafalgar Square, in London, 123
trauma, 5, 20, 23, 28, 54, 117, 119, 192, 211, 253, 279, 280, 293, 296, 312, 320, 342
Trouillot, Michel-Rolph, 13, 28
truth, 18–22
Tumbatu Channel, 191, 208
Tumbatu (island), 17, 191–212
TVZ. *See* Television Zanzibar
Twala, Abdul Aziz, 46, 49, 50, 127

U

Uamsho, 65n59, 178n71
Udende, Said Khamis, 167n44
Uganda People's Congress (UPC), 351
Ukutani, in Unguja, 39
Umar, Muhammad Mfaume, 46
Umma Party, 10, 12–13, 39, 41, 42, 44, 46, 49, 51, 52, 56, 58, 61, 63, 136, 288, 293
Umm Kulthum, 154
union, the (*muungano*), 5, 24, 50, 54, 99–100, 138–139, 179–181, 200–202, 209, 212, 233, 235, 239, 348–350
United Arab Emirates, 281
United Kingdom, 113, 117, 120, 237, 281, 284, 289
United States, the, 44, 50, 65, 237, 311, 316, 317
UPC. *See* Uganda People's Congress
Urdu, 111
USSR. *See* Soviet Union
ustaarabu, 102, 239n16, 283
Uvivini, in Tumbatu, 193
Uzi, in Unguja, 192

V

V.I. Lenin hospital, in Unguja, 15
vita vya mawe. *See* war of stones
Vipingoni, in Kenya, 87
visiwani. *See* isles
Vitongoji, in Pemba, 79, 88, 167
Volunteers, 167
Vuga, in Unguja, 113

W

Waarabu. *See* Arab(s)
Wabara. *See* mainlanders
Wagoa. *See* Goan(s)
Wafalme Wapya. *See* New Kings Football Club
Wahadimu. *See* Hadimu
Wahindi. *See* South Asian(s)
Wakati wa siasa. *See* "time of politics"
Wamanga. *See* Omani(s)
Wangazija. *See* Comorian(s)
Wanyamwezi. *See* Nyamwezi
Wakil, Idris Abdul, 44, 45, 46, 50, 55, 64
Warioba Commission, 349, 350
Warioba, Joseph, 202, 348
war of stones (*vita vya mawe*), 1961, 159, 160
Washoto, Said, 45, 46n20, 133n40, 136
washenzi, 123, 239
Washihiri. *See* Yemeni(s)
Washirazi. *See* Shirazi(s)
Waswahili. *See* Swahili, as population/people
Watumbatu. *See* Tumbatu
Weiss, Brad, 232–233
Western, 15, 57, 100, 111, 112, 114, 118
West, Harry, 242
Wete, in Pemba, 154, 161, 163
White, Luise, 83, 84
Wingwi, in Pemba, 161
Wolf, Markus, 45, 48, 53
World War I, 112
World War II, 83, 92, 110, 124, 129, 153

Y

Yemeni(s), 339n7, 370
Young Pioneers, 14, 45
Youth's Own Union (YOU), 39

Z

Zahor, Amur, 45n19
zama ya siasa. *See* "time of politics"
ZANU. *See* Zimbabwe African National Union
Zanzibar,
  independence ceremonies, 125–126
  nationalism. *See* nationalism, Zanzibari
  pre-revolution, 27, 53–54, 57, 63, 64n58, 66, 119–121, 211, 267, 315, 321, 339, 340, 344, 345, 346, 347, 348
  revolutionary. *See* revolution, of 1964, in Zanzibar,
  shifting meanings of, 7, 225, 226, 229–230
Zanzibar and Pemba Paint Workers Union, 89
Zanzibar and Pemba People's Party (ZPPP), 40, 45, 63, 159, 161, 162, 198, 200, 257
  and ZNP,
    See Zanzibar Nationalist Party
Zanzibar city, 42, 107, 111, 121, 227, 228, 239
  neighborhoods in, 42, 47
  population, 344
Zanzibar African Youth Movement, 50
Zanzibar Electoral Commission, 178
Zanzibar House of Representatives, 146, 181
Zanzibar National Archives (ZNA), 55
Zanzibar Nationalist Party (ZNP), 25, 27, 39, 63, 282, 321
  government, 17, 100, 126
  leader(s), 25, 123, 124, 209, 226, 234
  monarchy, 25
  secretary general, 39, 98, 125
  supporters/sympathizers, 161
  and ZPPP, 40, 45, 63, 159, 161, 162, 198, 200, 257
Zanzibari nationalism. *See* nationalism, Zanzibari
Zanzibar State Trading Company (ZSTC), 177
Zanzibar Organization, 284, 289
Zanzibariness, 17, 18, 223–227, 232, 238, 243, 313, 315, 328
Zimbabwe African National Union (ZANU), 11
Ziwani police headquarters, in Unguja, 15, 16, 42, 97, 126
ZNA. *See* Zanzibar National Archives
ZNP. *See* Zanzibar Nationalist Party
ZPPP. *See* Zanzibar and Pemba People's Party
ZSTC. *See* Zanzibar State Trading Company

www.ingramcontent.com/pod-product-compliance
Lightning Source LLC
Chambersburg PA
CBHW051347290426
44108CB00015B/1919